MW00588354

Showroom City

Globalization and Community

Susan E. Clarke, Series Editor

Dennis R. Judd, Founding Editor

(*continued on page 396*)

Showroom City

Real Estate and Resistance in the
Furniture Capital of the World

JOHN JOE SCHLICHTMAN

Globalization and Community, Volume 34

Foreword by HARVEY MOLOTCH

UNIVERSITY OF MINNESOTA PRESS
MINNEAPOLIS • LONDON

Portions of this book were previously published in a different form in
"Big City Problems: Private Equity Investment, Transnational Users, and
Local Mobilization in the Small City," *City and Community* 19, no. 1
(March 2020): 98–131.

Photographs were taken by the author unless otherwise credited.

Copyright 2022 by the Regents of the University of Minnesota

All rights reserved. No part of this publication may be reproduced,
stored in a retrieval system, or transmitted, in any form or by any means,
electronic, mechanical, photocopying, recording, or otherwise,
without the prior written permission of the publisher.

Published by the University of Minnesota Press
111 Third Avenue South, Suite 290
Minneapolis, MN 55401-2520
http://www.upress.umn.edu

ISBN 978-0-8166-9930-8 (hc)
ISBN 978-0-8166-9931-5 (pb)

Library of Congress record available at https://lccn.loc.gov/2021025891.

Printed in the United States of America on acid-free paper

The University of Minnesota is an equal-opportunity educator and employer.

28 27 26 25 24 23 22   10 9 8 7 6 5 4 3 2 1

Contents

Part III. The Fight to Reclaim Downtown

Foreword

Learning from the Outlier

HARVEY MOLOTCH

A nice thing about outliers is that they are inevitable—and ready to be found at either tail of any bell curve.

They can be teachers. As with deviant cases of any sort, an idiosyncratic city shows us things that occur in many other places, but not in such vivid ways. They are not featured as urban prototypes. Their qualities are not made central to paradigms. Organizations do not give out awards in their category, nor are there journals or curricula that speak their names. Rather than assembling cases that are similar enough to be given a common designation, why not take up a topic that does not easily fit—and make hay out of the distinctiveness?

With High Point, North Carolina, John Joe Schlichtman does exactly that, and *Showroom City* is the rewarding result. His diligent guidance leads us to a fresh understanding of how cities operate and, more important, how that can change. The peculiar and particular circumstances, the mode of marginality, inform us as to what goes on in urban realms more generally and has in fact increased in dramatic ways since Schlichtman began his fieldwork.

I have never been to High Point, but this book makes me want to go, just to see that a thing like this could be in the world. High Point, certainly as far as its downtown core is concerned, exists to show furniture, not to make it, not to finance it, not to ship it: to show it. And only for two "seasons," each about a week long. The rest of the year, many of the showroom designers, developers, and carpenters have a presence in producing the next show; some dabble in other pursuits, but the workforce of buyers and manufacturer reps mostly all go elsewhere. So do the cooks and cleaners, drivers and custodians who service the people who come to see the goods and place their orders.

We witness with a clarity seldom otherwise on view a readiness to turn things upside down in geographic and social terms. The urban essence— cities as places to meet, spark, and interact—is not of much relevance. Agglomeration benefits, such as they might be, are only oddly present. But unlike in the more common sagas of deindustrialization, High Point did not decay when its furniture and textile factories consolidated, went offshore, or de-skilled. In ways as never before, even with the need to dodge the evolving global pandemic, people come from across the world to see and touch furniture samples of goods that would increasingly come from elsewhere, especially China. At the higher end, some of the products still come from nearby in North Carolina, but mostly they do not— it is displaying them, not making them, that gives the city its resilience. Schlichtman shows us the face of small city success, as High Point beats out its primary exhibition competitors, Chicago and Las Vegas.

To make way for the triumph, everything else in the downtown had to go—shops, movies, restaurants, gone. Residents adapted as they cleared the path. Like at Disney properties, some townspeople became "cast members," greeting visitors at showroom doors, ferrying them around, serving food and drinks. With a lack of nearby hotels, High Point families turned their homes into furnished rentals; owners went elsewhere during season. In a glimpse of the gig economy ahead, students hired out as drivers, ordinary houses went into proto-VRBO/Airbnb status. As a wage system followed the enclosure laws, the showroom economy ushered in a rental of most everything, including service personnel. Temp Town was becoming, timed to furniture weeks, gig town—leadership of still a different sort.

The citizenry did not play a governing role in this shift. Their votes and statements did not dream up such a system. Yes, there has been the full panoply of organizational structures—mayors who come and go, city councils, planners, consultants, agencies, and commissions. There are civil rights leaders (about one-third of the city is African American), and there have been far-sighted reformers who wanted amenities for the locals. High Point University plays an active role in some town–gown affairs. But there is a clear hegemon: the furniture showroom. Through thick and thin, showrooms have kept multiplying in number and scale and expanding the support staff they entail.

Perhaps the most radical reconfiguration from High Point is the capacity to alter the meaning of time. The urban has long been associated with shifts in temporality, like the coming of factory-time as life organizer, or, at least in stereotype, a speedup of everything that city routines supposedly engender. Here in High Point, there is showroom-time; it changes not only what goes on during Market weeks but also life tempo in preparing for those weeks, much of it backstage where materials are assembled and arrangements worked out. In the downtime the emptiness, as Schlichtman testifies, astonishes. The city could not, in his words, "get more dead."

This is a place that has radical emptiness as its base. For cities where the niche is right, even the clock and calendar are thus strangely up for grabs. A city has many ways to bloom and to decline, and for depoliticization to work its way into materiality and civic consciousness. John Joe Schlichtman encourages finding them.

Introduction

An Empty and Impeccable Downtown

Encountering High Point

Curiosity got the best of me. It is about 4 a.m. in February 2001, and I find myself on the outskirts of High Point, North Carolina. I have just made the nine-hour drive from Brooklyn, New York, on a whim. Although I have been reading up on this small city from afar, the details are not adding up for me. So last night, I impulsively packed a bag, caught the subway to LaGuardia Airport, and rented a car to see High Point for myself.

I love road trips, so the drive has passed quickly. As I near High Point, signs welcome furniture buyers in several languages, and, although exhausted, I sit up attentively with a sense of expectation. It is short-lived.

I exit Business 85 and make a right onto NC-311, wondering if the trip was a mistake. Blight surrounds me. The road's surface is treacherous. Faded signs for regional fast-food restaurants speckle the dark pot-holed street, and the 1970s-looking establishments they advertise stand far behind; cracked parking lots span the distance between them. Dilapidated strip malls signal an atmosphere of rural poverty. The sidewalks—if they exist—appear broken or dangerous. Furniture liquidators with haphazardly painted signs occupy buildings that appear to have once been grocery and big box stores.

Is this it? Is this the city that claims the mantle of the world's furniture fashion center? Have I been duped by a shrewd marketing scheme? I assume the worst: High Point is really just a brief "Main Street" blip of US-311, and this highway will soon return to an ordinary, rural-looking state highway. I shudder to think that *this* is High Point.

1

Looking north at USA Pawn on South Main Street, with Elm Towers at left.

But once I pass USA Pawn and Sub-City restaurant (soon to become my favorite place to eat), a mirage-like image reawakens my interest. Just beyond the "World Famous Tiki Cabaret" cinder block bar, past the Elm Towers public housing, tall and stately brick buildings rise out of the strip malls into the sunrise, promising something more. This was my first time traversing High Point's stark line between marginal space and prime space, between global and local—an experience that would soon become very familiar.

Glossy black-painted streetlights replace deteriorating electrical poles. Dull traffic signals suspended from wires give way to brand-new fixtures. On my right, flags for Korea and Ireland hang in front of the International Home Furnishings Center, and dozens of other international flags line the sidewalks. Newly blacktopped streets with bright yellow lines meet my wheels. Fresh landscaping and brick trim highlight the bright white sidewalk. On my left, massive cranes are erecting what appears to be a touristy, festival-style mall.

Turning at Commerce Avenue and Wrenn Street, I get my first glimpse of Showplace, a curvy glass and steel structure on a lavishly landscaped property. Relieved, I know now my trip was not in vain: something *is* happening here. I walk through the empty parking lot to see Showplace's green-hued windows up close and peer into a striking five-story lobby flanked by twin escalators. The building is, unfortunately, locked. Back in the car, I am soon confronted by the massive rear of the Home Furnishings Center, a fourteen-story, aluminum-sided brown box that fills the entire block (imagine the biggest storage locker or rural carport conceivable). *What a contrast! There has to be a story behind these drastically different aesthetics.*

Excited to explore more, I take a one-way street that looks transplanted from Southern California. Brown and tan stucco buildings (are some single-family homes?) line the spacious road. Textured surfaces and lush greenery come into view. I see other "homes" surrounded by walls and gates, looking like a middle-class enclave in a global city in the developing world.

The "World's Largest Chest of Drawers"—a building whose kitschy facade is a four-drawer dresser—is on my right; I jump out to snap a photo. Soon I find myself in a New England–style retail neighborhood of wrought iron fencing and varied storefronts. I see trendy new-looking facades and unique hues painted on original brick.

The curvy glass and steel of Showplace furniture exhibition building.

The aesthetic difference between these buildings and those near the interstate a mile back could hardly be greater. The same types of storefronts that, just to the south, house businesses serving a poorer clientele are now cleverly transformed to gentrification chic. *What exactly am I seeing? What is this place?*

Now exploring on foot, I feel transported to a distant place as the environment envelops my senses. I pass the 220 Elm building with its facade of white glass framed by white steel, a design that would fit quite comfortably in downtown Los Angeles, and then the Commerce and Design building, a huge gray cuboid with silver stripes. The frosted white glass of the adjacent 220 Elm exposes eight floors of white escalator. This could be the setting for a compact SUV car commercial. To me, it is the aesthetics of advanced gentrification.

At the intersection of Elm and Commerce, a black building with the text "Natuzzi" is clearly designed to resemble a ship. A wooden gangplank with rope railings suspended over water draws attention to the

Looking north on South Elm Street with Natuzzi USA ahead. The white cubes of 220 Elm and the gray monolith of the Commerce and Design building are at left, and the rear of Furniture Plaza and Plaza Suites (at right) connect over South Elm via skywalk.

building's entrance. Hooked, I walk the plank and try to make out the dark, elegant lobby behind the locked door. "SHOWROOM CLOSED Between Markets" is permanently stenciled on the lobby windows.

Taking Elm to the railroad tracks in the center of downtown, I see a long, brick factory building that I take for a recent townhome conversion. New windows offset the weathered brick where Tomlinson Furniture Co., the original tenant, is visible in early twentieth-century lettering. Or was it all *made* to look aged, since the complex seems to be hip loft-style residences? At the end of the block is an apparently new office or residential tower, well integrated into the historic structure.

Who lives here—gentrifiers? But so many of the telltale indicators of gentrification are missing: no restaurant, no coffee shop, no pedestrians—just construction workers.

Approaching the tower at the end of the complex, I realize that the nineteen "townhome" facades adjoining High Street have no doors. This is simply one long building. And not particularly old. Up close, I can see new construction cleverly designed to mask one expansive open space.

The old Tomlinson furniture plant is now Market Square (center) with the addition of Suites at Market Square at left. The Market Square Tower looms overhead. Photograph courtesy of High Point Market MediaLink.

Not sure what to think, I gawk into the tower's plush lobby across the empty parking lot and see rich wood, expensive furniture, and thick carpeting. A security guard approaches and asks me to leave. I am taken aback. Walking through a large building in the middle of an imposing section of downtown, I thought I was blending in. *Why does he immediately assume I do not belong?* I inventory what cues he might be using to assess me: age, race, attire, gender. I ask him if a tenant could let me see their unit. The guard says all visits are only by appointment. He clearly assumes I have some background knowledge. With good reason: Who would venture into a landscape of empty buildings without a specific purpose? But I press the issue.

I keep pressing until the guard's nonchalant certainty that we are probably the only ones in the entire building convinces me that he is sincere. I leave, more puzzled about what I am witnessing in this downtown. On Main Street I chuckle when I notice the marquee of the nicely refurbished Center Theatre, presumably the city's old downtown movie house:

Now Premiering:
Jaclyn Smith's
Spencer Margaret Collection
Elegant Youth Bedroom

An actor's elegant youth bedroom on a theater marquee? On a plaque near the ticket window I read that Elvis Presley played the venue in 1956 and that "the Theatre was one of High Point's main attractions until 1980 when it was renovated as a furniture showroom."

Tensions: From Mill Town to Furniture Fashion Center

"This is one of the most peculiar places I've seen," urban planner Andrés Duany declared in 2013 as he tried to get a handle on High Point. As a student of cities and communities, I agree. High Point intrigued me well before my visit in 2001. My first walk there only illuminated and confirmed my impression of some seemingly profound tensions.

I came knowing that High Point was a site of global capital investment, but I could also see a distinct brand of poverty found in the U.S. South. I knew High Point attracted cosmopolitan visitors, yet it also appeared to be a rather parochial small southern city. Its human capital and its architecture marked it as a design center, but it also bore the marks of a deindustrialized "mill town." Although its name was recognized around the world, High Point ironically ranked far down the urban hierarchy even in its own state. The downtown seemed to be gentrifying, but I did not see a single resident.

Within urban studies, High Point was a place that defied common sense, at least as I had learned it. But just as I came to see that the loft conversion, the festival mall, and the homes were all showrooms, I also realized that it would require some digging on the ground to understand this place. A drive-through ethnography—a stay in a motel, interviews with a few key people, and then a written summation—would not do it justice.

Two regions dominate most conversations about the integration of North Carolina's urban economies into leading-edge enterprises of the contemporary global economy: Charlotte, a major global finance center, and Raleigh–Durham–Chapel Hill, a research hub in biotechnology and digital communications. High Point, population 116,000, sits directly between them in North Carolina's Piedmont region of "fiercely independent, thriving small cities": High Point, Greensboro, and Winston-Salem.[1]

Once known as the "Home Furnishings Capital of the World" for its manufacturing, High Point's gritty mill town heritage—as with many U.S. industrial towns—came to be more a liability than an asset. Unlike most deindustrialized small cities, High Point's downtown has witnessed intensive capital investment since the 1970s. Today this small city is integrated into a specialized circuit of global economic activity that both draws on and sharply departs from its industrial past. A new global identity has led ambitious city leaders to declare High Point "North Carolina's International City."

This investment recycled High Point's downtown in striking fashion, as various sizes of exposition buildings gobbled up real estate in the city center. The Natuzzi ship building where I walked the gangplank, designed by renowned Italian architect Mario Bellini and completed in 1999, exemplifies the city's new eclectic style. Such postmodern architectural spectacle in a small North Carolina mill town, along with a semiannual influx of visitors from 110 nations, invites some extravagant comparisons.

"Look at the Bilbao," said designer Raymond Waites, a reference to the wilting Spanish city turned international sensation after the introduction of architect Frank Gehry's celebrated Guggenheim museum building. "Nobody had ever heard of Bilbao before; now it's on everybody's wish list to go there."[2] Taking note of his "penetrating dark eyes, his thick furrowed brows and full beard" along with his "easy, Alabama twang," the *Chicago Tribune* called Waites "one of the most creative minds in the business of design."[3] Like several other High Pointers I knew, Waites had traveled from New York to High Point regularly for years before finally relocating there permanently.

High Point's architecture does not boast the Gehry pedigree that stamped Bilbao, and the Piedmont may not summon comparisons to the historic charm of Spain's Basque country, but like Bilbao, contemporary High Point is known around the world. Its renown is simply restricted to a smaller population of niche users. Twice each year, its downtown is the site of the largest furniture exposition in the world, the High Point Market.[4] The middle of nowhere for most, it is the center of the universe for many in the world's furniture fashion industry, a node of specialized global commerce.

High Point leaders' aggressive strategy to reinvent the city as a merchandising node was largely successful—depending on the measure— and has proved generations of doubters wrong. The area of the Market's wholesale furniture showrooms surpassed one million square feet in the 1960s, two million in the 1970s, six million in the 1980s, and ten million in the 1990s to become the world's largest wholesale furniture exposition. A preeminent node of global furniture exposition and merchandising, the High Point Market's footprint equals four Empire State Buildings and is larger than the combined area of the furniture expos of Cologne, Tokyo, Guadalajara, Milan, and São Paulo. More than seventy-five thousand marketgoers surge into town to attend each furniture exposition.

Come April and October, the downtown turns into what some residents call a Mini-Manhattan. "What Paris is to fashion, High Point is to furniture," many leaders, attendees, and residents have told me over two decades. "Not having the Market in High Point is like seeing a Broadway show outside of New York," a gruff rug salesperson from Brooklyn explained during my first Market. Downtown High Point during Market truly seems to be the center of it all.

Until the Market leaves town. Then downtown High Point is closed, and much of the visible activity halts, leaving it a ghost town to most observers. But closer inspection shows that it is not as stagnant as it looks. The Market is not equivalent to a circus tent or a resort town. Nor is it like the annual Burning Man festival in the Nevada desert, which erects Black Rock City, a temporary community of over sixty-five thousand resident-visitors, for a single week.

During its backstage months, downtown High Point is actually in flux with flows of materials, ideas, and capital investment as exhibitors carefully redesign their showrooms to best complement their next debuts. Even the downtown's recently renovated buildings become candidates for a complete renovation when a new tenant or an owner's new brand requires a makeover. The symbolic economy—a concept for the system that produces economic value via symbolic value—"recycles real estate as it does designer clothes."[5] Downtown High Point is the instantiation of this fact: an ever-recycled design showcase in six-month preparation cycles. When Duany was summoned to High Point in 2012 and charged with restoring a sense of community vitality (the topic of chapter 9), he found his traditional tool kit ill-suited to the High Point case. "The downtown looks empty and the store fronts are full and being paid for. Could you remind me what I'm supposed to do with this?" he asked.[6]

"Most empty downtowns are decrepit," Duany mused when he walked through the downtown. "*Your* downtown is empty and impeccable."[7] Called "the father of New Urbanism," Duany cofounded a design movement that envisions a diversity of residents comingling in a dense, walkable, mixed-use, vibrant common space, and Duany has spent a career championing such environments. In High Point, he *found* such a space. But its street life was limited to the seventy-five thousand visitors coming twice a year. And unlike Black Rock City, virtually none of High Point's downtown investments helped precipitate the makings of a community. During Market, to be explored in chapter 6, the leaders of High Point's great showcase must coordinate—choreograph, really—all the supporting functions such a huge gathering requires.

These huge "spikes" of downtown economic activity make "life incredibly difficult," Duany explained to an auditorium of High Pointers. "The only thing they're good for—absolutely uniquely—is your tax base."[8] For High Point leaders, that has been too good to pass up for the past seven decades, raising implicit questions. *What are the measures of downtown success? Who benefits from those measures?* That's where it gets complicated.

"I call downtown the perfect riddle," local leader Rev. Elijah Parish Lovejoy reflected. In his critique of High Point's development choices, Lovejoy often highlighted the five-billion-dollar annual statewide impact the Market produced, the hundreds of thousands of visits to and through downtown, and the twelve million square feet of showroom development. "So that's money, people, and real estate," he reasoned. "From a business model, that should be everything you need."

The crux of his riddle challenges traditional understanding: downtown High Point was desolate not due to disinvestment but to *investment*. It had what many former mill towns would covet: a global market for its downtown real estate. Wendy Fuscoe, the woman the city charged with downtown renewal efforts in 2010, noted, "The city is not losing a darn dime by having a dead downtown."

But for the city's 116,000 residents—half of whom are white, one-third Black, with Latino and Asian residents each making up roughly equal portions of the remaining population—the downtown hardly exists. We will come to understand it, especially in chapter 5, as an alienated frontstage landscape in relation to its surrounding neighborhoods and the city's permanent population. The hotels and exposition spaces that dominate it are a transitory and disembedded space. "Our downtown belongs to the world," Lovejoy explained.[9]

When he moved to High Point in 2008, Lovejoy's new friend, realtor and furniture consultant Audie Cashion, took him on a bike ride through the streets of the empty downtown, pointing out "which international company owned what section of Furniture Market." Kin to the American abolitionist of the same name, the justice-minded Lovejoy quickly concluded that High Point's center city was "occupied by showrooms" that had stolen what he described as its geographic "soul."

Creative Destruction: The Pursuit of Furniture Service during Manufacturing Flight

"If you're a person living in a city with a downtown that's devoid of any form of development, you'd probably think I'm crazy sitting here arguing with people coming in, redoing buildings, and making them nice again," laughed politician Jay Wagner. Like Lovejoy, we will come to know him as a critic of the tension between economic vitality and social vitality in High Point. This tension was relatively new.

The birth of the Market in 1913 coincided with the start of High Point's ascendance within the furniture manufacturing industry. The exposition was a small part of the city's diversified furniture identity. Over the next fifty years, wholesale furniture buyers "came to the Market, they bought their furniture here, and that money flowed into the factories that were *here*," explained Wagner. "And everybody from the president to the guy who swept the floor got paid."

The Market was one component of a vertically integrated industry, a seemingly natural merchandising complement to the region's manufacturing dominance. To quote the *High Point Enterprise* at the start of the Market in 1967:

> Somewhere in High Point today are the workers who made the furniture, fabric distributors who furnished the fabrics, executives who keep the plants going, the designers, the decorators, the night watchman, the workers who worked around the clock to get the [expanded space] ready, the buyers and the salesman, the press, and many others. They all make up the kaleidoscope of the Market.[10]

The global connectedness that swept through the U.S. South and changed High Point's relationship to furniture was not a wholly new phenomenon. The region has been heavily integrated into transnational economic flows since the days of the transatlantic slave trade and the export of tobacco and cotton. In fact, the U.S. South should be understood as the "leading edge of crucial new developments in political economy, including neoliberalism and globalization."[11] This perspective helps contextualize High Point's seventy-year tenure as a center of furniture manufacturing—*after* the industry fled the more costly Midwest and Northeast United States in the early twentieth century.

The move to the High Point region illustrates how "the timing of Southern entry into the wider economy, shedding its quasi-colonial status, left it as more or less virgin territory, its regional economy free to develop according to the logic of neoliberal, global capitalism."[12] During the United States' Sunbelt era of urbanization and industrialization that began in the 1950s, the South resisted union organization at every turn as it exploited cheap labor, affordable land, low taxes, and deregulation to lead the nation in both gross domestic product and foreign direct investment.

The city leaders touted industrial expansion, declaring in 1964 that "sound industrial growth is good for everyone" and demanding the community's support—cautioning "we cannot have this growth if we do not make arrangements for it."[13] Without growth, they warned, High Point would be stagnant. It was a growing manufacturing city and an argument that widespread vitality depended on industrial growth had validity.

Factory life in High Point had a "natural progression," said furniture industry veteran John Butt, recalling the former trajectory of a typical male factory worker. "You went to high school, you worked temp in the summertime weeding, tearing roofs off, painting fences," he began. In time, "you went to work at one of the plants; and you retire." Of course, you also took days off or went without sleep during Market weeks in order to bring in another few thousand dollars. These opportunities could support a comfortable, stable life in a small, affordable southern city. Furniture workers, William Lambeth explained, had a real sense of the craft, and it permeated the city. Unfortunately, he added, "the world has sucked their brains into a computer."

The South's ascent tracked closely with regions of the world that would develop decades later and absorb much of the manufacturing that left High Point during the era of automation. On the ground in High Point, this global competition began as a trickle in the late 1970s. In October 1978, a delegation of Asian furniture manufacturers came to the Market to, in the words of the group's head, "find out what is required of our countries to become competitive in your own market."[14]

High Pointers were proud of these early visits by foreigners. They did not foresee the speed and force with which nations such as Taiwan, Singapore, the Philippines, Malaysia, Thailand, China, and Vietnam would become furniture production centers in the 1980s and 1990s.[15] In the early years, U.S. furniture leaders helped Asian businesses navigate the craft because those manufacturers were relocating their manufacturing to Asia. Noting the steep learning curve in furniture manufacturing, one product developer joked that "the Chinese could not understand that we had 118 different textures of sandpaper whereas they thought that three's plenty." But learn they did, and eventually they transitioned from suppliers of U.S. furniture makers to their competitors.

"All the expertise we'd developed over the years and all the wonderful finishes and veneer work and carvings—we had to teach the Asians how to do it so they could provide us with more product," said the CEO of

Henredon Furniture. "The problem is, once that process starts, there's no stopping it."[16] Today the majority of High Point's factory jobs left the United States altogether in order to exploit the lower cost of labor, land, taxes, and regulation elsewhere.

Such interconnectedness is not new. What is unique to this era of globalization is the breadth (more areas of life are affected), depth (those areas are affected more intensely), and speed (innovations now occur months rather than decades apart) of this interconnectedness.[17] Capital mobility, which renders it increasingly easy for profit-seeking enterprises to choose the most profitable location for their investments, has structured a new reality for cities within the global economy.[18]

Capital had always been mobile to some degree, but new technologies "shifted the fulcrum of bargaining power in favor of capital to an unprecedented degree."[19] Also new is the degree to which capital investment in specific places seems footloose, able to unroot in one place and reroot in another with less friction than ever. Firms now exploit this flexibility as an explicit strategy to accumulate profits.[20] The era of Fordist production, in which manufacturers churned out large batches of standardized items for mass consumption, was replaced by the post-Fordist or "flexible specialization" era, in which manufacturers use flexible technologies to produce diverse, specialized products for discerning consumers.

In this swift transition, many communities and their residents never get the chance to reeducate and retool for the new opportunities. Instead, they are "carelessly discarded to make room for new ones."[21] High Point leaders have long feared the possibility of becoming just another discarded mill town. Urban leaders around the world have attempted various renewal strategies to avoid this threat of obsolescence, whether perceived or real. Yet few have responded to this global, structural transformation with the creative agency of High Point's leaders. Unlike many other small cities, when High Point lost its furniture manufacturing, its leaders identified a different but interrelated set of functions: they adapted and respecialized for a new era of growth.

Global interconnectedness and capital mobility fostered High Point's deindustrialization; these same forces incentivized High Point landowners to dedicate their downtown to global furniture expositions. Faced with the increasingly rapid contraction of the furniture manufacturing industry, High Point leaders tenaciously worked to secure their downtown's service industry niche. They prospered against competition from larger, wealthier peers including Chicago (in the 1950s and 1960s), Dallas (1970s), Atlanta (1980s), and Las Vegas (2000s) to become the largest wholesale residential home furnishings exposition in the world. Overmatched by the resources and amenities of its rivals, High Point leaders nevertheless doubled-down on their furniture showroom strategy, developing a "logistical genius," as Duany marveled, to "actually adjust to this very peculiar position."[22] Amazingly, it worked.

As with other cities, while High Point's blue-collar neighborhoods struggled to transition to the new postindustrial economy, its downtown became a center of experience. High Point strayed from a conventional small city strategy, which would relegate its downtown to a quaint Main Street of ice cream and antique shops with a localized theme for regional tourists. Flint, Michigan, paid homage to its industrial roots with a theme park; Roswell, New Mexico, specialized in attracting paranormal enthusiasts. In High Point leaders grafted new areas of specialization onto their furniture roots.

Like a literary character poised at the bow of a ship to challenge the threatening tempest, High Point encouraged the process of "creative destruction," which allows economic sectors to die and be reborn through relentless innovation.[23] Or, in a distinction that I return to in chapter 2, to be reborn without ever really dying at all. The result left contemporary High Point with a new set of specialized functions.

"The buying and selling happens here, the design work happens here," Wagner explained, but most of the furniture displayed is not produced in the region. "The very nature of Market and its depth of contact with our city is [now] different," he added. Wagner's perceptive observation about this "depth of contact" between an industry and a city stems from his work trying to reconcile the needs and wishes of High Point Market with those of High Point residents. As the owners, labor, and consumer base of the furniture firms grew increasingly dispersed, so too were the owners of downtown High Point.

Some of High Point's full-time residents are still employed in higher skilled and reskilled aspects of furniture production within what economists have identified as High Point's furniture cluster, a subject explored in chapters 6 and 7.[24] Formed through agglomeration, or the proximity of complementary functions, a cluster is a colocation of firms in a niche that develop a competitive advantage through their interdependence.[25] High Point's cluster has created a specialized expertise embedded in the city's networks, its culture—seemingly, its soil. Residents call it the "furniture DNA." For decades, the local government has largely overlooked these assets as merely the remains of a dying industry, focusing instead on the Market-centered downtown.

"Our downtown is the opposite of most cities," High Point planning director G. Lee Burnette told me when I first moved to town. In High Point, the center city amenities (such as restaurants, which operate year-round in most places) are temporary, and the exhibition functions (the exposition center, which is rented and used temporarily in most places) are permanent. In downtown High Point, the supplementary has become the essential; we might call it an adjunct city.

You can imagine that the strategy of a small city courting global investment and visitors comes with great risk. And the recent entrance of major private equity players into High Point's downtown real estate has raised the stakes. Today, the private equity firm Blackstone Group owns the majority of the downtown.

Yet this stunning reality is only a variation on a common strategy visible throughout the world. Blackstone is using its heft to acquire entire neighborhoods, often residential, and local spaces of daily life are reduced to financial formulas. When such formulas call for the displacement of the local fabric, it is not the result of "natural" forces. The turning over of locally owned spaces of daily life to globally owned spaces of capital occurs through a series of decisions by which such "expulsions are made."[26]

For local leaders navigating this flux, the way forward must be equally intentional. They cannot afford to adopt "silver bullet," off-the-shelf prescriptions, known as mobile or traveling policies, from another city.[27] "There's no rules to guide what we're doing," said Fuscoe in 2013. "There's no stuff we can read or other people we can go to [to ask] 'how did you do it?'" Chapter 9 explains how the city government charged Fuscoe with reintroducing *resident*-centered, walkable gathering spaces into the city's fabric. Her efforts had to counter a long-embedded social structure.

Structuration: A Card Game

Two foundational sociological concepts are worth mentioning here: social structure and agency. Social structure encompasses the fixed regularities and patterns that shape both perception and action in everyday life:

it is the durability and inertia of "the way things are." Structures are always present, but so is individual choice in navigating them—or agency. Any city or neighborhood's local situation has specific qualities that must be understood before a politician, an activist, or a policymaker can shape them. Yet there remains tremendous room for change, for creative agency. Past decisions may *constrain* future decisions, but they do not *determine* them.

The actions of social actors from factory workers to mayors actually help make up the very structures they are navigating. Every "new" action a person or entity takes draws on "existing conditions—that is, from structures resulting from their prior actions."[28] These structures can enable some outcomes and constrain others. For instance, local political structures can enable a city leader to take "good" actions (e.g., in support of education) or "bad" actions (e.g., extortion) or can constrain an actor from performing these same actions. Ethnography is a particularly useful lens to observe such complicated processes.

The on-the-ground learning, bargaining, and wrangling of city development is a bit like a card game, as urbanists H. V. Savitch and Paul Kantor note. Each city collectively and each politician specifically works with the structural hand they have been dealt by past actions.[29] Even efforts to develop a different hand—for example, one with more cards to facilitate new jobs in a particular sector—must *begin* with the cards they currently hold. Some cards in this hand are quite difficult or even impossible to get rid of. What basic structural factors in High Point foreground this book?

One durable factor is High Point's location between two cities: Greensboro, the seat of Guilford County where High Point is located, and Winston-Salem: both are a twenty- to thirty-minute car ride away. Although this geography is unlikely to ever change, its ramifications certainly could, such as if high-speed rail shortened travel time between the cities. Or if these municipalities consolidated their governments into a large tri-city.

Another durable factor is the state of North Carolina's position within a U.S. federal system of government in which higher levels of government are unlikely to meddle or assist in local development decisions. A related factor is High Point's council-manager form of government whereby the city council is in charge of general governing and the city manager executes city council policy and manages city departments.

The council comprises a mayor, two council members elected at-large, and six members elected by ward. The mayor, who presides over city council meetings, serves as the official leader and spokesperson of the city and represents High Point in interactions with both lateral (other municipalities) and vertical (county, state, and federal) governments.

Other factors are more variable, including the future of High Point's furniture heritage. It is conceivable (although admittedly difficult) to imagine a High Point no longer identified with furniture, just as it is to imagine a Detroit no longer identified with automobiles or a Paris disassociated from fashion. Another durable but potentially changeable factor is High Point's market (lowercase *m*) conditions: the circumstances that make High Point attractive or unattractive to profit-seeking investors.[30] Such factors—to which we could add the size of High Point's population—can ebb and flow, but are slow to change, with transformations occurring over decades.

Sociocultural factors that seem malleable in theory can prove quite durable in practice. The degree to which they actually change often relates to how social agents play their cards. One factor includes the "means by which citizens express their preferences and make elites accountable" for their actions.[31] *Do residents feel included? Do they vote and attend public meetings? What type of residents run for office? Do they form civic organizations that mobilize around common goals? What kind of civic causes do philanthropists support? What kinds of businesses do residents support?*

Cities' varying ability to bargain or play their hand can lead to vastly different development strategies and outcomes.[32] It is through these choices that even a huge, structural reality such as globalization "is variously embraced, resisted, subverted, and exploited as it makes contact with specific settings."[33] High Point illustrates this hybridity in which the local is inseparable from the global and exercises its influence through constant melding with it. Some urbanists use the term *glocal* to describe this interaction of global structural constraints and more localized agency.

With a global exposition such as the High Point Market, major world events can send shock waves through High Point. World War II managed to shut down the Market, for example, in 1942. The terrorist attacks on the World Trade Center in New York, the month before the Fall Market, did not. The global Covid-19 pandemic, however, led leaders to shut down the Spring 2020 Market. That year's Fall Market, though hobbled, was held in person over a longer period in tandem with an unprecedented online presence. By Fall 2021, as Covid-19 infection numbers decreased, the Market began to bear some resemblance to its pre-pandemic equivalents, even as supply chain struggles constrained some exhibitors' commitments to retailers. As it weathered the pandemic, it was clear that some of the Market's peculiarities offered advantages. Unlike at a trade show in a convention center, which has another event before and after it, the buyers tend not to arrive and depart all together, and exhibitors do not all erect and tear down their displays on a limited number of days, all using the same hallways and elevators. Furthermore, the many freestanding showrooms could accommodate the exhibition of furniture over a longer period of time to their and their visitors' comfort level. The result of past decisions, these peculiarities influence the cards that High Point leaders play as they prepare for the specter of future global pandemics.

The cards analogy helps distinguish between the cards in hand and the skills and philosophy of those holding them. The hand dealt to High Point was not unique, but some of its leaders played those cards in wildly unique ways. These leaders did not *ignore* the opportunities capitalism presented in an era of globalization, staring down the approaching train until it determined their fate for them. Nor did they merely *embrace* globalization, enjoying its anticipated benefits (such as inexpensive Chinese-made goods sold at Walmart) and accepting its anticipated costs (including the loss of local manufacturing) in the same way other places did. They did not attempt to *resist* it (by walling off the city from interconnectedness through tariffs or other tools) or *subvert* it (by undermining its core principles). Instead, High Point's political, economic, and social leaders worked together to *exploit* the opportunities of globalization.

They assessed their new cards and utilized High Point's peculiarities, converting them into subsequent hands that few could have imagined. Competing in high-stakes "place wars" with major cities (explored in chapters 3 and 4) took considerable audacity. Even critic Elijah Lovejoy respected the creative tenacity of High Point leadership in challenging "all of the [more prominent] cities that have gone after its furniture Market"—cities that "eventually gave up or just settled for a regional market."

Exploring the High Point Case

Shortly after my initial visit, I moved to High Point for more than two years. My immersive observation included living on Main Street, one mile from the Market district, and working in various jobs: as a front desk worker at Showplace during Market, an economic development intern at City Hall, an adjunct professor at High Point University, a shift worker at a group home, and an assistant manager at a gym, among others. I participated in citizen committees, most actively on the Downtown Improvement Committee. After I left High Point, I visited during Market and non-Market times, conducting field observations and taking photographs.

Throughout this project, I used multiple methods to achieve different ends. I formally interviewed just over one hundred residents. To access residents' sentiments about the city center, I placed a microphone to record their thoughts as we walked downtown (a "go along" interview) and looked at photographs of it (a "photo elicitation" interview).[34] To describe the downtown's transformation, I recorded land uses utilizing a data set developed from specialized city directories published by R. L. Polk & Company.[35] To access the public dialogue created about the downtown transformation, I conducted archival research and a forty-year content analysis of the city's daily newspaper, the *High Point Enterprise*. Finally, to document the aesthetics of the downtown, I created a photographic catalog of the entire downtown built environment, more than eighteen hundred images, and coded it with my research partner, Jason Patch. Overall, these methods yielded transcripts, field notes, archival artifacts, newspaper articles, photographs, and video.

The ten chapters that follow attempt to employ these data to answer key questions. Our questions are grounded within a theoretical approach that illuminates ideas vital to understanding High Point. Chapter 1 is an overview of these approaches.

How and when did High Point's development occur, both in the downtown and beyond? Why does that process matter? Part I overviews the past seven decades of High Point's development, taking a historical approach that spans chapters 2, 3, and 4. The overall goal of Part I is to gain a grasp of High Point's social organization of place building.[36]

How do different populations experience High Point? Part II departs from the more historical approach of Part I to examine the downtown from the vantage point of non-furniture-affiliated residents, Market organizers, marketgoers, and the designers and developers who live in the city year-round. Chapter 5 explores the downtown during its backstage months, and chapter 6 looks at the same space during the frontstage months when the community's massive Market performance is executed. Chapter 7 considers the more year-round components that, along with Market, round out the High Point region's furniture cluster.

In what ways have residents mobilized to reclaim the downtown for resident-centered uses? Part III is a chronological review of ten mobilization efforts by High Point residents on behalf of a more resident-inclusive downtown (chapters 8 through 10).

"We need to know much more than we currently do about how opportunities for profit from real estate are produced in place, as well as the time, extent and agents behind speculative investment in real estate," geographer Loretta Lees and her colleagues suggest.[37] *Showroom City* sets out to add color, nuance, and richness to our understanding as it addresses these inquiries. Rather than chronicling how the injustice of growth in a place like High Point "makes people miserable," the book uses ethnography to delve deeply into how power operates locally in one community, revealing often hidden aspects of larger urban processes useful to urbanists seeking new solutions for old problems.[38]

1

The Common Threads in High Point's Uncommon Fabric

One of the things that I find is that when I go to American cities, they
love to hear that they are unique . . . You know: *"we are unique."* And
they want to *hear* it from you. Sometimes, that's an easy white lie . . .
"Yes, you're unique." But they're really not. *This* is one of the most
peculiar places I've seen. . . . It's not exactly endearing, the way you're
peculiar, but it is *terribly* unique.

—Architect and urban planner Andrés Duany, High Point, 2013

Common Threads of an Uncommon Outcome

This book is designed to encourage a different way of seeing the urban
fabric by employing a community study approach. My goal is to extract
what are very common urban themes from a very uncommon urban
context. Is this misguided? As Andrés Duany suggests, is the High Point
case so peculiar that it is of little use interrogating it at all? Could it just
be a one-off: the postmodern, postindustrial condition writ large?

Urban studies should teach us that there is *never* a one-off, especially
in a globalizing world. The threads constituting the fabric of a seemingly outrageous story are never wholly unique. They merely combine
and cohere in different ways to create particular (and sometimes peculiar) outcomes. That is the value of methodically studying multiple places
and general urban trends: it teases out the general threads that constitute
a specific local fabric to reveal the common driving mechanisms at play
in cities and communities everywhere. What is the use of urban studies
if it cannot serve as a tool kit to help us tinker with varied contexts?

A case study of a single place offers the opportunity to dig deeper for
a more comprehensive examination of the threads that create a city's

fabric. This immersion provides a color, richness, and saturation difficult to achieve otherwise. Furthermore, investigating places not commonly studied has the potential to shake up our sometimes-stale understanding of the urban processes that shape communities. The High Point story both opens a unique window into the global economy and invites urbanists to reassess common issues.

What common threads are revealed by telling this story? First, we must consider the pursuit of profit in real estate, discussed here through the concept of *exchange value* and the related tenet of highest and best use. Second, it is not possible to understand High Point without grasping the *exclusion* that has helped shape our cities. Third, I look at the rise of *global interconnectedness*: its exhilarating opportunities and profound costs. Finally, the position and perspectives of different types of *users* of urban spaces are also important. In this opening "theory chapter," I have concentrated most of the abstract discussion about the thinkers and thinking that will help us contextualize the chapters that follow.

Thread of Exchange Value: Chasing Highest and Best

"You may have heard that our furniture market was the last bastion of free market capitalism," said real estate attorney Tom Terrell, talking about High Point's ascendance in the furniture industry. "I mean, it was run by real estate interests. If you could rezone for showrooms, you did it. It was loosely organized. But, truly, it was run by real estate interests, not by the furniture companies."

For its entire history, High Point has been dominated by various configurations of a growth machine: shifting alliances of local stakeholders who worked to "increase aggregate rents . . . for those in the right position to benefit."[1] This arrangement not only normalizes the celebration of elite growth goals as an assumed facet of civic life but also places localities in competition with one another in a way that actually harms their citizens.[2]

Although leaders in a growth machine do not always agree on the best strategies and specifics of growth, they do agree that *exchange value*—the monetary value of property determined by sale in an open market—should be at the core of what the local government does and the local community celebrates.[3] In this way, High Point's growth machine helps determine how local political, economic, and social life interact with the world around it. Observing their actions illuminates the links that connect "daily life and mundane local politics" with larger structures: economic and political systems that shape and are shaped by these politics.[4] The growth machine's pursuit of exchange value can come into conflict with residents' concern for *use value,* the worth derived from the satisfaction of *using* a property. The more commodified land is and the less its use value is debated in relation to its exchange value, the more its land markets will be facilitated by the unabated free market.[5]

Terrell's words are shocking: not only did the growth of the Market ignore residents' interests, but it also sidelined the interests of the furniture exposition it was presumably serving. A Market centered on excellent furniture exposition would have been designed differently. Chapter 4 reveals how the unguided High Point Market became a huge, chaotic, global furniture souk instead.

"The Market itself has challenges in that it is not under single ownership control," High Point planning director G. Lee Burnette explained. That allows each individual building to "decide when to turn the lights on and when to turn the lights off . . . Here, it truly is a market—small 'm'—phenomenon." In some other southern cities, "citizens expect and demand" regulation, whereas High Point is "more of a free market, this-is-my-property-I-can-do-anything-I-want-to-with-it type approach," he said. Some residents call it cowboy capitalism. Some academics will call it neoliberal governance. Whatever the perspective, few municipal governments have enshrined exchange value to the extent that High Point's city council has over the past six decades, and, correspondingly, few have witnessed such a radical transformation. "To some degree, you can argue that not having any regulation on it has allowed it to evolve and be here for one hundred–plus years," Burnette added.

Politician Judy Mendenhall has been a key player throughout this process. When I first met Mendenhall, she was the inaugural president of the High Point Market Authority.[6] Serving as mayor earlier in her political career, she was known for walking the downtown in tailored business attire and running shoes. To many, she exemplified casual southern sophistication. "I don't think it's the southern way to have a Plan B," she said from her Market Authority office in downtown High Point's brutalist white office building—often simply called "the white building" because its name changed so often as flagship tenants moved in and out. This was the first of many "No Plan B" conversations. In an unimpeded growth machine, owners are free to "manipulate property to 'highest and best use' by market criteria," as sociologist Harvey Molotch explains.[7] Not developing a Plan B and pursuing what real estate parlance calls *highest and best use* were complementary if not virtually synonymous. Throughout the Market's history, High Point leaders invoked the tenets of highest and best use to justify their pro-growth strategies, privileging development that is "physically possible, appropriately supported, financially feasible, and that results in the highest value."[8]

The brutalist downtown white office building, most recently called Showplace West, with the interior and exterior dining space of the shuttered J. Basul Nobles below. It once housed offices for Clinard's law firm, fabric producer CULP Inc., *InFurniture Magazine*, Phil Phillips's financial firm First Factors, the Market Authority, and so on. Showplace is in the background.

As the city's downtown stakeholders pursued highest and best use, the downtown became what urban planning theorist John Friedmann calls *economic space*. Driven by exchange value calculations—the instrumental logic of formulas—economic space seems endlessly expandable with little concern as to context.[9] Similar to the enterprise zones that have emerged worldwide in the era of globalization, High Point's local government has eliminated for downtown showrooms the red tape that developers would experience elsewhere in the city. As I show, the more High Point became wedded to the Market, the more local government leaders felt that they had to cede control to real estate investors to avoid losing the Market to a competitor. Unlike its company-town kin, also controlled by a single interest, High Point leaders had no representative with whom they could meaningfully discuss and negotiate. There was no single convention complex that managed these tenants. Rather, a plurality of owners and building tenants acting independently made up the High Point Market.

The control ceded to showroom interests has meant that High Point governance is remarkably nimble when it comes to the Market. Local officials are proud of how quickly developers erected major downtown projects, even when national, state, regional, and local bureaucracies were involved. They point to how the city quickly settled disputes between landowners or even between the city and exhibitors. The city has allowed showroom buildings in violation of fire and building codes to remain open for the Market, arguing in that instance that the government must "assist as much as we can to make each Market successful."[10] Such loosening of government control is evidence of urban planning theorist Edward Soja's "erosion of local control over the planning process, as the powerful exogenous demands . . . penetrate deeply into local decision-making."[11]

Burnette agrees. "Certainly our position in the furniture industry influences our policy," he said. "The city has had a laissez-faire approach to Market." But for local, nonshowroom business owners who have not enjoyed access to such expedited processes, the opposite is true. Like the many zones considered an "unregulated market," the downtown represents not merely the *absence* of regulations considered hindering but the marked *presence* of regulations favoring particular outcomes and effectively prohibiting others. As longtime students of municipal government know, one stakeholder's "let it be" environment often results in another stakeholder's "don't let it be" situation. Deregulation requires regulation so that market freedoms produce the outcome its champions desire. Or so that sovereignty is "sovereign in the *right* way."[12]

In High Point, the *right* free market has meant that the downtown would be shorn of locals. It has seen property owners and showroom operators frequently oppose the return of a resident-centered aspect to the downtown. Over the Market's history, they have favored suspending the use of buildings—and thus the entire downtown—between Markets to cut their costs and preserve their assets. In the words of architectural critic Ada Louise Huxtable, government used its power of zoning as "an instrument for maximizing real estate return" for investors rather than making the "city a fit place to live" for residents.[13]

"Realtors don't bother to even take people downtown anymore because they say you're wasting your time. The rents are too high," explained politician Jay Wagner. "If a property owner from a purely economic standpoint can rent the building for four weeks a year and have no wear and tear on their building and can make lots of money doing that, why wouldn't they do it? I understand simple *economics*."

Residents' biographies unfold in *life space,* explains Friedmann, which can present frustrating impediments to *economic space* stakeholders seeking unimpeded growth.[14] In life space, residents and their lives, struggles, and aspirations are forged: this is "the theater of . . . convivial life."[15] High Point's "complete dedication" to furniture exposition, as one Market official described it, did little for High Point's life spaces. When urbanists discuss control by capital, they often mean securing the cheapest labor or the most efficient distribution. Downtown High Point is a little different. Local leaders have allowed exhibition building owners what they sought most: a particular grip on the downtown's time and space.

Thread of Exclusion: Frontstage and Backstage

"Why is it that once you leave the showroom area of downtown, High Point looks like a slum?" former resident Mike Robertson asked in a letter in 2000 to the *High Point Enterprise.* "Why do the leaders place so much emphasis on this one area of the city when so much of the city needs help?" Robinson continued. "The leaders of High Point need to wake up . . . and start treating the citizens as something other than second-class people."[16]

Concern has grown over the past four to five decades that leaders around the world are increasingly fixated on using their cities as if they were a stage for productions for outsiders, whether gentrifiers, investors, tourists, or business visitors. This can produce two different types of exclusionary boundaries: a *geographic* boundary that marks *where* the privileged stages are and are not, and a *temporal* boundary concerning *when* those privileged stages are and are not under the spotlight.

I use the term *frontstage* to refer to a *place* that is a privileged geography during the *time* when the production is in process. *Backstage* refers to both the *times* in the frontstage when the production is not "on" and the *places* that are never in the frontstage. What transforms the dynamics of these terms? That variable is the gaze of an outside audience. In High Point, this gaze increasingly compares "everywhere in the world . . . with everywhere else," as sociologist John Urry has observed.[17]

The theater term *mise-en-scène* implies both concepts: frontstage and backstage. It describes everything the audience sees on the stage during a performance, including the arrangement of the actors, the props, costumes, and settings. A preoccupation with High Point's frontstage mise-en-scène completely dominates downtown High Point during the backstage months. This is a unique type of control over the urban landscape: control of its *temporality.*

Urban temporality is not unique to High Point. Every city has a temporality—times when it is "on" and times when it is "off" to particular audiences. Historians E. P. Thompson and Tamara Hareven describe how just such a reorganization of time accompanied the advent of industrial life.[18] Manufacturing cities had typically pulsed around the shifts of the local factory; their taverns and diners adjusted to match their workers' daily schedules. College towns are often ghost towns in June and July when they are in their backstage months. Come graduation, local hotels, apartment buildings, and even municipal services adjust their cycles; bushes are trimmed and even curbs get a fresh coat of paint. Major service-center cities also have their temporality, assuming an air of commerce during business hours with stints of lively street-level activity around lunch and perhaps evening times. Some residents lament that their city's business district is not "alive after five." Each of these cities may have influxes of outsiders, but their temporal rhythm is still driven largely by their residents and daily commuters.

The temporalities of most cities are similar. Certain scenes replay daily: during rush, work, and after-work hours. Even the dissimilar industrial and postindustrial eras share what sociologist Eviatar Zerubavel calls the "highly regular temporal structuring" that allows an observer to "tell the time by simply referring to the social environment."[19] Both operate on a visible cycle of weekdays and weekends, providing a "seven day beat."[20]

Downtown High Point operates differently: here the *month* most structures events. Observation alone cannot distinguish a Wednesday from a Sunday or ten in the morning from eight in the evening. This temporality became evident when I tried to create a year-by-year time-line of the downtown's rhythms with showroom designer Callie Ever-itt, who wracked her brain before confessing how difficult it was for her to translate the six-month rhythm of her life into my calendar of weeks, months, and years. "I think in Markets," she apologized.[21]

Before deindustrialization hit the city in the 1970s, the ideas of either a geographic or a temporal frontstage were less meaningful in High Point, where production and exhibition of furniture were then inextri-cable. However, in the era of globalization, the city's service-industry and manufacturing-industry fortunes began diverging. City and Mar-ket officials reprioritized and deprioritized particular regions and times based on the exposition. The downtown transitioned from being the main commercial district of a vertically integrated manufacturing town to the runway for furniture's fashion week. At the same time, the area around the red carpet was crumbling.

The use of terms such as *downtown* and *slum* is important here. They resonate with insights from urban studies, such as Friedmann's tension between the "citadel" and "ghetto."[22] These terms evoke a segregated city with spaces of lack and plenty, municipal negligence and priority. Cap-italizing on middle-class fears of what lies within the slum or ghetto spaces, developers build fortified enclaves in the downtown with designs that enclose and isolate buildings from the street. The result is a "citadel" or, in São Paulo, what urban planning scholar Teresa Caldeira called a "city of walls."[23]

These ideas can be subsumed under David Snow and Leon Ander-son's efficient terminology of prime and marginal space. They call *prime space* that which is desired "for residential, commercial, recreational, or navigational purposes."[24] Consider developing world cities where trans-national investment has historically enabled particular favored neigh-borhoods—deemed prime space—to grow very rapidly, fostering the development of globally integrated office, retail, and residential enclaves. Meanwhile, the remainder of the city, unhinged from these flows of investment, is left to carve out a life on the city's margins. For Snow and Anderson, *marginal space* has little exchange value and includes places where marginalized people such as homeless or poor residents, as well as marginalized uses such as informal settlements or single-room occupancy hotels, have more flexibility. These locations are peripheral, uncontested, and out of view. In marginal spaces, Duany noted, city inspectors only sporadically and selectively show up to monitor compliance with local ordinances.[25]

High Point's marginal spaces form a periphery around its prime space. Sociologist Stephen Sills and his team from the University of North Carolina at Greensboro identified more than 1,400 acres of vacant housing in the neighborhoods surrounding the downtown.[26] These census tracts had poverty rates of 32 to 87 percent, and the vast majority had labor force nonparticipation rates greater than 40 percent. City leaders refer to this area beyond the downtown as the "urban core." It consists of neighborhoods "plagued with blighted empty lots, vacant buildings, substandard housing, and whose residents have long experienced a lack of opportunity."[27] The ring of decay is interrupted at points, most prominently by Emerywood, the city's old-money neighborhood northwest of the downtown.

This southern landscape of bungalows, two-by-fours, shotguns, and low-rise public housing stands witness to the drastic devaluation over time brought on by mortgage redlining, federal defunding, municipal deprioritization, and physical deterioration. "It was really eye-opening to see how many houses are boarded up and that are vacant in town," began one civic leader discussing a 2012 tour with other leaders: "I had never seen that." Today, cities of various sizes include vast areas of unoccupied and unused territories that are invisible to residents with no connections there. Their laborers are redundant, obsolete, and often no longer trying to find work.

Gentrification gets most of the attention, but this is the *other* landscape of displacement: discarded neighborhoods. Although located just blocks from the frontstage, they are what urban sociologist Saskia Sassen calls unhinged: from the global economy, the commerce of the downtown, and the mental map of most visitors and many residents.[28] These unhinged areas can remain stubbornly disconnected from the global economy even as nearby areas become ever more connected. "It's awful. All the boarded-up buildings, all the houses that no one can live in," said

High Point nonprofit leader Maggie Mays. "But, you know, the only thing that matters is the showrooms that are open four weeks a year."

"There's a lot of job opportunities when the Market is here—and that's very beneficial for their families," explained community college administrator Janette McNeill, discussing prospects for students within the local economy. "But as a *community* we need to look at it a different way because that just keeps people in poverty."

Thread of Globalizations: Forging a Global Niche

To understand High Point, we need to grasp the "flows" of capital, people, information, technology, and products between it and other places around the world. According to sociologist Manuel Castells, contemporary societies are organized around such flows.[29] A city's role within networks of global economic, financial, informational, social, cultural, and political flows will shape everything from its business to its architecture to its spread of communicable disease.[30] The current "global urban order" is characterized by both dense networks of interconnection and intense interurban competition, as geographers David Bell and Mark Jayne explain.[31]

How are the city's flows articulated with cities that are further up the global hierarchy? Just as a human elbow is a different kind of articulation with a different function than a wrist, even though both are joint parts of the arm, flows in and out of cities can also be jointed and function in different ways. In addition, a particular flow—such as manufacturing investment—can be associated with two cities in very different ways. *What do these articulations of human interactions and economic transactions look like? What form do they take?*[32]

As a global merchandising and design center with a population of only 116,000, High Point has found itself in the limited company of other cities punching above their weight in the global competitions between places.[33] Bilbao is another such city; its name regularly arises in conversations of art and culture, unexpected from a city of just under 350,000.

In trying to make sense of the last fifty years of urban change, some theorists have retreated from the traditional understanding that cities occupying a "lower tier" in the global economy *must* "flow up" through higher-tier cities. More than two decades ago, geographers Donald Lyons and Scott Salmon noted how globalization was "expanding the global control potential of some cities further down the hierarchy."[34] Yet the traditional expectation persists that a city like High Point must stay within a particular lane, resigning itself to the so-called back-office functions (bookkeeping, call centers) that serve neighboring higher-tier cities.

Under the traditional model, one might expect High Point's articulation with the flows of the global economy to be mediated by (or first flow through) larger cities. Instead, downtown's flows of furniture people, products, information, and capital are connected directly to other higher-tier cities in the global economy. It is itself recognized as a node in global circuits (durable, predictable paths) of flows cutting across the globe, not just as a supporting player to a critical economic function in the larger southern cities of Charlotte or Atlanta, for example.

In the global economy, key nodes—whether neighborhoods in large cities or entire small cities—are integrated around shared functions (furniture merchandising) and shared meanings (such as a design aesthetic) in the name of garnering capital investment. I previously labeled High Point a "niche city" because of its significance within a specific portion of the global service economy.[35] This does not make it a "superstar city" on a par with New York, Tokyo, or London, but neither can it be likened to any typical local economy, which is experiencing rapid growth in global interconnectedness in more peripheral forms.[36] There are *many* places in between. As urban theorist Neil Brenner suggests, in assessing a city's relevance to the global economy, we need to expand our thinking beyond hierarchies and standard measurements (such as the number of transnational corporate headquarters or their supporting functions) to examine instead "the nature and extent" of a broader range of possible global-local linkages.[37]

In the abstract, we can envision the path of flows around the planet: they make up predictable, repetitive, and structural circuits of interaction.[38] Once these circuits develop, they have staying power and together constitute what Castells terms the *space of flows*. This helps explain why downtown High Point—so central to outsiders and so irrelevant to natives—just doesn't make sense *en vacuo*. We can really only understand a highly connected node via its location within these flows. It is less a product of its local geographic context than "a segmental unit of a larger entity" beyond its boundaries, as sociologist Guido Martinotti notes.[39] Sassen uses the phrase *terrain of centrality* to describe this context. In her language, downtown High Point's centrality stems not from its importance to the neighborhoods around it but from its significance to a "specific complex of industries and activities" that attracts flows from around the world.[40] When thinking about these terms, I envision models of plate tectonic theory showing the earth's continental plates as interlocked puzzle pieces (Pangea) with no oceans in between. Similarly, the nodes of the furniture world are thousands of miles and often oceans apart on a traditional globe, but are contiguous on the "furniture globe." In this light (and *only* in this light), High Point shares an adjacency, a terrain, a "larger entity" with Las Vegas, Shanghai, Cologne, Milan, and São Paulo. This centrality is not natural; it does not merely evolve or emerge but is strategized and created by economic and political actors.

The fact that this "specific complex of industries and activities" is of intense interest to buyers and sellers around the world distinguishes it from other, more local economic activities in the same city.[41] It constitutes what Sassen terms an *internationalized sector*.[42] She says that the internationalized sector imposes "a new set of criteria for valuing or pricing various economic activities," which makes it "increasingly difficult for other sectors to compete for space."[43] The local real estate market in which the tailor shop or local diner had once competed becomes overwhelmed by global capital.

"They think we're in New York City down here sometimes," said local historian Glenn Chavis. "Just because of the word 'furniture' you can charge all of these ridiculous prices." Chavis's comment illustrates how this node—the actual place where these durable circuits of capital, information, and people intersect with one another—also represents a local community that enjoys things like mom-and-pop tailor shops. This is what Castells calls the *space of places*. Just like Friedmann's life space, it has a specific history, vernacular, and peculiarity.[44]

The goal in such theorization is to shift our focus away from places and on to the processes that produce them. From this perspective, categories of developed and underdeveloped nations, city and suburb, and big city and small city are not particularly helpful in understanding how processes combine and cohere in specific places.[45] There are many "novel expressions of urbanization" today, as geographer Allan Scott notes, expressions that "generate new problems and predicaments of urban life."[46] High Point is a place that manifests clearly identifiable "urban"—and perhaps even "global city"—characteristics, while in other ways it seems to hardly resemble a city at all.

The current climate of global finance adds a new layer to this story of global interconnectedness. Today, exogenous private investment injects capital for projects that in the past were supported by infusions from national and state governments. This has precipitated a transition from small-scale localized ownership and financing to control by huge financial and private equity firms. Their influence can be broadly described as financialization: "the increasing dominance of financial actors, markets, practices, measurements, and narratives" at various scales of the economy and of governance.[47] While such acquisitions can seem like a radical departure, the underlying logic has "long been part of the urban land market."[48] For this reason, private equity's entrance into High Point, discussed in chapter 4, occurred with little fanfare. Only hindsight revealed how the underlying logic of highest and best use opened the door for a contemporary "scale-up" that Sassen notes "takes it all to a whole new dimension, one that alters the historic meaning of the city."[49]

High Point is not a mere allusion to "today's scale-up"; it embodies it.[50] This not only disrupts conventional understandings of small-city growth machines but suggests some unexpected lessons. For one, High Point's civic leaders may not have lost as much (relative) leverage vis-à-vis showroom owners as a result of international investment as one might expect. By some measures, they may have gained agency vis-à-vis the old growth machine days. One piece of evidence is persuasive: High Point's mobilizations on the behalf of local community, the subject of Part III of this book, were unsuccessful *until* the era of highest external investment. Our use of the growth machine perspective argues against over-romanticizing local power. While there is a story of *local* and *global* to be told, those terms should hardly be considered synonymous with *wholesome* and *malevolent.*

Thread of Users: A Gentrified Landscape for Visitors

Urbanists often classify redevelopment that creates a new infrastructure for a higher class of users as gentrification. This concept is essential in recognizing the production of High Point's frontstage mise-en-scène, which—ultimately—established a particular image of the city. But an image intended for whom?

As High Point began to focus on exhibition and compete with other exposition cities, it developed what sociologist Sharon Zukin calls a *landscape of power,* an area of the built environment dominated by government and business interests purposefully imbued with symbolism to support current power arrangements.[51] It contrasts starkly with the everyday spaces she identifies as *vernacular* that embody "the resistance, autonomy, and originality" of long-standing residents.[52] Its narratives contest the seamless gloss of the dominant landscape by celebrating local complexity. As vernacular gives way, a walk through the landscape of power can leave you asking, where's the *local*?

A place's reputation, its built environment, its politics, its social fabric, its history, its weather, people's experience of it, and many other factors all combine to co-create the image of a place, "the sense people have . . . of the cultural-material interactions" within it.[53] These various realms conjoin—they "lash up," in the language of philosopher Bruno Latour—like threads or strands in a rope to create a city's particular, enduring image.[54] Not only locals fashion this image; so do "those far away."[55] In High Point, a furniture world constituted of those physically located far away generates a defining impact.

Various populations constitute the contemporary city. Starting with the two traditionally recognized urban groups of *inhabitants* and *commuters,* Martinotti then adds the subgroup of city *users,* those who come to a city to utilize its private and public amenities.[56] Their increasing influence is especially important because, with little reason or opportunity to be cognizant of their impact on the city's aggregate footprint, this group can act in an "uncontrolled way."[57] The "direct competition or conflict of the users with the inhabitants" is always present, if not always apparent, and this is especially true in cities like High Point that—as Martinotti notes of Venice, Italy—has a "small population of inhabitants . . . but a vast population of city users."[58]

Some of High Point's users fall into another of Martinotti's categories: "a transnational middle-class" that lives a multisited life "between cities."[59] Sociologist Leslie Sklair explains that these distanced stakeholders "operate transnationally as a normal part of their working lives" and develop unique relationships to the social space they navigate.[60] For this cosmopolitan population, a city can play a significant role in their lives even though they might be in town only a few times annually.[61] Still, they may consider the place *theirs*—a type of home. Just the way many marketgoers regard High Point.

Geographer Eric Clark's intentionally broad definitions of gentrification and users also apply here. To him, gentrification is "a process involving a change in the population of land users such that the new users are of a higher socio-economic status than the previous users, together with an associated change in the built environment through a reinvestment in fixed capital."[62] His definition suggests that gentrification requires only three things: reinvestment, a dependence on new users, and that these users are of a higher socioeconomic class than the previous users.

Clark offers three causes of gentrification. First comes the commodification of space, which he describes as the transformation of human environments into a more or less indistinguishable good. The second concerns a polarization of power relations that enables some stakeholders to raise or suppress the value of places based on their economic, political, and social power. Third is the domination of "vision" over "sight" that characterizes the "vagrant sovereign," a concept first identified by cultural critic Wendell Berry. It connotes the "impulsive roamings" of distant investors whose visions and plans can be realized only through the disembedding and displacing of interests with an appreciation for the land tied to use value.

It is easy to see how this vagrant and uninformed supreme entity may not care about the convivial value of life spaces or the complexity of vernacular, seeing change as necessary for progress. Malice need not be part of the equation. Perhaps due to the loss of "ethical and economic interdependencies" that existed when investment was more localized within closed networks, the vagrant sovereign is unaware of the fragile boundaries it is broaching or the damage it is doing.[63] In other words, its violence can be structural. But the greater the power advantage, the greater the potential that the reinvestment will lead to a reinvention of the built environment for a new user of higher status.[64]

For most of the Market's history, the downtown's reinvention was unaccompanied by any permanent residential or retail infrastructure or the desire for any such improvements. Unlike typical gentrifiers—more-affluent in-moving residents who require the development of a traditional permanent infrastructure—High Point's users, the marketgoers, are participating in a structure of upgrading and displacement in their business lives rather than as residents.[65] Though my use of the term is untraditional, it still offers a vital tool for understanding both the displacement of present life spaces and the potential for future ones. As downtown land becomes increasingly appropriated by ever-larger, exogenous interests for use by a global middle class, there is the potential for these outside firms to act in ways both "sovereign" and "vagrant."

Tensions and Splintering

What is the impact of seventy years of privileging exchange value in a geography with such stark boundaries of exclusion? A property value map created in 2016 by the Asheville-based urban planning firm Urban3 offers a visual answer, showing the internationalized sector of the downtown real estate and the unhinged, disconnected areas beyond it. Land values are but one way to capture the sharp contrast between them.

Any consideration of exclusion, exchange value, globalization, and users must also take into account residents' right to their city. The right to the city was first articulated by sociologist and philosopher Henri Lefebvre in 1968.[66] For Peter Marcuse, this right aspires to "a place in an urban society."[67] To David Harvey, it is "a collective rather than an individual right" to "exercise . . . power over the processes of urbanization."[68] The discontent and alienation underlying "right to the city" demands can emerge from anyone "of any economic class" who opposes the "dominant system as preventing adequate satisfaction of their human

Tax assessed value per acre model presented by Joseph Minicozzi of Urban3 to the High Point City Council in May 2014 ("road diet" project in chapter 9 circled). Courtesy of Urban3.

needs."[69] That is, the same structural constraints can create discontent for residents with different levels of economic, political, social, and legal security.[70] This web of mutuality creates room for broad-based agreement, for collective action. A context without this interdependence presumably encourages injustice if, indeed, the "public realization of justice" requires community.[71]

The sociopolitical environments of engaged citizenries are more likely to lean toward values encouraging local community building: use value, local meaning or vernacular, life space, and fair treatment of marginal spaces. As High Point planner Burnette put it, in these environments "citizens expect and demand" regulation on behalf of broader community aspirations. Other sociopolitical milieus tend to cede control to powerful stakeholders' pursuit of exchange value, landscapes of power, economic space, and prime space. Burnette explains this as the "free market, this-is-my-property-I-can-do-anything-I-want-to-with-it type approach" that has dominated High Point's politics. Its lack of engagement over shared community issues can damage the "capacity for informed citizenship" that yields "more sensible and more ennobling decision making."[72]

Another binary from Berry—*exploitation* and *nurture*—can help frame the conceptual categories I have been discussing. Berry identifies efficiency as the motive of the *exploiter* and care as that of the *nurturer*. The exploiter's goal is to maximize exchange value and profit; the nurturer's is health.[73] The exploiter wishes to "earn as much as possible by as little work as possible; the nurturer expects, certainly, to have a decent living from his work, but his characteristic wish is to work as well as possible." The exploiter's service is often on behalf of an organization or an institution; the nurturer serves community and place.[74]

Applying any of the binaries discussed in this chapter, it is easy to imagine two sides "poised for battle," with the interests of residents pitted against those of "developers, chambers of commerce, and media boosters."[75] The latter group seeks unimpeded development in this oversimplified battle, while residents desire maximized participation and autonomy.[76] It is also tempting to characterize these two extremes as the political left and right, when in reality these contests play out much less neatly in particular places at particular moments. Besides the localized dynamics I have been discussing, there are also broader economic, political, and social factors acting on a place that require local leaders to respond by "accommodating, managing, or resisting" these forces.[77]

Faced with diverse dilemmas at multiple scales, local officials might find themselves promoting solutions they would never have imagined otherwise.

In this sense, each of our binaries is profoundly removed from the murkier positions people take in reality. Such measurements generally range on a continuum, not as either-or oppositions (such as 1 or 0, on or off, yes or no). Life is not this dichotomous. In fact, Berry adds a critical admonition to these debates about community, advising that his terms, *exploitation* and *nurture*, identify a division that exists not only between people and groups but also within people and groups.[78]

Although binaries risk portraying a false battle of opposite forces—as introductory college courses too often depict it—they remain useful for grasping the dynamics of development. After all, local mobilizations often emerge in response to residents' perceptions of polarization. I first heard of High Point through the lens of a binary: the revaluation of marginal spaces as prime.

In 2000, New York City building owners who helped transform a marginal life space for poor and homeless people into a prime economic space for showroom exhibition in midtown Manhattan petitioned for the right to reserve the space for their use as a showroom district—their landscape of power. New York City mayor Rudolph Giuliani, whose decisive actions against homeless activism had marked the 1990s, was more receptive to the campaigns of nonprofits serving the homeless by 2000, and he approved supportive transitional housing within this quasi-district. This act, not without its issues, was certainly more nurturing than previous Giuliani actions regarding the homeless.

Some showroom owners reacted with anger. They felt that the exchange values of this area had increased in no small part due to their

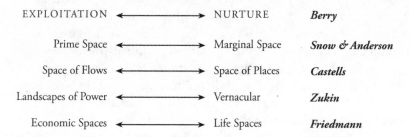

EXPLOITATION	⟷	NURTURE	*Berry*
Prime Space	⟷	Marginal Space	*Snow & Anderson*
Space of Flows	⟷	Space of Places	*Castells*
Landscapes of Power	⟷	Vernacular	*Zukin*
Economic Spaces	⟷	Life Spaces	*Friedmann*

Four binaries placed on a continuum from "exploitation" to "nurture," with corresponding authors.

efforts to establish it as prime space. The use of the area by marginalized residents—hardly a concern when it was marginal space—thus came under their scrutiny. Snow and Anderson explain that marginal space can be "ceded intentionally" to less desired uses by authorities, as with some skid rows or shantytowns, or it can be "ceded unwittingly" simply out of inattention.[79] In this case, Manhattan stakeholders fumed that the city was *intentionally* offering their prime land to uses for homeless residents *despite* their significant investments to change it. They forcefully argued that the area was worthy of the mayor's careful protection from marginal uses.

Nothing disrupts a landscape of power more than a sober reminder of poverty, especially in the form of homeless bodies, as Zukin observes.[80] The showroom owners explicitly articulated a need to conduct their business in a landscape free from what one called the "physical and visual confrontation" of homeless people. Another firm argued that it had just completed a major renovation that a leading magazine had recognized as a model of showroom design. But what does it matter *how* the inside looks, they asked, if the outside environment is "compromised"? The exhibitors concluded that Mayor Giuliani was uncooperative in promoting an adequate business climate. They argued that other cities had cleaned and swept—terms that surface in veiled antihomeless campaigns—this type of vernacular out of their global business districts. One such city, they said, was High Point.

These protests were how I first came to know about High Point and its "uncompromised" landscape. When I moved there two years later, I quickly discovered that the same landscapes exhibitors in New York considered uncompromised were regarded by High Point residents as highly compromised. "You get this splintering of the community," attorney and politician Jay Wagner said as he explained the social-psychological effects of this tension. "In a typical city you have a downtown where everyone feels *some* ownership, everyone feels like 'this is my downtown, this is my town,' and everyone in the city feels that. But you don't really get that here because our downtown is owned by someone else and it functions for someone else."

"A living room is to a home what a downtown is to a city," declared Elijah Lovejoy. "It is the heart. It is the place people gather. It is the one area everyone calls their own regardless of how they feel about people on the other side of town." High Point, he lamented, is "currently in search of its downtown—a place to collectively gather, dance, talk, laugh, and entertain"—because its downtown is "occupied by showrooms."

Displacement does not always occur in a particular moment. It can also be an enduring "loss of sense of place," geographers Mark Davidson and Loretta Lees point out.[81] Part I chronicles the history of this loss.

PART I

OUT OF THE MILLS

A Small City Goes Global

2

Hollowing Out

The "All-American" Downtown Goes Temp

Looking for Downtown

I was enjoying a meal with Elijah Lovejoy and Jim Davis, owner of the new Rosa Mae's restaurant in Thomasville, ten miles from High Point. Davis had closed his original restaurant in downtown High Point after concluding that the location was no longer tenable. Lovejoy was asking him what might replace the lost downtown.

"Essentially, it looks like the Palladium area," Davis said. He was referring to the new retail center in North High Point near the Greensboro border. This former greenfield area north of downtown was slowly incorporated into the city limits but was developed into a suburban landscape. "I mean, they're getting it all out there," said Davis.

"Do you think that's healthy for the community, for stuff to move to the Palladium? What do you think's the result of that?" Lovejoy asked.

"I think it divides us more than anything," Davis responded.

The rise of North High Point, located off Interstate 40 and near the regional Piedmont Triad International Airport, seemed a similarly natural evolution to many other High Pointers. Yes, the city had facilitated it, but such changes were happening nationwide. "The Market in its growth killed the downtown as a traditional downtown," politician Becky Smothers said. "But at that same time, traditional downtowns were changing anyway," she added.

This chapter explores the dynamics of downtown change through the lens of High Point's two downtowns: the official central business district and the Black downtown forged in the Jim Crow South. With a look at the impact of the *decentralization* of retail and other functions on the

43

traditional downtown, I discuss the development of the farms and green-space of North High Point, land the city annexed over time. Finally, I consider the dynamics that make downtown High Point unique—what some local players refer to as its escape from economic death.

Two Downtowns

"Everything in High Point worked on the Tomlinson whistle," said former floor-covering businessperson and civic leader Richard Wood, talking about a former downtown furniture company. "When that whistle blew, you knew it was noon. Again? It was three o'clock." In those days, he said, "the guy with the most dirty smoke coming out of the stack was the richest man in town. Tomlinson put out more black smoke than anybody." Jobs at Tomlinson, Adams-Millis hosiery, and other factories drew laborers to High Point from nearby and distant rural areas at a time when federal policies encouraging the mechanization of agriculture were pushing them out of farming communities. Downtown High Point of that era was a bustling place where families could shop in various department stores and small clothiers on Saturday mornings, where men and women would shoot the breeze while getting their hair done, and where mostly local talent—but also national figures such as Elvis Presley—would come to entertain on weekend nights in the Center Theatre.

As the number of rural Black southern migrants increased, they faced increasing hostility in downtown High Point. "We didn't hang out [in the official downtown]—let me put it like that," said Glenn Chavis, a Black resident who is a local expert on High Point history. "We did what we had to do and went back to Washington Street." Policy by policy, the High Point government limited Black residents to particular neighborhoods and solidified Washington Street as the city's Black commercial center, a separate downtown. The following two sections explore these downtowns in their heyday of the 1950s and 1960s.

High Point's "All-American" City Center

In 1962, as part of its annual competition, the National Civic League awarded High Point the designation All-American City. "I remember going downtown like, gosh, in the '50s," said realtor Ed Price. "Everybody in town would go and bop down there to the Saturday morning kiddie show at the Center Theatre. And then from there, you just hung around downtown. If you had any money, you get a hot dog or something." In the 1950s and 1960s, High Point was full of households with money to spend, the majority coming from the production of furniture and hosiery, and downtown was where many spent it.[1] For these residents, it was the town's heartbeat.

In this overview of the downtown's commercial transformation, I rely on what I and my colleague Jason Patch call a *temporal map,* constructed using data from the R. L. Polk city directory for High Point. The map tracks four different types of property uses from 1963 to 2003, beginning with the year High Point surpassed Chicago as the dominant furniture Market and ending with the year its Market area exceeded ten million square feet.[2] To help display the change in downtown uses, they have been divided into four types.

Retail establishments encompass places other than restaurants where a customer would purchase a tangible good. *Personal services* represents consumer services not involving the purchase of a tangible product, such as the dry cleaners, an income tax service, attorneys, and so forth. *Third place* designates those places away from home and work that constitute "hangouts," including pool halls, restaurants, lodges, and bars.[3] *Office* captures white-collar entities where people work but consumers typically do not frequent. I omit two obvious uses here for simplicity: showrooms (which rose from few to many) and factories (which declined from many to few.)

High Point's numerous downtown stores included independent retailers as well as regional and national chains. Sears, Alexander's, Gilbert's, Belk, Charles, Woolworth's, JCPenney, Richardson, and S. H. Kress & Co. speckled the central business district. Small men's and women's clothing stores provided an alternative to the major-store shopping. The diverse retail options in small-city downtowns like High Point inspired a feeling of sophistication and civic pride. For people fulfilling their daily errands, downtown High Point boasted nearly two hundred personal service establishments, an average of two each block in 1963.[4] The downtown's third places were the setting for chance meetings, spontaneous conversations, and a development of community consciousness. Cafés, grills, lunch counters, bars, pool halls, clubs, community group headquarters, and even laundromats offered sites for political discussion, gossip, and the exchange of community news. There were also

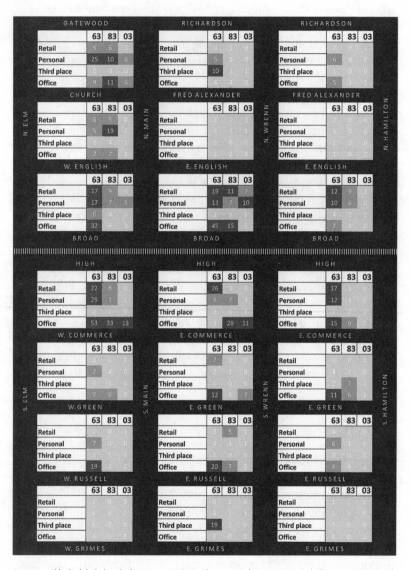

Downtown blocks labeled with their uses in 1963 (the year High Point surpassed Chicago), 1983, and 2003 (the year Market exceeded ten million square feet). Block proportions are for visual display only, and some city blocks are aggregated to allow for consistency despite road rerouting.

more than two hundred office establishments including, like many of its peer cities, businesses in finance, insurance, and real estate—the "FIRE industries."

Before geographic racial segregation increased in the 1920s and 1930s, both Black- and white-owned businesses occupied the Black downtown's Washington Street and the white downtown's Main Street, only half a mile apart. For instance, Black High Pointers Jesse and Minnie Edmondson owned barber and beauty establishments on both streets. By the 1940s and 1950s, Black ownership was more confined to Black communities.

During the era of urban renewal (1949–74) and slum removal in the United States, High Point inspectors searched for "the blight that's right." Overlooking the areas most in need, they instead concentrated on areas that promised higher exchange values for potential developers. In these targeted "sweet spots," usually near downtown, measurements of blight were artificially inflated and project boundaries gerrymandered by what one critical High Point councilperson called "captive" city employees— that is, actors given little latitude for critical input.[5] High Point leaders focused their urban renewal efforts on a six-hundred-acre project area they called East Central, which included part of the city center and the Black downtown of Washington Street.[6] Washington Street had connected High Point's downtown with its East Side until the late 1960s, when the city reconfigured nearby streets to bypass and isolate it, making the parallel Kivett Drive (today Dr. M. L. King, Jr. or MLK Drive) the new connecting thoroughfare.

During the same period, just one block south, the city acquired dozens of parcels and assembled them into a superblock that, illustrating the city's high hopes for it, leaders called the "Magic Block." Nationally, activists like Jane Jacobs decried the disruptions to the city street grid, loss of local architecture, and damage to local small business wealth that accompanied such single-use creations.[7] High Point property owners contested the project's questionable "blight" designations all the way to the North Carolina Supreme Court with little success.[8]

When the anticipated private market development never happened on the cleared block—a common occurrence in U.S. cities during urban renewal—the city sold the land to High Point University in 1964.[9] Recalling the "taking" of the Magic Block's thirty-three buildings through eminent domain, some High Pointers quip how small businesses, including

Black- and immigrant-owned, were "magically" wiped out.[10] High Point
University eventually leased the land to a Sears store in 1967.

Meanwhile, concentrating on areas near downtown, urban renewal
leaders continued to ignore the city's most deteriorated communities.
Under the national policy, the federal government covered two-thirds of
demolition costs, leaving one-third to the city. As a bonus, however, the
city could receive "credits" in lieu of its one-third contribution by completing public works projects such as schools, parks, or bridges. Mayor
Carson Stout informed the residents of the Southwest neighborhood
that with no public works projects underway there, the city would be
required to "lay out its whole share of [any potential Southwest] project in cash."[11] With federal funding readily available, that scenario was
not compelling to the mayor. It followed a bewildering but common
logic: because the city overlooked the ramshackle Southwest for local
public works funding, Southwest would get no federal urban renewal
help either.

The East Side's Washington Street

With its Quaker roots, High Point was slightly more progressive than
other cities in the Jim Crow South. "African Americans were allowed to
work in the factories, you see, and made fairly decent money—not as
much as their white counterparts but, still, it was good money," said
politician Bernita Sims, longtime head of the High Point Black Leadership Roundtable. "That's what started the influx of people from other
parts of the state into our community."

"They *needed* us for those jobs," said Chavis, whose mother did "piece-
work" for Drexel-Heritage furniture. "When the economy is going
[strong], you see all the Black faces in those places," Chavis continued,
describing the more difficult, "mankilling" jobs as they were called in
that era. "When the economy is bad, all of a sudden white people want
those jobs. And when they want those jobs, they push you aside, and you
don't even get an interview for the job." Chavis was illustrating what is
known as split labor theory in which a workforce that perceives divisions within itself—such as white versus Black—can be conveniently
exploited by employers who know that an alternate, desperate workforce will be waiting in the wings.

"African American folks stayed in their place and knew where that
place was," said Sims. Rules about racial boundaries were clear and passed

down. "You could go in Kress', buy anything you wanted to buy in that store, but you couldn't sit down at that counter and eat, that was the difference," she explained. "You could buy the garment, take it home, but you couldn't try that dress on in the store."

Like so many Black downtowns in the United States in the 1940s and 1950s, Washington Street was rich in commerce because virtually every aspect of life that segregation required to be duplicated—from places of worship to housing to banking to personal services such as dry cleaning, barber, and beauty shops—had generated distinct and flourishing Black business communities. "Washington Street was vibrant," Sims recalled. "We went to the pharmacy on Washington Street. We went to the movies. We bought clothes on Washington Street. Our library was on Washington Street. Our restaurants were there. Our cleaners, our shoe shops, everything we needed—beauty shop, barber shop—all that was on that street. There was no *need* to [go to the white downtown] unless there was some speciality item that you needed."

"Fifty-two businesses in a four-block area," agreed Chavis. "Seven doctors, two dentists, and an attorney practicing within a four-block area." He had recited these statistics so often they spilled out by rote. "Three Black hotels [the Hinton, Kilby, and Henry] on the same street at the same time." This Black urbanization, as sociologist Aldon Morris showed, helped foster organizational density, mobilize resources, and cultivate anchor institutions for Black thought in every arena of life.[12] Chavis proudly cited the prominent figures—Booker T. Washington, James Weldon Johnson, Mary McLeod Bethune, Walter White, Mary White Ovington, Langston Hughes—who came to Washington Street to speak, perform, or just visit kin and friends. Chavis fondly remembered the street's Kilby Hotel, where some of them stayed. "Unbelievable, heavy-duty stuff," he enthused. "We were being brainwashed to believe that most of the things that we had were inferior," he added. "We wanted to be a part of this world down here. 'Oh, they've got this. Look at the wonderful things they have' [in the white downtown]. But we *had* those things, you know?"

"Then we had this fabulous park," added Chavis, smiling. Washington Terrace Park, a twenty-seven-acre "Negro recreational park" project of the Works Progress Administration, was a community anchor. Sims, too, spoke with affection about the park's nurturing aspect. "During the summer, we'd go to the park every day," she said. "You didn't worry about where the kids were or what they were doing." She recalled the night-time baseball games and how when a fan's favorite batter came up to the plate, "they'd put a dollar in the fence for a home run. And, you know, if the guy hit the home run, he got to take the dollars out of the fence." She talked about the dance floor that would be set up adjacent to the baseball field, so "you could actually literally see the game from the dance floor."

"It's a mixture of everything, but we were all in the same boat," said Chavis—the park, the central business district, and the adjacent cam-puses of Griffin Elementary School and William Penn High School encompassed a one-mile stretch of public-centered activity. Bisecting Washington Street is Underhill Street, with the campus of the two schools on the west and Daniel Brooks Homes public housing development on the east. (Like other housing authorities across the nation, the High Point Housing Authority demolished the 246 units of Daniel Brooks in 2020, offering residents Housing Choice vouchers, and building new mixed-income housing on- and off-site.)

"Very few people remember Underhill Street," Chavis said. "That's where prominent Blacks lived. We used to call it Black Emerywood," a reference to High Point's elite white neighborhood. "Your doctors, your dentists, your principals, your teachers. All of these people lived on Underhill."

Jazz saxophonist John Coltrane grew up at 118 Underhill in the house of his grandfather, Reverend William Wilson Blair of St. Ste-phens A.M.E. Zion Church, after his father died. His father, John R. Coltrane, had owned a dry cleaning and tailor shop on High Street, an area later demolished when the roads around Washington Street were rerouted to bypass it. "Two big pillars," Chavis said, putting up his hands to illustrate the entrance to the neighborhood. The words *Underhill Avenue* made up a wrought iron arch that connected them. "You were so proud of being on Underhill," said Chavis.

"It is common today to become misty-eyed about the old Black ghetto, where doctors and lawyers lived next door to meatpackers and steelworkers, who themselves lived next door to prostitutes and the un-employed," cultural analyst Ta-Nehisi Coates warns. "This segregation-ist nostalgia ignores the actual conditions endured by the people living there—vermin and arson, for instance—and ignores the fact that the old ghetto was premised on denying Black people privileges enjoyed by white Americans."[13] Chavis was hardly blind to the fact that the very creation of the Black downtown was predicated on overt racism. However, he felt that the affirming Black space that residents created was valuable and laments the loss of it. "Integration destroyed Washington Street," he told me as we walked the downtown. "We were doing very well, we didn't *need* to come down here."

The era of integration reshaped Washington Street, triggering an artificially rapid exodus of the Black middle class coupled with disinvestment and loss of political leadership.[14] As the Washington Street community began unraveling, no central community space appeared to replace the rich public realm that was lost. In another walk through the center city, I asked Angela McGill, decades younger than Chavis, if she had any fond memories of downtown High Point. She remembered Bruce Lee movies with her father, but after the film, it would be a quick return to the East Side: "'Get in the car and get your butt back home. Get in the car and get—your—butt—back—home'" is how she remembered it.

The Beginning of the End of the Resident-Centered Downtown

Built in 1958, College Village, an L-shaped building with 142,000 square feet of strip-style retail storefronts connected by a roofed-over sidewalk and flanked by a parking lot, was the city's first mall. Although located about a mile and a half from downtown and not an easy walk, the mall was still a draw. "It switched from . . . going downtown every Saturday morning to going off to College Village," Price recalled. "That was brand-new. It impressed everybody." Although Black High Pointers were accustomed to shopping beyond the official central business district, for whites this was the first trickle of downtown activity siphoning off to another retail area, barely perceptible at first.

During this era, the Market area in downtown High Point was limited to three blocks within a still-active, resident-centered downtown. From today's urban planning standpoint, it was a healthy, mixed-use arrangement. Located at the corner of Main and Washington before Washington was truncated, Nugget House was a bustling diner from 1968 to 1982. It served as a *third place* that opened at 4 a.m. and closed at 9 p.m. "My father, he emigrated to Chicago in '48 and lived in Chicago for a few years," said Jim Davis. He cut his teeth working in the restaurant alongside his Greek immigrant father. "He heard about the High Point Market from the Chicago [furniture] market. And he came down." Stories like this, from seventy years ago, reveal High Point's small town cosmopolitanism rooted in its connection with major cities.

"When I was little, you had High Point Quick Lunch, you had Nugget House, you had Jimmy's Pizza, you had Steve's Sandwich Shop, you had Tracy's, you had Eagle Sandwich Shop," Davis mused. He could also reel off the names of all the clothing stores, drugstores, and shoe stores that were once in these few blocks. "Wilson Shoe Shop—first place I ever bought Converse shoes," he laughed. "It was just [a] tight community. Reminds you of something in Europe," he added.

The Rise of Malls and the Reworking of the High Point Landscape

By 1971, High Pointers were enjoying the city's first indoor shopping center, Westchester Mall. When anchor department stores like JCPenney and Belk moved to the mall, it significantly depleted the diversity of downtown shopping. Real estate attorney Tom Terrell recalled how exciting and innovative indoor, air-conditioned shopping seemed at the time. "I would go to see friends. You started doing all your Christmas shopping there," he said. Only in hindsight did Terrell, who also cherished downtown High Point's former vitality, fully appreciate the causality between the malls and the downtown. Next to go were the movie theaters: the Paramount Theater in the 1970s and the Center Theatre in the early 1980s. Utilizing the larger space available in malls, new theaters began shifting to multiscreen venues. "Back then," Price chuckled, "two or three was a big multiscreen theater."

The agglomeration of a former mill town's center city was unraveling, deagglommerating. To many High Pointers, the changes seemed a healthy, natural evolution, not the result of decisions made by local leaders. Larry Wilson closed his downtown shoe store—where Davis got his first Converse tennies—in 1982. "When a city reaches a certain size, they build malls and the downtown dies. I've never known one to come back. It's just a progression, a natural order of things."[15]

By the early 1980s, less than half as many retail establishments were there as in the 1960s. As traffic decreased, the niche retailers that remained depended increasingly on the occasional, planned purchase, such as sales of paint, musical instruments, office supplies, auto parts, jewelry, and clothes. Third-place establishments had fallen more than 50 percent in twenty years. The factories and retail that supported these third places had moved, taking with them much of the potential for spontaneous meetings that keep such informal community centers vibrant. Personal service providers followed the lead of the other downtown businesses, declining at the same rate over the same period. They, too, began to follow the city's residential population and traffic patterns to North High Point—"you know, your suburban paradise," as resident Nic Ruden noted.

The area around the downtown became increasingly Black and poor as white middle-class departures to the greenfield north of High Point became the norm—the local manifestation of a national trend of white flight. The white belief that Black residents deteriorated homes, schools, and neighborhoods became a self-fulfilling prophecy as it was institutionalized through policy at every level of government.[16] For most white residents, a suburban lifestyle meant not only a white picket fence but a homogeneous white neighborhood and school. In 1969, a High Point Board of Education member stated, "We are going to have to face the problem here of the present city becoming predominantly Negro. . . . As the Negro population density increases, there is a tendency for the quality of schools to deteriorate."[17] Served by the mostly white county school system, North High Point offered a safe haven for white residents fearing integration. "You would see this advertisement for real estate: 'county schools.' . . . It was a code word," said Terrell.

The High Point Market Growth Machine

Reinvestment often blazes a path created by disinvestment, but investors' initial forays can be "affirmed and strengthened by the state's selective response."[18] Much real estate speculation amounts to bets on this state response. After the mayoral election of 1975, downtown planning was given over to a new Downtown Development Board formed in 1976 that included Market, government, banking, and real estate players. Its composition undoubtedly reassured investors about the security of their bets on showroom real estate.

Robert Gruenberg, director of the Home Furnishings Center, was chair, and furniture industry insider Phil Phillips and banker Fred Alexander were on the board. White businessmen's dominance of local civic life was common practice in industry towns during this era. Within an environment of public disinterest in mundane civic affairs and a belief that "who, in material terms, gets what, where, and how" should be left to the experts, power had coalesced into "a dull but unanimous political façade."[19]

"There was a lot of cross-pollination between the furniture and textile companies and our city council," as Terrell saw it. It was an era when all the major downtown players were from the region; most lived either in or near town. Historically, consensus in High Point was reached in restaurant booths or at the Rotary Club, the country club, and other spaces where political decisions on important issues occurred in informal conversations among chummy city leaders.[20]

There is a storied table at the String & Splinter Club ("string" for textile, "splinter" for furniture), long High Point's favored setting for the meeting of elite minds. Many cities have such spaces; in Houston, it was "Suite 8-F" in the now-demolished Lamar Hotel. "It's all the cronies," said High Point furniture designer and full-time resident Raymond Waites. He repeated his version of the String & Splinter table story, noting (as politician Bernita Sims and others also did) that a weaker vestige of such a table still remained. A sense of inevitability attended the "back-room" plans devised there. Residents tended to understand the downtown development that resulted not as a series of decisions but, rather, as an organic process.

"So this is an evolutionary process like anything else," said one resident, offering a common accounting of downtown High Point's natural growth: "cheap land, place to build it. They built it to support local business. And there you go" was her neat summation. Yet even this account of virtual inevitability leaves much room for human decision-making. *How did their land get "cheap" in the first place? Who is doing the building? What "local business" does it "support"? When are affected parties and stakeholders brought into the decision-making process?*

In the mid-1970s, Samet Construction—the firm owned by downtown real estate owner and Phillips partner Norman Samet—announced its goal to develop showroom space both for firms currently with no presence in High Point and those needing room to expand.[21] While some argue about the degree to which the Market caused the departure of resident-centered uses from the downtown during this era, its unabated growth certainly undermined the business climate for the retailers that remained. In 1978, the city secured a federal Community Development Block Grant (CDBG) to add brick sidewalks and new benches to Main

Street and to eliminate nearly a third of the street parking. Storeowners insisted that they were not involved in this plan.[22] "They're eliminating parking when we're supposed to be fighting shopping centers," said a bewildered sporting goods merchant. "It just don't make sense."[23] But Market-oriented decisions *did* make sense if you considered the influence showroom stakeholders held over the city council, complained another store owner.[24] "Obviously, they were looking out for number one," retired *Enterprise* editor Tom Blount told me. "But removing parking from Main Street downtown . . . is a killer."

As showroom space burgeoned, additional surface parking also disappeared. "You were able to build something corner to corner on your lot without parking," said Terrell, who had witnessed many of these fights. Terrell believed that this lack of parking severely limited other possible uses for the downtown if the Market ever left en masse, but it worked for the current Market. "Everybody coming to your showroom was going to be walking anyway," he pointed out.

By the early 1980s, Samet headed up the city's Chamber of Commerce, then responsible for coordinating much of the Market's logistics. Ironically, the construction of Market showrooms by Samet's construction firm correlated with the failure of the very businesses that usually make up a chamber of commerce. This will recur at various points in the High Point story; all are "taken in by invocation of 'economic health'—including small-business people who are often displaced by the ill-conceived projects that take over their geographic as well as market space."[25]

A report on High Point development in the 1970s by city official Reggie Greenwood concluded that "people in High Point and people across the state feel that High Point does not offer the advantages of living in an urban area—specialty shops, good restaurants, cultural programs and night entertainment."[26] Still, optimism remained that a mixed-use downtown might eventually return. In 1983, editor Joe Brown issued a warning in the *Enterprise* to beware of "the nationwide trend toward similar looking malls" and "the emergence of a generic American landscape." He wondered if the downtown recovery efforts he observed going on around the nation could make "'going downtown' . . . mean something again" in High Point too.[27]

Resident-centered businesses wanting a central location fled to areas just north or south of the downtown where ample parking lots were possible. The result was the development of what High Point planning director Lee Burnette called "two strip downtowns—North Main and South Main. A lot of that is because of what's been pushed out of the downtown."

Meanwhile, the owners of downtown buildings that did not attract Market interest "warehoused" or "mothballed" them to await a Market buyer. The downtown became a landscape of speculation. "The Market, essentially, ate up the real estate," said Becky Smothers, "because of the attitude and perception by people that owned real estate that 'I'm not going to do anything with mine because it has *Market potential.*'" Once this mothballing set in, the shops still open grew farther and farther apart. "Are you going to walk past all those empty buildings?" Blount asked dubiously. By the 1980s, some businesses that had withstood showroom speculation were forcibly displaced for showrooms. Showroom developer Paul Fine evicted a gas station, a shoe repair shop, and a warehouse at the corner of South Elm and West Commerce in 1985.[28]

Looking North to a New City "Center"

Construction firms benefiting from showroom development also enjoyed the greenfield development that was simultaneously continuing in the lush Piedmont region. The 1987 announcement of Piedmont Centre, a massive high-end office park surrounded by tall oak trees in North High Point, was viewed as a potential anchor. With amenities such as sculptures and picnic areas for employees, a beautiful wooded setting at the eastern fork of Deep River and Bicentennial Greenway, and human-made water features, it would be a stunning place—mostly to drive through. Its development would encourage suburban-style, upscale strip-mall development near the Greensboro border for decades to come. From this point on, the argument that the downtown's loss of resident-centered uses and its accompanying Market-centered growth were the result of a natural or organic evolution became impossible to make. The twin ascent of North High Point's offices, housing, and retail and downtown's furniture showrooms came about through explicit city policy.

Looking back on this type of greenfield development in the United States, architect and planner Andrés Duany cites Norman Bel Geddes, a designer of the U.S. Interstate system, who warned that highways and the city don't mix well. One tenet of this warning is that the city must "not allow itself to grow along the highway." In other words, when "high-speed roads pass through the countryside," it is not an invitation for greenfield development.[29] North High Point was in direct opposition to this tenet: it was countryside development anchored on new highways.

In 1988, Mayor Roy Culler saw the potential problems in the city's sprawled development and proposed that the city slow down North High Point growth until it could better assess and strategize it. "I don't believe you need to strangle High Point," was council member Jay Bodenheimer's response to Culler's call for a reprieve.[30] If the city really wanted to take control out of the hands of private developers, "we ought to buy it," Bodenheimer reasoned. His assertion captured the local logic of cowboy capitalism: only owners have a say about their land.

"With that belief, I wonder why we even have zoning?" Culler replied.[31] Yet not even a mayor could turn the tide of what Duany called the era's "public sector's abrogation of responsibility for community-making to the private sector."[32] It produced a sentiment "that it's entirely up to the market to decide what gets built where. So much for planning!" writes Duany.[33]

In 1993, the *Enterprise* published an ostensibly noneditorialized news story celebrating North High Point's growth. It depicted a past when "consumers lived near downtown businesses, sometimes walking to work and enjoying a nice dinner in a local restaurant before heading home." It contrasted that scene with the present downtown: "a haven for drugs and crime, forcing businesses and homeowners into the countryside."[34] Residents have been calling High Point's core city "Little Chicago" for a full century, the moniker resurfacing at opportune moments to describe everything from bootlegging and criminal gambling rings to the city's high murder rate. From this perspective, developing North High Point for local retail and commerce and dedicating the downtown to a highly policed, temporary exposition center made sense to the city's white leadership. "The downtown concept has passed," said the city's Economic Development Corporation chief.[35]

Alternatives in the form of programs, incentives, or subsidies for year-round local downtown businesses never received serious consideration. From this vantage point—that most residents wanted nothing to do with downtown—it is easy to understand why the Market was referred to as a blessing, a gift horse, or a goose laying golden eggs. Downtown retailers did not fit into this perspective. "I don't see the city merging those two agendas in a way that will be agreeable to both parties," said the owner of the downtown Perkinson's Jewelers. "There's not a retailer in town who doesn't realize the importance of the furniture Market. But there's not a furniture Market person in town who realizes the value of retailers."[36]

From Greenfield to "North High Point"

Yet as bad as things downtown seemed, Rosa Mae's diner on Main Street—today a nostalgic artifact of a more recent "good ol' days"— only opened there in 1995, replacing a Chick-Fil-A that had left for Oak Hollow Mall.[37] Owner Jim Davis said he spent ninety thousand dollars renovating the space, and, although he considered it a high investment for a tiny storefront, the business boomed. "We could feed 150 to 160 people a day," Davis recalled. "During Market? 300. And that's phenomenal.

"I did more business in the first five years than I did in the second ten," he added. That was during his Main Street restaurant's peak in the mid-1990s. With a small but critical mass of businesses still downtown, plus the Market, Davis had a viable business. "It was a centralized hub. You still had businesses, you had offices," he said as he listed the furniture companies, the law firm in the white office building downtown, as well as the hundreds of employees at the telephone company across the street. And for four months of the year he could count on Market-related business. "I mean, you're looking at Pre-Market [a topic in chapter 6], you're looking at laborers, you're looking at designers, carpenters, painters, electricians, plumbers. That's one of the great things about High Point. I mean, you had it *all* here."

Resident-centered anchors remained downtown, but office space, personal services, retail, and third places had decreased at least 60 percent over the 1980s and 1990s. Business continued moving north to the North High Point area near the airport, now designated the city's "growth corridor," where population rose almost 50 percent in the 1990s through annexations and development. The view emerging among planners, journalists, and politicians was that North High Point, and perhaps all of High Point, had become a bedroom community of increasingly trendy Greensboro. Urban geographer Edward Soja uses the term *exopolis* to capture outer city urbanization that departs from, and even rejects, traditional urban characteristics as it establishes a new center.[38] It captures the office park and mall development in North High Point that began in the late 1980s and continued through the next two decades, which would cement the role of this exopolitan development in the lives of High Pointers.

Greenfield Growth

In an era known locally as the "mall wars," city elites fought over the construction of a regional shopping mall and debated environmental impacts, traffic patterns, and the choice of development firms. Political candidates differed over the details, but all agreed that High Point needed a large mall to catch up with the times. For all the heated discussion that followed, there was little debate where it would go: to the north side of High Point.

The nearly one-million-square-foot Oak Hollow Mall opened in 1995. "It's probably the most exciting retail development this city's ever had," then mayor Becky Smothers declared. "It should become the new town square," added the mall's general manager.[39] When the Sears on the Magic Block moved to Oak Hollow, no more department stores remained downtown. Despite all the excitement, High Point was characteristically lagging behind. Businesses were already venturing back into downtowns while the construction of enclosed, outlying shopping malls was tapering off.[40]

In the 1990s, a growing minority was becoming critical of the North High Point expansion. These opponents wanted to preserve the city's greenspace and wetlands in the north and invest in the downtown and the brownfields of the east, south, and west. Resident Marie Byerly complained that Mayor Smothers and her council "can't say no to developers." Byerly questioned their reasoning, arguing "their answer to crime, traffic congestion, and environmental threats is to bring in more cars and more people." In the future, she stated, "if we wish to escape the sounds of bulldozers and to see some big, beautiful trees, we can always go to Emerywood," the old-money neighborhood adjacent to downtown.[41]

Urban planner Duany's philosophy backed critiques like Byerly's. "The obvious goal here is to counteract the existing government and market forces that make it less profitable for developers to work in the city ('urban infill') than on the rural 'greenfeld' fringe," he concluded as he observed the rampant greenfield development going on around the United States.[42] But it was not to be.

By 2006, Piedmont Centre boasted two hundred companies and ten thousand employees. The center was in Foreign Trade Zone (FTZ) number 230, which gave it special storage, distribution, manufacturing, and customs privileges.[43] Smaller office parks clamored to locate in North High Point in the orbit of Piedmont Centre and the FTZ and were subsequently brought into the zone.

Lowell Easter, the developer who spearheaded Piedmont Centre, opened the seventy-six-acre open-air Palladium Shopping Center in North High Point in 2005. This area, close to Greensboro and seven or eight miles from downtown High Point, had been successfully attracting retailers.[44] Advertisements for the apartments and townhomes built in what is now called the Palladium Area crowed, "you may never need a car again," with the complex located "just a short stroll away from everything you need," including "coffee shops, restaurants, theatres, grocery shopping, medical services, and a multitude of retail stores."[45]

In recent years, suburban leaders across North America have attempted to restructure and repackage sprawl. Urban planning and design firms are making earnest and innovative efforts to densify or fill in sprawled development, organized by alliances like the Congress for New Urbanism. Projects by firms such as Duany-Plater-Zyberk (DPZ) promote this brand of walkable urbanism. In North High Point, however, the walkability was purely rhetoric—and actually laughable. "The public knows that these single-use pods are not places of culture, and that trading nature for sprawl was not a fair transaction," Duany argued in his 2000 book.[46]

"It's legitimate planning theory, to try to get people working and living in the same areas," argued mall developer Easter. "There's also a large amount of green space contiguous to the parcel, as well as the Bicentennial Trail and pedestrian access for people working in Piedmont Centre," he said.[47] True, the Palladium Area had retail, office, greenspace, and housing, but not in any semblance of order. It was a free market canvas, just like downtown High Point. Easter was essentially equating *proximate* with walkable, but the area was neither reachable nor easily navigable without a car.

Tom Terrell and I traded our experiences as pedestrians in the Palladium area. I recalled sometimes organizing my notes at the Starbucks "out-parcel," a regional term to connote the freestanding establishments dotting the outskirts of a mall parking lot. Some of these establishments were separated by concrete, greenery, ditches, or a lack of sidewalks. "Just a short stroll," as the advertisement said, could be treacherous. "There is a place in one of the out-parcels where you cannot go from one out-parcel to the next within the same center without getting in your car," Terrell explained, completely baffled. "What could have been a pleasant two-minute walk . . . , becomes instead an expedition requiring the use of gasoline, roadway capacity, and space for parking," as Duany described such design.[48]

"'Okay, yeah. *That* meets code. *That* meets code,'" Terrell added, imitating the city's planning department robotically approving projects.[49] "The Palladium complex is one of the worst things to ever happen to High Point," he said bluntly. "It created a suburbanized outpost that just sucks all of the life away."

People of the Third High Point

Whenever I've asked city leaders about the city's inequalities and divisions, they almost invariably bring up three different residential High Points. The typology begins with two categories: the traditional "haves and have nots," a legacy of the city's mill town history. "You've heard that High Point didn't have a middle class: It was mill owners and mill workers," said Smothers. Debate over High Point's lack of a middle class—and whether it was a problem—was a major political issue in the early years of Smothers's political career in the late 1970s and 1980s.[50]

Throughout her career in government, Smothers was part of an effort to create an unapologetically suburban-like landscape for middle-class North High Pointers.[51] The result, according to Sims, was a North High Point middle class that purchased real estate in High Point simply because it offered more "bang for the buck" than neighboring Greensboro. While these residents were willing to exploit High Point's deflated home values, she said, their "heart is somewhere else." This Faustian bargain was akin to what occurred downtown. "We know this arrangement is not ideal, but we'll make it worth your while," goes the bargain.

"North High Point? They don't even know they're *in* High Point," said Edith Brady of the High Point Museum, sounding a widespread sentiment. Local Nic Ruden agreed: "North High Point is Greensboro to a lot of people," he said.

Smothers did not mind such ambiguity. Asked whether she thought High Point had become a bit of a bedroom community, she said, "In the northern part, yeah." She noted its apparent assets—location, home prices, wide thoroughfares with flowing traffic, retail. In fact, she and former mayor Mendenhall not only allowed but sanctioned ambiguity during the development of linchpin Piedmont Centre when the city allowed the developer to give half the Centre's properties a Greensboro mailing address even though the entire office park falls within the High Point city limits. The developer sought this, Smothers said, "because from a marketing standpoint they were hedging the possibility that someone might want a Greensboro address." High Point knowingly allowed the obfuscation of its boundaries to satisfy potential business interests that perceived a High Point location as second rate.

Smothers recalled a 1992 visit with the president of a Piedmont Centre firm when she was trying to raise money for High Point's Arts Council. He was slightly confused by the solicitation. "He didn't know he was in High Point," Smothers said. His apparent slight did not faze her, however. "'Never fear, your budget director knows,'" she remembers answering.[52]

Once a node of locally headquartered manufacturing firms that created local wealth, beyond the High Point Market the city has become largely a location for the secondary, back-office functions of large corporations. "Yeah, they pay taxes in High Point and we get some benefit from that," said politician Jay Wagner, in response to such businesses. "But they don't serve on civic groups here, they're not on the boards. To me that's where you see the health of your community, you know?"

"Death" and the Rise of the Planetary Rent Gap

By the 1990s, the downtown renaissance and a "back to the city" movement were becoming the subjects of national debate. But due to the entrenchment of the Market, High Point skipped that moment altogether. So-called pioneer gentrification never took root in downtown High Point for one fundamental reason. "High Point is unique among the cities of the Triad," said Elijah Lovejoy. "Winston-Salem had tobacco as its primary identity. Tobacco died; they had to find something else. Greensboro was textiles. Textiles died; they had to find something else." Downtown renewal leader Wendy Fuscoe echoed the sentiment. "Those two downtowns were dead," she said. "They had nothing there 365 days a year." In contrast, she said High Point was "very successful and vibrant four weeks out of the year." The Market's investment in downtown High Point kept the real estate market from reaching a point where investors had to reconsider its use.

"So you've got a downtown," Fuscoe continued. "That's great for the tax base, great for the state of North Carolina, not great for bringing together the community of High Point." "It's *great* for them," she said, noting the presence of taxpaying properties without the accompanying police, fire, utilities, or sanitation demands. It seemed like a boon. "They don't have to provide *services!*" added Fuscoe. "And that's what makes it all the harder. Because you can't motivate the city to do *anything.*"

The Global Rent Gap and Investing in the Underbrush

In the terminology of gentrification, the "death" of real estate would be the point where the *rent gap*—the gap between a property's current value and its potential value under redevelopment—is enough to incentivize early gentrifiers, both businesses and residents, to take a risk. Downtown High Point has no *local* rent gap: local merchants have consistently found its real estate values highly inflated. There is, however, a *global* rent gap, an artifact of downtown High Point's global interconnectedness. What appears pricey to the local retail entrepreneur appears cheap on the balance sheet of a Milanese furniture exhibitor.

Furniture analyst and blogger Ivan Cutler offered a colorful metaphor to describe this situation. He said Greensboro and Winston-Salem have benefited from "burning the underbrush of the forest." In his analogy, the underbrush is the old economy and its accompanying built environment. While the larger furniture economy in its current form died, the downtown—due to the internationalized sector of furniture real estate—never dropped in value enough to attract locals with a new vision. With investment fortifying this underbrush, the analogy suggests, leaders ignored the assets (or mulch) that could generate a new ecosystem, such as the local craftspeople looking for new work. The landscape remained in a liminal, suspended state, propped up for a one-dimensional purpose.

Showroom investors experienced this propping up as deregulation. However, it was actually a form of regulation that steered the benefits of development: other inchoate resident-centered uses were blocked from nourishment. As I show in chapter 7, this is a very fitting picture of

High Point's furniture cluster beyond the Market—hidden from view, ignored, and needing light and nutrients.

Sims describes this point when the Market transitioned from *replacing* the uses that had left to actually *precluding* other uses from flourishing. As an illustration, she cited her time working in the corporate offices of La-Z-Boy subsidiary LADD, which occupied four floors of the white office building downtown. "'I'm not going to put my people through this,'" Sims recalled the management team feeling as they contemplated continuing amid the inconveniences of a desolate downtown. Instead, the firm moved to Greensboro in 1997.

The trade publication *Furniture Today* made the same move, to an office park. The symbolic and relational value of being in downtown High Point did not outweigh the inconveniences of its location, especially when compared to the benefits of the North High Point office parks. "I said 'Move back downtown, move back where you're supposed to be.' But they want the convenience," lamented Radio Building owner Candy Lambeth. Indeed, the white office building housed not only *Furniture Today* and LADD but also the edgy, glossy *InFurniture* magazine. It was also the inaugural home of both the High Point Market Authority and the furniture finance firm First Factors founded by Phil Phillips.

City leaders never publicly mourned such departures, nor did they try to incentivize cluster firms to stay. Therefore, leaders of downtown firms realized that if they stayed for the benefit of a greater good, they would be going at it alone. The local government saw the deterioration of the downtown's service-centered furniture cluster as a sign of the times. "Not many folks are moving into downtowns anywhere anymore," said High Point Economic Development Corporation president Kevin Johnson when LADD left in 1997. "Most developments are occurring in suburbs."[53] It was easy for the city to take this view; thanks to the demand by furniture exhibitors, it did not have to worry about the profitability of downtown real estate or the viability of downtown property taxes.

The Local Rent Gap and Burning the Underbrush

In contrast to High Point, leaders in Greensboro and Winston-Salem bought into the "burning of the underbrush" that was remaking other cities in the U.S. South and all over the globe. These cities were working to renew their downtowns, "justifying local arts agendas and new design policies as economic imperatives."[54] Their policies were "presumed to create attractive environments for educated residents who favor lively, walkable neighborhoods and a diverse mix of amenities that include live music scenes, bicycle paths, and a diverse menu of culinary options."[55]

When High Point's Oak Hollow Mall opened in the late 1990s, the neighboring *Greensboro News and Record* playfully derided its county cousin's aspirations. Although "to a casual onlooker" the mall appeared to be a "pale beige box surrounded by a pavement field," the paper chortled, Greensboro residents should tread carefully, since apparently to "many High Point observers," the mall was "a pearl."[56] Indeed, just as High Point was trying to play mall-building catch-up, Greensboro was heading in a completely different direction, toward a brand of gentrification that embraced a new southern cosmopolitanism. While the Market-related investors saved High Point's downtown core from devastation and discouraged local investment, downtown Greensboro's decades of struggles and devaluation gradually cultivated not only cheap real estate but also strong grassroots interest and participation in its rebirth.

In 1990 alone, Greensboro completed the Renaissance Plaza and First Union Tower office high-rises. These buildings, along with the expansion and renovation of the stately neo-Gothic, neoclassical Jefferson-Pilot Building from 1923, changed the downtown skyline.[57] "It was unprecedented that we had them all going on in the same two-year period," said Jim Melvin, Greensboro mayor from 1970 to 1980 and the cofounder in 1984 of Greensboro's Joseph M. Bryan Foundation. He had a major hand in the developments.[58]

The Bryan Foundation is evidence of another attitude characteristic of Greensboro: local wealth's willingness to take risks on their city. Funded by philanthropist Joseph Bryan, an executive of the insurance firm Jefferson-Pilot, the foundation infused large sums of capital into the downtown twice each year until Bryan's death in 1995, when it inherited $100 million from his estate.[59] Over several decades, the foundation has interrupted short-sighted, "highest and best use" development decisions to further what it considered more long-term benefits to the city.

When the only financially feasible site identified to locate the new Greensboro Children's Museum was outside the downtown, for instance, the Bryan Foundation footed the bill to make a downtown location workable. When support for a new baseball stadium flagged, the Bryan

Foundation, weary of advocating for it, funded the ballpark itself. Pockets of downtown Greensboro were starting to bustle. New occupants included a handful of midsize corporate headquarters—a regional "back-office" node, county government offices, and a cultural hub for a distinctive array of regional colleges and universities.

This reinvigorated civic environment provided the milieu for local actors such as Atlanta-native Pete Schroth, a University of North Carolina at Greensboro graduate student, to dream up the Green Bean coffee shop on Elm Street. Opened in 2002, when I arrived in the area, it became a vibrant downtown third space, music venue, art scene, and political center. Local growth leaders encouraged this investment. The Green Bean was part of a larger "alive after 5" movement that followed Greensboro's office renaissance of the previous decade.

In October 2003, I walked from the Green Bean to the Empire Room event space, grabbed dinner from the "mashed potato bar," and watched urbanist Richard Florida work the crowd. This was the beginning of Florida's worldwide tour in which he would lecture—preach, really—on what he saw as the realities of the global economy. These included the global competition for educated workers and the need for cities to be more aggressive in planning for the economic, social, and economic characteristics that attract them.[60] Much of what Florida was saying was already common sense to the crowd in that room, including his hosts, Action Greensboro.

After Florida's visit, Action Greensboro prepared a report, complete with plans for a trolley, to lure what Florida called the creative class. "The creative class consists of people who add economic value through their creativity," Florida explains. "It thus includes many knowledge workers, symbolic analysts and technical workers, but emphasizes their true role in the economy."[61] Greensboro had important assets in terms of culture, education (including a campus of the University of North Carolina, a private college, and a historically Black public university, North Carolina A&T State University), leisure, and technology. Florida's visit was proof of city leaders' commitment to package them into a coherent whole.

Lovejoy pointed out that amid Greensboro's transformation, High Point's old guard painted Greensboro as "chaotic, bizarre, out-of-control, fighting all the time, bickering." Meanwhile, High Point "prided itself on being more orderly, civil," he laughed. "The irony is that Greensboro is seen as a place of life and High Point is struggling with maintaining its life—in spite of all its civility and order."

If when High Pointers wanted to hit the town they enjoyed other cities' street life, that was fine with Mayor Smothers. High Point did not need the headaches. "You look at the real effort that Greensboro has made in terms of both private and public investment to have a residential downtown element, and the nightlife—and now they're at *war*!" Smothers commented. By "war," she meant city council squabbles over the residential-commercial mix relating to noise complaints and other issues. "I don't know if they're at *war*," she clarified, "but there's conflict. Some things are incompatible: like trying to sleep next to a bar."

Requiem for "Human Friction"

"You've got nothing to hang your hat on right now." Resident Heidi Allen was talking about possibilities for High Point's future.[62] "You've got this," she said, gesturing to the showroom architecture. "And you've got *him*." "Him" was High Point resident, motivational speaker, and local benefactor Nido Qubein who, without any experience in higher education, became High Point University's president in 2005. Known as one of the region's "main socio-economic movers and shakers," Qubein had been on several corporate boards, including BB&T (now Truist) Bank since 1990, and was also on the boards of various local and regional business alliances and civic groups.[63]

A common joke was to speak of the university's signature wrought iron fence as a living thing, in the same way residents spoke about the Market's "creep" or showroom "ooze." Lying in the strategic area where High Point's downtown transitions into North High Point, HPU's encroaching black fence seemed to appear first, followed by the demolition of buildings. With Qubein at the helm, campus acreage grew from 91 to 460 acres and building square footage went from 650,000 to 3.5 million.[64] The city council ceded a section of the thoroughfare Montlieu Avenue to the university so it could expand to the residential land on the other side of the street.

Like Market, as HPU grew, it was becoming a supralocal institution benefiting from the extremely low land prices of the real estate on its periphery. That included the Black East Side, which encompasses the greater Washington Street district and John Coltrane's childhood home on Underhill. Sims was very concerned that much of "the property that the university purchased was renter-occupied stuff. And when the owners decided they wanted to sell, it kind of left those folk at a disadvantage." Sims and other leaders would ultimately come to feel that as far as institutions go, the university was basically forthright in its dealings with residents who lived within the footprint of its expansion plans. No matter how well this expansion was executed, however, a considerable amount of exclusionary displacement occurred, as affordable, single-family homes were lost.[65]

Sacrificing the institution's bond rating and forgoing growing the school's small endowment, Qubein has leveraged well over one billion dollars to completely raze, rebuild, reinvent, and rebrand High Point University with amenities such as a "first-run movie theater, a steakhouse, and dorms with plasma-screen TVs and outdoor hot tubs" overseen by a new administrative position called the Director of Wow.[66] "It's bad when one of your nicest restaurants is on a university campus and only used by students," said young civic leader Nic Ruden. That "steakhouse" was a relaunch of a former downtown anchor, French restaurant J. Basul Nobles.

In 2009, Nobles vacated its first-floor location in the white office building and opened a new version on the grounds of HPU under Qubein's campaign to make the campus "extraordinary." Local historian Glenn Chavis shook his head in disgust—not over Qubein's boldness or the downtown's loss but at High Point leaders' ineptitude in cultivating their assets. "If *you* can't do it, *I'll* put a steakhouse on the campus," Chavis imagined HPU president Qubein saying. "If you don't want to make these things available for these people who visit this institution, then *we'll* do it. I love the thinking," he remarked, fully aware of its negative impact on the downtown. The onus to stoke the embers of downtown life was on High Point leaders, not Qubein.

Places like Nobles and Rosa Mae's were well suited for "bumping" into people, as Wagner noted, and created "the human friction where ideas occur." These accidental encounters build community, enhance politics, and increase opportunity. "It's one of the things that's missing about bringing this community together," Market official Sally Bringier said.[67] "Because when you went in there, there were city people, there were Market people. And you could have those conversations, which you needed to have to grease the wheels on both sides."

Rosa Mae's Jim Davis recalled how furniture company owners would come in and buy lunch for workers they had hired off the street to help unload trucks. "I didn't have a Market menu [with higher prices] 'cause that gentleman that was painting that showroom? That gentleman that was putting carpet in there? He ate with me all year-round." The diner served as a glue binding global and local, the white-collar furniture world and the blue-collar furniture world: High Point's unique *glocal*. Fairchild Publications' furniture fashion magazine *INFurniture* honored this authentic local diner in its editor's Market-time byline: "Rosa Mae's."

"You have the numbers out there," Wendy Fuscoe said of North High Point, "but then you've got the authenticity [downtown] that I think is what people want to see—something that is unique and different to their town." Meanwhile, the two malls that helped spur the downtown exodus both closed in the 2000s. Westchester had a thirty-year run and Oak Hollow remained viable less than half that long. Vacated before it was hardly broken in, it went on to enjoy internet celebrity as a "ruin porn" centerfold.

In the choices it made to sprawl to greenfield, High Point was merely a variation on a well-worn theme across the United States. As antisprawl crusader Duany has argued, "Perhaps the most regrettable fact of all, is that exactly the same ingredients—the houses, shops, offices, civic buildings, and roads—could instead have been assembled" using practices that promoted "memorable" places "of lasting value."[68]

3

The Golden Goose

High Point Becomes the World's Market Center

Embracing the Golden Goose

After examining High Point's general development over the second half of the twentieth century, this chapter focuses on the Market's ascent during the period, stopping just before 1990. This era saw the contemporary Market take form, beginning as the nation was reorienting itself after World War II. For the Home Furnishings Center, built in 1921 and enlarged in 1940 with a 65,000-square-foot addition, the adjustment was quite literal. The U.S. Army had commandeered the Big Building to house records during the war. Its transition back to peacetime use coincided with the postwar housing boom, a boon to the home furnishings industry.

During this era, the Market would come to be known as High Point's "Golden Goose," just like the goose that lays the golden eggs in Aesop's tale. This extreme protection of the goose amounted to High Point's local brand of neoliberalism, a philosophy espousing open markets, privatization, deregulation, individualism, and downsizing the public sector while increasing the role of the private sector. Growth leaders often pitch their agenda as the only viable solution. "There is no alternative" (TINA) is a simple phrase from philosopher Herbert Spencer that British prime minister Margaret Thatcher appropriated to support her free market policies. TINA's take-it-or-leave-it orientation implies, for instance, that capitalism can accommodate no alternative to gentrification but ghettoization, no alternative to corporate incentives but disinvestment. The principle aptly describes the rhetoric of growth in a variety of contexts. It certainly describes High Point.

Under the TINA principle, mistreating the Golden Goose would be both unconscionable and nonsensical. "Mistreating" could be a mere discussion about the ramifications of growth. Considered in the local context of growth machine development, other agendas are overwhelmed so that "there is, without explicit conspiracy, control over ideology, over discourse, over issues.[1] This shift makes the local elite's plans for "development 'value free'—ipso facto good and not appropriately subject to critical analysis."[2]

High Point had defeated larger rivals and gained global prominence as a furniture center. However, it was incumbent on the entire community to protect its prize. The way to do that was simple: *build.* Home Furnishings Center director Leo J. Heer exhorted the Rotary Club in 1967 to come together in the name of Market growth:

> Now we stand having accomplished something big . . . the greatest furniture market in the world. High Point has brought here this great Market and now the community must build the things to keep it and expand it. It is simple as that. That is our challenge.[3]

For many years, *High Point Enterprise* editor Holt McPherson was a classic "cheerleader for development," someone who greased the wheels for the plans of High Point's industry and political leaders with "peerless boosterism."[4] The newspaper was careful to "congratulate growth rather than calculate its consequences, to compliment development rather than criticize its impact."[5] McPherson shared the plucky mill town's attitude, motivated by a chip on its collective shoulder to beat its more-resourced rivals. "To the extent that a search for meaning is a general condition of culture, the deployment of a discourse of 'us' versus 'the rest of the world' becomes a seductive binary around which to construct a sense of group identity and belonging," explains sociologist Mark Boyle.[6]

McPherson encouraged High Pointers to maintain an "attitude that nothing will be allowed to steal our valued market from us."[7] The Home Furnishings Center developed "Smile and Say 'Hi,'" a campaign designed to "make [our] honored guests feel at home with a real Southern welcome, and extend to them every extra courtesy and privilege in our places of business—in our homes—on our streets. Let's make them feel that their [marketgoer] badge is indeed 'the key to the city.'"[8]

McPherson was not the only "cheerleader" in town. *Enterprise* editor Joe Brown made growth goals a community affair and allegiance to the Market a litmus test for local citizenship. "If there is any pride left in the quality of Southern hospitality," he said in 1973, "will it not be enhanced if we demonstrate it to those who visit?"[9] "Any who fail to practice it," he added, "can be sure that they are out of step with a majority of their neighbors.[10] While it can't be said definitively that this rhetoric either influenced or mirrored community sentiment, cheerleading was certainly a consistent element of the city's boosterism.

High Point and the Figure 8

The burgeoning Market was reflected in a burgeoning Home Furnishings Center, whose owners expanded it piecemeal to meet rising demand. Despite the industry's increasing appreciation for showroom design, aesthetic concerns over the Big Building's exterior facade seemed to diminish with each addition. In 1959, the seven-story Wrenn Street Wing was added and connected to the original building by a skywalk over Wrenn Street. Four more stories were added two years later. The building seemed to grow like a living organism, both taller and wider, in fits and starts.

In 1960, a second furniture exhibition building entered High Point's downtown landscape with the appearance of the Furniture Plaza, seven stories of new construction just under half the size of the original Home Furnishings Center, built facing it on Main Street. Like the Big Building, the Furniture Plaza would also grow windowless appendages in response to Market need.

There was little doubt that High Point was the symbolic center of the Market during this period. However, the exposition's showrooms were actually scattered over two hundred miles of poorly paved road that came to be known as the "Furniture Highway." Also called the "Figure 8" for its shape (although it looked more like an infinity symbol ∞ with its eastern and western loops), it was flanked by the towns of Lenoir, Drexel, and Hickory on its western side, and High Point, Lexington, and Thomasville on the eastern side. Industry analyst and blogger Ivan Cutler called the Figure 8 Market of this era "a mercantile bivouac . . . an arduous, arduous enterprise," so convoluted that some used helicopters to navigate it.

Us against Chicago

"Everyone agrees that these two sessions should be held in Chicago, but everybody keeps coming here, in ever-increasing numbers," noted Ray Reed.[11] A commentator for *Home Furnishings Daily* and a longtime critic of the Market, Reed acceded the crown of national furniture exposition to the one anchored in High Point in the early 1960s, calling it a "miracle of modern distribution."

"Buyers who become infuriated waiting a few minutes for an elevator at the Furniture or Merchandise Mart in Chicago think nothing of dashing forty miles between factories" in North Carolina, Reed marveled. "For years on end, industry spokesmen have insisted that, on the basis of convenience, accommodations, difficult coverage, [and] lack of sophisticated after-hours entertainment, there is absolutely no reason" for the southern Market.[12] These complaints remain a prime topic of conversation today.

Yet the nation's furniture fashion node was moving out of Chicago's two buildings of more than five and a half million square feet of exhibition space—the Furniture Mart and the Merchandise Mart—to the Market's two million square feet of expo space spanning six towns. Other rival expositions had emerged by this time, in Dallas, San Francisco, and Atlanta, but they all seemed to become more regional than national.

By 1963, the tide had clearly turned. That year Chicago discontinued one of its shows, New York was visibly floundering, and Grand Rapids had announced that it was discontinuing its entire exposition. The next year, Big Building chief Leo Heer claimed the city needed to "consider adding to the geographical designation, 'Furnitureland, USA,' the additional phrase, 'And The World.'"[13]

According to Heer, "World recognition is heady stuff, but it can be handled in stride." He added, "Now the challenge is whether we can be just as militant and aggressive in our merchandising presentation as we have been in the other phases of production and design progress."[14] In 1964, the *New York Times* declared High Point the winner in the battle for furniture exposition supremacy. Editor McPherson announced the news in the *Enterprise*: "Thus ends one of the classic wars in furniture wholesaling with the Southern Market victor."[15]

Noting that the High Point–anchored Market had been the leading national exposition for some time already, McPherson remarked that "the

New York Times might well put on its masthead an addendum to its slogan 'All The News That's Fit To Print': . . . 'When We Get Around To It.'"[16] What geographers David Bell and Mark Jayne perceive as small city "emulation mixed with jealousy" was especially evident in McPherson's comment that the bespectacled *Times* reporter was examining High Point while looking "down the full length of her New York nose."[17]

Why did High Point win the battle over Chicago? One key reason is that the exposition's buyers were individual mom-and-pop furniture stores that had little choice but to travel where the furniture manufacturers decided to display their creations. Manufacturers were increasingly choosing to display the furniture where it was made. Thus the answer to why the exposition was not in New York, Chicago, Dallas, or Atlanta was "This is where the manufacturers are, this is where the furniture is."[18]

A second reason is that the schedule of production and display within this network of furniture showrooms and manufacturing was synchronized with the furniture industry's business cycle. The showrooms were located on or near a manufacturer's production site and were designated for the manufacturer's exclusive use, allowing a showroom to be conceived in concert with the design, development, and marketing of the furniture itself, so that, as Ray Reed noted, "New lines are always introduced *first* at the Southern Market."[19] Showrooms were just another facet of the vertical integration that was penetrating most manufacturing industries during this time. To Heer, the Market represented "the importance of style and glamor going hand in hand with efficiency of production."[20]

Reed described how manufacturers' control over display led to the production of "dazzling" showrooms that were "more attractively displayed" and "more imaginatively presented."[21] The sensory importance here is much more than merely visual: furniture industry professionals wanted space to *experience* furniture—lean on it, touch it, sit on it. High Point would come to specialize in this niche of aesthetic and tactile experience.

The confluence of these factors, supported by North Carolina's vast amount of cheap land, made the Market a must-visit destination for buyers, designers, manufacturers, analysts, and media who wanted to keep a finger on the pulse of the industry. High Point's mushrooming showroom complex expanded to three blocks with the addition of a third major building also across the street from the Big Building. In the Fall 1964 Market, the National Furniture Mart building was introduced by fabrics supplier J. L. Fine and his grandson Paul, who would serve on the city council in the next decade. At the opening of the 85,000-square-foot building, Mayor Floyd Mehan declared that the "progress of the city is symbolized by this building," telling J. L. Fine, "The citizens of the city thank you through me."[22]

In 1967, the Big Building received its sixth addition, considerably larger than the original building, with the Green Drive Annex of 350,000 square feet. "I'm supposed to go to the lobby," a journalist overheard a cleaning person say to a salesperson in the Big Building at that 1967 Market. "Do you know where the lobby is?" "I'm sorry," replied the equally bewildered salesperson, "I don't even know where I am."[23] It was an era marked by buildings used as cash cows with architectural designs made "for the stockholders," as Richard Wood said. "Don't give a damn *what* it made High Point look like," he added. Individual exhibition building owners would simply glom utilitarian appendages onto their existing buildings, much like the accretions of informal settlements seen in the developing world.

In this age of strong local ownership, wouldn't the owners care about the effects of their actions on High Point's image? When I asked Wood, he explained that the dominant view at the time privileged profit over reinvestment. "They wanted to see that money come back. [Stockholders] wanted those big ol' divvies to hit every year," he said, referring to firms cutting profits dividend checks for shareholders rather than investing money back into the buildings. Therefore, while the Market's metamorphosis to a fashion week helped realize the city council's ambitions for growth, it produced little urgency to accompany this new prestige with a more creative, less utilitarian built-environment. Like the Home Furnishings Center, the National Furniture Mart would also continue to expand. In 1969, the building almost doubled in square footage.

A precedent had been set. When High Point leaders got nervous about their market position vis-à-vis other cities, they built. Upon constructing National Furniture Mart, Fine stated that "anything which is put in High Point helps High Point . . . keep the Market."[24] In this era of the local growth machine, it was possible to see some wealth "trickling" down and out to the community at large through taxes, civic boosterism, and philanthropic gifts to local institutions.

Moreover, the Market's footprint was large, but not imposing. Despite all the major projects, it had swelled only about four hundred feet to the east (with the Home Furnishings Center expansion) and the west (with Furniture Plaza and the National Furniture Mart.) High Point Market's square footage was still less than 1.5 million square feet, the size of a large regional shopping mall today.

"It was an exciting time because it was local ownership of those buildings then," said Wood. "Those guys were taking some risks for High Point." High Point maintained a diversified downtown, with retail, offices, manufacturing, churches, and showrooms all comingling. Showrooms represented the diversification of an industry presence: the vertical integration of marketing and distribution within the region's existing complex of manufacturing. High Point was the rare small manufacturing city with a prominent service-industry presence. It seemed like everyone was winning. And then Dallas threatened it all.

Fighting Dallas through Ceding Land

Some of the visiting buyers and manufacturers who showed in High Point began to grumble that the furniture-producing behemoths at the far ends of the furniture highway were stubbornly insisting on keeping their showrooms near their factories. "Personally, I liked the spring and fall shows in Chicago, when everyone was together," complained an executive of Hickory Manufacturing, whose showrooms in Hickory, North Carolina, were a major cause of the sprawl. "A buyer could look at one line, then go down the hall or to the other building, check another line, and make up his mind within 15 minutes which one he wanted to buy," he continued. "Now the buyer . . . can't remember how a line looked from one showroom to the next.[25] Market leaders claimed that buyers could put well over one thousand miles on a car during the Market.

Throughout the 1970s, the Dallas Market Center complex developed into the world's largest with an expansion that brought its campus to over five million square feet. "Dallas was going to kill us, so they said," Wood remembered. "They're going to take this Market away."

"High Point without a furniture market?" asked Brown at the time as he tried to rally residents. "It boggles the mind."[26] "Every citizen has an individual responsibility and an individual role to play in assuring that we never have to discover that fancy can turn into fact."

For many residents, the Dallas exposition exposed High Point's embarrassing small-city flaws. These concerns would crystallize into Market leaders' focus not only on the city's perceived lack of adequate showroom space and accommodations—Dallas offered nearly twenty-five thousand hotel rooms—but on the prohibition of "liquor-by-the-drink" by High Point's county, Guilford, and its effect on the quality of restaurants the city could attract. Local leaders believed that the prohibition, which ended in 1979, would be its narrow-minded, "old mill town" death knell in the contest against cosmopolitan competitors. They lobbied for a local option referendum on the issue. Even though such issues were symbolically significant, the consensus is that they were not what made the difference: High Point built itself out of the Dallas threat.

High Point's lack of central planning ran counter to the coordinated approach most cities were taking to court large conventions. In the early 1970s, a 750,000-square-foot Commerce Wing was planned for the Home Furnishings Center, its seventh and largest addition (again) to date. The Big Building was transitioning leadership from Leo Heer to Bob Gruenberg, who had recently left his position as executive vice president of the National Home Furnishings Association in Chicago to take the post. Gruenberg's first action in his new stewardship of the building was to prioritize expansion.

The problem with the planned expansion was that a "special citizens advisory group," as it was appointed by the city council, had recently determined that three adjacent downtown properties owned by the city—a former fire department headquarters built in 1917, City Hall, and the Paramount, a vaudeville theater turned movie house built in 1923—should be developed into a theater and exhibition center. Early in 1972, voters endorsed a $350,000 bond issue to create a "civic center in a prime location in downtown High Point" that the advisory group felt would be unique in the state.[27] This was an important, insightful move to establish resident uses in the downtown. As it turned out, however, the prime location was *too* prime.

Legal representatives for the city and the Big Building determined that the city could honor both the referendum and the lease if the buildings were razed and the easternmost side of the massive addition was developed into a theater. In 1973, a decade after it opened to Black patrons, the city leased the Paramount Theatre project land to the Home Furnishings Center. All parties seemed to agree that showroom was the

Old High Point City Hall (here circa 1937), voted by referendum in 1972 to be part of a larger performing arts center together with the Paramount Theatre. It was demolished for Big Building expansion. Durwood Barbour Collection of North Carolina Postcards (P077), North Carolina Collection Photographic Archives, Wilson Library, UNC–Chapel Hill.

highest and best use for the location. In fact, there is almost no public recollection of this muted tussle.

In 1975, the cast-concrete, one-thousand-seat High Point Theatre near the old Paramount site stood awaiting its first event. Greunberg touted the theater at the ribbon cutting as "the first such facility between Washington and Atlanta to be built in decades with funds totally from the business community." He added that "presenting this theatre to High Point is our way of thanking everyone in the city for showing our Market visitors that we are glad to see them and appreciate their business."[28] Mayor Paul Clapp announced that the theater ushered in a "new era." In retrospect, this era would give the furniture industry final say over the kind of downtown High Point would have. The High Point Theatre remains in the same location today, swallowed up by additions to the contemporary 3.5-million-square-foot Home Furnishings Center.

Like most residents, Elijah Lovejoy was unaware of these transactions from the 1970s. He had always considered the theater a victory: "a corner of life, a toehold of life—local, year-round, community life." Even so, he recognized how this location had to overcome a "tidal wave of opposition to going downtown due to the sense of it 'not being for me.'" Indeed, reuse of the historic resident-centered buildings for the use of residents, as the citizens advisory group originally planned, would have warded off the current situation in which some High Point residents do not even know the Big Building has a theater. While the plain 1970s-style theater seemed like a boon to some, an arts complex developed from four early twentieth-century buildings adjacent to the Magic Block appears enlightened in hindsight.

The Primacy of "Highest and Best Use"

Some of the regional consolidation of the exposition in High Point took the form of freestanding, single-exhibitor showrooms. In 1971, the eighty-year-old Grand Rapids furniture powerhouse Baker began shopping for real estate in downtown High Point to join the handful of other firms that had developed freestanding showrooms there. All noted that not only was downtown High Point where the "traffic" was, but the extra space in their new showrooms enabled them to showcase their entire lines in one place for the first time.

J. J. Cox wholeheartedly embraced the Market's move into the old buildings of the downtown. He remembered sitting in front of his home on the 100 block of South Main Street as a boy in 1919, watching the Southern Furniture Exposition Building go up, today the oldest of the Big Building's fourteen segments. Joseph J. Cox had quite a High Point pedigree. Other well-connected kin aside, his paternal grandfather served as mayor and his uncle founded one of High Point's most important early businesses, the J. Elwood Cox Manufacturing Company.

Cox had managed the Furniture Plaza building, the city's third major exhibition center. His family owned another building down the street from the Plaza. Although it had housed retail tenants for decades, Cox had furniture aspirations for the property. During the 1960s, as exhibitors began constructing freestanding buildings, smaller exhibitors would take short-term leases in unused storefronts, clean them up a bit, and display their wares for the Market.

In the early 1970s, Cox began urging such manufacturers to do something that seemed good for High Point: take long-term leases of these spaces. This would allow them to amortize the costs of their showrooms rather than pay high rents twice each year, Cox reasoned; it made good business sense. He went on to outline a rationale that appealed to both manufacturer and city, one that real estate owners would echo for the next three decades.

First, Cox maintained that furniture manufacturers with long-term showroom leases could become known for their location. He envisioned an era of image making in High Point that city leaders around the nation were only beginning to grasp. Surely not realizing just how prescient he was, Cox argued that buyers would become familiar with the space and associate it with the exhibitor's brand. Today, for example, buyers take selfies in front of the Baker building and share them on social media. Their posted selfies enforce the symbolic value of Baker's more-than-four-decades-old location at 319 N. Hamilton, a building designed to resemble a stately Italian courtyard, with wooden doors from Verona. Taking and sharing the selfie reinforces the symbol and its significance. Insiders who see those Veronese doors as a backdrop know where the photograph was taken, at Baker.

Second, manufacturers could customize their spaces to suit their specific needs and image. Enthusiasm for this idea launched the disorganized chaos that helped keep the High Point Market rooted in the downtown. Manufacturers could improve, renovate, and rearrange their spaces on their own schedule and at their own discretion during the Market's backstage months. Their showroom, both inside and out, could become a symbol, an extension of their brand, a signature. Exhibitors could alter their showrooms as they altered their lines.

Cox directed his third argument at High Pointers at large: a building in use simply "looks better than having a lost tooth."[29] Again, Cox was discussing image, here asking High Pointers to consider the image they were portraying to outsiders. Did they want to be known as a dead place with vacant storefronts? It was the beginning of a decades-long preoccupation with how the downtown looked rather than how well it functioned.

Overall, Cox explained, showroom use "represents the best current use for otherwise vacant buildings," bringing immediate investment to the downtown.[30] And with the buildings "otherwise vacant," he said, there was really no loser in his proposition. A photography shop, a record shop, a clothing store, a shoe store, a hat shop, and a jewelry store had all turned over to Market use by the Fall 1972 Market. So did

F. W. Woolworth's, the site of High Point's major sit-in a decade earlier. A closed café was transformed into a replica of an old-fashioned meat market for marketgoers. In 1973, a manufacturer's representative with showrooms in Florence, Barcelona, Valencia, and London leased the former JCPenney department store to show his collections.

While relationships with government officials are vital in maintaining a nimble growth machine, even more important is the degree to which property is liberated to operate as a commodity.[31] The rationale that Cox promoted and the city later accepted would precipitate a new commodification of downtown real estate. This new revaluation of the downtown raised the stakes to a level that would incentivize the politicking of real estate interests and the maintenance of loose land use laws. Highest and best use became synonymous with Market use.

If there had been regulation of the downtown in the form of government-owned land or land bound by strong controls, then the furniture growth machine would not have had such agency. Under such conditions, only some of the downtown would have been available for manipulation by the free market—or, in our case, the free Market (uppercase M). Had such controls been in place, there might not have been the critical mass of interested investors needed to generate the ideological and political control it would take to develop downtown High Point.[32] But there were neither controls nor the will to regulate showroom demand. High Point leaders created an unimpeded growth machine able to manipulate land freely under the rationale that any Market growth is good growth. Under these conditions, growth leaders can pitch their plans as necessary for citizen well-being: the favored development becomes a community affair framed as being for the good of everyone—landowners, politicians, the unemployed.[33]

Social science's hindsight can be unrealistically judgmental. When the demand for downtown real estate was declining nationwide, who would expect owners to question the sudden demand for their property or its community-level ramifications? From the perspective of the building owner seeking to lease, "it was so effortless," said politician Bernita Sims, noting the light use the buildings would receive. "I can get me a three- or four-year lease on this space. I don't have to worry about it. I can lock the doors!" she declared.

For those wanting to sell, it seemed too good to be true. "You are an old-line drugstore in downtown High Point and somebody comes up and offers you an unusually exorbitant amount of money for your building," added resident Geraldine Dickins.[34] "So you sell, you retire and disappear. But that takes you out of the economic life of High Point."

Such a scenario offers up no obvious villain other than the government leaders who were unwilling or unable to extrapolate the community effects of such individual decisions. At a moment when disinvestment was a national urban problem, both foresight and fortitude would have been required. "At the time, when people are throwing money at you and buying buildings and fixing them up and building new showroom buildings and whatnot, you know, it's hard to look and say 'wait a minute, are we doing this right?'" politician Jay Wagner explained.

High Point and the Tourist Bubble

In the early 1970s when Cox was articulating his "best use" philosophy, city leaders around the world were investing in regeneration strategies directed at the promotion of events and conventions.[35] Looking back at this time, scholars describe a "tourist bubble" approach that encouraged the creation of fortressed leisure areas and superblock convention centers.[36] In this model, planners separated workplaces and work times from spaces of consumption.[37] High Point's competitors, such as Dallas, emphasized safety and navigability. They sought to separate the visitor experience from the unpredictability of interaction with residents beyond those in roles serving visitors. High Point could not offer such containment and was really too small to try. However, various informal policies introduced in High Point during this era encouraged residents to "stay out" of the downtown area so as not to disrupt the Market experience. Local "sweeps" and "stings"—vagrancy, prostitution, drug dealing—were the norm, undertaken with the unspoken understanding that the Market's veiled, higher-end offerings of drugs and sex work had replaced the local version.

Of course, High Point's efforts to offer exhibitors a controlled visitor experience would never be completely successful because the city was not a centrally owned and managed complex like a convention center. It was still in many ways a downtown. And it was hardly a hospitable anchor for an inhospitable Market sprawled across the region.

McPherson dryly lamented the lack of amenities and accommodations, recognizing High Point's lack of polish, its provincialism, and its noticeable grit as weaknesses that needed addressing. He sarcastically equated the migration of buyers to downtown High Point to unfortunate but natural migratory instincts. "In Africa, the wildebeest makes an annual migration under conditions of severe hardship. In Norway, lemmings make a suicidal dash into the sea," he noted. "All over the world, various migratory birds battle thunderstorms, blazing shotguns, and other discomforts or hazards through instinct, or reasons known only to them."[38] Apparently lured by a similarly brutal intuition, the "brightest and boldest buyers make a semi-annual trip to High Point. . . . the only trip he makes where he can't live better than he lives at home."[39]

Deindustrialized Spaces, the Rise of Design

"We felt that the whole Market was going to start migrating to this town away from . . . the Figure 8," manufacturer and showroom owner Dave Phillips explained. Brother of Earl "Phil" Phillips Jr. and son of former mayor Earl Phillips Sr., Dave Phillips had the inspiration that the old High Point Tomlinson furniture plant could accommodate the growing demand for showroom space. The idea occurred to him on his regular route to work when he passed the factory. It was the mid-1970s, and he had just returned from a San Francisco furniture exposition where he had seen a similar building called the Icehouse. The building on San Francisco's Battery Street "was a wonderful old plant that had been turned into a furniture showroom complex for decorators," he said. Originally built to supply ice to the city's fishing industry, the conversion was the brainchild of San Francisco developer Henry Adams, who been general manager of that city's Western Furniture Mart. The aesthetic-minded socialite Adams would eventually grow the San Francisco market to a quarter million square feet by redeveloping Market Street's warehouses.

In urban planning circles, the San Francisco practice of reuse became the favored model for a peaceful coexistence between preservationists and developers.[40] In this approach, preservationists maintained old buildings while developers got space for commercial uses. Critics see such a model as celebrating building preservation without any regard for the social preservation of the surrounding community fabric. Proponents see it as salvaging possibly doomed buildings not only for present use, admittedly maybe less than ideal, but also for alternative future uses.

Dave Phillips had just invested in a firm owned by advertising executive Richard Behrends, which also employed Leo Heer, no longer director of the Home Furnishings Center. From their quarters in the white office building, they could see the Tomlinson plant. At a meeting one day where Heer was telling Phillips and others that High Point needed more showroom space, Phillips pointed to the old plant and shared his idea.

Phillips remembered his colleagues saying he was crazy: *Who would show home furnishings in an old factory loft?* Phillips persuaded them to visit San Francisco to see the Icehouse for themselves. When they saw it, they understood. Phillips approached the owner of Tomlinson about buying portions of the factory building over time, and the owner agreed. The stage was set to introduce a grimy old furniture plant into the Market's fashion show.

One decade after urbanist Ruth Glass coined the term *gentrification* in London, this account from mid-1970s High Point follows the development of a global design trend: the repurposing of old factory lofts, in this case to display furniture lines. As with the residential gentrification that was gaining momentum in New York City's SoHo, cost considerations were driving the transformation. The concept of factory loft showrooms did not yet mean hip and edgy to most people. The buildings were simply available, unwanted, spacious, well built, and *cheap.*

The constitutive ramifications of these decision-making processes in San Francisco and High Point are interesting. Such buildings, with their industrial backdrops of tall exposed ceilings and brick walls, would provide the settings for "mom-and-pop" furniture buyers to first see new furniture and (through furniture photography at expositions) the contexts for local retailers and furniture consumers to get a first look in advertising materials and magazines. While this cultural transition was already underway in San Francisco, the idea was still unspooling in High Point.

Phillips needed to find potential tenants to make the old Tomlinson factory financially viable. "Century Furniture Company were good friends of mine, fraternity brothers of mine," he said. "I called [Century president Harley F. "Buck"] Shuford and I said, 'Buck, would you consider coming to High Point?'" Buck's response reflected the current power dynamics: manufacturers were in charge. "We used to have all the showrooms in the back of the factories, and the product would just go right upstairs and be set up and displayed," said Buck's grandson Alex Shuford III, as he recalled Century's adjoining exhibition building.[41] His grandfather produced and marketed his product from one local place, Hickory, the place he also called home.

"I don't want to come down there and live in a motel room," Phillips recalls Shuford saying; the latter preferred to show his merchandise where he made it. The anecdote illustrates what Phillips characterized as the attitude of the time: "It's not what the customers want, it's what the suppliers want." Large manufacturers like Century had the stature and influence to sway the industry; they controlled both the goods and the means to produce them. Mom-and-pop furniture retailers, lacking agency, went wherever the large manufacturers displayed. Phillips's push for High Point's Tomlinson plant conversion proved to be ahead of its time. Without an anchor like Century, the bid died.

Manufacturers did not yet see the design potential of a converted industrial loft space. Even in fashion-forward San Francisco, Adams's associates considered his now-visionary reconceptualization of former manufacturing space folly. "The decorators aren't going to go in there!" one said.[42] Meanwhile, other High Point exhibition buildings continued to expand in increments in response to rising demands for more space from new exhibitors and from existing exhibitors with expanding lines. The National Furniture Mart additions in 1976 and 1978 tripled the size of the original building.

Two summers after Phillips's bid failed, Tomlinson Furniture went bankrupt. Until then, the firm's highly customized, craft-dependent manufacturing processes not requiring automation had allowed it to weather the regional decline that forced out its peers. Even when desired, automation was not an option for many High Point furniture makers, with their aging facilities or lack of investment capital. The building of new furniture factories in North Carolina slowed as production in Indonesia, Taiwan, Singapore, and the Philippines increased. The hefty savings promised by overseas production increasingly sealed decisions against investing in local factories.

Amid the regional decline in furniture production, local furniture leaders Chuck Hayworth and Jake Froehlich purchased the Tomlinson business. Froehlich had been one of the first furniture manufacturers to import hardwood from Southeast Asia and would use that expertise to move Tomlinson's case goods manufacturing to Indonesia. Each manufacturer navigated this sea change differently, but eventually all would have to address automation's impact on efficiency and potential profit.

"The free market is working very, very well in America and will continue to work," an executive from Furniture Industries assured a Market audience at the Fall 1983 exposition.[43] A Lane Furniture executive told the same audience that major firms such as the manufacturer Henredon were "making treks to Europe to investigate" the highly automated furniture production there.[44] Designer Raymond Waites remembers his days with Lane Furniture after the firm fully automated its U.S. production. "When I went to the factory for the first time, the factory was over a mile long. They were on a railway stop. At one end, the train came in and they unloaded lumber, and they pulled the cars to the other end of that mile and they were loading furniture on the same train," he recalled with wonder.

A major transition was occurring in all design-centered industries. In Phillips's smaller operation, production had become "computerized to where our creativity could be translated on a piece of machinery in a very short period of time. Instead of months, we could do it within days," he said. With this shift, the concentration of labor moved from manufacturing to design and innovation, and from "a couple" of "styling staff" to "twelve full-time designers creating product," he added. With a more prominent role and flexible manufacturing practices on the rise, innovative designers were now freer to jettison design catering to mass-produced suburbia.[45] It presaged what was coming: value was more dependent on the image of the furniture rather than the tangible good itself.

It was a new era, and, at the Market, there was more optimism than alarm until the late 1980s. The issue of imports was always "treated delicately" at the global exposition, where such import relationships often began. Cornell University's Curtis Tarr spoke with rare candor when he told a room of furniture executives at the Fall 1986 Market: "Some of these people are eating our lunches."[46] He argued that footloose investment would continue migrating from favorable to more favorable contexts. "There are all kinds of places where there exists that entrepreneur spirit and a cheap labor rate," he warned them.

Postindustrial Aesthetics and
Increasing Retailer Power

Undeterred by their previous setback, Phillips and ad agency owner Behrends approached new owners Froehlich and Haywood about a new plan to renovate the former Tomlinson plant in stages using federal historic preservation tax credits. They called the project Market Square. Their plan, really a microcosm of downtown redevelopment, would transition usage from manufacturing to exposition within the complex. The new owners would be responsible for removing the machinery in phases while Phillips and Behrends developed showrooms and moved in exhibitors.

Once again, Phillips needed an anchor tenant. And once again, he approached Century president and fraternity brother Shuford. "Buck Shuford said that the time had changed," Phillips recalled. The decade of the 1970s *had* brought changes.

First, the cultural interpretation of old buildings completely transformed. There was a new sense of importance for both art and history in popular culture.[47] In 1977, *Apartment Life* magazine renovated an old home in downtown High Point for its showroom, recognizing the emerging "commitment to urban living."[48] Older buildings enabled this pursuit of authenticity because they could lay claim to gritty vernacular vis-à-vis new construction.[49] Over time, this revaluing of the old would intersect with a growing distaste for modernist designs that had been "cheapened and standardized after they were adopted on a massive scale." Every new building seemed like a "big ol' box," as Richard Wood told me. In such contexts, old brick buildings seemed increasingly distinct.[50]

Second, as sociologists Joseph Bensman and Arthur Vidich note, by mid-decade "artistic cultivation, sophistication, and consumption" had become a "new basis of status and lifestyles" for the middle class. A new melding of high design with popular culture had set in. It was the era when, working from his New York apartment, Waites introduced the middle class to the designs of Finnish Marimekko through Crate and Barrel and to Gear Design through Sears. Bloomingdale's promoted a SoHo-style furniture line as loft-living homeowners maintained a status of avant-garde even as they became mainstream.[51] Magazines featured residential lofts that rivaled the offerings of any suburban home and with items familiar to the middle class, such as "the oriental rug, track lighting, polished wood floors, comfortable sofa and chairs," all effectively integrated into this new type of residential space.[52] Factory lofts were the preferred canvas for experimental décor.[53]

Furniture retailing had changed, too. Retailers were merging and gaining power. No longer did they have to place an order at the Market to stock their shops with finished goods they had touched and assessed in High Point. Instead, large retailers had begun working closely with a select number of manufacturers, discussing their needs and wants before and during production.

It used to be that "the manufacturer would say 'hey, if we *want* to do business with you, you come out to *our* office,'" furniture finance analyst Kris Reining explained. This was the privileged position from which Buck Shuford declared that he would prefer to sleep in his own bed rather than a hotel room in High Point. In the new climate of huge retailers, said Reining, "you sit down in *their* office and they *tell* you what they are going to pay for it, how much you're going to give them, and how quickly you're going to deliver it." Shuford foresaw these new days. "He felt that he *had* to go to High Point because his customers told him he had to," Phillips stated bluntly. In 1984, Century Furniture announced plans to make the ninety-mile move from Hickory to the new Market Square, becoming one of seven initial partners.[54] Within two years, Market Square was fully leased.

"We found people like Natuzzi, a bald-headed Italian with a great flair," said Phillips, describing one of his most prominent recruits. As head of Industrie Natuzzi, then a twenty-five-year-old firm in southern Italy, Pasquale Natuzzi had mastered the vertical integration trends of the 1970s. He "grows his own cows, has his own tannery, makes his own foam, makes his own furniture, puts it in boxcars, and ships it all over the world on containers," Phillips marveled. "We came across him in Copenhagen, Denmark in a furniture show," he added. "He's phenomenal, but he had never been to the American Market. He came here, rented a little space, took off, and now he does close to a billion dollars around the world." Furniture journalist Francine Liddelle also noted Natuzzi's swift rise.[55] "He loves High Point so much," she said. "He really does. He truly thinks it made his career to come here."

High Point's growing dominance in presenting the fashion element of furniture amid the deindustrialization taking place paralleled the course of another highly aesthetic industry sector that Market players often referenced: the garment business. In that international industry, Paris, New York, London, and Milan became or remained the chief debut sites even as apparel manufacturing migrated to Asia.[56] New York, like High Point, orchestrated a deliberate transition from production to runway. The city created awards and held special ceremonies near the garment district, not for leading local *producers,* but for global *fashion figures* such as Calvin Klein.[57] High Point followed a similar campaign, establishing the Furniture Hall of Fame (and its accompanying downtown Walk of Fame modeled on Hollywood's star-studded sidewalk) and the Bienenstock Furniture Library. In these institutions, the distinctions between furniture production and furniture design are bridged.

Despite the city's appointment of a committee to explore how to retain traditional resident-centered businesses in the downtown, High Point officials hailed the announcement of Tomlinson's conversion to showrooms as progress. As the value of the buildings and infrastructure around manufacturing decreased, the city worked to cut its losses by promoting the value of other uses.[58] In New York, this disused manufacturing space was converted into residences for its highest and best use. In High Point, the conversion was to showrooms.

Building Booms and Growing Pains

The remaking of the Tomlinson plant was proof of High Point Market's ascendance. It was a turning point of a scale that "scared everybody," said resident Geraldine Dickins. "Nobody thought that building would ever be anything except for a hot mess."

By 1985, when furniture-making giants Bernhardt and Broyhill moved from Lenoir, North Carolina, into the Home Furnishings Center, one year after Century's pioneering move to Market Square, all but 30 of the 1,500 manufacturers in that year's Market showed in High Point. That same year, the Home Furnishing Center's eleven-story Design Center, an addition of more than half a million square feet that opened in three stages, was completed. High Point Market showrooms were a seller's market. "We could pick and choose who we wanted to be our tenant and how much space we would allow them," said Ivan Garry, then the manager of the National Furniture Mart.

The developers of large furniture buildings had no problems maneuvering through the city's zoning requirements during the construction frenzy. Most of their battles were internal ones mediated by each challenger's political networks in the city. In one confrontation, the clout of Market Square leader and furniture industry fixture Jake Froehlich was apparent. The Market Square partners had purchased the air rights between their building and the Furniture Plaza / Holiday Inn property across the street to build a skywalk. However, the city had also granted a permit to another alliance of local developers to build the high-end Commerce and Design (C&D) Building in an area that overlapped these air rights.

In a remarkable demonstration of the city's deference to local influence, the city council determined that although Froehlich's skywalk would intersect the new Commerce and Design Building, the C&D Building would have no access to it. "It was strictly a commercial decision," explained Froehlich. "It's ludicrous," said a tenant, marveling at the city's failure to intervene in Froehlich's cutthroat maneuver. Realtor Mike Quinto, a member of the city council, was candid about the city's dereliction of leadership: "We should have made the rules, but we were afraid to," he admitted.[59]

Downtown development began to boom—everywhere. *Sprawl*, a term you might expect to have disappeared once the Market was consolidated from six towns to one, resurfaced in a new form. The Market that once sprawled across two hundred miles was now becoming newly difficult to maneuver on foot as it stretched over a growing number of downtown blocks. Charlie Greene, president of local upholstery producer Classic Galleries and then chairman of the Chamber of Commerce, calculated in 1986 that with 1,500 manufacturers, a buyer putting in ten-hour days and limiting each visit to twenty minutes per manufacturer—virtually impossible for major showrooms—would still not scratch the surface. "Working the Market" became a common phrase to describe the skill set required to adequately cover it.

Plans for new multitenant buildings emerged with regularity. The simple and elegant C&D Building added 250,000 square feet with its completion in 1988. The Market Square investment group announced that it would add a fourteen-story Market Square Tower to its historic site. Billed as the "first mixed use high-rise in the state," the tower featured five floors of showrooms that were an extension of the old building's showroom space, with the remainder dedicated to fabric businesses and residential condominiums.[60] The residential component of the mixed-use plan was deceiving. Market players bought or leased the condos for use during High Point visits in lieu of renting hotel rooms for themselves or clients. In recalling the project years later, Dave Phillips explained: "We sold the condominiums to anybody," adding without a hint of irony or humor, "whether you're a retailer, manufacturer, or supplier."[61] Today, a penthouse unit can rent for eight hundred dollars a night.

The Rise of the Freestanding Building

In the current post-Fordist manufacturing landscape, IKEA reigns as the world's largest retailer of ready-to-assemble furniture, as both producer and seller. "There used to be a tradition that if you bought furniture, it was for a lifetime," Waites explained. Companies such as IKEA changed the landscape, he said. They offered highly aesthetic furniture that customers, as old-school Richard Wood put it, will fall in love with in the summer and then "burn it in the winter for heat."

But when the RTA (or Ready To Assemble) Center opened in High Point on North Hamilton Street, this transition was inchoate. IKEA had just opened its first U.S. store in Philadelphia, and most people were still calling RTA furniture "KD" for "knock down." Smaller furniture stores that sold RTA furniture were ordering their inventory at Market. In 1985, the RTA Furniture Association renovated the city's landmark Pittsburgh Plate Glass Building to accommodate this growing niche.

Freestanding showrooms remained popular with exhibitors for the expansive and flexible space available to accommodate their lines and for the control it offered showroom designers. Almost every year since the 1980s—right up until this writing—one or more furniture companies have moved to a freestanding building, saying that this was their first opportunity to show the breadth of their line in its entirety and in an environment that does it justice. "We were reaching our limits," an executive at Pennsylvania House explained in 1987, "and we can now present the product in an environment that can be reviewed, seen, and understood." He saw the new showroom as "a symbol of the direction we're heading in the home furnishings industry."[62]

"We can use this building in advertising and be recognized," Charlie Greene said of his former law building, adding, "freestanding showrooms are a key to keeping the furniture market entrenched in this area."[63]

The Cash Cow's Final Hurrah

Although change was imminent, the 1990s began with the most traditional method of Market construction: more additions to old buildings
by the local growth machine. A twelve-floor, three-quarter-million-
square-foot Hamilton Wing was added to the Home Furnishings Center in two stages in 1990 and 1995, the eleventh and twelfth additions.
Additions three through ten had taken over the entire city block bounded
by Commerce, Wrenn, Green, and Hamilton. The Guilford County
Courthouse was the sole non-Market holdout left on the site, eerily
overshadowed by the three-million-square-foot exposition behemoth.
"We're just filling in the 'U'," explained Big Building president Bruce
Miller as he announced the demolition of the courthouse in 1989.[64]
"The exterior will look just like the rest of our buildings," he added,
meaning a blank aluminum-clad wall. "It's the interior we are excited
about," Miller said at the time.[65]

While exhibitors meticulously maintained their showroom interiors,
the building owners were cutting corners not only in the exteriors but also
in the upkeep of common areas inside. "We'd push our dollies down
the hallway and they'd fall right through the floor, they were so rotted
out," recalled showroom developer Matthew Tallon of his experience
working for clients in the Big Building.[66] Sarah Simpkins noted that
during the 1980s when she worked in the building, management had
planned to replace the very worn and dated "IBM blue" stairwell car-
pets.[67] However, when new management took over after a stock buyout,
the investors sought "more and more money for themselves and did not
put it back in the building." I knew exactly what she was talking about;
that tacky carpet was still there when I arrived twenty-five years later. "It's
just a mindset of old," Tallon concluded of this maximizing of short-
term revenues.

The additions had also taken a toll on the navigability of the Big
Building, which was in fact multiple buildings deceptively sheathed in
the same exterior aluminum cladding. A visitor entering the building
interprets it as a single large building enveloping one square city block.
Unconsciously, the mind's eye starts mapping the interior, which is
actually a collection of independent appendages combined to create one
massive assemblage. The resulting clash between perception and reality produces a panicked "mirror maze" sensation, like running into a

seeming corridor that turns out to be a mirrored wall. I felt profoundly lost the first time I entered the building; the lack of windows and the scrambled irregularity of the escalators, stairways, and elevators offered no sense of direction. Feeling claustrophobic when I finally exited, I stayed outside for hours. "We probably lose people in that building that are never found," quipped Becky Smothers, shaking her head after I told her my story.

Center of the World

The Market grew without oversight. "If there had been, you know, the city fathers would have saved the street-level storefronts for retail," said Aaron Clinard, an advocate of resident-centered usage. As long as the Market goose kept laying golden eggs, the mere suggestion that its growth should be managed could be interpreted as lack of support.

"High Point is immensely proud to be known in every corner of the globe as the true furniture market of the world," exhorted *Enterprise* editor Joe Brown in 1985. "Every citizen has a stake in its success."[68] Local radio personality Bobbi Martin agreed: "Information is now being placed in every U.S. embassy and consul in the world . . . we are a known commodity throughout the world."[69] In the words of resident Tom Terrell, the Market had become the city's "championship team."

Martin's comments extolling the Market in 1988 came the same year that geographers Kevin Cox and Andrew Mair made their observations about business coalitions pitching "the pseudo-community of the locality" to residents.[70] Amid weakening neighborhood networks, a stubborn identification with lost manufacturing strongholds, and the growing competition with distant places, local pride promised residents "the vicarious hope of living in a major league or world class city," they noted.[71] Although typically it is use value we connect with sentiment, in this way exchange value of downtown properties attaches to residents' sentiment as use value does.

As a result, residents who feared that High Point would be viewed as a tired old mill town seemed to show a hint of pride when they noted that High Pointers' "can't afford the dirt" of downtown real estate. "Feeling that their locality is the center of the world . . . is now important to people," sociologist Mark Boyle maintains.[72] In this environment, the alternatives to supporting the growth machine's plans appeared senseless and illogical. After all, "the Market has made the difference between High Point being just another manufacturing town and the internationally known furniture exhibition center it has become," as Phil Phillips put it in 1977.[73] Political scientist Richard Fogelsong found a similar sense of gratitude regarding Disney's presence in Orlando, one that makes political leaders uncomfortable with opposing it.[74] This environment leaves investors and developers free to revalue the entire downtown. In High Point, landowners were able to sell or rent their property at whatever price the showroom real estate market allowed without interference from the community or government regulation. This pro-growth orientation left High Point vulnerable as it entered its most tumultuous era yet.

4

The Cruise Ship and the Forbidden City

Aesthetic Flair and Private Equity Come to Town

The Golden Goose's Huge Basket

Cam Cridlebaugh Jr. was my landlord in High Point. I would see the dapper septuagenarian, sometimes wearing a light-colored suit and a pastel tie, at the office where I would pay my rent. One day in 2002, he invited me into his office, where he explained the Market's ins and outs (he also owned a showroom). Regarding the 51 percent share of the Big Building that was locally owned, he said that no offer could ever be high enough to get the owners to sell. I pressed him on this. Albeit still few, my experiences thus far had taught me that everything in downtown High Point had a purchase price. Why wouldn't they sell? Cridlebaugh cringed at my naivete, growling, "They don't want the damn Yankees to own it!"

That summer, I was at a community meeting when a city council member leaned over and asked me if I wanted to hear what he called a "dirty little secret." "People don't come because High Point has the Market," he whispered. "High Point has the Market because people come."

The first anecdote illustrates the Market of the previous era, when it was a homegrown extension of "us," a merchandising variation on what Big Building chief Leo Heer previously described as High Point's "militant and aggressive" approach to production. Local realtor Ed Price characterized the old generation of showroom owners: "They lived here, they had their plant here, they invested in the community, their workers were here." The Market was simply the place where white-collar "furniture men" debuted the furniture that their quirky designer colleagues had conceived and their proud blue-collar coworkers had constructed.

97

The other anecdote points to the changes that began in the 1990s. The contemporary Market seemed more sleight of hand than organic outgrowth, a disembodied tax benefit justified in the name of community pride. Not surprisingly, calls for support of the Market had grown less lofty and more pragmatic. "Quitcherbitchin," *Enterprise* editor Tom Blount admonished High Pointers in the early 1990s: "Be glad Market is here."[1] "If we're hosts and hostesses with class, they tell a lot of people," he added in another editorial. "That's always to our benefit. If we're not, they tell everybody. That hurts."[2] "Remember your heritage if you're a Southerner," he reminded readers the next year. "Show hospitality."[3]

In High Point, said columnist Josephine Goodson, "good-natured people roll up their sleeves and roll out the red carpet to accommodate and entertain tens of thousands of strangers (some more strange than most), proving that Southern hospitality is not a forgotten tradition."[4] She likened Market to an "annoying or peculiar relative" that her mother would remind her to "be courteous and hospitable to." "Without a threat or bribe, my mother could convince her children that listening to the litany of Auntie's aches and pains, or sharing our favorite toys with a cousin prone to hair-pulling and hissy fits, was a test of moral fortitude," she recalled.[5] Aunties, cousins, Markets, New Yorkers—all just inconvenient and incontrovertible facts of life.

As a city council candidate in 1989, Judy Mendenhall took the position that "growth can be a good thing if it's a controlled thing and well thought out."[6] But that type of considered, reflective approach was not to be. Fostered by the inaction of the 1980s, it was in the 1990s that High Point's dedication to the growth of both Market and North High Point became seemingly irreversible.

"It is not the Southern way to have a Plan B," Mendenhall said thirteen years later, when she was Market Authority president and the downtown was amid a construction flurry. This was less a statement of her own attitude than a description of the political context in which she was operating. By the 2010s, it was apparent to any observer that there was no Plan B. "This place," urbanist Andrés Duany said as he reflected on the city's situation in 2013, "all the eggs are in one basket. That's unfair, because this is a huge basket."

Since the 1990s, the *Enterprise* has been pointing with pride to Market real estate transactions, because of the prominence of the firms purchasing buildings and the downtown preservation and renovation that was occurring as a result. That decade was ushered in with the purchase of the Center Theatre by an investment group from the Tupelo, Mississippi, furniture exposition, a group that would increase its downtown footprint as the decade progressed. The newspaper applauded the renovation for preserving the "spirit of the movie house."[7] "Much of the building's character has been retained in its renovation," it cheered. "Outside, the marquee has been restored and new lights installed to maintain the character of the building."

More was at play than contending with out-of-town marketgoers and building owners. Increasingly, these out-of-town investors came backed by private equity. Looking back, my 2002 conversation with Cridlebaugh in the time capsule of Atlantic Realty's offices seems like something from a bygone era. Global real estate speculation has become a mainstay of the global urban economy, and small High Point has not been exempt.[8] This shift had general, macro-level implications for the world's flows of capital, but it also affected the dynamics and structure of elite power on the ground in High Point.[9]

The idea of globalization as a "speeding up" of interconnectedness is useful to frame the changes that were occurring.[10] In the era discussed in this chapter, economic shifts of a magnitude that once took place every few decades now began happening every few years. In a general sense, the same rapid increase in global interconnectedness that enabled the speedy transfer of furniture production to Malaysia, Thailand, China, and Vietnam also facilitated a surge of real estate investment and Market participation in High Point. Before the advent of capital mobility, when local manufacturers like Dave Philips found their investments in a new factory or new machinery suboptimal, they were stuck with their decisions for a certain period. In an era of capital mobility and multinational investment, however, backers were less bound to their place-rooted investments. The lure of bigger profit margins elsewhere due to cheaper materials or labor made cutting loose from a manufacturing investment easier. In a similar way, investors sinking money into a showroom development project today could transfer the same capital elsewhere tomorrow; they might even abandon a newly renovated building if the numbers were right.

The transformations seemed seismic. With the advance of some economic arrangements and the simultaneous decline of others, explains Sharon Zukin, it can feel as if "the ground shifts under our feet."[11] The players seated at the table were different and so were the cards that local leaders could play. It behooved High Pointers to grasp what was going on in their midst—and quickly.

With the Eyes of the World upon It

"There will be a quote placed in the pre-cast concrete that reads A CITY UPON A HILL WITH THE EYES OF THE WORLD UPON IT," Chris G. Kennedy, son of Senator Robert Kennedy, declared at the announcement of the Suites at Market Square, a new High Point exhibition building. Kennedy's uncle, President John F. Kennedy, had referenced the same biblical passage to argue for American exceptionalism. His nephew was employing it here as president of Chicago Merchandise Mart Properties Inc. (MMPI), a successor to the Kennedy family's legendary real estate interest in Chicago's massive Merchandise Mart building, to trumpet the firm's new investment in High Point. It confirmed a local trope, refined through four decades of repetition and recitation and now assumed to be undeniable: High Point was a globally prominent city.

MMPI had recently felt the eyes of the world on *it* when it was acquired by Vornado Realty Trust in January 1998. In two transactions soon after, MMPI acquired Market Square, National Furniture Mart, Furniture Plaza, and several surrounding downtown High Point properties constituting more than 1.2 million square feet. "These showroom buildings . . . are part of the heart and soul of the home furnishings industry," Kennedy said of the acquisitions.[12] Vornado Realty Trust's assets as a firm totaled just under ten billion dollars when I arrived in 2002.

MMPI's investment revealed just how relatively local—how human— the Market had previously been. In the age of Vornado, the behind-the-scenes arm-twisting by characters such as J. J. Cox, Dave Phillips, and Jake Froehlich in High Point and Henry Adams in San Francisco seemed like the distant past. To be fair, Kennedy and his firm were familiar with furniture exhibition. The Chicago Merchandise Mart, MMPI's flagship holding, was one of Chicago's furniture anchors when High Point stole the Market in the 1960s. MMPI was, by various measures, a solid corporate citizen.

"We have worked with industry partners in Los Angeles, Toronto, Miami, New York, Washington, D.C., and Chicago and have been embraced by those communities and look forward to developing relationships with High Point's community," Kennedy promised.[13] MMPI had an active and engaged representative on the Downtown Improvement Committee during the years I also sat on that civic body. Notwithstanding MMPI's place in the community, its use of terms like *corporate citizen* sounded a bit jarring. Such terms would have been redundant in previous eras.

"What the Kennedys own now, that was local people. And that's just changed," said realtor Price. "These local entrepreneurs aren't here anymore. I mean, to somebody buying a building down here now—somebody from San Francisco or Chicago or whatever—it's really a dollars-and-cents investment no different than if they were buying a building in Phoenix or New York." These holdings would be valued in global city offices by metrics such as their "adjusted funds from operations" or "net asset value." "The Market is a very small part of their overall portfolio," said Market leader Brian Casey, "but to High Point it's a very big thing." To Casey's point, even Chicago's MMPI was small in comparison with its parent Vornado.

A sign of this new era would be the weakening agency of big High Point players in the local growth machine. A regional business commentator noted at the time that the majority locally owned Big Building "usually gets what it wants to the chagrin of other showroom building owners and managers." But he observed that the "high visibility" of new-player Vornado could "displace some of the power and prestige" that the Big Building had enjoyed for decades "with little interference."[14] A firm like MMPI would not pinch pennies. The Big Building's days of getting away with bizarre additions and outmoded IBM blue carpet seemed numbered, as MMPI's investment in large-scale anchors like Market Square, Furniture Plaza, and Commerce and Design helped elevate other exposition buildings and draw attention away from the old stalwart.

The Rise of Signature Architecture

Historically, it was common for government to lead the development of iconic architectural designs, such as with High Point's old city and county buildings. In this global era, architectural critic Ada Louise Huxtable explains, "the dominant forms of architectural iconicity . . . are increasingly driven by those who own and control the corporate sector."[15] This is the era of what some call starchitecture—and small cities are not immune. Individual, freestanding showrooms were popping up all around downtown, and the quality of architecture began mattering in a new way. Trophy or signature buildings, boundary-pushing architectural designs from risk-taking architects, became a type of symbolic capital. These "identifiable corporate images" grew more common with "the entry of new property investors, especially foreigners, and inflation of property values."[16]

"I'm a crusader that architecture can be a draw," said Raymond Waites, High Point's own prominent transplant. He went on to cite the "Bilbao Effect," the extraordinary surge in international visitors and architectural prestige that this small Spanish city enjoyed with the opening splash of the Guggenheim Museum structure in 1997 and a rebranding of the formerly ailing city. The phenomenon connotes city leaders' facility in transforming the symbolic capital of unique architecture into other forms of capital, most notably cultural or economic.[17] Frank Gehry, the designer of Guggenheim Bilbao, has called the "Bilbao Effect" "bullsh*t," and some detractors consider it "sinister code for tearing the heart out of communities and turning their inhabitants into service-sector drones."[18] Yet there is no doubting the influence of Bilbao's experience on other cities around the world.

Italy's Industrie Natuzzi gets the credit for pioneering High Point's aesthetic arms race. In the late 1990s, eight years after investing in its first showroom space in High Point, the firm began contemplating how to put its architectural stamp on the city. At that time, Phil Phillips, brother of Market Square's Dave and president of furniture finance firm First Factors, set in motion a real-estate domino effect that forever altered High Point's architectural footprint. Phillips owned a showroom building at Elm and Commerce that he sold to Natuzzi. Phillips heralded the handover, saying it meant a great deal "for High Point to have a company like Natuzzi on that corner," one that "strengthens High Point's hold on the Market internationally."[19] In 1997, with the sale to Natuzzi, Phillips opened a new pop-up exhibition space: a 65,000-square-foot tent that, during Market, connected to the structure of the former Sears property on the Magic Block.

While some argued the Magic Block could become resident-centered and help High Point establish a mixed-use downtown, a topic taken up further in chapter 8, others argued that the Big Building could have utilized the Magic Block to replace the one-dozen-addition behemoth appended to its original structure. Tulane University architecture professor Grover Mouton had recently remarked, "Someone must come to terms with how unbelievably ugly that . . . building is."[20] For some, this was the moment for the Big Building's leadership to act and demolish the building. "They would have owned the world," predicted Matthew Tallon, a showroom developer at the time. To him, the cash-cow mindset was still too ingrained in the showroom industry, just as it had been in manufacturing.

Meanwhile, Industrie Natuzzi, by now one of the world's leading leather furniture firms, announced its plans to transform Phillip's former property at Elm and Commerce Street into its showroom and U.S. headquarters in 1996. The president of Natuzzi USA revealed only that "this project will be a significant one," promising "it's not going to be a 'how fast can you put it up and how cheap can you build it' showroom structure."[21] The company's Italian founder, Pasquale Natuzzi, commissioned fellow Italian Mario Bellini as architect. Described as "one of the last great protagonists of Italian design" by the *New York Times,* the Milanese Bellini has twenty-five works in the permanent design collection of the Museum of Modern Art in New York. His architectural credits include the Islamic wing of the Louvre in Paris and the iconic Milan Convention Centre.

"We expect, together with architect Bellini, to create a building which will properly showcase Industrie Natuzzi's products in the most important market in the world and add significantly to the High Point skyline," the firm's president declared.[22] From its inception on the drafting board, Bellini's design was intended to be iconic: a building made to resemble a ship cut in half. With this design—Bellini's only project in the United States—Natuzzi would challenge the former conception of High Point's showroom buildings as spare, utilitarian, blank containers, or what furniture blogger Ivan Cutler once called a "mercantile bivouac."

"[Natuzzi] chose this because he really wanted to make the point that he is coming in on a boat, that it is international," said journalist and industry strategist Francine Liddelle. "He's one of the first to make the 'this is international, let's not forget that' statement." "High Point has entered into the world's dialogue on design," a Greensboro architectural expert noted at the time.[23] It was a fitting end to the decade and a sign of what was to come.

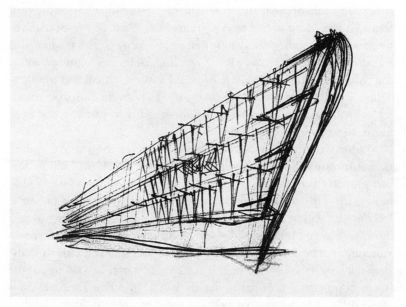

The sketch of the Natuzzi USA headquarters concept by architect Mario Bellini had drafting board iconicity. The firm said it would not be another "how fast can you put it up and how cheap can you build it" project. Photograph courtesy of Mario Bellini Architects.

The influx of international investment could be intoxicating to local officials. "High Point is as exciting as Fifth Avenue in New York," boasted High Point Economic Development Corporation president Kevin Johnson. How far could it go? "The market determines that," Johnson argued. The TINA philosophy witnessed thus far in the High Point story is straightforward: either investment is flowing in or it is not. If it is, then it is virtually preordained where and how it will occur. What is the alternative: to refuse investment? Who would be that foolish? "Those of us in the business development area can't control how well an industry is doing," Johnson demurred.[24]

Aesthetic Wars

The year after Industrie Natuzzi's ribbon cutting, two other Italian interests joined Natuzzi to add another significant marker to the High Point landscape in 2000. Manufacturers Delma Arredo and Rossetto leased the courthouse building formerly housing fellow Italian manufacturer Gabriele Natale. Like Industrie Natuzzi before it, the Natale firm vacated the building for its own freestanding headquarters in the former Adams-Millis hosiery factory. It offered the increasingly familiar explanation for the upscaling: the factory loft building would allow them to "showcase their collections in their entirety . . . in the diameter of an average dining room, bedroom, or dining room."[25]

Also like Industrie Natuzzi, Natale would add its North American headquarters to the new space. Natale expressed hope that the planned renovation, led by High Point–based designer Sid Lenger, would include a resident-centered component including a banquet facility and a sports bar. Market real estate strategist Ivan Garry recalled his pitch to Natale for marketgoer condominiums: "'$100,000 [for] a two-bedroom, two-bath, little living area condo . . . we can sell 'em like hotcakes to reps.'" The investment of an amortizable fifty thousand dollars (per sales representative) for a room in downtown High Point would be worthwhile

The Factory, occupied by Bermex of Quebec. Formerly the Adams-Millis hosiery plant, it was converted to Market use by Italian manufacturer Gabriele Natale and has been a part of many resident-centered visions up to the present day.

for both Market and intra-Market visits. This rationale was similar to that of purchasing, rather than leasing, a showroom. When the renovation estimates proved too costly, Natale sold the second hosiery building behind his headquarters. Most of Natale's community-facing plans never materialized, although he did attempt to develop a music club, the Aquarius, in part of the old plant. A small group of resident-centered downtown loyalists talked about those hopeful days for years after, noting how Natale would hold court at club events. "Bald head, glasses and everything," said resident David Williams. "You can tell an Italian guy, designer." Natale could not coax audiences downtown.

In 2000, Vornado/MMPI opened its first new construction in High Point, across the street from Natuzzi. The Suites at Market Square—the one inscribed with the "eyes of the world" quote—was a 750,000-plus-square-foot addition to the Market Square development. Market Square's substantial presence, its powerful backers, and its new aspirational quote helped normalize a downtown of distinctive but uninhabited showrooms as it celebrated the city's international prominence. It also made the Market considerably more navigable. One could now walk indoors from Furniture Plaza to Market Tower—half a mile via sidewalk, a quarter mile as the crow flies.

MMPI's next construction project, Plaza Suites, coincided with the peak of the Market's real estate boom. This building on the former site of the downtown Holiday Inn was nearly half a million square feet. Replacing the Holiday Inn with a simple but well-constructed edifice changed the aesthetic of the intersection of Main and Commerce and simultaneously wiped out a block full of memories for many High Pointers. At this time, a twelfth floor totaling 250,000 square feet was added to the Home Furnishings Center—its thirteenth addition. The floor was built across the top of the eleven-floor Commerce, Hamilton, and Green wings. The days of the Big Building, which then stood at its current 3.5 million square feet, essentially *being* the Market had long passed.

On the Magic Block, Showplace owner Phil Phillips and his partners, Jim Millis—a fixture of High Point's hosiery wealth—and furniture giant Paul Brayton, developed a local project designed to be of equal aesthetic magnitude to MMPI's and Industrie Natuzzi's developments. It replaced their original makeshift combination of a tent and the former Sears building that stood on the property. When it opened in 2000, the executive vice president of the American Furniture Manufacturers Association hailed the signature Showplace as a physical embodiment of High Point's national and international stature.

Showplace chief operations officer Joanna Easter utilized her office within the developer's new iconic, high-design building as a bully pulpit to blast the cash-cow approach represented by the Home Furnishing Center visible outside her window. Her disdain for utilitarian showroom buildings is evident in a story oft-repeated in furniture circles. After adding cloth awning to embellish the facade of the Big Building behemoth, its president (well aware of Easter's aesthetic tastes) called her to gloat. He suggested she take a look and call him back. As the story goes, Easter called a few minutes later with her response: "You don't mean that sh*tty brown thing hanging off the front of your building?"

This incident illustrates several shifts that occurred within this period. Besides a greater emphasis on aesthetics to showplace exteriors, attention to women's sensibilities and priorities in the industry became more acute as the number of women exhibitors and buyers rose. This new respect was accompanied by a perception that these sensibilities clashed with the culture of both the furniture growth machine "cronies" and the industry's marketing practices. Author Beth Macy recounts an anecdote from that period about advertising consultant J'Amy Owens, who began a presentation to Bassett Furniture executives by remarking that they had not redecorated their own conference room since the appearance of the song "Muskrat Love" in 1973. Capturing furniture's male-dominated, tone-deaf corporate culture, Owens showed a storyboard featuring "grimy black-and-white smokestacks and white guys in ties sitting in wingback chairs, smoking cigars and drinking scotch."[26]

This was also an era of expanding global participation and ethno-racial diversity at Market. High Point's Forbidden City building dates to this time. Lifestyle Furniture founder William Hsieh built his stylized replica of China's Forbidden City as a statement of Asia's ascension within the world furniture industry. It was no longer merely the supplier behind the scenes. The company's managing director stated that "the company's Chinese heritage is something we should boast about and talk about."[27]

"Scary man with big plans who likes shiny suits." That's how one furniture insider characterized Hsieh's reputation. Hseih lived in the region, and High Pointers regarded him as an eccentric character in the vein of the region's other visionary "creatives." He had had the fragile components of his signature building shipped from China by the exclusive licensee of Forbidden City reproductions. "Some people think this is kind of China sticking a flag on the peak at ground zero of the Market," I remarked to a journalist, attempting to interrogate the veracity of other accounts I had heard about Hsieh. Her response took me aback. "It's Mr. Hsieh saying 'here you go, up yours,'" she replied. Her comment echoed earlier accounts of Hsieh's statements I had heard—I just hadn't believed them. "That was his exact phrase when he described this building: 'Screw you!' That's *exactly* what he said," she insisted.

While it may be true that every city has leaders dreaming of a hometown "McGuggenheim," High Point did not develop an ambitious plan to attract its signature buildings.[28] Looking back at this shift, it would be misleading to frame this aesthetic moment as "architects being deployed" by High Point's growth machine "to foist onto local populations landscapes that promote forms of civic pride" to advance their own plans, as Mark Boyle describes.[29] Although this aptly describes other cities, in High Point architecture was a tool wielded by the newly influential outside players rather than by the city. The city's continuing free-market preoccupation encouraged global investment, and those new players (Natuzzi being the perfect example) infused the landscape with international design. The reality is that if firms had built the same "big ol' boxes," as Richard Wood described the early showroom buildings, the city would have certainly approved them. These flashier plans just fit a particular moment within a particular facet of a particular industry: an increasingly postindustrial, postmodern, design-centered furniture world.

"It's So Much"

"There are buildings all over the place that were just parking lots when I first started coming here," I overheard a man muse to a friend while strolling down Hamilton Street at the Fall 2002 Market. That year, when I would walk to my job as an intern in the downtown City Hall, I saw all the signs of a construction boom: yellow Caterpillar machinery driving down the street, cranes towering over buildings, and seemingly ubiquitous signs with architectural renderings advertising a coming showroom's square footage. The unregulated Market had reached a new level of sprawl

The Cruise Ship and the Forbidden City · 109

and increased by two million square feet in 2000 and 2001. That was more than the Market's total square footage before 1975.

"I've grown up in this Market," Waites recalled. "I've been coming here since I was a young man and basically learned who I like and what I want to see." He continued, "I've often thought if [you were] someone coming from Turkey or coming from Qatar and had no knowledge of what and where to go, how would you approach it? You know, because it's *so much*. And if you don't know where to go, you can miss so much of the really special, wonderful things here."

"I'd probably throw my hands up and get back on the plane," concluded another veteran marketgoer as he contemplated the prospect of a novice encountering the Market's sprawl.[30] Having worked at the front information desk of Showplace for two Markets in the era just before the Market debuted a helpful navigational phone app, I saw many "get-back-on-the-plane" reactions firsthand. It was instructive to watch flagging buyers leave the labyrinthine, 3.5-million-square-foot (the size of three U.S. shopping malls) Home Furnishings Center and warily cross the street to Showplace, mistakenly believing they had conquered *most* of the Market. From my position at the information desk, I would either apologetically or humorously—depending on the potentially jet-lagged visitor's disposition—pull out a map to reveal the other 180-odd buildings still left to conquer.

The Authority

At the turn of the new millennium, the Market was still coordinated by the High Point Convention and Visitors Bureau, the American Furniture Manufacturers Association, the International Home Furnishings Marketing Association, and the Furniture Market Development Committee. In 2000, the latter two groups were combined to become a new Market Authority. The other two groups were members of the Authority board, along with the mayor of High Point, and major showroom owners.

The Authority was primarily supported by state funds from the Departments of Commerce and Transportation, a High Point showroom tax, and a city budget line. It was charged with coordinating overall Market-related services such as promotion, accommodations, parking, and transportation. The formation of the Authority marked High Point's most coordinated effort to exercise control over its showroom presence. The market manipulation and interference suggested by such public–private authorities sits "uneasily" with the "free-market imaginings" evidenced in High Point.[31] However, what we can call regulated deregulation is more the norm than the exception. The united front cultivated by organizations like the Market Authority has been "a basic guiding force" in reducing the friction of capital flows around the world.[32] "We're going to have one solid, strong, effective voice for solving any problems with the Market," City Manager Strib Boynton said at the announcement of the Market Authority.[33]

Inaugural Authority president Judy Mendenhall's first Market was in October 2001, the month after the attack on New York's World Trade Center, when coordinating new security measures for the state's most global event became the priority. That included the enlistment of sharpshooters on Market building roofs, dedicated FBI agents, patrolling canine officers, a mobile command post, and an on-street parking ban. Amid her first, frenetic Market, Mendenhall clarified the Authority's main objectives going forward. Among the low-hanging fruit was centralized registration, a very helpful addition for a Market once so minimally coordinated that each major building required its own entry badge. Other Authority objectives were more complex. Mendenhall understood that the downtown's free market sprawl required an innovative transportation system to make it navigable. "We are creating, with the city of High Point, a new transportation system for the Market," she announced.[34]

Additional potential interventions were more controversial. A decades-old industry scuffle regularly broke into the open during my time in High Point. Referred to locally as "price gouging," the practice referred to local hotels, restaurants, and other businesses up-charging Market visitors. "Take one feather at a time and it's not too noticeable. But you pluck enough feathers over time and you'll have a bald goose who's likely to take flight," warned the head of the county restaurant association with another reference to the fabled goose laying golden eggs.[35] Yet when Mendenhall tried to broach the topic that first Market, the exposition's most prominent player criticized her for meddling in the free market. "There's no role for government to play in pricing," declared Chris Kennedy of MMPI. "Let market economics play its role and the marketplace will respond accordingly."[36] Kennedy, who would go on to run as a Democratic candidate for Illinois governor in 2018, added, "The people who can't afford to come to two Markets a year probably aren't our target audience."[37]

At the most basic level, the Authority was responsible for organizing chaos. I remarked to Mendenhall's successor Brian Casey that of all the directors of the world's major exhibitions, he probably had the least control. "I'm used to having the whole bucket," he admitted, reflecting on his previous roles. "I can't control lease pricing. I can't control category acquisition or targets for that. I can't control stealing of tenants from one entity to the next." He continued, "You know, we make up one large 'Market,' but I tell people it's kind of like the largest *co-location* of a show anywhere in the world."

When she was new to the role, I asked Mendenhall how this chaos can be coordinated. "Everybody does not agree on everything," she acknowledged, "but they do agree on Market." Once the growth machine's "dull unanimity" is established, disagreements are fine because they leave untouched the consensus for growth itself.[38] This is not exactly a healthy milieu for either community development or innovation, however, as industry blogger Ivan Cutler observed: "They grudgingly—all of the landlords and opponents who hated each other's guts—agree to say 'okay, maybe we are kind of in the same ship.' But they still don't row together." Coordination mattered again, as a new competitor would soon be upping the ante.

A Market in the Mojave

In 2000, investors announced plans to construct a 7.5-million-square-foot complex dedicated solely to furniture exhibition in Las Vegas called the World Market Center (WMC). MMPI's Kennedy used the term Chicken Little to describe the overblown panic around the announcement in the media—that is, a warning that "the sky is falling." This was consistent with the general haughty attitude among Market leaders. Pro-Market commentators called it a "trial balloon that's probably going to be popped" and a "pipe dream."[39]

"Vegas was different," said real estate attorney and civic leader Tom Terrell, "because when Vegas came along, we were arrogant in our superiority." At first, the confidence of High Point leaders seemed well placed. Las Vegas faced several years of delays due to red tape.

World Market Center leaders commissioned Los Angeles–based architect Jon Jerde to construct "an icon."[40] Jerde's previous design spectacles included the Fremont Street Experience and Bellagio hotel in Las Vegas, as well as Horton Plaza in San Diego, and Roppongi Hills in Tokyo. The WMC asked Jerde to create an "architectural language" flexible enough to accommodate an "internationally recognizable," evolving "collage" of buildings.[41] On the eve of High Point's Spring 2005 Market, WMC leaders made a bombshell announcement: they planned to expand their project in stages to twelve million square feet—the size of the entire High Point Market.

It was difficult for High Pointers not to take the announcement personally. Las Vegas ex-mob-lawyer-turned-mayor Oscar Goodman did not help matters when he began "trash-talking" the mayor of High Point. "If I lived in High Point, North Carolina, I'd either be committing suicide as I stand here right now, or I'd be looking for a ticket to come out here to Las Vegas," jibed Goodman. "I'd be worrying about the new furniture capital of the world: Las Vegas."

High Point's major advantage had been its willingness to accommodate manufacturers' display needs—the malleability of its built environment.

"Mob lawyer" turned Las Vegas mayor, Oscar Goodman touts the plans for the World Market Center. Photograph courtesy of Steve Marcus / Las Vegas Sun.

Large manufacturers like having a stable show space that they can innovate from exposition to exposition. Some also want to occasionally open their showroom by appointment during the backstage months. Although they tried to coordinate into a cohesive network, High Point's unregulated development had left this latter group of exhibitors scattered throughout the downtown.

High Point's area, flexibility, and diversity of exhibitor types provided the blueprint for its well-financed rival to perfect. The first phase of the Las Vegas Market featured ten floors of exhibitor space. The exhibitors' clients could access the bottom two floors year-round and the top eight only during the furniture markets. "While combining conventional showrooms and year-round trade exhibits is not unique to Las Vegas," the *New York Times* noted, the WMC was a major innovation in regard to convenience.[42] "It's never been done on this scale before," a WMC official explained.[43]

As momentum seemed to shift in Las Vegas's favor, local Market players appeared more worried. Cutler envisioned "the Golden Goose flying away and building its nest in Las Vegas."[44] Exhibitors around the world were reassessing the odds. Some buyers I spoke to were giddy that the Vegas Market would rid them of High Point's less-polished elements, like the downtown hotel's breakfast buffet. "Vegas can't come soon enough," said one buyer said as he scooped what he called the "crap" from the buffet table onto his plate.

He wasn't alone. Many High Pointers considered this buffet a particular embarrassment. If there is one meal in which the South takes pride, it is breakfast. High Point's penny-pinching proclivities only appeared starker in comparison to the extravagant amenities promised by Las Vegas—not least, a good buffet. Like Dallas before, the threat posed by Vegas motivated High Point Market leaders to begin exercising greater influence over the Market's supporting amenities.

Jerde's design for the World Market Center was constructed in multiple stages, starting with Building A (1.3 million square feet) in 2005, Building B (1.6 million square feet) in 2007, and Building C (2.1 million square feet) in 2008. As I stood before the WMC just after Building C was constructed, the eye-catching complex seemed to rise out of the Nevada sand like a mirage. *Here's the end of this story, I thought. High Point stubbornly put its eggs in one basket and it cost them everything.*

The first Las Vegas exposition in 2005 attracted fifty-three thousand attendees. Their market had thousands of parking spaces on-site and a shuttle that connected more than thirty downtown Las Vegas hotels. In comparison, High Point offered only park-and-ride lots and budget hotels sprawled across multiple cities and towns. Las Vegas had ten times the number of hotel rooms of High Point, Greensboro, and Winston-Salem combined. Finally, when fully built, the Las Vegas Market would offer twelve million square feet in a single campus with a coherently planned "architectural collage," rather than the High Point sprawl of nearly two hundred buildings, most originally built for other purposes. High Point's purported centerpiece, the Big Building, was itself an "unbelievably ugly" and intimidating assemblage of fourteen pieces. And yet High Point won.

An Idea Whose Time Has Come?

The battle of Vegas versus High Point had the highest stakes of any exposition competition in the industry to date. Even so, for those in the furniture world—including those who worked at both the High Point Market Authority and the Vegas World Market Center—loyalty to interdependent furniture networks always trumped place-based rivalries. They were "furniture world" people first. Sociologist Saskia Sassen notes that an identifying characteristic of a globally connected city is not its dominating independence but its stark interdependence on global networks of collaborators and competitors; this idea is exceptionally pertinent here.[45] "We're friends with all of them," said Sally Bringier, citing other furniture exposition centers around the world. "It's something that plays out in the media much more than it does here. Other than [Las Vegas] Mayor Goodman, it's really not the stone-throwing kind of thing."

"To me, it's very hard to look at it like one market is cannibalizing another," said designer and executive Jason Phillips from his office in High Point. "We love the people in Vegas, we love the people in High Point," he said. "We have similar-sized showrooms in both locations. We depend on both markets. But High Point is a *staple*."

Both cities had to navigate the financial downturn of the late 2000s, and High Point stood up to Las Vegas in a way few, me included, would have imagined. High Point was the one playing with house money. The Las Vegas threat had exposed not only High Point's weaknesses but also its strengths. "[Our] buildings are paid for," remarked Candy Lambeth, owner of High Point's Radio Building. "You can't fill those eight buildings with [enough revenue to justify] what it costs to build them," Kennedy argued regarding the infeasibility of the fully built WMC project. Las Vegas was anywhere from two to ten times more expensive than High Point for exhibitors, depending on the specific comparison. "That doesn't seem like a good deal, does it?" Kennedy asked.[46] As Vegas developed, exhibitors who owned their High Point buildings held on to them. Those leasing space from local building owners renewed their relatively inexpensive leases in High Point while they also tried out Las Vegas.

Another "fallacy of Las Vegas," enumerated local booster, former furniture professional, and showroom owner Charles Simmons, was that "it doesn't make sense to build a building for a company that can go bankrupt in three Markets." Many others in the industry echoed this statement. "Most of the High Point companies, particularly the creative ones, are smaller and it's hard for them to afford those big expenses," Waites said of Market exhibitors. Waites and Simmons were highlighting how few "anchor tenants" the furniture industry had. The upstarts that innovate the industry tend to have a more precarious existence.

In contrast to other global fairs meticulously controlled by their organizers, downtown High Point's built environment has nooks—from hallways to old gas stations to tents on parking lots—where scrappy, high-risk, high-reward companies can find spaces to put their products in front of buyers' eyes in a way that is impossible elsewhere. "We would always say 'that little guy who is getting an eighth of a page in the back of the book today is going to be your full-page advertiser in a year,'" explained furniture journalist Francine Liddelle. "[If] you've got the right product, you could blow up and own a building three years from now."

High Point's small-city built environment was important beyond its inexpensive buildings. In a globalizing era that seemed to spell doom for "place-bound cultures and local identities," as Zukin noted, cultures and identities that people perceived as local and rooted seemed more authentic, more legitimate.[47] "Tourist bubble" development dominated U.S. cities in the 1970s and 1980s, as noted in the previous chapter, and in the 1990s and 2000s visitors were tiring of visitor-centered districts that amounted to what critics called a "parody of the unique" or "sanitized razzmatazz."[48] Business users also wearied of superblock convention centers unfriendly to pedestrian navigation and disconnected from the local fabric.

Experiences that celebrated local vernacular and local authenticity, including explorations of bohemian and ethnic neighborhoods, appeared on official tourist maps.[49] These were neighborhoods with high-density, walkable city blocks of the type celebrated by urban planning thinker Jane Jacobs.[50] Research on small cities has uncovered how they utilized their historic and walkable downtowns as assets to attract visitors and residents regionally.[51] Downtown High Point's greatest growth parallels this privileging of the local fabric.

High Point's claim to furniture industry authenticity was particularly relevant in this era of disdain for simulation.[52] A city's origin story substantiates the value its leaders can derive from its authenticity. Market leaders could lay claim to these origins. High Point Market was "the original" global furniture node and the only one with a history as a center of furniture production and craft.[53] Its claim to craft authenticity was augmented by the authenticity of its downtown built environment. High Point designer Sid Lenger recognized this connection in 1993, when he recommended that downtown High Point "capitalize on" its "great architecture" and the "nostalgic . . . powerful charm we have."[54]

High Point's built environment boasted three distinctions. First, noted Market professional Sarah Simpkins, the downtown isn't enclosed like a self-contained convention center. It offers marketgoers opportunities to step outside the exposition environment and catch their breath. It is easy to get "overwhelmed with all the products and sites and sounds and people and food," she explained, but "you can go outside and clear your head. You get fresh air," she continued, "you see the flowers—you just get a mental break when you walk from building to building." More than a decade after the Las Vegas threat subsided, in the midst of the Covid-19 pandemic, the ability to breathe "fresh air" would take on an entirely new meaning, and High Point's outdoor spaces became a different kind of asset.

Second, the High Point Market is made up of hundreds of distinct places filled with intricacies, nooks, niches, and secrets to explore. They range from "high-rise" buildings that allow marketgoers to see many exhibitors in one building to others that are "still like shops," as Emil Khoury, the former proprietor of a showroom serving mainly Middle Eastern and African customers, noted. The fact that many downtown edifices—from the theater to the post office—retained symbols of their former use lends to Market the character of a functioning community. The Market has enveloped about two hundred buildings in the downtown, offering a staggering amount of architectural diversity compared with other expositions. "In High Point, every building has its own personality and its own quirks," Simpkins agreed. "Design types really like this." They note "rolling metal doors" or gush that "every creak in the floor makes me happy." Liddelle interprets High Point's reuse of factory lofts such as Market Square as "a homage to what this industry used to be."

Finally, Market's downtown location also offers veterans a sense of satisfaction. "They know their way around," said Khoury. "If you go to Pennsylvania House, they have their own showroom. If you go to Baker, they have their own showroom. If you go to American of Martinsville, you know where they are." To the marketgoer, there is a comforting permanency to each area of the downtown—in fact, today the Market's districts are now officially called "neighborhoods." Once marketgoers develop a comfort with their Market routine, they have opportunities to explore and discover new areas. "That's a very important distinction, in my opinion," said Khoury.

High Point's peculiar situation was that this now-appealing setting of walkability, localness, historic preservation, and high-quality architecture sat empty and unappreciated until its distant users arrived. As sociologist Harvey Molotch has framed the High Point paradox in our conversations over the years: "Jane Jacobs, eat your heart out!"

New Private Equity Players

The ownership structure of downtown High Point property continued to undergo major shifts. In 2005, Showplace, the white building, and three affiliated properties were sold by Phil Phillips, Paul Brayton, and the Millis family to High Point developers Coy Willard and Maurice Hull, along with a third Charlotte-based developer. Walton Street Capital, a Chicago-based private equity firm, financially backed the trio's firm, Capstone Property Group. As part of the deal, the storied white office building was to be converted into showrooms, named Showplace West, and connected by a skywalk to Showplace. The restaurant J. Basul Nobles, Clinard's law firm, and the Market Authority were tenants of the white building at the time.

Asked whether there were any concerns about losing these local anchor tenants, Terrell said: "There may have been, but the decisions are made by the people who own it—who don't talk to you and me and the City Council members. Monday was a normal day [without any indication that a major transaction was brewing] and Tuesday there was this big article in the paper. It's not a conversation that anybody's a part of." In this social and political climate, it is laughable to suggest that democratic processes, with all their inefficiencies, be invoked and potentially drag down economic transactions.

In a move seemingly unrelated to furniture, Jefferson-Pilot, a corporation founded by Greensboro's Joseph M. Bryan, was taken over by Lincoln National Corporation in 2006. As a result, Lincoln National, a holding company with more than two hundred billion dollars in assets, inherited Jefferson-Pilot's share in the Home Furnishings Center. With the other 47 percent of its shares owned by Bassett Furniture, the Big Building's remaining Triad-based ownership (by the former publisher of the *High Point Enterprise*) quietly became a minority. Although most residents were not aware of this change, it would turn out to be consequential for future transactions.

In 2008, the national financial collapse hit High Point. The financial world was in a freefall; lenders wanted to cut their losses and minimize potential damage. The next year, the same five Showplace properties owned by Walton Street Capital were placed in receivership by their lender, Bank of America, when the group defaulted on an eighty-one-million-dollar note. The two High Pointers overseeing the properties (including a planned overhaul of the white office building) stated that Walton Street "would not fund improvements we wanted to make to the properties and had withdrawn most of their capital."[55] "You end up with [an] owner that comes in and doesn't make the right decisions," Brian Casey said, explaining the Market Authority's lack of agency in situations pertaining to the exposition's spaces. It was as if the director of a convention center could only stand by, helplessly watching pieces of his building disintegrate, with no power to intervene.

"When we heard that it was going into foreclosure, I called the city manager and said 'well, you know, it wouldn't make a bad convention center,'" Mayor Becky Smothers recalled, momentarily imagining Showplace as a resident-centered space. "We could just buy it.'" While this was a chance to make good on the local "renaissance" promised by

Showplace's original developers, there was no reason to believe that the city manager or Smothers would suddenly break with precedent.

The transactions involving Vornado, Capstone, and Lincoln were significant to local pastor Elijah Lovejoy. To him, each of these situations illustrated how "a faceless company is making decisions based on their multiple property holdings—one of which *happens* to be High Point—about what's in *their* best interest." German sociologist Georg Simmel's words describing economic transformation, written well over a century earlier, seem especially apropos here. "Unknown purchasers who never appear in the actual field of vision" had stripped the human, "emotional tone" from commerce.[56] It was only the beginning.

The Ground Shifts under Our Feet

In March 2010, MMPI's umbrella firm, Vornado Realty Trust, cut its losses. In lieu of foreclosure, it turned over control of its five High Point buildings to the special servicer that administered the company's loan within a pool of mortgage-backed securities that were owned by global investors. The firm viewed "the exiting of the mart business" as necessary for its portfolio.[57] With Vornado shares falling in value, "people want[ed] to see Vornado simplify" and concentrate on its core assets, as a Wall Street analyst explained. Distant analysts were evaluating the economic space of downtown High Point according to profit algorithms, just as High Pointers had feared. Vornado's High Point holdings, Casey noted, are "a small investment for them," and they just decided "'this is no longer important for us.'" In *Wall Street Journal* jargon, they simplified and exited.

In early 2011, rumors began to circulate that "a group of dispassionate lenders and private equity investors" was considering purchasing a large swath of downtown, as Phil Phillips put it at the time.[58] The weight of this potential transaction and its relationship to the world economy prompted the European Commission to examine it. As the story unfolded, it felt like huge macro-level forces were landing on the city with an almost physical impact.

In January 2011, Bassett Furniture announced that it was selling its 47 percent stake in the Big Building. The next month, Bassett and other Big Building shareholders—Lincoln National Group and the charitable foundation of Randall Terry, the former *Enterprise* publisher—said they had a buyer. A series of tediously slow transactions followed, as High Pointers tried to piece together the story of what was happening to their town.

In March, newspapers reported the sale of the High Point show-rooms held by Vornado/MMPI to the mysterious High Point Acquisition Co. Then, in April, the Big Building was sold to an entity called IHFC Acquisition Co. In May, the court-appointed receiver for Show-place properties (which, due to the Walton Street Capital transactions, included the white office building and buildings in the Hamilton and Wrenn Avenue district) filed a motion in order to sell to Showplace Acquisition Co.

What was happening? The month-by-month machinations to un-recognizable buyers appeared secretive, ominous, and unending. Due to the similarly named ("Acquisition Co") entities, it seemed that there was one interest behind all these transactions. The talk in High Point barbecue spots, coffee shops, and barbershops was that an outside rival was behind the buyouts, intent on shutting down the High Point Mar-ket and transitioning it en masse to its own exposition site. While such a plan hardly seemed likely, the underlying assumption that global capital could simply "write off" a loss on major High Point real estate holdings had already proved true.

Bloomberg provided clarity in May, when it reported an "investment of approximately $1 billion to unite iconic showroom assets in High Point, N.C., and Las Vegas, and create an effective, efficient and com-pelling world-class business-to-business platform for both buyers and sell-ers."[59] Downtown landowner (and my landlord) Cam Cridlebaugh Jr. passed away one month before the first transaction in January. He did not live to see the fear he had articulated in his office in 2002 now transpir-ing: Wall Street controlled the Market. Outsiders owned not only the Big Building but all of its major competitors. Local allegiance had a price.

The investor, International Market Centers (IMC), was majority-owned by funds managed by Bain Capital Partners, with total assets of more than sixty billion dollars. IMC was a subsidiary of an investment fund managed by Oaktree Capital Management, a firm with approxi-mately eighty billion dollars in assets. Related Companies, a well-known New York–based real estate firm, was a partner in the deal. "Of course we're concerned," said Mayor Becky Smothers. "We have to assume that nobody's got enough money just to buy something frivolously" or, as she restated later, to "throw around a billion dollars."

The purchase gave IMC ownership of the majority of downtown High Point and the entire World Market Center complex in Las Vegas. "We are bringing together the best minds in the business, the most coveted properties and the deep financial and operating resources of leading firms who share our optimism about our industry's growth prospects," announced IMC chief executive officer Bob Maricich.[60] "This significant and strategic investment creates the world's greatest marketing stage for the home furnishings industry," added a Bain executive.[61]

The list of IMC's High Point properties included the original Home Furnishings Center and its thirteen additions, Historic Market Square, Market Square Tower, Suites at Market Square, Plaza Suites, Furniture Plaza, National Furniture Mart, Hamilton Market, Showplace, Showplace West (the white office building), and, later, the Commerce and Design Building, plus several other freestanding buildings. Maricich said IMC had inherited thirty million dollars' worth of "neglected infrastructure from former owners who invested nothing in preventative maintenance."

Simpkins mused about the loss of another familiar aspect of local industry culture. "There was a rivalry between IHFC and Market Square, Showplace; there was a lot of trash talk," she explained. After this mass conglomeration, these competing interests were suddenly "all in the same family," she said. It was a huge shock to those intimately involved.

"Sixty-three percent of the people [the Market Authority works] for are now under one owner," reflected one official as she contemplated the Authority's role in the future. It would be difficult now to make the case that the Market was an exposition put on by High Point and coordinated by its Market Authority. "Things are starting to get a little squirrely in Raleigh," Mayor Smothers shared, speculating about continued funding from the state of North Carolina. "Does the state really want to be putting dollars into a major international trade show that is so heavily dominated by just one company?" she asked, articulating legislators' concerns. The year after the takeover, Governor Pat McCrory did cut the state's Market appropriation in the 2013 budget. However, after a coordinated campaign by Market leaders, he restored funding, and state support has continued to date.

High Point's Market buildings were not only suddenly in partnership with one another: "Now, we're *all* in the same family with Las Vegas," said Simpkins. "That might be the quirkiest thing," agreed Mendenhall. "Us walking hand-in-hand with our supposed archenemy."[62]

Sovereignty

Residents were grappling with the new landscape promised by Bain's investment. It could no longer be framed as a commitment to the "home team" community of High Point in the sense of Fine's 1964 investment in the National Furniture Mart, Phillips's 1983 investment in Market Square, Natuzzi's 1999 investment in the cruise ship, or (even) Kennedy's investment in five Market buildings. "These are private equity companies," a riled Maricich was reported to have said while speaking to city council members at the High Point Country Club. "They get into an investment and they get out of an investment, so we have to find a way to monetize their interest."[63] Downtown High Point was now an interest to be monetized, a formula to be maximized. For this small city, it was a lot to take in. "We've painted ourselves into a corner because we've sold the middle of our town to people that don't have any interest in it whatsoever," said High Pointer David Williams.

"They could have never even *attempted* to do anything like that had it been a prior day when they were all still family-owned," noted former showroom developer Matthew Tallon. Yet, viewed from a wider perspective, the path to the present situation could be traced directly back the earlier, family-owned era. The pursuit of maximum short-term profits led the original owners to put off maintenance, favor leasable space over creativity of design, and sell off properties to incrementally more resourced and, in Phil Phillips's words, "dispassionate" buyers. The Bain transaction merely marked the moment when incremental change had accumulated to become a sea change.

Jay Wagner ticked off what was lost in the erosion of this old growth machine. "They served on the YMCA board, they were in the Rotary Club, they were in the country club, they supported charities, supported all of these civic groups that are now all having trouble," he said. Glenn Chavis agreed, although he acknowledged that Black High Point was not necessarily "getting big bucks out of it." He valued aspects of the old growth machine that "invested back into the city" and were "always thinking about the community." In the previous era, High Point's wealth offered at least the *possibility* of trickling out to the community at large and—for all its warts—it was local.

This new form of investment is "blind to geography," creating "profit for faraway shareholders that have little connection to a local area," observe policy analyst Atif Shafique and colleagues.[64] We are reminded of the idea of the "vagrant sovereign" to describe an entity that is extremely powerful but wedded to no place, just passing through.[65] When High Point's investment was localized within closed networks, the enemies and the allies of any particular interest (e.g., civil rights, resident-centered amenities, deregulation) were clear. But the new arrangement removed the "ethical and economic interdependencies" that had existed.[66] Within the contemporary changing structure of financial arrangements, even local players with "honorable intentions" can unwittingly support processes with "abusive" results, argue geographer Elvin Wyly and colleagues.[67]

"I'm envious," said High Point council member Britt Moore, thinking about those positioned to benefit from the shift. "Excellent short-term visionaries," he added. "Of course, it is well known that I am stuck in the twentieth century. I'm hung up thinking more about the long-term effects to a country, a culture and a people, a municipal tax base, cities—sovereignty."[68]

PART II

TEMP TOWN

*Spaces and Seasons of the
Furniture Capital of the World*

5

Hibernation

The Downtown Landscape during Backstage Months

You take the blue pill, the story ends. You wake up in your bed and
believe whatever you want to believe. You take the red pill, you stay
in wonderland, and I show you how deep the rabbit hole goes.

—Morpheus to Neo, *The Matrix*

Moraines and Pills

The sounds of John Coltrane's obscure, haunting, and sensual jazz standard "Naima" bounced off the buildings near the intersection of Commerce and Hamilton. A stately bronze statue of Coltrane stood near the
kiosk emitting this melody, intended to be a love letter to his wife. "Music
filled the air" in Coltrane's "house on Underhill," the kiosk informed
passersby, as "his father played the ukulele and the violin. His mother
was a trained singer and often played the piano."

The memorial expressed the tension between local history—specific,
individual, and, in this case, African American—and the large, swoop-
ing glass surfaces that seem unattached to specific persons, experiences,
or vernaculars of contemporary High Point. The intimacy of the tune and
the warm image of the Coltrane home only exacerbated the contrast. As
"Naima" continued to play, what *DownBeat* magazine called Coltrane's
"sheets of sound" began playing tricks on the acoustics beneath the terminal, which serves as the Market's depot.

It is easy to see why residents liken being downtown during backstage months to being in a campy science fiction film. One resident said
it looked like the victim of a Stephen King–inspired "green ooze" that
gobbled humanity; architect Andrés Duany called the feeling it emoted

The John Coltrane statue at High Point City Hall, with the Mendenhall Terminal (left) and Showplace exhibition building (right) in the background.

"Zombie Town." I was walking this downtown with Angela McGill, who saw a parallel with *The Matrix*.

"Coming out of my social environment," said McGill, who grew up in High Point's all-Black public housing, learning about the Market-centered downtown always seemed "a whole new thing." Our walk downtown reinforced that. "Even now, I'm realizing: 'Wow, *really?*'" "Like how *you're* doing me now," she laughed. What I was doing was asking Angela to walk through the desolate downtown as I recorded her thoughts, a process called the go-along.[1] After half an hour, I told her that I could not help but feel like I was leading a counseling session. Although she had been born and raised in High Point, I was the one very much leading the way.

"I grew up here," said McGill with an incredulous tone. "It's not that I am clueless. It's just that the design is there [to steer her away from it]. It's like *The Matrix*. You see what's designed for you to see. Take the red pill or the blue pill. *Which one will you choose?*" she chuckled. "Some people that walk through here will have taken the red pill and some have taken the blue pill."

"Domination" was what McGill saw in the unpleasant truth of her red pill orientation. She repeated this word more than a dozen times in our walk. Those living in the blissful ignorance of wonderland took the blue pill. They saw something completely different. "When was the last time you walked downtown?" I asked.

"When I was little—I mean, seriously," she said. "So I didn't see all this growing up," she added later as she gazed at the scene from a pedestrian's vantage point for the first time in several decades. Without intending to, McGill was implicitly chronicling how, as a Black child in the 1970s, she had been relegated to High Point's Black neighborhoods and then, as an adult, she was excluded from the furniture-"dominated" downtown. It was not that she was uninterested, she reiterated. It was just that, for her entire life, "daily living did not require I be in those environments." The downtown never mattered to McGill, and that, she suggested through her *Matrix* analogy, was by design.

"I can't think of another city that has such a dichotomy," public–private renewal director Wendy Fuscoe said, referring to the difference in how downtown is experienced by High Point's users and residents. High Point is a place of seeming dichotomies: resident-centered or Market-centered, rich or poor, global or local, the downtown or the slum. These themes arise in conversation because a tension between two polarized types resonates with the way residents and stakeholders understand High Point. For the remainder of the chapter, I discuss six themes that emerged in my walks with residents, alluding to the binaries discussed in chapter 1. These six themes are that the downtown: does not matter to leaders, is aesthetically disconnected from the city, has lost its local meaning, crafts a history for outsiders, has seen its life spaces intruded on, and—despite all of this—remains a part of the identity of High Pointers. The goal of this chapter is to use these themes to organize our discussion of the tensions that residents perceive in the landscapes around them.

In the words of Harvey Molotch and colleagues, "places not only give material resources and shelter, they also 'give off,' as [sociologist] Erving Goffman might say, messages."[2] In this tradition of analysis, we can understand the built environment not just as wood, steel, and bricks but as a text that can emit stories of accumulated decisions and power struggles. Such stories are evident to those who know it well, but fresh eyes examining a landscape—a city block, a park, statuary—can also discern them at times.

This chapter explores the messages downtown High Point gives off outside Market times. Using photo elicitation and go-along interviews, my goal here is to excavate residents' relationship to their city's downtown by exploring it with them. We will stroll through the spaces of downtown discussed in Part I while working to incorporate some of the insights and theories of chapter 1.

"When geologists examine deep incisions in the Earth's surface, they often observe moraines, the glacial deposits of soil and rocks left at the margin of an ice sheet," I once observed together with my colleague Jason Patch, trying to glean a geographic lesson from geology.[3] "The glacier has long since retreated or disappeared altogether, but evidence of its earlier presence remains."[4] I assume a city's physical landscape to be an aggregate of expressions (i.e., moraines) of how major exogenous factors (i.e., glaciers) interacted with what geographer D. W. Meinig described as the "cultural values, social behavior, and individual actions" on the ground.[5]

Neither the exogenous factors nor the values, behaviors, and actions are immediately observable. But the expression of their conjoining, the built environment, is a moraine that marks their impact. Urban built environments are, after all, the accumulation of decisions and the motives that drove those decisions. If one desires to understand the motives that formed a place, the built environment is a good place to begin.

The Days That Don't Matter: "We Just Don't Matter at All"

"They don't care about the citizenry," community college administrator Waymon Martin asserted as we walked the littered and shuttered downtown. "They're just waiting for the people to come back from outside the city." Martin's observation illuminates a distinction between the city's frontstage and backstage, a tension that has come to structure how High Pointers interpret the rhythms of daily life. This tension structures the city's geography, but it also structures the city's temporality. A High Point Market Authority campaign in the early 2010s hailed the High Point Market as "the next six days that matter." High Point leaders have historically not been overly concerned with the state of the downtown during its backstage months because, as Martin noted, there are no eyes that matter gazing on it.

One can find signs saying SEE YOU AT NEXT MARKET or some variation taped on the windows of exhibitors who departed the city a few hours or days early. To the exhibitor, this sign is akin to a proprietor who owns a Monday through Friday business departing early for the weekend and leaving a quickly scribbled sign on the way out to say "See you Monday!" in the unlikely event that any customers visited on Friday afternoon. When the tenant returns the next workday, they will remove it. Because that day in the High Point case is six months away, the sign will hang, yellowing in the sun, until the exhibitor returns. Perhaps no image better reinforces the idea that in the collective mind of the furniture industry downtown High Point is simply "paused" until its users return to the show.

Similarly, on Elm Street, a simple piece of printer paper announces a noon lunch hour for laborers at the loading dock. If this were a traditional resident-centered space, the sign would have most likely been removed by the person who put it up or by a city worker (as it fronts the sidewalk.) Instead, the crispy sign has been battered by sun and rain since that meal ended about ninety days earlier. As in an apocalyptic scene of a campy science-fiction film, only nature had remained behind. A similar artifact was the outdoor newsstands used exclusively to hold Market-week publications. At the Center Theatre, there is a stack of warped, yellowed *Market Press* newspapers, including a free "Market edition" of the local *High Point Enterprise* dated April 20. It was July 10.

On Wrenn Street, the storefront of the empty Oly showroom illustrated a common practice, which prevents pedestrians from peering into disheveled showrooms during backstage months: the interior papering of windows. Looking through an unpapered section of another building, you could see evidence of a hurried departure as if an evacuation had occurred. Exhibitors dashing to catch their flights home left desks uncleaned and small items—like fans, McDonald's packaging, and crates—strewn about. There is clearly little concern for the appearance of the spaces. Dust and spider webs were visible in showroom interiors, and nature had also affected the exteriors, as residents walking on Hamilton Street could observe.

Marketgoers describe Hamilton Street as the Beverly Hills of the Market, and I quickly came to enjoy its aesthetic as a motorist due to

The Oly Studio showroom on North Wrenn, during backstage months with windows papered.

its clean lines and smooth surface. However, the unoccupied street I enjoyed during backstage months cannot compare to the landscape's "blue pill" actuation during the Market performance, when—in sociologist Erving Goffman's words—"the impression and understanding fostered by the performance . . . saturate" the moment, and, therefore, the onlooker is "guided by the definition . . . the performance fosters."[6] With cocktail parties streaming out of the doors onto the sidewalk and exotic cars parked on the street, it is quite a show.

One showroom contributes to this glitzy scene each Market by showcasing a luxury supercar parked diagonally on the brick sidewalk leading up to its main entrance. "And then you go by [in off months] and it's like the *Omega Man*," a reference to the campy 1971 sci-fi film with Charlton Heston that was forerunner to Will Smith's *I Am Legend*. "Those people have enough money to hire somebody to come in and clean that mess up between Markets so we don't have to look at it," agreed nonprofit leader Maggie Mays, who had no ties to furniture or the Market. "We just don't matter at all until it's time for Market. It's that simple."

Disconnected Stories: "Plop This Thing Down"

Clearly, the Natuzzi Americas building is what sociologist Leslie Sklair would classify as a structure that is purposefully "different and unique, intended to be famous" from its conception, bearing symbolic and aesthetic qualities that "can be proclaimed iconic before they are built."[7] As one faces the building, the left side is covered in glass that exposes the inside floors of a ship, while the right side is a markedly real-looking steel hull complete with round portholes. Unlike other buildings that emphasize their street-facing facades, it offers a complex view from any angle. It is also completely out of context.

Decades ago, sociologist John Urry foreshadowed our current realities as he grappled with a symbolic economy in which "everywhere in the world can be seen and compared with everywhere else."[8] A globalized landscape bears this mark. It is a compression of time and space he noted, a hodgepodge of disconnected stories.[9] The literature on global urban landscapes is laden with inventories of the design cues characteristic of locally disconnected built environments. In the late twentieth century, this "global" look implied impersonal steel and glass construction with smooth-surfaced, high-gloss, computer aided design–inspired exteriors.

Ada Louise Huxtable warned that a landscape's "recycling and adaptation" would fail to maintain a sense of local "place, identity, and meaning."[10] Locally disconnected, globally connected landscapes such as High Point are best understood in relation to their peers, those nodes with which they are connected through global flows.[11] This *space of flows,* quite different from the specificities, peculiarities, and vernacular that make up the *space of places,* is palpable to residents when they breach it. It has uprooted local experiences and histories by obscuring the relationship between architecture and community.[12]

High Point home furnishings players contest what "contemporary" design looks like in their own work. Designer Raymond Waites asked, for instance, "Where in the dictionary does it say that contemporary is defined as steel, glass, and chrome?"[13] We can see these same tensions play out in High Point's unregulated showroom architecture. "We have a design core here," said recent High Point University graduate Nic Ruden, noting that these designers seem to embrace aesthetic unpredictability. "People that . . . do this for a living, with furniture. We have architects that come together with them and they have this vision of what they want it to look like. And that's what makes the city so unique. You have a ship downtown, you have this cube-looking thing downtown, you have the wave building, and the Chinese—it's like a hodgepodge of different things." Ruden's sense of the collaboration and cross-fertilization between internationally minded furniture and building designers is insightful. However, not everyone agrees with him that all of the creativity is positive.

"I just think that's ugly. Is that *global*?" Fuscoe asked, concerning Lifestyle Furniture's replica of China's Forbidden City to which Ruden referred. "I just think it's *tacky*." Residents couched such comments in the context of the city's planning and zoning function, over which they felt showrooms clearly had carte blanche.

"They're taking us over and so they come here and build a cute building that says 'We're Chinese!'" said resident and nonprofit professional Trish Perkins. "I just think it's a stitch that we're like 'Suuure . . . whatever! Come build a completely stereotyped Chinese building in the middle of like ultramodern, swoopy *whatever.*' It's ridiculous."

"It's out of place. It's out of place," said resident Tom Williams, laughing heartily as he echoed a common sentiment.[14] "You take our jobs and then you want to come and plop this ugly thing down?" This use of *plop* here is interesting. Molotch and his colleagues used the verb to describe a land use (e.g., a stadium) that has no ties to the context.[15] However, as Lifestyle's president argued at the building's debut, the celebration of Chinese heritage in downtown High Point made perfect sense.

Calling it "kitsch," attorney and civic leader Tom Terrell disagreed with framing the campy Lifestyle building as heritage: "I did not ever feel like it had anything to do with China. I just thought it was the stupidest thing and I was ashamed."

Standing at the corner of Green and Centennial, atop a small hill, downtown High Point's splintered hodgepodge fabric is clearly evident. To the left is the Forbidden City; on the right, the postmodern Showplace exposition center. Between the two buildings, we see the cinder block side of a characteristic U.S. storefront. And in the foreground? The city's main post office parking lot filled with its fleet of U.S. mail trucks.

"How in the world did they decide that that stuff went together?" asked Williams as he surveyed this vista. The answer quite simple: no one

This architectural hodgepodge features the main High Point post office in the foreground, with Lifestyle Enterprises' Forbidden City showroom and Showplace exhibition building in the background.

did. These themes—a lack of context, a lack of planning, and a fragmented landscape—so important to theoretical approaches developed to interpret the landscape of globalization, emerged regularly in High Pointers' interpretations of the downtown. To High Pointers, they were not abstract, a level or two removed from street-level reality, but emanated from their raw experiences.

"It's hodgepodge," Williams continued. "I don't know what designer thought that was cute, but it didn't turn out too good," he said as he laughed. McGill said she had become "blind" to this fragmentation. "Except that I have a lot of people that come visit me from out of town and we ride by and they're like 'what the *hell* y'all doing here? What is *that*? And *that*?'"

The Radio Building's showroom tenant directory orients meanderers to its changing occupants.

The Mendenhall Transportation Terminal, an airy canopy of classic "contemporary" glass and white steel that anchors the Market's temporary transportation system, is one block away from Lifestyle. To the European or Asian visitor, it is similar to the large train enclosures found in global cities. It is no surprise that this placeless aesthetic would be carried into an international transportation hub with users from more than one hundred nations.[16]

As an international airport depends on signage to orient navigators assumed to have no map, buildings in downtown High Point have historically relied on signage for marketgoers. Only the most seasoned have a "generalized mental picture" while navigating downtown High Point, to use urban planning scholar Kevin Lynch's terminology. The rest are unable to synthesize their "immediate sensation" with "the memory of past experience"—the ability that typically guides pedestrians as it helps them interpret cues around them.[17] It makes sense, then, that many downtown buildings have large directories attached to their exterior to inform Market pedestrians of the current commercial tenants.

Loss of Meaning: "You Get the Feeling You Are Not in High Point"

When I would ask residents where they felt like they were when standing in specific places, they would respond by saying either Los Angeles or some other global city, even on another continent. "You get the feeling that you are not in High Point when you walk down this street. No way," Ruden remarked while walking down Elm Street. The intersection of Commerce and Elm with Natuzzi, 220 Elm, the Commerce and Design building, and Market Square often evoked this sentiment. "For some reason, right here," Ruden offered unprompted, "I always see the set from Universal Studios." He interpreted the site as a theme park's interpretation of a city, an "ahistorical, acultural" landscape.[18] This is High Point's landscape of power, bearing the imprint of powerful business and political interests on the built environment. It is in stark contrast with the city's vernacular, the spaces where everyday life unfolds that call attention to local peculiarities.

On a walk through downtown High Point, it was disorienting for residents when vernacular seemed to appear: it was jarringly out of place. For instance, as local historian Glenn Chavis and I were walking downtown and he was making personal recollections about High Point's segregation, something caught his eye. He stopped midsentence. "Is that a café over there?" he asked with enthusiasm about a new space reminiscent of a northeastern deli or pub. "It looks like a sandwich shop," he said. "Someplace I'd go to have a quick snack." The Market's aesthetic tricks fooled a septuagenarian born-and-raised High Pointer. "It's signaling to you," I said, "but it's signaling the wrong stuff. [The signal's] not accurate." It was a showroom, a boutique line of an international conglomerate—a fact I knew only because I had had the same experience with the same newly renovated building days earlier.

Residents misjudged Market spaces as local, but they were also unaware of the resident-centered functions that actually remained in the downtown. Some did not know, for instance, that the Big Building also housed the city's community theater complex. There was an overwhelming sense, as Elijah Lovejoy noted, of "that's not for me."[19] The stage is directly across the street from the front steps of City Hall, but there are no indications of its existence—just the huge unbroken, blank wall of the Big Building.

Given the rarity of downtown walks, other residents were seeing iconic showroom buildings—ones they had heard about for years—for the first time. "Everyone always goes 'you know, the ship building,'" said resident Heidi Allen, as we discussed the Natuzzi Americas building. "And I'm like 'huh?'"

Sharon Zukin's landscape–vernacular binary, as any, betrays the blurry boundaries of everyday life. For instance, given High Point's longtime status as a global furniture node, the downtown's placeless landscape seems to have worked its way into the local vernacular. While perhaps surprising at first, this is no more revolutionary than, for instance, Roman columns being at home in Detroit: "not like High Point" was slowly becoming distinctively High Point.

However, as discussed in chapter 4, this was not a plan by elites to improve the city's architectural standing. Milanese architect and designer Mario Bellini's imprint came to High Point in the form of the Natuzzi building, for example, but High Point had not been "Bellinized" from the top down. Contrary to the common narrative of an arms race of cities competing for signature architecture, most High Point leaders had not even heard of Bellini at the time his building was erected. Regardless, his impact on the landscape was significant. "You bring an international

The Natuzzi USA building is designed to look like a ship. The west elevation has the hull cut away to reveal decks, while the east elevation is an intact hull with portholes. Photograph of west elevation courtesy of Mario Bellini Architects.

architect in to do a project and they are kind of imposing their art on you," said Peter Freeman, who, like his father, is one of the city's leading architects, with many showrooms to his credit. "The architect has a responsibility in that." But at the same time, Freeman said, the community should be flexible. "It's nice to have their eyes open to what *can* be, you know: '*what's happening here?*' This *is* a global city. We do have people coming from all over here and it should be represented in the public art that is architecture. You've got to embrace that."

While there are buildings with intricate detail from multiple vantage points, such as Natuzzi and Showplace, other parts of the downtown feature expensive-looking, high-quality facades that stand in sharp contrast to their blank cinder block or dryvit (a common, inexpensive surface material) side walls. One freestanding showroom building on Hamilton, built as the JeffCo building, is an excellent example of this. The building features an elaborate, ornate facade complete with marble columns, wrought iron, huge wooden doors, and textured concrete. Eye-catching facades that contrast with a lack of attention given to the other three sides of the building is common among downtown buildings, an aesthetic akin to a Potemkin village. Huxtable noted that some buildings "are not meant to convince; they simply supply architectural identity; in fashion it is known as a look."[20]

The attempt to create a classic pastiche includes faux external effects mimicking "accumulated, accidental, suggestive, and genuine imprints that imbue the artifact with its history and continuity."[21] Whereas a neoclassical structure, perhaps in France, might be missing a sculpture (long since destroyed or removed) yet retain the sculpture's original frame, in the JeffCo building a faux-worn appearance was created using an empty frame. High Pointers are quick to call such buildings "campy" in a derogatory tone. This is appropriate, as cultural analyst Susan Sontag highlights: the camp sensibility openly celebrates the "indefatigable patronizing" of the past, which includes attempts to create "instant character" by making new things look old.[22]

The "windows" of the facade are the essence of this patronizing of the past. They are merely faux window frames "bricked-in" with a brick-textured finish. This is a strategy that some showrooms have used to break up the monotony of blank, windowless walls, an imperative for exhibitors who want to eliminate unwanted light in the highly controlled showroom spaces. Few architectural details get politician Jay Wagner worked

The JeffCo building on North Hamilton Street is a postmodern mix that tends to evoke love–hate reactions with its busy front elevation and a blank north elevation.

up more than "buildings that were designed with windows that look like they've been bricked up." He actually considered crafting an ordinance against such design—another sign of how ersatz environments can breed frustration—but ultimately chose bigger battles, as seen in Part III of the book.

The notion that the built environment is not meant to convince (by itself, at least) is revelatory in a walk downtown. This part of High Point is a stage set manipulated to "send messages rather than fulfill needs."[23] Some residents feel this: they live in the barrenness of Disneyworld after hours, without the cast, lighting, and music. Like a closed theme park, it clearly communicates that its messages are targeted to other eyes at other times. As with other environments of great initial visual impact but little deeper connection to a place—from theme parks to universities— positive reactions can give way to a bland hollowness and even resentment when it is encountered more regularly. The substance of vernacular is conspicuously absent for some. "It's just like icing, you know?" said Perkins. "It's just like plastic that you put in front of the world."

Costumed Extras: "There Is Confusion There"

In the meetings of the Downtown Improvement Committee (DIC), which I discuss in Part III, downtown proponent and attorney Aaron Clinard often expressed a desire for the downtown to "look, feel, and be more international." The DIC wanted to stake a claim to the downtown, to communicate "we have some substance," as Clinard would say, to the visitors who walk its streets. However, to some residents, High Point leaders had, to echo Huxtable, exorcised the legitimate ghosts of the past and replaced them with "costumed extras."[24] Residents laughed when they came upon a plaque to honor Baseball Hall of Fame shortstop and coach Luke Appling, known as "Old Aches and Pains" for complaining about his ailments. Although born in High Point, Appling moved to Atlanta as a child. "Whooo?" was a common response.

The Furniture Walk of Fame built by Chicago Merchandise Mart Properties—an installment of bronze plaques in a brick sidewalk bordered by cast-iron benches—provoked a similar sentiment. Marketgoers snap photographs of these inscribed plaques recognizing inductees of the Furniture Hall of Fame, formed in 1989. Not surprisingly, some residents I walked with were not aware that these plaques existed.

"Do you know a lot of people don't know that the memorial for the sit-in is there?" McGill said of a striking bronze plaque commemorating High Point's Woolworth protests in the 1960s one block away from the Walk of Fame. The plaque was outside what residents characterize as the downtown hotel's "scary" (due to underuse) back entrance leading to Showplace. Residents do not use this path—that is, back and forth from the hotel to the Market buildings: it is the marketgoer's path.

Feelings about the local homage to High Pointer John Coltrane were especially complex because the city had made so many recent efforts to promote the jazz icon: a festival, a statue, historical markers, a children's music workshop. Some High Pointers were happy to see a local Black man receive due for his brilliance; others questioned what motivated the statue all of a sudden. Terrell felt that High Point's embrace of the jazz pillar was utterly disingenuous. "I can't tell you how many conversations I've had with people—or was on the receiving end of a conversation—about 'Oh, we have to make use of John Coltrane. We have to exploit John Coltrane,'" said Terrell. "Go down to the street and you grab the first hundred people you see and you ask them if they can name one song that John Coltrane wrote or performed—one song. You won't find anybody." Chavis cited a meeting of the group that planned the statue in which he recalls someone calling Coltrane "the most important person to come out of the African American community" in High Point.

"I said 'are you *ooouuut* of your *miiiiind*?'" shrieked Chavis before delving into his encyclopedic knowledge of Black residents who have made an impact on the local fabric. Chavis noted that when they called Coltrane's son Ravi, a Grammy-nominated saxophonist, for the dedication ceremony of the statue, "that's the first time he ever heard of High Point." Chavis was also troubled by the statue's location, outside City Hall, rather than in Coltrane's neighborhood. "They should have put his arm pointing down toward Underhill," he said, laughing dryly and pointing toward Coltrane's street in the old Black downtown. Chavis and Terrell are exposing the use of Coltrane as a "costumed extra" exploited for his symbolic currency within the furniture leaders' economic space, their landscape of power—imbued with symbolism that reinforces current power arrangements. The statuary and plaques, as DIC chair Aaron Clinard acknowledged years later, were "primarily for all of those folks who are walking around downtown during Market time, so that they can see some of our heroes."

"This is a discourse in which localities are defined, by their residents and by outsiders, as more or less 'worthy,'" as geographer Mark Boyle explains. In determining what is worth commemoration, "moral evaluations are being made" in the effort to gain "some sort of national, or better yet, international recognition or visibility."[25] For Terrell and Chavis, these evaluations seemed disingenuous—both to Coltrane and to High Point. It felt liked a sanitized, insincere attempt to tap into global prominence and cosmopolitanism. "You see, there is confusion there," said Chavis. "He gave *nothing* back; he contributed *nothing*."

High Point leaders were exorcizing the more mundane ghosts—the everyday heroes—of High Point's past. While he was not interested in the Coltrane statue, Chavis spent much of his time fighting for a downtown plaque to honor the Black laborers who died in the project to lower the city's downtown railroad tracks below street grade. This story revealed local complexities that, to Chavis, equipped onlookers to be better citizens. To him, this was High Point's true vernacular.

Of course, on-the-ground realities complicate simply labeling a particular object as resident-centered or outsider-centered. As inauthentic as the Coltrane tribute might feel to some residents, this presentation of local heritage is an act of resistance to others who see any nuance, any hint of vernacular in the global downtown, as "pushing back." On my first day in High Point, my twenty-something artist neighbor Luke had expressed that Coltrane, like other homegrown aspects of High Point, was "downplayed by the 'furniture people.'" No longer. To Luke, to "play Coltrane up" was equivalent to celebrating High Point's vernacular. Regardless of how we categorize a specific part of the built environment, the tensions inherent in our binaries help assess it.

Homage or Obscene? "You've Intruded on Something"

Furniture producers repurposed not only factory and warehouse buildings but also office, government, and consumption spaces. In the case of the Center Theatre, the original facade with the billboard and awning remained. For the Market, "the genuine historical fragment" of the Center Theatre was "a plus" because it offered a sense of place, of authenticity, of realness.[26] Although common local sentiment held that there was a better use for the old theater than showrooms, there was also a widespread concern that similar buildings in other small cities had decayed and been demolished. "I'm glad they preserved the movie theater marquee and the entrance like that," Heidi Allen said. "I don't know much about it, so I just enjoy looking at it." Her comment could be the downtown High Point preservation mission statement, which established the idea that the cost of preserving something is losing community input as to its use.

As showroom development expanded to exclude other uses, government spaces moved westward into new and uninspiring public buildings on the downtown's western fringe. Meanwhile, showrooms now occupy the stately former government buildings: a U.S. post office (built by the Works Progress Administration during the Great Depression), a county courthouse (on the national registry of historic landmarks), the old central public library, and a fire station. Like some of the other repurposed buildings already mentioned, these designs are considered familiar, repeated, and cherished, thus iconic on these grounds.[27] They are icons, says Sklair, of "the aesthetic and urban achievement of the past."[28] Their renovations have preserved the exterior messaging but transformed the interior. In the courthouse, small plaques next to the entrance doors are the only indicator that the interior is no longer for public use. The buildings' permanent markings ("Guilford County" etched in metal and "United States Post Office" in stone) remain unaltered. The high prevalence of such inaccurate labels can make navigation difficult for marketgoers who have not studied up on the downtown.

As Perkins and I looked at the old post office, her response surprised me. "Isn't that sad?" she remarked. Since she had not grown up in North Carolina, I was not sure why the reuse of a post office in a downtown she barely knew would be particularly sad, especially in the context of a discussion about many dozens of buildings. When I asked, Perkins explained, "It was a post office. It was a *noble* building." *A noble building?* High Pointers had developed a rather thick skin when it came to repurposing buildings, which made it surprising to encounter such emotions. Nevertheless, this turned out to be a sentiment commonly expressed by residents in various interviews. They understood the post office as a life space, which we recall from chapter 1 is John Friedmann's name for an almost sacred place where the mundane happenings of daily living occur, where the theater of life unfolds. It was easy to grasp the importance of these everyday spaces as I engaged with residents' emotional responses.

Former U.S. post office, county courthouse, and city firehouse: once government buildings but today all showrooms.

The global stakeholders who operate in what Friedmann calls economic space do not perceive value in the conviviality of these life spaces—or may not even be aware of it. Residents perceived this disrespect of local meaning. "You hate to see that be a showroom," said Fuscoe, trying to make sense of her sentiment about the post office. "I want to say *obscene,* but that's too . . ." Fuscoe broke off, trying to clarify further. *Obscene?* "You can take a theater. You can take a hotel," she continued. "You can take lots of buildings, but . . . every time I drive by there, it bothers me."

"It's like you've intruded on something you shouldn't intrude," Fuscoe concluded. Perhaps it was the meaning of "post": the sometimes exciting and place-based process of going to get your mail, marked by unplanned encounters with neighbors who were going to get theirs. Similarly, glimpsing a photograph of the post office hit Terrell like a load of bricks. It was a beautiful moment and a testament to the power of places to connect the present with the past.

"Ahhhhhh," he said gently when his words got caught in his throat looking at the photograph of the building's exterior. "P.O. Box 1551," he added, his eyes moistening as he recalled his grandfather's post office box. Like many at the time, his grandfather would wear a suit and tie even to check the mail and would often take a young Tom along. "It was one of those federal buildings that would be built only in the 1930s," he said, seemingly back in the building at that moment. "And it echoed inside. Everything was concrete or marble or metal—high ceilings. *Everybody* was there."

"I remember going in there as a kid and it was just kind of awesome: marble, sunlight coming in. Sorta like our Grand Central Station," said theater administrator Paul Siceloff, who is younger than Terrell. "So I miss that. I miss being able to go in there. That had a great aura to it." Given this sentiment, of course, it is not surprising that Siceloff, Fuscoe, and others would prefer to see such buildings returned to residents' life spaces. "That should have been off limits to the furniture Market, as far as I'm concerned," former city dispatcher Larry Diggs stated as he walked by it.

Ours: "That's My Town"

Residents actually cared about the downtown architecture. They lamented that the uninspired buildings of the 1950s through 1970s hold on as anchors of the contemporary Market. "It always frustrated me that the furniture buildings, although housing some of the world's greatest design pieces in home furnishings," said Terrell, "were themselves the most functional, square blocks. That's all they were: functional buildings, ugly as they could be." "Nothing but damn big ol' boxes," as resident-centered renewal advocate Richard Wood said. Showroom developers built most of the major exposition buildings with few windows so that exhibitors could control and manipulate internal lighting. When developers of larger buildings failed to design creative exteriors (unlike JeffCo's false bricked-in windows), the result was massive walls lining the downtown streets. These monoliths, said Siceloff, "seemed to be consistent with the fact that 'this is not open to you, it's just for the industry.'"

"I don't know what shifted," Siceloff noted, highlighting as I did in chapter 4 that the 1990s saw a change in the approach to building aesthetics. "The Natuzzi building, certainly Showplace, a lot of the restoration of Market Square—which has windows, it's a cool, inviting building—were more open. I mean 'open' like free-feeling and showed creativity too." While facing the same design constraints as that of the older buildings, the new cadre of designers and architects tried to break up their exterior walls—often with windows opening to lobbies

Blank walls line many High Point streets due to windowless designs that permit the manipulation of interior light for showroom displays. Here is the corner of South Elm and West Green Streets.

or stairwells—and even curve them, which meant additional construction costs and reduced floor area.

While it may seem contradictory at first, it was the norm for residents to feel a degree of pride in the new buildings of the downtown landscape. Residents expressed satisfaction that the city's position in the furniture world had resulted in spaces of prominent architecture just as some New Yorkers—who wear clothes with the silhouettes of buildings they have never entered—might be proud of the architecture of Manhattan financial firms vying to outdo one another by adding their aesthetic signature to the skyline. The pride they evidence relates to the fact "that their locality has all the qualities to pin down global forces."[29]

"I love my city," said Houston transplant Trina Johns. "There's something going on in there that's shown in magazines all over the world. Cool, that's my town," she nodded.[30]

"It's so cool, High Point being a design, fashion-forward center, to have cool buildings that reflect that," said consultant Audie Cashion. "A lot of pride in that. Many, many times—anybody comes into town, I'll go around the other way to come down Elm Street and take a look at it," he said of Natuzzi. Residents with and without ties to Market referenced this: driving different ways either on special occasions or in their daily rounds to enjoy the architecture in distinct areas of the downtown. Waymon Martin did it on his way to church, as I did, since the downtown was completely free of cars on Sunday morning. "Architecture," said Martin, "is sort of an art. And art depicts beauty." Before the aesthetic turn in showroom design in the late 1990s, Martin noted, "the downtown needed more beauty."

"I still am very proud of Showplace and Mendenhall Station because I feel that was a way of saying to the world that High Point and its showrooms have now emerged into the twenty-first century," opined Terrell. In 2000, the Showplace exposition center opened its doors on the city's Magic Block with much fanfare. Showplace's original investors, High Pointer Phil Phillips along with hosiery executive Jim Millis and furniture executive Paul Brayton, called it the "beginning of a renaissance of downtown High Point," which was a nod to the potential for community use of the space during the backstage months.[31] After noting that High Point's newer buildings such as Showplace were creative, free-flowing, and open-looking aesthetically, Siceloff went on to say that some of these buildings actually were open—that is, unlocked. They became, he added, "some of the buildings that High Point could use—a little bit."

"It's not built for them," Fuscoe deadpanned, directly contradicting all the inclusive fanfare directed at residents about Showplace. "I mean, it's gorgeous, but it's built for Market people. With an ancillary use, with a *nod* to High Point . . ."

"CVB *tries* to book that as a convention center. But there's lots of things wrong with it—the pillars, the ceilings—lots of things keep it from being used like that. We try to—again—put that round peg in a square hole," Fuscoe said. "*Make* it fit." Yes, residents tried. The local Dancing with the Stars charity fundraiser had been held at Showplace, as were Rotary Club galas, fishing shows, and proms. People hosting resident events merely rented the lobby or an unoccupied showroom within this edifice of economic space. Having admired the building's exterior, Johns's "jet-setting" daughter wondered if she should have her wedding there. "I said 'well, outside it is fabulous,'" Johns recounts, "'but inside it's pretty mundane.'" Johns said she was fine with this; common wisdom stated that there was no sweet spot where resident use and Market use truly coexisted.

The Market's newer outdoor areas elicited similar sentiment. They meant more grass, benches, and plazas, but the bar had been set very, very low, with almost no greenspace in the downtown. "They tried to make this the gathering place for High Point," former showroom administrator Sarah Simpkins said, pointing to the open space between Showplace and the Mendenhall Terminal, a highly landscaped parking lot divided by a huge landscaped walkway.

"It's not a park. It's got all of that concrete," Simpkins added. This area, which Lovejoy (and later Duany) would term High Point's "town square," was actually Showplace's parking lot. "Showplace has done the most amazing job in making that walkway as beautiful as it could be," Simpkins conceded, "but it's still a parking lot. And there's something that's very cold and not welcoming. During Market, you can truly fill it up with people," she noted, adding that this adequately obfuscates the fact that it is a parking lot.

Further illuminating residents' connection to the city's former life spaces that are now economic space was how often they noted specific sections of the downtown that could have been set aside for resident use. As the city rarely solicited their visions, I attributed the effusiveness of the responses to their being pent-up. A two-block section of MLK Drive just east of Main was one site that elicited lively conversations. Residents said that they appreciated its "Main Street" feel.

"Oh! This could be so fantastic," said Simpkins, who came to High Point to work in marketing at the Big Building in 1980. "That is the 'quaint kind of southern town' that could be fixed up, a walking community, restaurants—could be just very, very vibrant," she continued. When he is on this block, John Butt said that he is reminded of High Point's old "juke joints" near the factories where the "working class worked hard and partied hard." He added, "There's enough character there, enough of the old flavor that can be recaptured."

The use of aesthetic language such as "Main Street, USA" employs "already known symbolic codes and historic forms" that serve to prompt associations for the onlooker, according to urban historian M. Christine Boyer.[32] This space also evoked associations because it was once a unifying

Storefront showrooms on Dr. M. L. King, Jr. Drive on a stretch where many residents can imagine local businesses.

space across age, race, and income. "S. Rabinowitz used to be here and I used to go in and buy work boots," said Terrell of the immigrant clothier formerly there, before expanding on how difficult it was for Jewish immigrants like Rabinowitz in the South.

Terrell said he enjoyed patronizing such shops. "It was a *different* type of international flavor for High Point that I look back on with a lot of nostalgia." Rabinowitz was down the street from the Nugget House restaurant, owned by a Greek immigrant. In the early twentieth century, there were also Black-owned businesses on this same stretch, which once connected the thoroughfares of the Black and white downtowns. Although hardly a utopia of diversity, it had been a district of small-town cosmopolitanism, similar to the one that Jane Jacobs experienced in her enjoyment of "Mr. Halpert and his laundry, the Cornacchia family's deli, Mr. Goldstein's hardware store," and other proprietors during that moment in her New York City community.[33]

Residents were quick to point out that local businesses such as clothing boutiques did operate in some of the smaller spaces as pop-ups, exclusively during Market time. "During Market, these little shops right here are bustling little shops, man," said Market official Sally Bringier. *"Do a killing."* Geographically, this region lies in the sweet spot for a mixed-function space, furniture journalist Francine Liddelle explained. The "Main Street" district is walking distance from some of the year-round businesses north of the downtown and immediately adjacent to the Market. This mixed-function area had served this hybrid function before Market showrooms encroached on its real estate. The renovations of these shops into showrooms have mimicked the vernacular look of a Main Street pub or deli because the "Main Street, USA" aesthetic has an exchange value to exhibitors; recall that the look of a "local sandwich shop" was the cause of Chavis's mistaken identification earlier.

Residents evidenced ownership of the downtown in their embarrassment over traces of local vernacular—what one called "pimples"—that they felt do not befit the downtown's status. As with any of the other kitschy sites included in lists of the United States' top "Roadside Attractions," the World's Largest Chest of Drawers elicits polarizing responses. Local furniture designer and civic leader Sid Lenger, who arrived in High Point shortly after graduating from the Kendall School of Design in 1964, created the chest, which locals also call "the Bureau," thirty years later. Some residents felt that it was too much vernacular to be within the city's global frontstage. "I don't know why we hold that in such esteem around here," said market shuttle driver and resident Tom Williams. "That's a redneck piece of art." Terrell agreed: "Before I knew the word 'kitsch,' it was kitschy."

"Too campy, wish it would go away," Liddelle said. "I'm a little sensitive to it. I spend a lot of time defending High Point." The giant dresser is, to her, embarrassing. It undercuts her hope for the city's cosmopolitanism—its claim to higher culture. "I see the snob factor," she said in a stern assessment of the Bureau that it clearly failed. "I see people go 'reeaally?'"

"I mean, you see campy," replied a colleague of Liddelle upon seeing the jumbo dresser. "I see—as people are approaching this, they are saying 'Look up here! Look up here! Have you seen this?' she laughed. High Pointers who appreciated it noted its specific design features: not only the specific type of chest (Duncan Phyfe) but also the cleverness of adding a sock to represent the city's twin industries. "What an icon— a perfect icon," said John Butt, articulating this perspective. "It's soooooo High Point. It's so specific," Siceloff said of the Chest of Drawers. "And it's cute and it's playful." It makes sense that the term *camp* emerges in such debates. According to sociologist Andrew Ross, it issues "a challenge to the mechanisms of control . . . that operate in the name of good taste."[34] Sontag notes that campy objects, "from a 'serious' point of view," may be considered "either bad art or kitsch."[35] But camp is "serious about the frivolous," values objects that are intensely specific, and appreciates artifice like the Bureau's facade or JeffCo's bricked-in windows.[36]

In 2018, the Bureau was renovated and its color changed, going from stained cherry wood with brass hardware to a painted surface of what is often called "gentrification gray," with nickel-shaded hardware. It is as though a millennial maker had found the old chest at a flea market and resurfaced it. Having changed the connotation of the edifice, this facelift has won over a few skeptics.

While the chest appeared marginal to some, it is extremely difficult to find regions of the downtown that were truly marginal: areas seemingly dismissed by global capital. Residents observed one glaring exception, however. A decrepit building with a sign reading HAIR-N-STUFF TANNING CENTER stood just blocks away from the imposingly global "Universal Studios" landscape Ruden identified. Walking from one

World's Largest Chest of Drawers building on North Hamilton Street, post-makeover. Photograph by Daniel Burapavong.

to the other, the feeling of stepping in and out of flows of capital was palpable. It is a sensation that jarred marketgoers and residents alike— akin, perhaps, to what it would be like to encounter a tiny, raggedy storefront church on New York's Wall Street. Nobody passed Hair-N-Stuff without a comment. "All of this is terrific," said Johns, gesturing south on Elm Street. "And then you get a little pimple," she said, providing a colorful analogy for an unrenovated non-Market building.

"If you walk down there, you feel like you're in a downtown," said Ruden, pointing toward the intersection of Commerce and Elm. "When you turn the corner—" he added with an eye toward Hair-N-Stuff, "then you don't." "There's the 'grotesque High Point,'" he added.

"Where the *hellll* is that?" asked Market official Sally Bringier when I showed her a photograph. Terrell had the same reaction when I showed him the same image. "Ohhhhhhh, Hair-N-Sh*t," he said after he got his bearings. "Less than a block away from the main part, and you've got 'Hair-N-Stuff.'"

Hair-N-Stuff beauty and tanning center on North Elm Street and West English Road. The C&D building is visible in the background at far right.

"There's the area that could stand to be torn down. Great real estate for somebody to put a big showroom," Ruden added. He appreciated the architectural and planning aesthetic that the Market brought to the downtown. As we walked, he truly fretted over each blemish, each pimple, or, as J. J. Cox said in chapter 3, each lost tooth. Ruden pointed them out and took note, as if he planned to report them. He was concerned with what it said about his city. These walks revealed an insecurity that such complex vernacular—depending on the speaker—spoke poorly of a mill town heritage, the South, or small cities.

Not far from Hair-N-Stuff, the Market has enveloped similar buildings that retain evidence of their once-marginal uses despite minimal renovations. I questioned designer Raymond Waites about the exhibitors' crafty incorporation of things like lightly renovated former gas station buildings into the Market. "Number one, the gas stations are there. Number two, they're relatively inexpensive," he noted, displaying his own design sensibility and aesthetic inclinations. "I just think that's a part of the humor and whimsy—it's fun, it's fun." Like the giant chest, gas stations were part of High Point's messaging of bizarre charm. However, being neither global nor campy, Hair-N-Stuff was embarrassing to all. "That's pitiful," said Johns. "*That* gotta go. It looks like Detroit."

No Ghosts: "The City Dies before Their Eyes"

To Lovejoy, people who came to know High Point after the mid-1980s "have no communal or institutional memory of a downtown." For them, there were no ghosts of the past, present, or future that inhabited the space. Recall that John Butt could envision the old juke joints, and others were transported back to the post office. Siceloff experienced a ghost in our walk when he passed the Radio Building and "saw" the blind man who had run the candy counter there. Likewise, Chavis "heard" the William Penn High School marching band at the customary parade grandstand near the Center Theatre, recalling the drum line cadence aloud in a series of *boom-cah-tahs* as we walked Main Street. For High Pointers who were adults in the 1980s, the downtown landscape is still a "repository of . . . memories and of the past" and "a receptacle of cultural symbols" in the words of philosopher Walter Benjamin.[37] Lovejoy concluded that without communal life spaces to gather, such common ground begins to "fragment." The past no longer maps onto the future. Some people just leave, he said, while others, disenfranchised, "withdraw to their section of the city."

On my walks with residents, I questioned the community's capacity to vision together—what political scientist Stephen Elkin described as "social intelligence."[38] Residents did not feel that city leaders were interested in their hopes for downtown. This confirmed for them that local problem-solving abilities were unappreciated. Without locally emergent ideas represented at the table of public dialogue, policy is "likely to be ineffective simply because some desirable alternatives will go unexplored."[39] In their drive to residualize any concerns beyond short-term growth, growth machine systems tend to "erode the capacity to collectively solve problems."[40]

Lovejoy worried that High Point leaders' singular orientation and disregard for residents' misgivings had resulted in a downtown understood only as an aggregate of material transactions. If leaders "don't have the worldview to see intangibles," Lovejoy warned, "their city dies before their eyes." To Lovejoy, that is exactly what was happening.

Nevertheless, Martin remained convinced that any true community center for all of High Point must be downtown. To him, the downtown's size and architecture presented a "flavor" and "a total atmosphere" that could not be duplicated elsewhere. "The streetscape in our downtown, the tall buildings, the wide sidewalks, it longs for that kind of use," acknowledged Fuscoe. "But everything is driven by economics, really. And if we've got a billion dollar trade show—successful still, in the downtown—I don't know creating that urban feel can compete economically."

Still, residents used words like *us*, *our*, and *we* in describing the downtown landscape. While one could interpret such identification as an indication of the elite's brainwashing of everyday High Pointers, that seems overly simplistic. I wondered if it was an asset that could be mobilized for the community good. This emotional investment evidenced that the apparent disenfranchisement was far from complete.

Several people I walked with downtown stopped to note aspects of the city center that they felt were particularly "urban" or evoked the meanings and associations of "downtown." "I even like the ads on the sides of buildings," Johns said. She liked what she called the "urban" look of colorful furniture advertisements decorating those large, flat, otherwise-blank surfaces. Indeed, well-designed, colorful ads on blank walls are usually reserved for larger cities. At times the scale of the murals on Commerce Avenue in High Point transport me to the intersection of Houston and Lafayette in Manhattan.

The cavernous alleys created by the large downtown buildings were another such "urban" feature. "Now, places like New Orleans, Savannah and those places, you would *never* have an alleyway looking like that," said Chavis as he eyed the neatly kept but unutilized alley. "There would be something in here. It would be painted up—the sides—and somebody would use it." It is interesting that someone like Chavis, who cited the unjust dynamics behind gentrification (he called it "sanitizing"), viewed the downtown as inferior to its peers because it lacked amenities such as alley cafés with murals. This lesson often arises in gentrification research: what would seem to be *symbols* of gentrification—edgy alley cafés, bookstores, street festivals, and so on—need not be inherently divisive. Some of these elements are merely cultural elements of the moment. It is often the representation in and execution of *implementation* that produces division: the who and how, not the what.

One asset of the current built environment is the vibrancy it communicates. Downtown *feels* like "the real thing, the real deal," Johns added. "You pick up an energy when you go into a city," said Heidi Allen. Walking downtown, she felt it awakened certain "big city" meanings for her. "It's like you just start feeling that vibe: like 'Whoa! This is cool! It's exciting,'" she noted. However, that vibe quickly dissipates: "It's like *waaah waaah*," continued Allen. "It's empty. It's dead."

"What's today?" Chavis asked rhetorically, looking at his watch as we walked the stretch of former storefronts on MLK Drive that residents valued. "It's Thursday, and about twenty minutes to one. And what's going on in this town?" Pointing to the storefronts, he paused for effect, waiting for my answer. "Beautiful buildings over here," he added as he continued to wait: "*Nooothing.*"

6

Choreographing Mini-Manhattan

Visitors Experience the Market

Making the Six Days That Matter

Martha Stewart, "making her first appearance at the fall Market in two years now that she's out of jail, strode in looking lean in her taupe Yves Saint Laurent pantsuit and towering Hermes pumps," a *Washington Post* reporter dispatched from downtown High Point in 2005. Stewart was in town to promote her collection for Bernhardt Furniture. "She'd flown in that morning from a conference in Puerto Rico and was leaving that night for New York to shoot her how-to show *Martha*," the article continued.[1]

"Getting off the shuttle and seeing Showplace—the iconic High Point Market image—[is] like walking into Disney World for the first time." That's how interior designer Arianne Bellizaire reacted to her first glimpse of High Point Market. Writing on her blog, Bellizaire said she was "overwhelmed, anxious, and excited all at once."[2] She described the enormity she felt being at the scene where the furniture world witnessed "tens of thousands of new product introductions each Market." She named the "interior design rock stars" she encountered in various spaces. Venturing into the International Home Furnishings Center's Interhall, Bellizaire was immediately overwhelmed. Interhall, on IHFC's first floor, is often a marketgoer's first stop. There the Market's "freshest new ideas," "high-design products, chic displays, and unusual finds" are featured, curated through a "rigorous juried selection process."[3]

As she went on to explore the downtown's Hamilton-Wrenn Design District, just a few blocks to the north, Bellizaire likened it to "the Rodeo Drive of Market." As for the Hamilton Street building seen in chapter 5

161

Hickory White showroom on South Hamilton Street during Market. This area is sometimes referred to as the "Beverly Hills of Market."

with crabgrass overtaking the sidewalk between Markets, its supercar was now in place and the sidewalk tidy. Walking through the west side of downtown, Bellizaire was smitten by Market Square, one of her new "favorite destinations," citing the charm of its "exposed brick, wood plank floors, and rustic appeal."

"I defy you to find another city of this size anywhere in the world, where [in] Milan and Paris and Cologne and London [you] say 'High Point' and people know what you're talking about," Market official Sally Bringier told me. "You go to Shanghai and the same thing happens. Guangzhou, Taiwan, Vietnam," she added. "It's an international city," furniture powerhouse Alex Shuford III of Hickory Furniture said in 2013. "Everybody is willing to come here."[4]

The preparation rituals and strategies that buyers devise to work the vast Market resemble the training secrets of an athlete. Designer Alexa Hampton shared her survival techniques: "hair appointments on various mornings throughout Market so I can look and feel human," she said, and "occasionally schedul[ing] a massage."[5] Bellizaire created a how-to video with her tips to "conquer this beast" and what tools she uses: "my resource guide, my High Point Market app, flats, and a rolling suitcase." She recommended "fabulous for-sitting-only heels" and shared how she avoids being "overwhelmed": by "spending the night poring over my resource guide and the High Point Market website." Her hectic first day began on the Market shuttle at 7:30 a.m., preceding a nonstop day—with "the occasional bite" for "energy levels"—before her "exhausted return" to the shuttle at 7:00 p.m., "eagerly looking forward to a shower and bed."

"Wash, rinse, repeat . . . for five days," Bellizaire added. "Market is sensory overload. There is so much to see, do, experience, and EAT! It was sort of like a marathon. It required planning, pacing, and endurance!"

On social media (especially Instagram, ideally suited to the visual universe of Market), the hashtag #HPMKT brims with accounts like Bellizaire's. To juxtapose the backstage downtown that residents described in the previous chapter with the downtown Market visitors experience is stunningly diametrical. The storefronts of Dr. Martin Luther King, Jr. Drive—the "Main Street, USA" buildings that residents often covet for themselves—bustle with crowds both inside and out during Market. As the *Enterprise*'s resident ode to Market put it: "Am I still in High Point? Yes, and isn't it wonderful?"[6]

Storefront showrooms on Dr. M. L. King, Jr. Drive during Market.

To call the transformation of the downtown an illusion would be inaccurate, but production fits the bill. And although Market, as life generally, is not really a stage, "the crucial ways in which it isn't are not easy to specify," to cite sociologist Erving Goffman.[7] From the choreography of the Market's performance to the managed performance of each showroom, the downtown is a stage, the exposition building is a stage, and each showroom is a stage. In offering a preview of the Market, a leader affirmed in the 1990s: "The players are on the stage . . . and everybody is ready to play their parts."[8] A market analyst in the 1980s cautioned High Pointers not to assess Market before its "final act" and its ultimate "audience reception."[9] An *Enterprise* columnist writing in the 1970s called Market a "Broadway opening," and a trend analyst reporter described how "everyone works feverishly to set the stage for the big production."[10]

"The next six days that matter," as noted earlier, was the tagline of a recent Market Authority campaign. This chapter is about the production of these frontstage days when Market is in full swing. Especially important for Market days is what in discussions of films and theater is called the mise-en-scène: the assemblage of props and everything an audience sees onstage that help legitimate the performers for a particular period of time. This mise-en-scène assemblage—seen in certain districts of High Point, on individual city blocks, within buildings, and ultimately within showrooms—works to "fix a kind of spell" over the downtown.[11] Goffman maintained that such legitimating "assemblages of sign-equipment" warrant greater attention.[12]

Choreographing for "the Man in the Armani Suit"

"The entire issue of what happens with the High Point Market," said Big Building General Manager Robert Gruenberg during the Dallas threat of 1978, "is related to the environment buyers find themselves in when they come to Market—accommodations, eating facilities, general amenities."[13] This is a problem, since many marketgoers are what sociologist Guido Martinotti called "expert urbanites" who "tend to know their way around" furniture exposition cities like New York, Shanghai, Paris, São Paulo, and Milan.[14] Global cities in developing nations have created separate, distinct spaces specifically for such selective visitors. In the extreme case of Lagos, Nigeria, for instance, the privately developed Eko Atlantic—a four-square-mile city within a city—is under construction.

High Point leaders feel similar pressure to simulate "the kind of world" their higher-status audience "is thought to take for granted."[15] "They have all of the things that a bigger city would have," County Commissioner Bruce Davis asserted. "The only thing is that when they're gone, it goes with them." Leaders discuss, note, and correct breaches in the performance of "world class." This is apparent in oft-repeated Market anecdotes that offer admonition, such as stories of the "man in the Armani suit." In this trope, to be discussed again, embarrassing small-town vernacular jolts a sophisticated European marketgoer.

"Twice a year people come here with the imagination of, with the image of being in a town," High Point transplant Trish Perkins said. "They *like* the fact that this is a town," she added, marveling that tens of thousands of marketgoers, exhibitors, and Market laborers become players within the choreography, even dressing for their parts as they collectively help co-create this space of Mini-Manhattan. "They themselves are walking back and forth and carrying satchels and looking like business people that actually work and live there!"

Hustle and bustle around the Commerce and Design building (left) on South Elm Street during Market. Market Square (right) and Market Tower and the Suites at Market Square (center background) are also visible.

High Point may seem like a fantastical outlier, but it is just another city that has thoughtfully sculpted spaces to which users conform with little thought.[16] This is a difference in degree, not kind. Yet the difference in degree is profound: we see this in the production of the Market's entertainment, cuisine, accommodation, and transportation amenities.

Entertainment

The streets during Market burst forth with a marked energy. Parties sponsored by individual exhibitors or media outlets such as *Architectural Digest* and HGTV spill out of the showrooms on to outdoor courtyards, city sidewalks, or parking lots fashioned into venues festooned with white tents. A street-corner musician playing the sax suggests a cosmopolitan ambiance although he has no open case to receive donations; the police would be quick to ask such an unpermitted performer to move along. The jazz band playing in the corner of an exquisitely decorated loft showroom, their metallic instruments conspicuous against their black clothes, lends an avant-garde edge to the room of exposed brick and wood beams, reminiscent of New York's "loft jazz" movement of the 1970s.

High Point's niche blends high-culture sophistication with low-culture commodification to produce a campiness longtime Market observers describe. One such mix of world-class taste, local tradition, and campy flair could be found at the 2012 black tie grand reopening of a Canadian-owned building, The Factory. The Factory was Québécois firm Bermex's rebranded name for the old Millis hosiery plant originally renovated by Italian leather furniture leader Natale. A drum line from High Point Central High School, a unicyclist, a hip-hop deejay with break dancers, body-paint artists working on posing women, and stilt walkers lent an atmosphere of revelry and spectacle to the event.

A local nonprofit program manager working to reduce human trafficking explained that Market is like other large expositions, where "escort services are provided at parties, and hookups happen at those parties."[17] Several activists have described prostitution sweeps by police to displace the city's regular sex workers for Market days. Not so much *dis*placed as *re*placed by "a different category," quipped one High Pointer. Another longtime resident similarly observed the appearance during Market of "a high class" of sex work, "the more high-society-type situation."

Market's parties are discussed at length in trade magazines, insider's guides, and even the *Enterprise,* which has been repeating its "wish-I-could-take-you-all-with-me" style of reporting for more than sixty years—in those very words by a regular Market lifestyle reporter and columnist. At the Fall 1984 Market, he reported "chatting with fascinating people from all over the world and drooling (in an urbane, sophisticated, 'oh-isn't-that-nice' kind of way, of course) over much of the furniture."[18]

"The *Architectural Digest* cocktail party is always a highlight," one designer advised marketgoers in an insider's guide. "It's a great time to see friends that you haven't already run into at Market."[19] A second singled out "the gang" at one showroom for their "BBQ dinner with live music that brings out a great group." The Oly showroom, whose papered-over windows were noted in chapter 5, is on full display during Market. "We always hit the Oly party for creative hors d'oeuvres and fun hats," added a marketgoer, calling it a "charming get-together from a company we love and adore." Another recommended New York star designer "Laura Kirar's karaoke party, hands down."

Marketgoers in Oly Studio showroom window, now unpapered, on North Wrenn during Market.
Courtesy of Jill Seidner Interior Design.

The parties and concerts are important ingredients of the High Point "bling" cited by the *Washington Post* columnist previously quoted. Market also can mean seeing famous faces or their surrounding entourages. One expects to see renovation stars (such as Drew and Jonathan Scott, Chip and Joanna Gaines) and designers to the stars (e.g., Barry Dixon, Todd Oldham, Jonathan Adler). A common sight at Market over the past fifty years are lifestyle magnates such as Vern Yip, Martha Stewart, Kathy Ireland, and Bobby Berk, fashion giants on the scale of Oscar de la Renta and Alexander Julian, and celebrities like Miranda Kerr and Donald Trump, all promoting their branded furniture lines. To celebrity is added spectacle, as exhibitors try to top each other. International contingents often employ elaborate costumes, scripts, and props from their home country to stand out. The Brits brought a town crier to herald their arrival in 1975, the Danish group brought Tivoli Guardsmen from Copenhagen in 1985, and Indonesians hosted traditional dancers from Bali in 1989.

The furniture world has its own celebrities, and, as Goffman suggests, those inclined to take a "modest role" in other company will "be much concerned to make an effective showing" when their "professional competency" is on display.[20] Personally warm and endearing designer Raymond Waites transforms into Artemis the artiste, widely known for his lavish parties. "I think of myself as an introverted, shy guy, but I know when I present a collection, I have to be a showman," he explained, "so I'll put on a red jacket or something that goes with the collection, and it's part of the showmanship."[21] William Hsieh, the Taiwanese chair of Lifestyle Enterprises, also has a reputation as a showman. "Remember his silver bullet suit?" one journalist asked. "These are our rock stars," said local furniture consultant Audie Cashion, sharing past Market stories about Hsieh giving away luxury cars and offering to take clients from the simulacra Forbidden City in High Point to the real thing in Beijing.

Raymond Waites points to his "Artemis" nameplate at Market: "When I present a collection, I have to be a showman," he notes. Courtesy of Home Accents Today.

"What is Hsieh going to do *this* time?" is a question I have heard more than once.

Yet no matter how hard High Point works to craft an entertainment landscape, it will never be Las Vegas, Shanghai, or Milan. Wouldn't a larger city with more street life be a better fit for the Market's showrooms? I asked the enduring question of a group of young buyers walking the streets on a breezy Market night at the height of the Las Vegas threat. In a response that would hearten Market leaders, one woman laughed and deadpanned: "We are three twenty-somethings out here looking at furniture at 9:30 p.m." Millennial Jason Phillips, whose firm shows at both Markets, echoed this sentiment ten years later. "I can surely tell you that serious buyers making serious purchase decisions do not care that they are going to see a Cirque du Soleil show at night—or that they're *not* going to see the show that night."

Cuisine

"There are New Yorkers and they're used to picking up the phone and saying 'yo, I want a pizza,'" said Market worker Heidi Allen. "And I go, 'Yeah, good luck with that!' New York is the place that never sleeps. This place sleeps all the time." As restaurants left the downtown in the 1970s, '80s, and '90s, the exhibitors and laborers in the growing showroom district had few places to eat during the Market.

In 1978, parishioners of the downtown's First United Methodist Church opened the Parson's Table in the church basement. Hungry exhibitors looking for somewhere to eat promised the congregation paying customers if the church would start serving a reasonably priced meal at lunchtime. Today, about one hundred volunteers (often white women in their sixties or seventies) dish up homemade southern favorites such as banana pudding in a "church basement" atmosphere, itself an American trope. The sound of myriad accents and the sight of exquisitely dressed cosmopolites sitting at Formica tables in a church basement marks an "only in High Point" moment.

Local restaurants that managed to endure the downtown's hostile seasonality were often culprits of the practice known locally as "price gouging" and more broadly as price surging. At French restaurant J. Basul Nobles, year-round customers would go in for their "usual" meal during Market and, as one said, get "half the food for double the price." They were a Market "icon," Bringier noted, so that if marketgoers failed to get a reservation, it was like "they hadn't been here." Looking at the higher prices from the vantage point of the restaurant, she said, "They could get it." And they probably needed it.

One lesson learned from feeding marketgoers was that high-culture cuisine such as at Nobles worked and so did low-culture fare such as at Market hangout Biscuitville. But some hit neither target, like Market Fest, a project of the local Arts Council that debuted at the Spring 1986 Market. The food stalls featuring local vendors were rejected as too functional. "Aesthetics are important," a Big Building player noted at the time.[22] Of course, the kiosks were no more functional than the Formica tables of the Parson's Table, but they were a misfit within the high–low trope.

As attendance surged by tens of thousands each decade, civic groups and the smattering of restaurants could accommodate only so many. Exhibition centers and a surprising number of freestanding showrooms began operating their own well-appointed temporary "restaurants" in spaces designed to look permanent. Following the downtown's real estate consolidation, around twenty of these shell restaurants came under the control of IMC. Today, locally owned restaurants and caterers run some, and nearby national and international chains (e.g., Jersey Mike's) operate others.

The rising popularity and cachet of food trucks was a fortuitous coup for the Market. Up to ten trucks now line the circle drive of Showplace during each Market, offering a diverse selection of food from throughout the region. They also contribute to the Market mise-en-scène, providing a lived-in, local feel, as if they were *always* there during the lunch hour—a laughable presumption to any hungry resident who works at the neighboring City Hall.

While the satellite restaurants and food trucks offer no-frills sustenance, frills are in evidence elsewhere, ranging from "local done right" to world class. Exhibitors host their own chefs, sometimes flying them in to cook the cuisine of a specific region of the world (e.g., the French Riviera). Local caterers work in various contexts. For its New York clients, Allen's firm enlists a chef to cook tableside in their rental homes. IMC offers exhibitors a list of about twenty suggested caterers, half of them from High Point. According to a 2013 study from Duke University, exhibitors and showroom buildings spend an estimated $24 million on Market catering each year.[23]

Food trucks occupy the circle drive at Showplace exhibition building during Market. The white office building is in the background.

The amount of free alcohol at Market rivals the amount of free food. Temporary mini-bars appear in the halls of multitenant exhibition buildings. Fully built, well-appointed bars crop up within both multitenant and freestanding showroom buildings for Market use. Examples of the former are the Boiler Room in the basement of Market Square and MIX in the Big Building. UK-born, Vietnam-based furniture designer Jonathan Sowter operates Jonathan Charles' Woodman Inn pub inside his showroom, an example of the latter.

With marketgoers' appetites sated by Market-orchestrated vendors, local establishments and regional chain restaurants can assume a more manageable and symbolic role: serving food representative of Market tradition or the authentic local vernacular. New York magazine editor and stylist Cara Gibbs recommends the "homemade pies at The Parson's Table," which she considers "a great little insider spot to relax, rest your feet, and have a delicious lunch served by smiling faces while at

The temporary MIX Bistro and Lounge in the Home Furnishings Center during Market.

Market."[24] Like many travelers today, marketgoers seek the local flavor of such insider spots. "When in Rome, you eat pasta. When in North Carolina, you eat Barbecue," advised designer John Call in an insider's guide to the Market. "Carter Brothers BBQ is some of the best I've tasted. Don't miss their homemade pies and cakes, too," he said.[25] Designer Barry Dixon echoed his suggestion: "I like the opportunity to eat 'southern-style' food while there—local diners and 'dives.' And Krispy Kreme!"[26]

Some marketgoers are looking for Bringier's campiness: the risks and rewards of the city's hidden culinary vernacular. Martha Stewart has a weak spot for Washington Street's Becky and Mary's restaurant, a place so hidden it has no sign. "If you really want the flavor, we're going to give it to you," Bringier said of marketgoers looking for the backstage, the "real" and authentic High Point. I sat down in the Big Building's café with two such marketgoers as they talked to their colleagues. One noted the "charm" and "ritual" of what she called her "High Point life," which included billiards at a spot she considered slightly seedy. Another suggested that her rookie companions drop by a particular bar for "a great way to say goodbye to the crew and 'see you in six months.'" She talked about how in her most recent visit she ran into friends who delayed her at the door; by the time she reached the bar, the bartender had already fixed her favorite drink.

Marketgoers' ideas of their "High Point life" form an important narrative. Sitting in Starbucks in a strip mall landscape north of downtown at the close of a recent Market, I noted one furniture buyer with a huge cup of coffee to go. Halfway out the door, he stopped briefly to announce to the patrons of the shop that this marked the beginning of an annual ritual: a slow, relaxed, post-Market road trip on the scenic route from that coffee shop to his home in New York City, taking in the colors of changing leaves. Acquaintances inside waved their goodbyes and called out his name: someone standing in line, another person seated at a table, a barista behind the counter. Here was evidence of a level of social cohesiveness one would see in a healthy neighborhood, yet it was among people who see each other only a few times each year.

Accommodations

"You can't build churches for Easter Sunday; you can't build hotels just for furniture Market," industry analyst Rick Barentine has often said. The Market Authority sanctions just five hotels in High Point at prices

J. H. Adams Inn in Uptowne features thirty-one guest rooms in a historic home and its South Wing addition. Courtesy of Freeman Fotographics.

ranging from about two hundred dollars to four hundred dollars per night. Besides the High Point hotels, the Market Authority promotes about forty-five hotels in Greensboro, about twenty-five in Winston-Salem, and another ten or so in suburban Kernersville and Archdale.

Early on, the accommodations crisis prompted thousands of High Point residents to rent out their homes, rooms, and apartments. Having no other choice, Market leaders cemented the arrangement, framing it as a "tradition among High Pointers."[27] "Imagine," *Enterprise* editor Holt McPherson asked residents in 1969, "Chicago or New York . . . opening homes to furniture visitors."[28] To coordinate home and room rentals, the Chamber of Commerce created a temporary Housing Bureau consisting of "three women manning the telephones and multiple-colored cards" coordinating thousands of bookings.[29] "We desperately appeal to you for that extra room and private bath, if you can spare it," the *Enterprise* urged readers on behalf of the bureau.[30] The newspaper called on locals' civic responsibility and esprit de corps, declaring the Chamber of Commerce to be "entitled to all the cooperation that private homes can give."[31] North Carolina's congressional representatives joined the battle by fighting for decades to keep Market rental income tax-free, allowing people to pay no tax on rentals of up to fifteen days.[32]

"It's difficult to get a place to stay," a puzzled Indonesian entrepreneur commented in 1988. "Why does the United States have such a rich market in such a small city?"[33] Just like the lack of adequate choice of cuisine, this breach of amenities was an embarrassment to Market leaders. In 1997, the Chamber of Commerce dissolved its Housing Bureau and encouraged the formation of home rental firms, while Market leaders tried to standardize the temporary rental process for both owners and renters.

As the Market approaches, these rental firms inspect the proposed homes using various proprietary tricks of the trade. Pets or any evidence of pets are removed, filling the local kennels to capacity during the Market. Homeowners vacate their premises to go on vacation, stay with family, or go camping at Oak Hollow Campground, a local Market-time tradition. Homeowners take to their mobile homes or campers, purchased specifically for Market time usage often with the earnings from their Market home rentals. "One Market they *didn't* rent," said a home rental firm owner, relating a common anecdote, "and they stayed out at Oak Hollow campground anyway." As rental firms became a fixture of High Point life, some residents began checking with them about a home's Market appeal before renovating or buying property.

"It is kind of campy to stay in someone else's house," admitted one Market leader. Head in hands, designer Raymond Waites blushed to recall the old days when an imaginary designer staying in "a bedroom that's mold and blue" would have to tiptoe home "late at night" for fear of "bothering the little old lady that's rented [the] room." Plenty of uncontrollable human intrusions arise at Market, frontstage breaches that would be unacceptable if not for a campy forgiveness that "relishes . . . awkward intensities of 'character,'" as cultural analyst Susan Sontag observed.[34] The colorful stories could fill volumes, such as the one about the sanctimonious homeowner who, during an unannounced visit to tidy up, threw out what she thought was a male exhibitor's costumed female escort. It turned out to be the exhibitor's wife, the story goes, sleeping in following the firm's masquerade party.

As the number of major chain hotel rooms in the region slowly increased and the home renting process became more selective, the homes chosen for Market tended to be those offering what Market leaders and marketgoers refer to as the "Camp High Point" experience. Homes rent for eight to ten days for $1,500 to more than $5,000. I asked Richard Wood, whose family showed in the first Market expositions a century ago and who has rented out his home for decades, what "Camp High Point" meant to him. "Warm, comfortable, homey," he said. "Everybody has one big night where they have a big ol' steak cookout—bring two cases of beer and a bunch of wine." Added Wood, "These furniture people, when they come here, they *work*." He outlined a typical itinerary of a large company's buying team. "Some will go see upholsterers at one price. Someone will go see lamps at another price. Some will see accessories at another price," he said. They are not just evaluating furniture but also absorbing emerging design vogues, taking notes on ideas for arranging their retail store's floor. Taking in all this information for an entire day, the buyers need somewhere to relax, debrief, reflect, and team build. "That's what makes *home* so attractive to 'em," Wood explained. "They'll sit down in that home and say 'here's what I saw,' 'here's what I saw,' and 'here's what I think we can put in the store.' And usually by week's end, they kind of have plans of how they are going to merchandise everything."

Long-term home renters form relationships with their tenants. "They exchange Christmas cards, give their kids presents at graduation," noted Edith Brady of the High Point Museum. "We'd miss them if they didn't come," one resident said of his Market tenants of two decades. "They're almost like cousins," his wife added.[35] This couple is a rarer case today of homeowners who stay at home *with* their marketgoer tenants. "We've shared the good times and the bad," said the tenants, mentioning the deaths and marriages of loved ones. "When we leave the Market, it's like going home at night."[36] Some Marketgoers feel so much "at home" that they leave behind liquor, coffee makers, and other belongings to await their return. In one revealing anecdote, Charles Hicks recalled how when he moved to High Point from New Jersey in 1969, his new home's long-standing Market tenants from Mexico "contacted us before we closed on the damn house!"

Today, High Point's entrepreneurial home rental firms, along with their distinct curation of Market properties and knowledge of market-goers' preferences, are under increasing pressure from Airbnb.[37] The Market Authority now lists Airbnb as another home rental option. Just as with the food trucks, a decentralized free market solution arose to answer a mega-event need, in this case housing.

Mobility

Considering the dearth of downtown parking and that all but a paltry half dozen of the ninety or so hotels the Market Authority recommends are ten to twenty-five miles away, the Market presents a daunting transportation problem. In 1966, one report estimated the parking deficit at two thousand spaces.[38] That report, by the High Point Merchants Association, hitched the long-term prospects of local downtown merchants to that of the Market, arguing that "parking required for Market visitors automatically provides abundant parking facilities for business in downtown."[39] At this point, the merchants still saw the Market as compatible with a resident-centered downtown. Part I showed how that would change over the next decade.

That same year of 1966, the Chamber of Commerce began offering volunteer drivers HAIL ME / FURNITURE CAR signs to display in the windshield of their cars for the privilege of shuttling marketgoers between lodgings and showrooms. By the end of that year's Fall Market, frustrated marketgoers took matters into their own hands and simply began ignoring "no parking" signage en masse, their solution to what the *Enterprise* dubbed "The Great Parking Snafu." High Point's Law and Public Safety Committee implored all nonfurniture "businessmen," all furniture exhibitors who lived in town, and all "city officials, from the top down" to be "driven downtown, take a bus or walk" (a practice that has endured).[40]

As attendance continued to rise, the only chance for a sustainable Market was to make the exposition navigable by foot and shuttle. At the Fall 1972 Market, organizers introduced two double-decker London-style buses to shuttle marketgoers between the downtown and outlying park-and-ride lots. Later, men from local churches volunteered to drive vans and buses along set routes throughout the downtown and to the distant lots. The shuttle expanded to include hotels in the mid-1980s. This practice persisted until the early 2000s, Engineering Services Director Keith Pugh said, embarrassed that twenty-first-century Market transportation still relied on school buses and church vans.[41] The appearances were unbecoming. As Bringier explained, "If this is the first thing you see when you are stepping out of your hotel—'I'm in my Armani suit and I'm getting on a school bus'—this is a problem."

From rickshaw to helicopter, the unregulated Market has seen a full array of transportation gimmicks. One day in 2004, I grew worried when my workout partner did not appear at the gym for our usual routine. Later, I found him newly equipped with a brilliantly waxed black Lincoln, business cards, and a dedicated cell phone. He was playing showroom chauffeur for six hours, providing the buyer clients of his exhibitor-employer with a touch of personalized luxury. As with High Point's less pleasant aspects of accommodations and cuisine, Market leaders felt that transit failings needed to be remedied and the more pleasant aspects, such as the personalization of my friend's dedicated limousine service or the fun of bike taxis, continued in the name of character and tradition.

"When I think about going to Disney World," Authority president Judy Mendenhall said in 2001, "every transportation step is typically taken care of before you leave your front door at home. There's no reason we can't provide a seamless transportation approach here as well."[42] Even after Mendenhall and the Authority turned Market transportation and traffic control over to a transportation logistics firm (a role that is today internal to the Market Authority), coordination of the Market's

A bike taxi waits for customers on the Showplace walkway during Market, with the white Mendenhall Transportation Terminal and the hulking Home Furnishings Center (the Big Building) in the background.

seventy coach buses on the Magic Block's current configuration re-mained outright dangerous. In 2003, a delegation of state and federal legislators visited High Point to observe its transportation conundrum; their emphatic response was to construct the Mendenhall Transporta-tion Terminal.

"Visitors from around the world will see this facility and associate it with High Point," Pugh said.[43] The terminal serves as the Market's central transportation node and includes service to North Carolina's three major international airports, all Market-sanctioned hotels, out-lying Park and Ride parking lots, and downtown showrooms. These are supplemented by a "Go Anywhere" service that will pick up or drop off a marketgoer anywhere within three miles of the terminal. "It gave us a starting-off point and made the navigation of Market a million percent easier. Because you knew where to start, you had a frame of reference, and it sort of made everything come into focus for how the plan of Market worked," a Market official shared.

"In combination with [adjacent] Showplace, it really kind of sets up the iconic identity for furniture Market," added High Point architect Peter Freeman, a further illustration of the legitimating role buildings play in the mise-en-scène. "People would get off the bus—and at some point in our history that was a school bus or a church bus—they'd get off the bus and go 'oh, this is *it*?'" said Bringier, mimicking disappointment. "Now, it's, 'Awwww, *this* is *it*!'" she exhaled. "With the transportation system today, you feel like you're at a world class market."

With transportation under control, the nagging question "what would the man in the Armani suit think?" turned its attention to the routes the buses traveled. As one neighborhood leader shared, officials seemed more interested in the appearance of neighborhoods from the window of a passing Market bus than with the amenities they could offer Market. "There's a subtlety to it; you don't realize the perception," said one transportation official.

"I knew that going down Centennial meant going back past some things that—it's really ugly. Strip mall dying, you know, the perception of High Point is right there," she continued. The city's transportation

Inside the Mendenhall Transportation Terminal during Market, where marketgoers get free transport to showrooms, park and ride lots, three international airports, and all Market Authority—approved hotels.

logistics team designed a new, slightly longer route that would take travelers "past a whole lot of High Point University," a meticulously maintained streetscape, before continuing on to MLK, Jr. Drive. "Even when you got to what would be considered a not-so-great part, it had a lot of tall trees and a lot of it was blocked," another official added. "And suddenly, your whole perception of High Point is different." Strategizing to optimize visitors' transportation experiences is familiar to convention planners. But in High Point it marked a new phase in the long-standing practice of manipulating transportation routes to skirt the Black East Side. "We don't want the furniture people coming in here, having to sit in traffic and observe *this*," local historian Glenn Chavis imitated with feigned contempt.

Designing Showroom Exhibition

"Renting exhibition space permanently to be used for only a handful of days a year may seem counterintuitive," explained the *New York Times,* "but such an arrangement has advantages for furniture manufacturers who find it cost-effective to maintain a single showroom, rather than to bear the cost of shipping, erecting, and dismantling a trade show booth every year."[44] It would be misleading to label most of the Market displays, such as that for Mexican firm Taracea in the Radio Building's ornate former bank, with the convention-industry term *booth.* You'll be hard pressed to find a typical "pipe and drape" trade show setup at Market. Furniture sets itself apart from other consumer goods with the belief that a real "furniture person" would not dream of buying furniture without touching, feeling, and experiencing it.

"My friend just bought a building," a first-time Market attendee mused during a conversation we had at a 2015 Market. His friend's handsome, prominently located, four-story brick building from the early twentieth century was seven thousand square feet and worth about $750,000. "It's open only two times a year," he marveled. I am certain I have seen people puzzling out similar calculations in their heads dozens of times.

"It's complete dedication, which you don't get anywhere else," said Bringier, referring to downtown High Point's sole focus on Market. "Furniture cannot just be shut down and stored and then brought back out again like T-shirts and key chains and lamps—whatever—fashion, make-up," she said. In addition to an estimated $130 million in annual

The Taracea showroom in a former bank within the Radio Building on South Main Street, complete with travertine marble walls, thirty-foot ceilings, and a twenty-four-ton vault. Courtesy of Taracea USA.

rent, Market exhibitors invest $211 million in the construction and setup of their showrooms, according to the 2013 Duke study.[45] Goffman mentions furniture as a typical "background item" that sets the scene for a performance. In High Point, furniture is an inanimate star with a mise-en-scène crafted to accentuate it.[46]

The Temporality of Showroom Design

Showroom designers like veteran Callie Everitt transform individual exhibitors' visions into exhibitions. The process for the next one begins while the current one is on display at Market. Once they know what the product is going to look like from the product developers, each exhibitor assembles a team of "designers and creative people," such as Everitt, who "start looking at layouts for that space," explained Judy Mendenhall. Given all the planning required, "I've got to be a Market ahead," said Everitt. For as Goffman observed, giving a room a "quiet dignity" can, ironically, require one to "race to auction sales, haggle with antique dealers, and canvass all the local shops" to create the setting that emotes such calm.[47]

Showroom renovations can range from a sprucing up to a complete reconfiguration of the space. Mendenhall described how the exhibitors' "creative people" (design, merchandising, and marketing staff) usually collaborate with the showroom designers to determine "the best way to show any nuances in the existing lines." A showroom developer coordinates any actual construction and that process can take many variations. Former showroom developer Matthew Tallon recalled one experience in which he completed about twenty million dollars in work for an international exhibitor he never even met. The project was transacted solely through transmitted showroom blueprints and money wires.

Exhibitors' renovation schedules depend on whether the showroom is participating in Pre-Market, which is a sneak preview of the Market performance for A-list buyers. The exhibitor traditionally puts up these privileged guests at a Greensboro resort. At Pre-Market, the buyers can make early purchase commitments and suggest possible improvements for manufacturers' planned Market product mix. In response to this feedback, "any adjustments are made," Mendenhall said.

"Pre-Market *used* to be . . . two dressers and fifty sketches," said Everitt. Today her Pre-Market exhibitor clients have access to "the whole showroom in all its glory and glamour four to five weeks before Market opens." In 1999 a frustrated Market leader, concerned about Pre-Market "chaos," remarked that "Market is planned out twenty years in advance so that everyone can have plenty of notice of when and where they have to be at Market."[48] More recently, IMC CEO Bob Maricich has also been extremely critical of Pre-Market. "Can you imagine Fashion Week saying to Ralph Lauren and some of these other retailers, 'Why don't you guys come in before everyone else does and see what's new before them?'" he asked in 2014.[49]

Pre-Market took on a new meaning during the Covid-19 pandemic. After the Spring 2020 Market was canceled, the next two Pre-Markets saw more than three times the usual number of both exhibitors and attendees. "It's like the twilight zone. We know the overall economy is not good, but our business has never been better," said the Pre-Market chair of the consumer's desire for furniture during the pandemic.[50] Pre-Market offered exhibitors more control over who was in their showroom and, rather than using it as a sneak peek, some attendees seized it as an opportunity to avoid Market crowds altogether. This temporarily exacerbated the issues Maricich cited, as it kept the entire kaleidoscope of the furniture world from sharing the same space at the same time. However, during this exceptional time this was a better option than most. "We've got twelve and a half million square feet of space here, and we're spread out, so social distancing is no problem," current Market Authority president Tom Conley said.[51]

Even though their factories are rarely nearby anymore, the exhibitors do make changes to their products based on Pre-Market feedback—reshipping the adjusted furniture only to get it "half right and half wrong *again,*" Everitt said. But Pre-Market is no longer the primary site of such buyer input. "In between the Markets," clients typically "are going to be over in China, Vietnam, wherever, looking at those samples at the factory with me," product developer Phil Hood explained. Exhibitors who produce locally have an added advantage at Market because they can adjust their product samples even during the exposition.

As the Market approaches, designers work fourteen- to eighteen-hour days for two to three weeks. During "the last two or three days, trucks are coming twice a day with the stuff . . . from the West Coast [ports]," Everitt said, delivering furniture to exhibitors who did not participate in Pre-Market. Movers blanket the sidewalks. During this time, furniture executive William Lambeth is grateful to own a freestanding building with its own loading dock. As a teenager in High Point, Lambeth said he found himself at the city jail twice for fights that broke out over jockeying for position on exposition center docks. "You're trying to get your stuff in," he said. "You've got people waiting upstairs. You've been in line for twenty hours and somebody else is paying [off] somebody to get *ahead* of you?"

Working sometimes with only a sketch and a color panel, Everitt creates a showroom design to complement the exhibitor's line, then awaits the arrival of the furniture. The trope this suggests—that of a brilliant showroom designer orchestrating her vision under pressure—is strong in Market lore and is reinforced by print media photographs and coverage. It presupposes a dramatic reveal, a rising curtain. "Before we would have to black out the windows, and make sure nobody could sneak in to see what we were doing," Everitt said. No longer. Exhibitors and their customers "all see it in that plant over there—and we're not hiding it," she added.

Temporary exhibitors who rent booths in the dedicated temporary spaces not owned or leased year-round join the flurry of activity. Exhibitor representatives attend training sessions to learn about the items they

The new showrooms and offices of China-based Markor International Furniture Company on North Hamilton Street called Markor Art Center. A collaboration between architect Peter Freeman and designer/founder Richard Feng, its huge dome floods the interior space with muted light. Photographs courtesy of High Point Market MediaLink and MP Productions NC/Michael Blevins.

Showplace at night. The Showplace exhibition building is rarely illuminated. Here its textured walkway is front and center, surrounded on both sides by parking lots. Photograph courtesy of Showplace.

will sell during the Market. Outside, hundreds of tons of discarded cardboard and emptied crates sit on curbs awaiting garbage collection. Contractors rush to put finishing touches on the latest signature buildings. In Spring 2019, for instance, the most anticipated debut was Chinese conglomerate Markor's showroom and U.S. offices, a concept designed by founder Richard Feng with local architect Peter Freeman to reflect "the creativity and artfulness" of his company's brands.[52] Commercial window-washing firms are suspended from the downtown buildings, cleaning dusty showroom windows. And inside Showplace, Natuzzi, 220 Elm, and the other showpiece buildings, the lights are back on.

Innovation in Showroom Design

"It is a major difference, there is no question about it," said longtime exhibitor Emil Khoury. He summed up what "differentiates this international market from other places: the other places are exhibit centers, this is like a home." He explained that "the normal" exhibition is concerned mainly about cost per square foot and break-even formulas. "If you go to the Shanghai Market versus our Market," agreed journalist Francine Liddelle, "they still see it as a commodity, a complete commodity. They don't see the romance in it." That's High Point's chief difference to them, the romance.

High Point's common wisdom is that one cannot assess furniture without touching, feeling, and experiencing it—an argument for the sensuousness of furniture. Yet, to be clear, the High Point Market is not a high-end exhibition. Although the Market offers a range of goods, it has been a "commodity" exposition for its entire one-hundred-year history, featuring design for the masses. It developed in tandem with both mass production and mass culture—a collective culture cultivated by people's exposure to the same sources of information.

The rise of mass culture also introduced the sensibility of camp, which, as Sontag describes, is unconcerned that mass appreciation undermines good taste.[53] Camp, says Sontag, is concerned with "all of the elements of visual décor," and it privileges "texture, sensuous surface, and style."[54] By this standard, a "doorknob could be as admirable as a painting."[55] Camp puts a premium on "the *love* that has gone into certain objects" and therefore can see triumph in unexpected places (see the Bureau in chapter 5).[56] High Point designer Raymond Waites coined the term *love objects* to describe frivolous accessories full of unabashed personality. Interpreted from this vantage point, the High Point Market concedes that home furnishings are a commodity, but one that should be lavishly feted.

Notwithstanding this narrative of romance, sensuousness, and love, it is precisely economic formulas—accounting for the city's cheap, unregulated land and labor—that anchor the Market in High Point. This advantageous cost formula allows exhibitors to experiment. In the same way low-rent areas offer pioneer gentrifiers extra flexibility to take investment risks in pursuing entrepreneurial goals (opening a bookstore or music club, for instance) or placing more emphasis on architectural design, dependably low costs allow exhibitors to dream up schemes that would be unaffordable elsewhere. It is doubtful that Pasquale Natuzzi would have built his Bellini-designed ship in Milan or that William Hsieh would erect a stylized replica of China's Forbidden City in Paris. Affordability invites experimentation, which helps cement the Market and gives it staying power, making High Point "sticky."

Unlike most other expositions, which just pack up "like a circus and leave town," High Point exhibitors make strategic, "elaborate investments" to contextualize their pieces, Brian Casey points out. Khoury said exhibitions like "Frankfurt or Milan" offer "*styling*, you know, but nothing like [High Point]. You have your bedroom, you have your dining room—it *looks* like a dining room," he explained.

"Design styles start here too," said Sarah Simpkins. She credits it to the "free rein" accorded to High Point designers. The innovation within the Market's showrooms also makes it an important exposition for interior designers. Exhibitors have the luxury to showcase "a whole merchandising program" to convey exactly how they envision their pieces fitting into a home. After a century of engagement between the Market and the local community, even temporary Market workers understand this innovation and accommodate the flexibility it requires. "There's just this mentality in High Point that you do whatever it takes," Simpkins explained. No one in High Point says "I'm a carpenter, I'm not an electrician" when asked to change something, she added. "Nobody says that unless they *can't* do it—and *then* they'll say 'I'll call my friend John. It's no big deal.'"

High Point's history of dozens of competing exhibition buildings also helps explain this phenomenon. "Basically, if I get somebody in here, I keep 'em," said Candy Lambeth, who owns one of the few multitenant exhibition buildings not currently controlled by IMC. "I treat 'em like a damn stewardess, if you want to know the truth."

Creative designers assembling their vision will *always* want adjustments. "There are no unions here," explained Simpkins, unlike other expositions where "it just is outrageous what you can end up paying." While some designers profess to be pro-union, they still describe the red tape and the constant cost-benefit analyses they encounter in completing a design under pressure at other union-controlled venues as extremely frustrating. In expositions like Las Vegas and New York, Raymond Waites said, "they can't put in a light bulb, they can't move an object—*ca-ching, ca-ching, ca-ching.*"

International Market Centers intends its Suites at Market Square building to be its "incubator" for showcasing new tenants with "innovative products." However, it cannot compete with the flexibility available in the unregulated downtown buildings just beyond.[57] "I think the Market has become two industries," observed one exhibitor in a freestanding building: "Stock it deep and sell it cheap."[58] To him, it's the difference between commodity and craft. He was among the exhibitors who helped form NED, the North Elm District abutting the Suites that debuted on the Market site map in October 2015. "It's kind of like an arts district," said another NED exhibitor. "It's where you go to find people who think differently."[59] From the pedestrian's perspective, NED feels distinct from the rest of the Market, a gritty space for the indies in the shadow of the downtown's sleeker architecture on Elm Street. "The 'makers' of the industry are moving out and away from the big buildings and the mass importers," the exhibitor added.

During my first experience of the reinvented North Elm, I was grateful that I knew nothing about the new exhibition district, an area then including Hair-N-Stuff. Encountering it unawares, I was struck by how palpable the boundary was. Broken-down streets and sidewalks deteriorated into mud and gravel. Cars were strewn about for lack of legitimate

North Elm showrooms, originally called the North Elm District but now dubbed a "neighborhood." Here, South Elm's crisp lines give way to a bohemian dingy chic on North Elm.

parking spaces. Many of the building exteriors bore the recent marks of inexpensive facelifts (e.g., brick painted black). Some of the bohemian-looking exhibitors had arranged their goods outdoors like a yard sale. This was "grit as glamour," in gentrification parlance: craftspeople gleaning energy from reused marginal space.[60] "We love coming to work in these buildings," one NEDer declared.[61]

These exhibitors were creative risk-takers taking a chance on investment in undervalued, underused land adjacent to prime real estate. Although overlaid with a strong cultural agenda, their venture was economic at its core. Like struggling artists securing loft space in New York's SoHo neighborhood in the 1970s, they were there because the real estate was cheap. The old industrial buildings of NED embodied the Jacobsian idea that "the best way to encourage entrepreneurial mitosis is to supply small spaces, perhaps somewhat dilapidated, at modest rents."[62]

Niche Specialists in the Exposition

The niche functions that support the Market are "*mainly* rooted here [in High Point]," observed furniture executive Jason Phillips. As a result, it "would be very difficult to fully displace them," he argued. High Point's showroom designers are "skilled people who can do all kinds of creative things in the show—that can do faux, that can do murals, that, with their hands, can make the showrooms look phenomenal," Simpkins enthused. Brian Casey agreed that expertise is what makes the furniture industry's "fashion component . . . come out," creating "a whole different feel, look, experience."

"You get hooked," Everitt said as she tried to convey the allure of showroom design. Her crew takes "a possession of the showroom. It's not so-and-so's showroom—it's *my* showroom," she explained. "Some people get it and some people don't. But those of us who've been here for twenty-something years? We've got it *bad.*"

The degree of expertise found within this niche is evidenced in the number of veteran showroom designers from Everitt's High Point circles who were called on to help Las Vegas put on its early exhibitions. "*All* of us," Everitt said. "It was supposed to be cookie-cutter, but the people I work for are not cookie-cutter kind of people," she added. "That was a tough Market," she recalled, "but we lived through it." High Point showroom designers would teach Las Vegas, just as High Point manufacturers taught their future rivals in Asia one generation earlier.

Another example of High Point's niche expertise is in photography. On my first day in High Point, I was surprised to learn the profession of my neighbor Luke, an artsy-looking student in his early twenties who introduced himself as a *furniture* photographer. The Duke University study estimated that Market exhibitors spend some forty million dollars annually photographing the furniture debuting at each Market.[63] Every type of furniture publication requires extensive photography. About ten days before opening, furniture photographers begin shooting the new lines of furniture round the clock. Some are done in the showrooms' home settings, others in local homes. Exhibitors do not rent only well-appointed houses; an unadorned setting can also be the desired canvas. The disappointing part of renting out your home for a photo shoot is seeing everything removed afterward, "like it never happened," complained resident Trina Johns. Some exhibitors have purchased homes to serve as combined photography sets, showrooms, entertainment spaces, and Market accommodations.

Furniture photography has also spawned a Hollywood-style supply of sets, designers, props, and lighting experts in High Point. "The most difficult problem is to capture the very sensitive, subtle color that is so important to furniture," said photographer Sidney Gayle Jr. of Alderman, a business dedicated to furniture photography, founded just before the turn of the twentieth century.[64] It is not alone. Albion, Kreber, and Tri-Group are all local photography studios specializing in furniture photography and its nuances. Kreber boasts a "creative playground," with forty-five room settings that are "constantly transformed." Just like downtown High Point.[65]

High Point's unique real estate market is another example of exhibition-related expertise. Although the unregulated landscape of downtown creates an unparalleled range of options for exhibitors, finding the appropriate space to display an exhibitor's vision to full advantage remains difficult. Enter Ivan Garry. Garry's more conventional exhibition career ended when he organized an unsuccessful effort to buy the National Furniture Mart, the building he had managed since 1976. In 1998, he found himself in a bidding war pitted against the Kennedy family's MMPI and its new parent Vornado. Garry was dislocated by a transnational player that, as Loretta Lees and her colleagues note, raised "the potential ground rent to a point that existing local demand was not allowed an opportunity for profit."[66] Soon after, Garry offered help to an exhibitor looking for showroom space in High Point. An intuition honed over decades of experience lent authority to his advice: "You don't belong anywhere else, you really belong at Hamilton Square." Then, drawing on his history of relationships, he closed the deal. When the exhibitor asked him, "What do I owe you for this service?" Garry's firm was born: part real estate agency, part strategy firm, part design consultant—and completely unique to the city's exhibition niche.

Temporary Market Jobs

Goffman wrote that the frontstage roles of any performance are reserved for those perceived to make the proper impression.[67] Six years later, in 1965, civil rights leaders Ralph Abernathy and Elton Cox addressed the exclusion of Black labor from the High Point Market's frontstage roles. Throughout the Market's history, one group recruited for the frontstage has been young, mostly white, women. One High Point University student who entered unknowingly into this long tradition, traceable back to the use of beauty pageants to find young women to fill temporary Market roles, told me her Fall 2003 Market job description was "look cute." Suspicious, but assuming she was "going to be hostessing," given the good pay, she showed up for work in an elegant dress. When she learned that her role would be to coax male buyers into a leather showroom, she quit the first day.

Many temporary Market jobs are behind the scenes. When Everitt traveled to Las Vegas to assist that fledgling exposition, she—tellingly —brought with her a crew of four High Point laborers. These laborers, classified as "unskilled" in quantitative data, had an invaluable tacit knowledge. "The labor out there does not know how to unpack it, put it together, pick it up, or set it down," Everitt said. Setting up a showroom inevitably brings minor emergencies that require creative problem-solving. So, while "it's not cheap," she explained, "I like to take my guys . . . that know furniture." Added Everitt, "The people I work for are so picky . . . They should be. *I'm* picky," she laughed.

"About a month, six weeks before Market starts, people are standing on street corners waiting for jobs, waiting to hear 'jump in, we need all this furniture moved, we need this and that,'" community college administrator Janette McNeill said. International exhibitors often paid local workers in cash. Even when exhibitors did not contact temporary laborers in advance, they managed to find "their" exhibitor. I once witnessed a friend with a criminal record that affected his work history go off to meet an exhibitor without any communication beforehand, simply reporting for anticipated work based on the rhythms of Market time. The cash-paying Middle Eastern exhibitor he worked for knew all he needed to know about my friend: he had a great personality, he worked hard, he always showed up, and he knew how to work an exposition.

The arrival of the furniture world each Market season—and for visits between Markets—brings a cosmopolitanism to High Point with far-reaching ramifications. City leader Angela McGill shared a common experience about how Market introduced her to people she never would have met otherwise. In a showroom job as a teenager more than thirty years earlier, furniture manufacturing tycoon Paul Broyhill encouraged her to attend college. "I remember seeing all these different people from different parts of the world and talking to these people. That *did* inspire me. I happened to be in the right place at the right time. I was a high school dropout."

It is not certain that these two people would be working in the same capacity today. In the past, said Chavis, leaders would recruit labor for particular communities through their networks within churches and other institutions. Chavis's father, a chef at the now-closed downtown Sheraton hotel, was one such liaison. Furniture leaders relied on the wisdom embedded in their contacts' local networks to send them workers who fit the job. Replacing informal mechanisms with formal, "sophisticated" ones (global temporary labor firms like Manpower) had an obvious effect, said Chavis: "Quite naturally, to me, it doesn't filter into the community." Resident Larry Diggs echoed his complaint. "Citizens here could really make money at Market thirty years ago because they were like their own agents," he said. Today, the firm gets "the big money at the top," while the labor gets a dollar or two over minimum wage, he pointed out. Politician Bernita Sims considered this an unfortunate cost of progress. "As we have become more sophisticated in the Market," she said pragmatically, "we tried to eliminate some of those things that were negatives as it related to the Market. Some things went away."

Camp High Point

Just before the specter of Las Vegas appeared, several marketgoers shared their view with me that the High Point brand served as a powerful counterforce against global homogeneity and the encroaching "Walmart-ization" of the industry. Their message was that commodification could persist without soullessness.

Walmart has mastered predictability, navigability, and efficiency. High Point claimed none of these attributes. What interior designer Arianne Bellizaire called "conquering the beast" entails a rite of passage to make the transition from Market outsider to insider. This transformation permeates narratives about how one must *learn* the High Point Market. "You know, the component of this Market—that it's very difficult to shop?" said Brian Casey. "The plus side of that is that those that come in here and acclimate themselves and become familiar, it's enjoyable for them because they come across these special treasures that they may not normally find."

In a world overfull of tourist-bubble downtowns that would become a "parody of the unique," the High Point built environment stands out, especially to seasoned designers who have been around the world and seen it all.[68] The "High Point mystique," showroom executive Joanna Easter's name for the aura of Market, is unimaginable to someone who only experiences the landscape of downtown High Point out of Market season. It's "the tale of the cities" said the Radio Building's owner Candy Lambeth, except that this tale is geographic *and* temporal. It is similarly unimaginable to stand in the barren desert of Nevada and envision a temporary community of more than sixty-five thousand people creating something called "Black Rock City." Yet organizers of Burning Man, the name for this one-week-only "metropolis dedicated to community, art, self-expression, and self-reliance," have managed to create a thick but temporary community there.[69] In both places, the performance of the temporary space saturates the moment so convincingly that it guides the participant into the organizers' desired impression.[70]

In addition to mastering the physical environment, learning the culture of "Camp High Point" also helps delineate insider from outsider. As Sontag notes of the camp sensibility, there is an appreciation of the city's idiosyncrasies and quirks that offers marketgoers "*a private code, a badge of identity.*"[71] This code generously embraces breaches in High Point's performance of Mini-Manhattan in the name of fun, whimsy, and authenticity. The resulting stories "detailing disruptions" in the performance of the frontstage—"real, embroidered, or fictitious—are told and retold," just as Goffman would expect, but High Point's campiness permits and assimilates these breaches.[72]

"Twice a year you have got everyone in the world coming here," print advertising specialist Geraldine Dickins colorfully observed. "You have a truck that is driving down Main Street during the Market that has a flag for the Confederacy and he's got the hat and he's got the gun rack. And right behind them is a Jaguar with a nice Italian lady who is chatting on her phone. And it's like, this looks like a movie—I don't know, maybe Coen Brothers? What's going to happen next?" Skeptics have long framed High Point's cosmopolitanism-cum-parochialism duality as a disadvantage against its big-city competitors. Yet it has consistently defeated them. Could aspects of this milieu also be ingredients of the Market's glue, a secret to its endurance? Hints of this go all the way back to 1963, when High Point overtook Chicago's expo and furniture analyst Ray Reed enumerated High Point's considerable shortcomings only to conclude that its Markets were "friendlier, folksier, and more fun than the cold, calculating, big-city shows."[73]

7

The Fragmented Year-Round Design Cluster

The Cluster

"I think [High Point] is still the artistic, creative center," declared furniture designer Raymond Waites. "When I moved here, I found that there were some of the weirdest, creative people—much more than New York—I mean, really idiosyncratic, brilliantly creative people." Jason Oliver Nixon of Madcap Cottage agreed. He had made the same move himself: "Everyone thinks Brooklyn is creative, but this region has its own gems—there's a real environment of makers, creators and carvers. Plus, I can double-park for deliveries, and my upholsterer picks up furniture at no charge!"[1]

"We've got more Parsons, Pratt, RISD, and SCAD graduates per capita than anywhere else in the world," so local real estate owner, former Bernhardt employee, and civic booster Charles Simmons would excitedly tell anyone within earshot. In fact, a 2013 National Endowment for the Arts report corroborated that "no metro area approaches" the High Point and Greensboro region in the number of design firms per capita.[2]

As we examine the year-round elements that make up High Point's furniture cluster in this chapter, it will become clear that High Point's furniture presence does not turn on and off with the flick of a switch. A cluster, such as the agglomeration of firms that has sprung up in High Point, develops a competitive advantage through its members' interdependence on and geographic proximity to one another. High Point's furniture cluster facilitates the sharing of facilities and infrastructure, the matching of workers to firms, and the dissemination of new processes of furniture design, production, and merchandising.[3]

"This Market's been around for a hundred years and so when you look at it, yes, manufacturing may have gone overseas," said Market leader Brian Casey, "but there's still a significant amount of industry cluster that's here. . . . You can't just take something like that and put that in place overnight in the desert in Las Vegas." Various economic and cultural assets have adhered to create a context that can be found only in High Point.[4] Its niche is very specific, but most globally connected regions are not jacks-of-all-trades articulated to the global economy across a broad range of expertise areas. Rather, they are specialized nodes cultivated by specific economic histories that foster and produce a unique brand of innovation.

The innovations that occur in some clusters within prominent global cities depend on time-sensitive transactions, such as creating a financial instrument in New York or lobbying against particular legislation in Washington, D.C. In these cases, assembling a broad range of experts quickly can make or break a deal. In contrast, the innovation that occurs in High Point is a slower, sustained steeping. It relies on the ongoing collaboration of a rich network of complementary functions. This slow innovation is also more inclusive than that of the more bifurcated global city variety, requiring meaningful engagement by everyone from furniture firm CEOs to community college instructors.

Cluster functions operate quite differently from regional economies of old. As Michael J. Piore and Charles F. Sabel note, a Fordist mode of production—the mass production that dominated High Point in the mid-twentieth century—"calls for the separation of conception from execution." But they explain that the niche specialization of post-Fordism "often demands the reverse: collaboration between skilled designers and skilled producers."[5] Contemporary forms of collaboration have a unique milieu in High Point that has been difficult for local firms to delineate, but the industry recognizes its influence.

It just makes sense for people with furniture aspirations to be near this activity, Simmons and others say. It's akin to an aspiring actor waiting tables in Manhattan, where she might serve a Lin-Manuel Miranda. Or an aspiring clothing designer in Paris who finds himself pouring the coffee of an Oscar de la Renta. Similarly, furniture designers like Joanna Gaines or Thom Filicia might be waited on by just any "down home Southern girl" or by a "student at High Point University studying textile manufacturing," as Geraldine Dickins described.

Take the case of my first conversation with Dickins, which began in the newspaper office where I was placing an advertisement to recruit interviewees. I was surprised when our discussion quickly turned to High Point's furniture buzz, never imagining that Dickins, an advertising professional, would consider herself part of that aspect. But Dickins described the expertise she had gathered in creating "furniture ads forever and a day" and through innumerable "conversations at dinner on Sunday" with family members in the industry. She told me that the culture has given High Point a distinct advantage. "You *have* to speak their language," she advised. "It's an ongoing lexicon, and it changes."

The furniture cluster's flexible, connective tissue supports the High Point Market, as we saw in the previous chapter, but it also helps extend Market synergies into the rest of the year. These year-round aspects of High Point's furniture industry are the focus of this chapter, which explores High Point's furniture design and product development and then moves to the industry's "creative people" who have carved out a full-time life in the High Point region.

Collaborative Design

"Art is very subjective. Beauty is in the eye of the beholder," mused product developer Phil Hood. "Well, in *our* world, beauty has to be in the eye of a lot of beholders," he laughed. This design sensibility succinctly describes High Point's role as a center for commodified, mass-market furniture that celebrates both art and profit. Hood said that people might understand the designer as a mad scientist, a pied piper, or a savant. "But usually there's a product person that helps take this very creative . . . idea and [tries] to turn it into something where the masses say 'yeah, I wouldn't mind having that in my home,'" Hood explained. "I have never in my life had a designer walk in and lay down this product and say 'you oughta do this.' Not once. Ever."

Product developer William Lambeth, who lives in nearby Thomasville, agreed. Only one designer—a big name—ever sent him drawings prescribing the final product. Most designs evolve through a collaboration between the designer and the product developer, often drawing from a palette of various design elements. "Knowing how to take that version of this chair—the leg from this chair, and the seat from this chair, and the micro-weld instead of the big thick weld—and put it into

a blender and grind it up and come out with that?" said Lambeth, pointing to an image of a chair as he made his case that the process is "an
art." "That's a huge talent. And to me it's as important as the first guy
who designed the first chair." He observed how the designs of the eigh-
teenth- and nineteenth-century pieces combined design elements in the
same way: "If you look at Chippendale or you look at Sheridan or you
look at—any of the original credited people—their designs came out of
architectural functions that were just a component part of *this,* adapted
to *this.* But the idea that you adapted that and it was that good as a
concept? *That* the average Joe can't do," he asserted.

"The spot for art," agreed Hood, is how the product developer com-
bines design elements in new ways. Pushing the envelope means first
knowing the envelope. "A slight variation but not enough that people
are, like, 'what the heck is this?'" he clarified.

Did design professionals feel more freedom to take a risk because they
were more independent than in the past when a firm's product development was in-house? "Oh, my gawwwd, *yes,*" answered Hood. "Infi-
nitely more." Even what feels like "a total departure" from the design
norm can work if it is "a total departure that the masses can relate to,"
he noted.

"Oftentimes the least practical is the most successful," observed Waites.
"I've spent my career, you know, saying 'this isn't going to be the number one seller—we know that—but it will bring all of these benefits to
us and the line." Although designers may have more latitude to conceive
an idea today, that freedom can end once a proposed design is accepted.
At that point, it might get "whittled and shoved to fit into a particular
potato sack," said Hood. Therefore, "designers need a champion," as
Waites often counseled, so that another player somewhere down the
line—such as an accountant—does not make a decision that compro-
mises their entire vision.

Each person in the design process brings a unique skill set to its
development. Lambeth works with someone who, by his report, travels
the world and sends photos of things he discovers, accompanied by
notes such as "I want the arm to flare a little bit more." His firm's product developers then translate those design cues from concept to reality.
Lambeth's mother, a Parsons graduate who designed home interiors for
celebrities, had a similar gift. Although she could "visualize every piece
of furniture, every fabric," he said, she could barely "draw stick people."

She needed an artist collaborator to translate her ideas. "All of these people are very important to me to keep throwing things at the wall," said Lambeth, referring to the others who contribute to the process. "I'm able to look at the wall and tell what I believe will be successful."

The division of decision-making roles within the design process illuminates another valuable feature of the High Point Market: it is a twice-annual fashion show that keeps these players' fingers on the design pulse. The line between keeping one's finger on the pulse and stealing, however, is murky. That's why a designer with a well-known luxury furniture importer/retailer hesitated when at a recent Market I asked him what his role was since he wasn't exhibiting or buying. Apparently, he was developing ideas for his design palette—and the product developers I spoke to told me "fair pool" dictates that Market's too early for that.

"We made a *rendition* of it a few Markets later—or we made it cheaper," said a member of a well-known furniture family while offering me a primer on how to incorporate a trend without unethically "knocking off." Thankfully for designers, lawsuits have shown "rendition" to be open for interpretation. In one notable court case, High Point designer Leo Jiranek once copied Dixie Furniture's suite called Arrival for Bassett Furniture, sold it for less, and had the chutzpah to call it Departure.[6]

Nimble Firms

Why do product developers and designers end up in High Point? In today's mobile world, couldn't they be anywhere? Hood clearly had not thought much about it, but after some thirty minutes of talking it through, he arrived at a conclusion: "It's really logical—if you show here two Markets, [have] several customer visits between that, [and] your product is sitting here in your showroom—to put your office here," he declared firmly. Nobody realizes how "poor" the furniture industry is, he said, pointing to the "alarmingly high" cost of raw materials and the narrow profit margins. "Furniture is made of . . . little entrepreneurs out there scratching away at things and thinkin' they can make something work," Hood continued. All the vacancies in High Point's buildings beyond the downtown means "there's waaay waaay plenty real estate over here for what's required," he added. Affordable real estate offering the legitimacy of an address in the world's furniture fashion center is a major bonus.

Like the sculptor in 1970s SoHo New York, these designers and product developers would not be in High Point if it were not cheap. They locate on undervalued land, and, much like the NED exhibitors, they see themselves as industry disruptors and purveyors of the craft of furniture. The innovations of product developers, designers, and small manufacturers located in the High Point cluster (many on the periphery of the Market district to attract visitors during Market) have a major influence on the dynamic of the High Point exposition vis-à-vis other furniture centers. "It's kind of like the old West. We're all kind of gunslingers at heart. . . . We are a little bit sensitive to anybody wanting to corral us," Lambeth observed.

Some of this "gunslinger" nimbleness was evident as these product developers discussed how technology transformed their distribution chain. Choosy consumers ordering specialized products often do not want to wait for shipment from abroad. Even aside from delivery schedules, it is not financially feasible to make these custom items through sustained production runs in a large factory. However, small High Point manufacturers were able to produce unique pieces targeting buyers who had never been the Market's primary audience.

"I used to carry $2.5 million worth of inventory," Lambeth said. Under the old model, this was necessary because a production run required at least twenty-five to thirty units of an item to be cost effective. "Today, we buy sheets of plywood, we put it on a CAD [computer-aided design program]," he explained. "When I say 'I want to see the sample,' it's eight o'clock; at noon they have it." The idea of inventory is completely transformed. Rather than selling many similar units to a single retailer, a manufacturer today can sell a single, customized unit to the end-consumer or an interior designer. During Market, while some exhibitors focus on the "stock it deep and sell it cheap" buyer, Lambeth draws about one hundred interior designers and their clients to his facility.

Such smaller players within the cluster were "scratching away," as Hood put it, clawing to adapt to the flux of technological and economic change. The High Point context offered them the flexibility to innovate. Lambeth joked how he explained to his banker that he now lives by "five-*minute* plans" rather than "five-*year* plans." The niche of flexible specialization that he has developed cannot be duplicated everywhere. "China can't respond to anything other than container loads; they can't individualize their projects," he said. "That . . . *could* be us," he mused.

Matching Cluster Need with Semiskilled Labor

A product developer's design choices have to be "grounded against the skill set of the factory making the thing," Hood told me. Success depends on a balance of design, labor and material costs, and structural quality and integrity. He likened it to a puzzle—a Rubik's Cube—and technology was a part of solving it. "Hey, you know, you could ladder-press this shape, and do it out of veneer and MDF [medium-density fiberboard], instead of having to do it out of big, heavy, solid lumber," he said. "And because of that, this could make its way to a particular price point that would allow it to be sold in volume." High Point's forty- to sixty-something-year-old furniture makers described an urgency they felt to teach those who will succeed them how to solve this puzzle.

The solution was at the intersection of digital literacy, design skill, and artisanship, and it entailed higher-technology, small-batch production. Automation has deskilled furniture work, said Lambeth, noting how new upholstery-cutting equipment can cut fabric to a thousandth of an inch. "But you still have to have the know-how. You've got to be an adequate cutter to run a cutting machine," he explained. "When the machine says '*ehh! ehh! ehh!*'—it doesn't match—somebody's got to know how to lay the pattern out and match it so they can tell the machine what to do. The problem is finding someone who can do *that* who [also] understands computers. Suddenly I've got an avenue for that next generation that I wouldn't have had otherwise."

Here community college administrator Janette McNeill also saw opportunity. "There are upholstery jobs, but we have difficulty attracting students because the perception of the public is there's no jobs available," she said. "The same thing could happen with design." The region's younger residents were actively avoiding jobs in furniture manufacturing after witnessing jobs disappear due to deindustrialization. "Parents would say, 'Stay away. You will lose your job,'" a human resources executive for Lexington Home Brands in Thomasville said.[7] The same trend was playing out nationally, leaving manufacturing jobs unfilled.[8]

"I walk around our factories every other day and am spooked by what I see," said Alex Shuford III, executive of Century Furniture in nearby Hickory. "The retirements are coming and I can't find enough people."[9] His concern followed a decade's mismatch between the specific job competencies needed by the furniture cluster and the skills of the region's available labor force. Amid a labor shortage in 2019, Craftmaster

Furniture, located one hour from High Point, was offering job applicants a two-thousand-dollar signing bonus. The moment presented High Point with an opportunity to prepare residents, including those most in need of livable-wage jobs, for the industry's relatively high-paying positions expected ahead.

In response to this skill mismatch, more than a dozen area firms collaborated to create the Guilford Technical Community College–High Point Campus's (GTCC) first furniture sewing program in 2017. The campus's historic disadvantage (its downtown South Side location on the fringes of the Market District) now became an asset. "The largest challenge in the furniture industry today is not the threat of foreign competition, but the lack of skilled labor to fill the jobs that we do have," said Andy Greene, vice president of Swaim, Inc., whose Design Center building at the time was in the city's old public library, just down Main Street from the campus.[10]

Many industrial cities have seen skilled, longtime craftspeople disappear from the local economy after the aggressive automation that occurred at some domestic firms and the departure of others for cheaper contexts. In these cases, the craft purveyors were gone long before millennials with a pro-craft disposition arrived. With its industry cluster still intact, High Point had a chance to exploit these specialized assets, but the window was closing. "You look at the workforce that is available here, the craftsmen that are available here," said architect Peter Freeman. "An incredible history of true artisan craftsmanship." In the area of smaller-scale furniture production, High Point remained well positioned to draw on this history to purposefully map a new future.

A lack of foresight and planning by past High Point leaders was partly to blame for the current skills mismatch. The next chapter notes how architect and consultant David Crane began calling for a downtown school for the industrial arts in the 1990s—and, a decade later, Raymond Waites met with local institutions proposing a similar idea. These ideas never gained momentum.

Designers Need Cluster Expertise

The numerous points at which the full process of creation and innovation intersected with High Point's furniture cluster was part of local common sense and thus difficult for people like Hood to enumerate. Once they began to do this, it was clear that the cluster made their High Point location somewhere between convenient and necessary. "I'm here because the Market's here," Hood concluded. "I'm here because the design, and finish, and the supporting cast—if you want to say—are here."

"Every client I have here . . . they're close enough for me to run over there," said Waites. "I mean, I've got drawings for them and I send them without going over there personally. But then when they want me to come and have a meeting, it's not getting on an airplane and going away, you know. They're right there."

"But even the [firms] who aren't here, by definition *must* spend some time here," noted Hood. That is, many prominent designers still live in places like Miami or New York, but much of the connective tissue that binds them to the industry is in High Point. The rooted milieu offers firms outside the region year-round access to a critical mass of specialty services and expertise.

To illustrate how the industry depends on the cluster, Hood proposed the hypothetical of a product developer living and operating a successful business in Albuquerque. At some point, this product developer will have to leave Albuquerque for High Point to confer with an array of proximate specialists—one example might be face-to-face "meetings with three designers who are developing different stuff." Then he might go with a designer to visit one of the High Point region's coating firms. There, they can confer with a color specialist and make sure they have the right color "in the works." The fact that a variety of these meetings can occur in a single trip to High Point helps highlight the complex network of interdependencies that exists both within the cluster and with firms geographically external to it.[11]

Creative Clash

But within High Point, the meshing of design minds and sensibilities into local community life has not been as seamless. Waites was floored, for instance, by what he saw as the city's misguided efforts to rebrand the emerging Uptowne neighborhood, an effort discussed more fully in chapter 9. In the late 2000s, the organizers of this campaign installed streetlight banners designed by local community college students aimed at giving the place a hipper image to lure creative types into what the City Project termed Uptowne's "urban style of living."

"I think the Uptowne concept is completely ridiculous," said Waites as he joked about the streetlight banners—this coming from someone who has supported plans to draw on the region's professionals to train local design students. Grabbing a piece of paper, he started to brainstorm and to sketch. "What if they had done . . ." he began, as he started drawing a more eye-catching alternative. "What if they had done" is a sentiment commonly heard among High Point designers. As a designer, Waites is in the habit of scanning the city's landscapes; he sees where High Point's design expertise is in evidence and where it has been neglected. "Create some big, bold beautiful patterns. That's not expensive," he suggested as he continued to sketch. "But you see it. It floats down the street. The wind blows it all kinds of crazy ways," he added, pointing to the design for long, colorful, tapered banners he had just created.

"There's a thing in Liverpool, England, called the super lamb banana," said a former journalist for *InFurniture* magazine, a defunct Fairchild publication once headquartered in the white building. She began reminiscing about the super lamb banana (a bright yellow sculpture of a cross between a lamb and banana) and the wildly popular "cows on parade" fiberglass sculpture installations that spread across the globe from Zurich to Madrid to Chicago at the turn of the twenty-first century. "It is camp," one participating artist said of the cow installation in Chicago. "I am really for public art projects that will take a little bit of the elite out of art." Art scholar Stanley Murashige agreed with this assessment of the playfully lowbrow Cows on Parade. "One of our myths is that art—if it is art—has to be serious," he said.[12]

In this same vein as the cows and the super lamb banana, *InFurniture* created an installation of chair sculptures painted with different themes scattered throughout downtown High Point. "We did six of them and what we wanted to do was install them permanently across the city and, in fact, do more," she continued. When I first saw the chairs, I recognized their gesture toward the street art found in other cities. Marketgoers clearly enjoyed taking photos of this unique sculpture. However, city leaders felt differently. "We got *nowhere,*" the *InFurniture* journalist said. "Everybody thought it was the dumbest idea they had ever heard."

"It's hard for a designer to be their own champion," Waites intoned regarding civic life. "The second you lose your champion, you lose your right for being. It's that champion who helps clear the way." Leaders in other North Carolina cities that are experiencing a resurgence of

"Chair Affair" installment by Fairchild Publications' *InFurniture Magazine*. The unashamedly campy exhibition never got local buy-in.

downtown development along with an influx of new middle-class residents and accompanying gentrification have consciously created entry points to attract new, creative ideas. "There's holes, and hooks, and niches," resident Trish Perkins pointed out, ways to jump in or grab on to processes already in motion. She mentioned Elsewhere, a Greensboro museum and artists residency where visitors can explore a collection of junk accumulated over six decades by a local hoarder and now made available as material for artists. "You've got to have that weird, funky, cheap, off-the-wall stuff if you're going to have life. And none of the people I know in High Point understand that. They want the big places," Perkins said.

High Point leaders have a history of seeking national and international retail stores to legitimate what they consider the city's key spaces. "Their idea of how you develop has to do with getting a big department store or that kind of thing, a big chain," explained Perkins. And when Starbucks, or Fresh Market, or Belk did not respond to High Point's overtures to move near downtown, civic leaders would regroup for the similar next attempt. To Perkins, such single-minded thinking "causes leaders to overlook small potential changes" in their midst. "That's like the *end* of the process, you know?" she said. "You don't get the big money that moves in until all the funky people have made enough money so that they are not poor and funky anymore." In Andrés Duany's parlance, this is when "the boring gentrifiers called 'the dentists from New Jersey'" move in.[13] In the now-familiar gentrification narrative, this is when the place loses its authentic character.

Perkins's frustration that the leaders of a creative hub like High Point would remain fixated solely on recruiting a national or transnational chain to anchor the downtown is like Waites's exasperation over a global design center that would call on community college students to create city street banners to lure creative professionals without soliciting their creative expertise. While High Point politicians express extreme pride in their city's furniture fashion heritage, outside the Market they have operated as if this were just another small southern city. "The creative class is a creative *clash*," quipped blogger Ivan Cutler. "It clashes with the business interests that are only present-minded. They are looking at the most immediate return on their investment for now versus the long term."

"It is funny that the city and a lot of the decision makers have kept a lot of the design community outside the decision-making process," architect Peter Freeman observed. "I think there is a lot of frustration, and I think that other designers feel that . . . 'we'll go to Greensboro or Winston.'"

"High Point *has* to open its arms to the creative class," Freeman continued. "It *is* and always *has been* a really important part of shaping the city." The immediate issue for High Point has been how to retain and exploit what it already has to make its advantage sustainable. "These people are here for a reason," said politician Bernita Sims. "They *come* for a reason. And I think it's important for us to find out what that reason is and ask, 'How do we build upon it? How do we capitalize on it? How do we make it be our own?'"

Creators as Citizens — of the Region

"Having been a part of the Hamptons for thirty years," said Waites, "you have Southampton, you have Bridgehampton, you have East Hampton, you have Amagansett, you have Montauk. They are at least thirty miles away from one to another." Tapping the table to underscore each word, he continued, "People in the Hamptons go to—*all*—the—Hamptons. For lunch, you'll meet somebody in Southampton or you'll meet 'em in Montauk . . . you *jump* between the Hamptons. And Montauk is twenty-something miles. But it's no [big] deal to go out to Montauk and go to the docks to watch the boats come in and out. So we've always been used to traveling a little bit for your recreation, for the restaurants, the things you enjoy."

Waites used the example of how he entertained his well-known designer friend, Norwegian Ristomatti Ratia, when he came for a visit to High Point. "My goal," he said, "was to show him that we're not a bunch of rednecks down here." He went on to describe how he drew on the resources of the whole region to entertain him—from Charlotte to the beaches of the Atlantic Ocean, each for their different strengths. "If you make use of this area, you have everything you could possibly want," he said.

Jason Phillips was still a teenager when his parents, Mark and Julie Phillips, moved their firm Phillips Collection from the New York area to High Point shortly after the terrorist attacks of September 11. In 2005, Jason repeated his parents' path and moved to High Point from New York City to work at the Phillips Collection. He views local living broadly, like Waites: "We work in High Point, I play in Winston-Salem, I live in Greensboro."

Market leader Brian Casey agrees that to view High Point as being in competition with neighboring cities is unproductive. "I think the *region* itself as a cluster brings more strength to the table," he said. Casey is not alone. Since the 1980s, other High Point leaders have recognized the benefits of balancing local with regional while preserving High Point's small-community life. "Hollywood is not just Sunset and Vine," remarked Ivan Cutler. "As Hollywood is a frame of mind, so High Point is . . . not just Commerce and Main Street. It's an arc from Raleigh to Hickory," he explained.

What position does High Point hold within this regional picture? Must city leaders resign themselves to the lesser status of a bedroom community of better-known Greensboro and Winston-Salem, a suggestion made by urban planning scholar David Sawicki during a planning charrette in the 1990s? "Well, it's High Point *too*," Waites replied.

"I like High Point a lot for what it *doesn't* do. I like that we're a small community."

"I think what a young designer needs more than anything else is the ability to have a low cost of living, which this region definitely allows," ventured Phillips. "You don't have to be immersed in a bohemian hotbed of culture and hippies and art galleries and free thinkers," he added, debunking a stereotype about the role of creative milieus. He believes that Google searches or a trip to High Point's furniture libraries are where most designers find their inspiration. What matters most to young creative thinkers is having a lifestyle that supports their preferred stimuli, and he offered examples such as a housing market that allows them extra funds for travel or a community with plenty of hiking trails.

In 2014, Jason Nixon and his partner John Loecke, the owners of New York–based firm Madcap Cottage, packed up their Brooklyn brownstone and moved to High Point. After visiting High Point for the Market for the past twenty years, they purchased a 1930s Regency Revival home and a former pharmacy storefront on the edge of the North Elm Design district. "The resources here are just unbelievable," explained Nixon.

"High Point is a unique place," said Loecke, as he recounted many of the themes already described in this chapter. "The (furniture) industry is still here, whether it's made here or overseas. All the capabilities are here: designers, artists, refinishers and furniture manufacturers. . . . We had nothing like this in New York," he said. After three years in the downtown's former pharmacy, the duo moved their Madcap Cottage headquarters to suburban Thomasville in 2018, just up the street from Lambeth.

In 2017, Nixon and Loecke joined designers Thom Filicia, Alexa Hampton, Tobi Fairley, Barclay Butera, and Celerie Kemble in redesigning a seven-thousand-square-foot Market District home built in 1905 into a luxury boutique inn and event space. Pandora's Manor was the brainchild of Ridvan and Siw Tatargil, owners of Chicago-based Eastern Accents, who had been eyeing the building for thirty years during Market visits. Each designer had control over individual guest spaces, creating, in effect, "an immersive showroom" for guests.[14] While projects like this and the Nixon–Loecke home privileged historic preservation of large, traditional houses, others looked to the revival of High Point's deteriorating "downtown core," the area surrounding the Market district.

The designers of the interior of Pandora's Manor pose on its wooden staircase. The boutique hotel and bed and breakfast, which is located in the shadow of Market Tower, has six rooms. Photograph courtesy of Elements Studio, High Point, North Carolina.

Creators as Pioneers

At the time Duany visited High Point, a subject of chapter 10, he had grown concerned that development in centers of innovation like Brooklyn was pricing out and displacing risk-taking creatives so that "a generation of pioneers has been chased away, only to reappear at the next Brooklyn."[15] Duany felt that High Point was positioned to offer an environment for such creative risk-taking. In 2018, the publication *Business of Home* similarly mused whether High Point was furniture's "new Brooklyn."[16]

Duany was certainly not alone in seeing potential waiting to be realized within deindustrialized and devalued sections of numerous U.S. cities, including broad swaths of rust belt cities such as Detroit, Cleveland, and Chicago. As one Youngstown, Ohio, native confidently described it, "hitting that low point could be the best thing . . . because it has made property so cheap . . . that you can kind of blow up and start again."[17] Amy Cotter of the Lincoln Institute suggests that some disinvested industry centers provide "a quality of life and authenticity you can't find elsewhere, and at an affordable price."[18] Old buildings—suddenly considered assets of authenticity—still stand, often because local governments lacked the means to tear them down.

High Point's West End section is such a neighborhood. The area's racial composition has been durably diverse. It is just under half white, with most of the remaining population evenly split between Black and Hispanic residents. Thirty percent of its housing was deemed substandard in a 2016 survey by sociologist Stephen Sills, and 40 to 50 percent of the population was living in poverty, with similar numbers recorded for those outside the labor force and without a high school degree.[19]

"The low rent world is also the creative kind of world," said Perkins, voicing a conclusion previously heard from Duany, Jane Jacobs, and Sharon Zukin. Perkins had a daydream of living in the West End and starting a pay-as-you-can program shuttling locals to area farmers' markets. "I fantasized about [it]—and my husband was like 'What? You're going to do what?' My idea was to spend a year living in the West End."

She was partly drawn by the houses. "Beautiful," she said. "You know, just really nicely built. Lots of beautiful little lines. I mean, cottage-type lines. It's a great neighborhood. There's a lot of like low-income but proud people" she noted as we looked down the block. "Look at those," she said, pointing to rows of uniform shotgun homes. I recalled my own first impression of their striking uniformity. "Just like the single artist place, with real life. That's one of the things that artists like, is to have real life around them. This is *real life*," she declared. "This is a crack house, or was—so was that," she added. Perkins knew the neighborhood from her days as an AmeriCorps fellow at its nonprofit West End Ministries. The organization had long collaborated with Pastor Jim Sumney, an activist for restorative justice whose work using the Drug Market Intervention approach of criminologist David Kennedy has been widely documented. Perkins cited Sumney and Kennedy's work as she continued to talk about the neighborhood's decrease in crime, but added, "The artists, they don't care if there's *some* drug dealing. It might actually be good for them."

The "accumulated mythology of the artist in the city," explains Richard Lloyd, frames "elements of the local landscape that many would find alarming as instead being symbolic amenities."[20] He noted the complex and dynamic way in which artists "fold the representation of urban decay into their picture of authentic urbanism, even as their presence contributes to the reversal of many of its effects." Zukin seems to interpret this relationship between grit and artist as organic to the development of an art enclave. She contends that in New York, for instance, "low rents and the gritty local character of the streets *generated* an art scene."[21]

"Working-class history is not very sexy to some people," High Point preservationist Dorothy Darr said in 2012, with the implication that it *was* appealing to a select few. "Some would just as soon blow the factories up and deal with flat, open land. But these historic structures give flavor to an area and make it authentic," she explained. "The challenge is, how do you create buzz and a twenty-first-century plan for an area that has been forgotten or that people never knew about?"[22]

Market exhibitor Jim Koch has operated his fine art gallery in the historic Melrose Mill in the West End neighborhood since moving it from New York in 1988. "It was so perfect because it didn't have any posts and it had high ceilings. In Manhattan, I was in a five-story walk-up. Having one level was fantastic because it didn't have the stairs. It was just raw, empty space with wires hanging everywhere," said Koch, singling out the building's "character."[23]

"You need revitalization from *something*," Trish Perkins reasoned pragmatically, "and it takes a while for a whole artsy fartsy community to be really gentrified. Because the artists," she added, "have a stake in it being low-rent."

Artists were also reevaluating the deteriorated East Side. Phyllis Bridge's Yalik's Modern Art had been operating on Washington Street there since 2008. In 2014, Greensboro-based artist Beka Butts and her 512 Collective opened across the street with a grant from a local philanthropist. "We need the artists," said Wendy Fuscoe. She revealed that the owners of the Collective first spoke to her about locating in the Uptowne neighborhood, until she "connected them with the Washington Street folks." Explained Fuscoe, "We need more of those different-thinking kinds of people to get involved." For better or worse, it is not unusual for such edgy uses and "different thinking" dreamers to locate in Black and Latino neighborhoods that are relatively cheap from years of devaluing, deterioration, and defunding.[24] Butts entered with little fanfare and no resistance—not that many organizations or businesses were trying to locate on Washington Street.

"It's a vibrant street. I just don't think a lot of people pay attention to it," said Butts. To Butts, the city was overly fixated on Market. Meanwhile, High Point's marginal areas were in a state of worsening

The Kilby Hotel on Washington Street after its collapse, with historic First Baptist Church on the right. Photograph courtesy of Patrick Harman, Hayden–Harman Foundation.

deterioration. Just down the street from Butts, the Kilby Hotel, described as a linchpin of Washington Street's architectural and historical contributions, collapsed after a rainstorm in June 2014.

"We need to reinvent the city, and there's some real talent here," Butts said of High Point.[25] Over time, nonprofit leader Maggie May had come to embrace such gentrification-fueled reinvention in High Point's marginal areas for pragmatic reasons. "You can't imagine how hard it is for our . . . people to try to find a job in High Point. They're just destitute," she said. "It's a huge, unnoticed population of poor people. So, if there were more jobs, regardless of where in High Point they are or what kind of jobs they are, at least they're jobs. It's something," she concluded.

The Salon

"It is in the DNA." That's how Sarah Simpkins and many other locals view the cluster's complex competitive advantage. "This is a five-generation region of furniture builders and distributors and suppliers and designers," said Phillips. Furniture's full-century presence in High Point has given the city myriad intangible advantages.

Over this time, High Point's economy has specialized and respecialized, not only incorporating furniture manufacturing, design, and product development but also encompassing showroom design and photography, as well as finance, trade associations, and journalism.[26] High Point's most important asset alongside cheap real estate is the extant buzz embedded in the connective tissue of furniture relationships and the inimitable culture that has developed around them. This raises the potential for "cross-fertilization" that urban studies theorist Richard Florida recognized in his notion of the creative class.[27]

"The mirage of the exposition in the Las Vegas desert was that it sought to create a market without making the cluster. You need a foundation first," said industry blogger Cutler. "Inherently, Las Vegas is transitory. The people fly in and fly out. Discontinuity is the continuity," he said. "In High Point, people live here. They interact with each other. There's kind of a—without a formality—a salon. *Everybody's here.* But nobody has taken the golden thread and tied it through and pulled it together," he added.

For much of the past seventy years, High Point leaders have been negligent in looking for such a thread and complacent in identifying, preserving, steering, and cultivating the cluster's assets. If High Point had conscientiously inventoried such synergies, relationships, and cross-fertilizations in the past, its leaders might have responded differently to significant losses over the past two decades, such as the departure of furniture firms from the white office building. The variety of former tenants—headquarters such as La-Z-Boy subsidiary LADD, trade publications such as *Furniture Today*, the Market Authority offices, and the furniture finance firm First Factors—represents just the type of clustering that contemporary policy approaches would attempt to actively court and incentivize. Such firms are similar enough to benefit from co-location, but diverse enough to bridge the vicissitudes of their individual business cycles.

The creative "friction" forged in this co-location of furniture designers, journalists, showroom designers, and executives was reinforced in informal meetings in places like Rosa Mae's or J. Basul Nobles. It strengthened High Point's economic and social fabric as a home furnishings center. High Point's constellation of assets—and how they cohere—is unique to High Point. Through this lens, a place like Rosa Mae's may be under-appreciated in its role as the furniture cluster's "water cooler or coffee machine where colleagues and work mates gather."[28] If it did have this value, then why should its existence be left solely to market forces when thoughtful government intervention could foster the sustainability of such small, local anchors?[29] The "golden thread" Cutler talked about could come only from a hyperlocalized brand of innovation, one that respected and welcomed the diverse voices of the city's local and global stakeholders as part of its distinct glocal. This would require a specific style of governance. On that front, Phillips noted in 2012, "the city has some catching up to do."

The argument that High Point won and kept this exposition because of its dominance as a furniture manufacturing center has been obsolete for decades. By this measure, the Shanghai market should have been crowned the world exposition long ago.[30] High Point's endurance illustrates how specific "regional legacies" can help shape "global enterprises."[31] It suggests another way in which the "Southern convergence with the world economy" is actually driving rather than merely reflecting broader trends within the process of globalization.[32]

Possessing the unique "indigenous assets" of its industry cluster, High Point has an advantage over other places that crave a similar milieu but lack High Point's industry-concentrated heritage.[33] "You can cut the tree off, but the roots will still be in the ground" is Callie Everitt's metaphor for this difficult-to-quantify expertise. High Point's furniture future will certainly hinge on how the city can orient these locally rooted assets through a changing global context. "I don't want you taking my baby anywhere," declared William Lambeth. "I want my baby right here."

PART III

THE FIGHT TO RECLAIM DOWNTOWN

8

Poking the Golden Goose

A Brief History of Local Protest

The Streets and the Conference Table

The sixty-three-year-old, three-time Grammy winner Michael McDonald was performing on a stage in front of the Home Furnishings Center during the Fall 2015 Market. The baritone's voice cut through the sweet autumn air as his audience enjoyed catered food and free alcohol. I overheard those from the United States explaining the cultural meanings behind the songs of McDonald's Doobie Brothers band to people from around the world. They were leaning in to hear each other over the loud music. McDonald did not know what to make of this cosmopolitan crowd holding their drinks and dancing in the shadows of the glass and steel architectural backdrop. "I've never been here," he said in a tone of voice that seemed best translated as "Where *am* I?" The environment was electric. Just having returned to High Point myself, the uniqueness of the setting felt palpable and jarring to me, too. Looking around, I saw High Pointers who had lived their lives around the rhythms of this global exposition. I also savored the free show as I stood next to a Market worker, a Brooklyn transplant I had met at the concert. It was one of dozens of such moments I had experienced over the previous two decades that left me thinking, "Only in High Point!"

The buildings surrounding the Magic Block provided ideal acoustics for the concert's powerful finale, "Taking It to the Streets." While McDonald should not be construed as a protest song writer, his song aptly captures the back-and-forth of social movement politics. "Ohhh *you*, telling me the things you're gonna do for me," says the frustrated, untrusting activist in the lyrics. "I ain't blind," he says to the adversary that has not gained his trust, "and I don't like what I think I see." The powerfully delivered song concludes on a triumphant note with the background singers repeatedly delivering the activist's decision: he's "takin' it to the streets." And when the activist in the song runs up against the establishment leader's placating statement of "We'll discuss it further," suggesting the resolution of the dispute in due time at the conference table, he meets this response with the negative: "nah."

The song echoes the strategies that a local High Point civil rights leader, the Rev. B. Elton Cox, employed over the years. In 1963, Cox had threatened to enact what he called his "ace in the hole": a direct action in which one thousand Black men would lie on the ground in front of the Big Building during the Market. He knew this show of messy local vernacular, laden with complexity and discomfort, was not something leaders would stand for in the Market's frontstage. McDonald's rousing 2015 performance would have made a fitting commemoration of Cox's tenacious efforts a half century earlier. However, exposing High Point's rough edges during Market was no more acceptable in 2015 than in 1963.

This chapter's broad sweep through four decades of resident-focused history lays a foundation for interpreting the more recent past. It begins with the era of Black mobilization, which examines the activism for Black access to downtown in the 1960s. The era of mayoral agency will outline two municipal efforts, led by Mayors Judy Mendenhall in the 1980s and Becky Smothers in the 1990s, centered on whether resident usage deserved a role in downtown development. The Downtown Improvement Committee era looks at the 2000s when this city-endorsed advisory group of local civic leaders strategized about how to carve resident-centered meaning into the downtown landscape. The Party on the Plank era advances us to the 2010s, through the evolution of Elijah Lovejoy's tactical urbanism campaigns encouraging residents to take psychic ownership of the downtown and reconsider it part of their life space again. These campaigns employed different tools—nonviolent protest, municipal power, civic engagement, and grassroots intervention in the built environment—but they all sought to question the dominance of showroom use in the downtown.

The Era of Black Mobilization (1960s)

In the 1960s, downtown High Point, the stage of the Market, also became the site, object, and stage of the struggle in High Point for Black civil rights. Rev. Cox would repeatedly cross the boundary between the Black East Side and the downtown to protest segregation in white-dominated spaces using the tactics of nonviolent direct action. "I see a dividing line that I knew when I crossed over, I was in another world," said Glenn Chavis. He was referring to the role Centennial Street played in demarcating east (Black) and west (white) High Point. Chavis explained that even after Washington Street was physically truncated at the Black downtown, erasing West Washington Street, white High Pointers maintained this symbolic line by referring to the Black downtown as "*East Washington Street.*"

Nonviolent Protest on the Stage of the Town Center

In 1962, the National Civic League awarded High Point its All-America City designation, an accolade due in no small part to Rev. Cox and his assertion of the city's relative racial progress. The thirty-two-year-old Cox had come to High Point four years earlier to become pastor of Pilgrim Congregational Church, one of the many movement-conscious leaders who had moved to the South from more progressive northern environments via the church.[1] He had developed a nonviolent direct action platform of seventeen "ins," a repertoire of integration protests that ranged from wade-ins at pools to watch-ins at theaters to bury-ins at funeral homes.[2] In 1960, he led High Point high school students in a direct action sit-in at the city's downtown Woolworth's with the co-founder of the Southern Christian Leadership Conference, Fred Shuttlesworth. The next year, Cox joined the Congress of Racial Equality, where he became one of the original thirteen CORE "Freedom Riders," and eventually rose to the office of national field secretary.

Cox intended to use the influence he had gained working with the All-America City campaign to the movement's advantage. High Pointer Peter Mason called Rev. Cox a "thorn in the side" of the white power structure that they nonetheless "had to deal with because he was persistent, unafraid, courageous."[3] His boldness in words and actions was related, to be sure, to the resolve he had developed in response to many threats on his life. Friends recall how Cox's audacity and humor reflected a plucky zeal for living. Numerous anecdotes—from his suggesting that an attorney prosecuting him in Little Rock had "Negro concubines" to his progressive vocal stances on the interracial relationships of his CORE members and on interracial marriage—illustrate his fearlessness in a perilous time.

"I think we are still ahead," Cox noted, strategically straddling a line regarding High Point's civil rights protests and his endorsement of the All-America City accolade. "We are not, however, at the goal."[4] In 1963, the year after High Point won the designation, the local CORE office sought to provoke controversy by handing out leaflets that questioned whether High Point should be recognized as "All-American City or Jim Crow Town."[5] CORE pointed out the continued segregation in the city, including at the downtown Paramount Theatre, located on city-owned land. Civil rights attorney John Langford, who was affiliated with the NAACP, argued the case against the Paramount, contending that "a city can't lease its property to concerns which will discriminate against certain citizens."[6] In an act of rhetorical gymnastics, Mayor Carson Stout countered the suit by claiming a proprietor's right to serve "any person whom they choose regardless of race."[7]

In September 1963, nonviolent protests became potentially incendiary due to the increasing presence of white counterprotestors.[8] On September 3, 1963, a counterprotestor struck Cox in the face as a mob of an estimated one thousand whites surrounded a "drive-in" demonstration he led.[9] "It was really something. It heated up night after night," recalled Ben Collins, a Black High Point police officer who was on duty those evenings. "The numbers of Blacks who were demonstrating—the numbers increased every night," he said. "And the numbers increased of the whites who were against it."[10]

Demonstrations continued throughout the downtown: at the Center Theater on Main Street, the Paramount Theater on Commerce Avenue, the K&W Cafeteria on High Street, and the A&W on Main Street. A victory at the latter drive-in had seemed imminent when the national president of the A&W chain wired CORE leaders offering his assurance that he would not allow segregation in his establishments. However, on September 6, the local store manager defiantly placed a message on A&W's revolving street sign reading "We are not integrated."[11]

The protests and counterprotests continued each night. On September 10, more than 550 antisegregation demonstrators were met by a crowd of about 2,000 whites at A&W. "There were so many whites protesting the march," Officer Collins recalled of that Tuesday. By his account, the white counterprotestors barely left enough room for the police to usher the demonstrators through. "They were up on top of the building, down the sidewalk, out to almost the middle of the street," Collins remembered.[12] The next night, in a story that made national news, the police used tear gas bombs to "quell a near riot that developed when two thousand white persons began throwing rocks, eggs, tomatoes and other missiles at Negroes conducting antisegregation demonstrations."[13]

Each day, before heading off from Washington Street for the protests, the marchers met in a church and turned over any firearms. However, as politician Al Campbell explained with a playful smile, the route from the church to the protest site passed the pool hall. When the protestors passed, the men from the pool hall would get on the back of the line. Those who joined the march at the pool hall had not stopped by the church to relinquish their firearms.

"We could always hear the message [that the pool hall crowd was present] get up to the front of the line: 'They're back there!'" Campbell recalled.[14] "It was rather funny, to some extent," Campbell said of this mix, "but on the other hand we were very glad they were back there [participating]." The story adds a missing element to the standard narratives that have characterized participants of the nonviolence movement as martyr figures. Even Rev. Cox was vocal about the fact that "nonviolence" was a strategic *choice* that he made for the purposes of direct action. "I had two German Shepherd dogs, and five guns loaded," Cox shared of his home security. "I am a nonviolent person while *demonstrating*," he quipped.

Black physician Otis Tillman was in bed with a fever when one of his closest friends called during what he called this "fiery time in 1963." The caller was Jimmy Millis, a white hosiery manufacturer whose family would come to be recognized for their forward-thinking attitude about Black labor issues.[15] He told Tillman that Black residents were lined up on one side of the street, whites on the other. "I'm afraid they're going to burn the town down," Tillman recalled him saying. "So I got out of my bed, went down there, went and found him on that side— the white side," Tillman continued.[16] Millis told Tillman he would reason with the white side of the street and asked Tillman to do the same with the Black side. Tillman agreed, but when he arrived there, he had a change of heart. "I got down there in front of the A&W Root Beer place and they were singing 'We Shall Overcome,'" Tillman said. "And *all* of the past experiences came back to me." When the police told Tillman to move, he refused. "And I was carried to jail like every other person in sight that was Black that didn't move on when they said 'move on.'"[17]

During that summer, dozens of Black demonstrators would be arrested and overwhelm High Point's infrastructure, a key tactic of nonviolent protest. The city simply did not have enough paddy wagons to hold them all, forcing some of the arrested protestors to walk to their booking. The jail was also grossly inadequate to accept the influx. Each night, a county sheriff's officer would lock the overflow in a courtroom and stand guard. Those locked inside would respond by singing songs of the movement. "We would sing until three o'clock in the morning and it would make them so mad they couldn't stand it," Campbell remembered, shaking his head and smiling. "They'd say 'what the *hellll* are y'all singing for?'"[18]

Nonviolent Protest on the Stage of the Furniture Market

As the summer protests and counterprotests escalated and continued into autumn, the Fall Market grew closer. At a Sunday mass meeting on September 8, Cox threatened to assemble one thousand Black demonstrators to lie in front of furniture buildings at the October 1963 Market.[19] Downtown High Point, like most southern downtowns at the time, was a distinct symbol of the local white power structure. It was also the stage setting for a highly synchronized Market performance during this influential furniture fashion week. And if the power structure did not respond satisfactorily to local demonstrations concerning the day-to-day—the right to attend a movie matinee or buy a hamburger—Cox would take the protest to a larger audience. In the language of McDonald's song, it was Cox's ultimate "Nah."

Cox's campaigns exemplified how the "urban environment provided the stage on which the drama of the Civil Rights struggle unfolded."[20] Nonviolent direct action required a protagonist, an antagonist, a moral confrontation, and either a live audience or a camera to document the event. Cox's threat to take his protests to the Market—his "ace in the hole"—would have introduced the High Point Market to most Americans not as a furniture fashion week but as a front of the civil rights fight.

White leaders cautioned Cox that he should be content with the pace of progress. The *Winston-Salem Journal* warned him and his High Point contemporaries "in the wake of marked progress, if Negroes persist in demonstrating, they in their turn run the risk of building up the very resistance they are trying to tear down."[21] However, Cox understood that direct action in the street empowered, rather than weakened, his work in the boardroom. In the words of the song, a willingness to "discuss it further" and a call for "takin' it to the streets" were not mutually exclusive.

Any activity that compromised the preeminence of the Market was met with outright disbelief, if not anger. The fact that this threat to disrupt Market was both willful and orchestrated by "agitating" Black residents (led by a leader raised in the north) roiled white High Pointers. Occupying downtown space in June was disruption, but protesting in October would be utter betrayal. *Enterprise* editor Holt McPherson termed the threat "arrogant blackmail."[22]

As the Market approached, the city had little choice but to ensure Cox's Market protest did not occur. The mayor established a permanent Human Relations Committee to continue the work of the temporary Biracial Committee. CORE agreed to suspend its demonstrations from September 20 to December 6, a period that included all Market activities, to work out the details of how the city would proceed. John Langford, who had been a vocal antisegregation champion throughout the period of unrest, contrasted NAACP's legal approach to that of CORE's direct action orientation, saying, "I am glad this issue is back around the conference table. That's where it will be decided."[23]

The success of Cox's "ace in the hole" (threatening High Point's image during Market) is not surprising when considered in the larger context. With the nation and the world descending on the city, its leaders sought to project an image of harmony in line with local boosters' promotion of a "New South" at this time.[24] They delivered that message in an OPEN LETTER TO HIGH POINT BUSINESSMEN that was published in the *High Point Enterprise* on the last day of Market, October 25, 1963. The letter declared:

We, white citizens of High Point and area, in support of efforts being made by white and Negro leaders, do hereby stand by the principle of equal treatment of all persons, regardless of race. We are convinced that there is only one solution to the present racial problems in our city—the immediate removal of the color bar in all places of business and institutions to which the public has access. We urge the managers and operators of such businesses and facilities to proceed immediately to remove from their operations all segregation and discrimination.[25]

Cox never let up the pressure. After a large protest in May 1966, he presented the city council with a list of twenty grievances.[26] On the issue of housing, Cox complained that with few housing relocation options, Black residents displaced by urban renewal projects "must buy white slums."[27] Concerning employment, the Reverend Ralph Abernathy, co-founder of the Southern Christian Leadership Conference, noted that the furniture Market did not have a single Black furniture sales representative.[28] Except for female showroom designers and hospitality volunteers, the structure of exclusion in furniture merchandising and marketing applied to nearly everyone but white men.[29] Abernathy's indictment and recognition of Black exclusion was prescient. It came just as the automation and flight of furniture manufacturing—the jobs that had attracted Black migrants initially—began taking shape.

While Cox counseled his Sunday evening church audience on May 15, 1966, to keep their "marching shoes" ready, the enemy was becoming more ambiguous. Like much of the South, High Point had concluded that displays of overt racism were bad for business. Due to the efforts of people like Rev. Cox, Black High Pointers slowly gained access to downtown High Point, but it was not the same downtown. As historian Thomas Sugrue noted in his seminal study of Detroit, at the moment when Black mobilization gained Black access to the center of the city, the city center began its rapid decline.[30]

In High Point, an important variation on this general narrative occurred. The very period when Black residents gained full legal access to the downtown, downtown became less accessible to *all* High Pointers with each passing year. During the "fiery time" in 1963, Biracial Committee Chair Major General Capus Waynick had warned that High Point must eliminate Black residents' "second-class citizenship" and allow them full rights to the amenities downtown.[31] By the turn of the century, the *majority* of High Pointers would feel like "second-class people" in their downtown, thanks to a transformation Mayor Judy Mendenhall had seen coming in the 1980s.[32]

The Era of Mayoral Agency (1980s and 1990s)

Market real estate in downtown High Point was burgeoning in the late 1970s and early 1980s when all the other center cities in the region were starting to suffer. To the degree that small merchants could hang on, they became "both an irritant and an impediment" in the transition to the more profitable use.[33] Showroom developers were counting on local officials to support the revaluing of the downtown real estate for their purposes.

One important strategy for contesting development plans is to disabuse proponents of the expectation that growth benefits a community merely because it raises tax revenue.[34] Easier said than done. "If somebody wants to come into your city and pay millions of dollars to develop a piece of property that's going to add tax value to your city budget, it takes a lot of courage to say 'no you can't do that, we're going to keep that property for *us*,'" said Lovejoy. "Or the city is going to buy it . . . and keep it for the people." Why would a local government incur costs to supervise, regulate, or manage properties that—without lifting a finger—would produce revenues? *What is the city's role?*

A timeless urban planning quandary—what I call the *regulation dilemma*—would emerge in High Point repeatedly: the point when things are bad seems the wrong time to regulate and manage growth. However, when things are good, as Lovejoy outlined here, is an even worse time to manage growth.

Many High Pointers later criticized local leaders for only belatedly trying to control Market growth. Politician Bernita Sims said politicians in the early days of growth should have put something in the "mix to allow for businesses and other retail to grow" alongside the showrooms. Looking back, Jay Wagner thought that "about 1980, the city should've seen this coming and [been] willing to do something about it then."

Mayor Mendenhall's Showroom Bout

The city's first woman mayor, Judy Mendenhall, first brought Market development decision-making into public debate in a serious way. In the early 1980s, the Market had reached 2.5 million square feet, the size of two large U.S. shopping malls. At that time, she and the city's Economic Development Commission began to take on small property owners who were operating in the landlord's utopia that J. J. Cox had promoted in the 1970s: leasing downtown buildings to small furniture manufacturers who were willing to pay above-average rents year-round but required only seasonal attention. She called on them to consider the ramifications of this for the community.

230 · Poking the Golden Goose

The *Enterprise* identified the opponents in the "battle" in October 1986. "In the far corner, looming extremely tall, and with the weight of state redevelopment statutes behind it is the city of High Point."[35] In the near corner, standing proud and resting on the weight of societal trends and High Point's furniture orientation is a determined group of downtown property owners," the paper wrote.[36] These state redevelopment statutes entailed the use of *eminent domain,* government's power to seize private property without the owner's consent in the name of the public good while paying a fair market value.

When the mayor invoked the idea of eminent domain regarding more than forty-four structures in the targeted area, it raised suspicions that the public "would be the losers."[37] Skeptics warned that property owners would not get fair market value or the city would use a technicality to swiftly condemn land it coveted. They worried that the plans had nothing to do with the public good and everything to do with backroom deals in the works before the plans came to light. Given the abuse of eminent domain in the United States, this scrutiny was healthy and well-founded. Mayor Mendenhall tried to assure property owners that condemnations would be pursued only if the plan was "overwhelmingly good for the community."[38]

The area in question encompassed three of the four blocks at the intersection of Main Street and the railroad tracks, with the city's new downtown hotel and prominent white office building occupying most of the fourth. The mayor expressed concern that the appearance of these occupied but dormant storefronts was injurious to the center of the downtown. "To the mayor, the targeted blocks are a largely unattractive and abandoned looking cluster of buildings that contribute little to the greater community and dress up only twice a year," according to the *Enterprise.*[39]

The gradual, unregulated, and seemingly inevitable transition of individual properties and blocks to Market use came to be known in local planning circles as "Market creep." Mendenhall's questioning confronted the city's unimpeded free market approach by implying that it was not in the "public good" to have every vacant property turned over to Market. Concurrently, she was arguing that turning over properties to resident-centered uses could be "overwhelmingly" in the public good and she was willing to utilize one of any city's greatest and most contested powers— eminent domain—to fight High Point's most powerful interests and their foundational tenets of highest and best use to achieve it.

"For the longest time, Knox Bridge, right there at the train tracks, all the showrooms were south from there," said restaurant owner Jim Davis, looking back to the era when the railroad tracks demarcated Market uses from other uses. Land speculation was breaking down this informal boundary that not only benefited residents but, as Davis noted, also encouraged a synergy between resident- and Market-centered uses. "On the [north] side of the bridge, it was all retail," Davis said. "That was the line. People who came for Market, they would come up because they knew where to get their eyeglasses fixed. They knew where to get some shoes."

The response of landowners was predictable. As the attorney for one property investor put it, "the best benefit to the people of High Point is to protect the furniture industry." He cited J. J. Cox, who had just sold his building for more than one million dollars. As he further pointed out, "the buildings' value to the furniture industry increases their worth" along with city tax revenues.[40]

"I don't understand fooling with that," said one property owner. "Anything that hurts the exhibitors hurts High Point."[41] This "we feeling" legitimates the idea that a favored industry is *us* and its economic success means communal success. It makes exchange value, as opposed to just use value, seem important for community cohesiveness.[42] If it's good for the Market, it's good for High Point.[43]

The city's plans to control properties on these key blocks through eminent domain failed. As Market showrooms continued to replace resident-centered uses, one of the downtown's signature enterprises closed after almost seventy years in business. "Downtown is becoming all Furniture Market," complained the owner of High Point Cleaners and Hatters, who had grown up in the shop his father founded in 1919 when he emigrated from Greece via New York City.

"I don't know what happened," said resident Larry Diggs, one of the few people I spoke to who had followed Mendenhall's effort as it unfolded. When I asked Lovejoy about the Mendenhall eminent domain campaign, he was shocked. "I didn't know about it and 95 percent of the city doesn't know about it," he said.

"It's like, systematically, it was blocked," offered Diggs. "She was trying to catch it, just right before it took off," he added with an insight and interest I rarely saw in High Point. Not only real estate and furniture interests rallied against government regulation; residents and small retailers also had opposed Mendenhall's proposal. This exchange—the little retail shop owner imploring the city to leave all property owners alone—would be repeated for years to come. It represented unwavering allegiance to the philosophy of the unregulated market on the part of small property owners, either for its own sake or in the hope that the demand for showrooms would one day benefit them too. "It's big bad City Hall," Mendenhall said of this broad resistance to intervention.[44]

Mayor Smothers's "Magic Block" Charrette

During the 1990s, the Market burgeoned from six million to ten million square feet. Mendenhall, now heading the Chamber of Commerce, was among those calling for resident-centered space to be included in the plans to redevelop the seven-acre Magic Block. In her view, a resident-centered *component* (she conceded showrooms) could have been nearly anything: housing, retail, restaurants or cafés, professional offices, meeting space, or public space.[45] The Magic Block had been home to a Sears Roebuck store since 1967, but Sears was moving to the new Oak Hollow Mall. "It was a huge chunk of real estate smack dab in the middle" of the downtown, said real estate attorney Tom Terrell, and there was debate as to "what could that mean as a supplement to the Market or as some complementary use that would actually give us a chance to replace what furniture took away."

Mayor Becky Smothers, who had shared High Point's unique downtown real estate conundrum at a conference for the Mayors' Institute on City Design, an initiative of the National Endowment for the Arts, planned a High Point design charrette with some of the institute-affiliated architects and planners in August 1994. They included Richard Dagenhart, David Sawicki, and Douglas Allen of Georgia Tech; Grover Mouton of Tulane University; and David Crane of the University of South Florida. Smothers promised not to disclose her personal preference during the charrette, which took place in the art gallery of the High Point Theatre immediately adjacent to the Magic Block. But she did disclose that she was "fiercely protective of the Market."[46]

Residents also were excited about the "creative discussion" the charrette generated. "There was talk about a park, you know, some sort of creative greenspace, fun, recreational space," said Paul Siceloff. The planners emerged from the charrette with two possible development paths as well as a third suggestion to not intervene in the use of the space at all.

The first would have High Point University take the lead on developing a mixed Market–resident district. The second would give the lead to the City of High Point for a similar space that would include a Market transportation terminal. Dagenhart, an urban planner at the Georgia Tech School of Architecture, thought the public-led scheme was the most plausible plan. Crane, an architect, suggested that the space bridge the city's past and its present with an anchor such as a school for the industrial arts.

"It just had a dreamy sound to it," Terrell recalled, waving his hands airily as he spoke. "Everybody acted as though this was *their* moment to—through being in the room—to control or have an idea that changes High Point's destiny," he said. He included himself among the gullible participants who believed that a resident voice actually mattered in the solicitation process. "I think there was that sense that the city . . . was going to somehow be the muscle that would make something work," he recalled. "That there would be that connective tissue between idea and action." He did not see the writing on the wall at the time.

"Now I'm experienced enough as a land use and environmental attorney—and I hope wizened enough—to have thought about something that I did not think of then," Terrell added. "The city *never* tried to gain control by zoning it. I think that's probably because if the city had thought of it, they didn't have the backbone to do it. But until you downzone it to seize some control for the people wanting to come in, to then change it to a usable function? The city has no control," he explained. "We were kibitzers," Terrell concluded.

Siceloff concurred. Even at the charrette, Siceloff said he sensed "there was already some talk that the Market is going to snap that up." In retrospect, realtor Ed Price recognizes the importance of the invitation to stop and think. "Highest and greatest use would have been for showroom," said Price. He thought a charrette to question that dynamic as a community was the right approach. "That was probably the last chance to save downtown as a retail center," he added.

A new variable also emerged during this era, a "pull" of resident-centered uses that amplified their "push" from the downtown. The city, state, and federal governments were investing in road and utility infrastructure development in the greenfield of North High Point. The real estate market was structured so that resident-centered uses in the furniture district were now in competition with greenfield prices. Crane called these the city's "two warring forces." Price noted that for the retailer weighing the economic feasibility of a downtown location, it had become "a real stretch when you start thinking about what you pay per square foot for that land" compared with the greenfield.

In the common view, it was simple: the growing sprawl of North High Point was a natural, inevitable response to consumer demand. But consumer demand alone does not turn farms into subdivisions. Such conjectures leave out the agency that key decisionmakers were wielding behind the scenes. They give the misimpression that change is "legislated by historical circumstances rather than by the conscious collective action of individuals."[47] The Mendenhall and Smothers efforts marked two situations when visionary leadership could have explicitly communicated the alternative paths facing the city and thus illuminated a moment for decisive, collective action.

Immediately after the charrette, *Enterprise* editor Tom Blount wrote perceptively that it "will have little if any bearing on what eventually happens to the block" because the development would be determined by highest and best use. "That's how the free enterprise system works," he stated.[48] Blount, who would be a nuanced public voice for decades, understood why High Pointers "worship Market," but argued, "we need to take care of ourselves at the same time."[49] Crane agreed with this balanced approach, concerned with how "many people are not connecting" due to High Point's lack of community-building spaces.[50] The city's perspective was closest to urban planner Sawicki's. "It might be best just left as it is, to the furniture Market," he said. "I think you're going to be a bedroom community, folks, but revel in it."[51]

Without Market showroom investment in downtown High Point, the valorization of the greenfield as a new "bedroom community" would have likely produced a downtown rent gap large enough to warrant the return of local or regional investment to the city center. That might have resulted in more traditional gentrification akin to other North Carolina cities, bringing its own benefits and problems. Instead, Market showroom investors exploited the rent gap as it emerged, driving rents up. Growth leaders promoted the "common sense" that if showrooms were in demand, then the city should encourage showroom construction. "I don't think a dramatic change will occur imminently," Mayor Smothers stated just after the charrette in what appears today to be a massive understatement.[52] Six years later, the Showplace exhibition center and parking lot would consume the entire Magic Block.

The Downtown Improvement Committee Era (2000s)

The work of the Downtown Improvement Committee (DIC), which began in 1993, was originally aesthetic. "I'm not naive enough to think we can come up with grandiose plans of redeveloping downtown," a realtor with almost four decades of experience said at its inception. "We'd like to leave as good an impression as possible with our out-of-town visitors," he added.[53] His words show how peculiar High Point's situation had become. Similar committees in other communities during the 1990s were brainstorming ways to redevelop their downtown to attract visitors. This longtime realtor thought it "grandiose" to imagine a downtown for anyone *but* visitors.

After a hiatus of a few years, the city-sponsored DIC resumed meeting in April 1999 with the support of Mayor Smothers and chaired by local attorney Aaron Clinard. The owner of a downtown staple, Perkinson's Jewelers, had noted in 1993 that establishing a vibrant downtown would require not only the cooperation of resident- and Market-centered interests but also the "the [city] money and willpower to do it."[54] Absent that, he said, the committee would be limited to "pretty landscaping." When the DIC reconvened in 1999, it valued both approaches, calling them "functional" and "aesthetic."[55]

The DIC was officially a citizen committee of the City of High Point. Besides the jeweler mentioned, the committee's board of directors included representatives from banks, realty companies, restaurants, a financial firm, a law firm, the phone company, hotels, a stationery store, an architecture firm, and a construction company. The two furniture exhibition representatives on the board during these years (Joanna Easter from Showplace and Lisa Shankle from Chicago's MMPI) had a decidedly local bent. What I witnessed during DIC meetings I attended from 2002 to 2004 was middle-class and upper-middle-class professional residents working to cultivate a downtown street life that included residents and traditional tourists. Their most ambitious plan was beginning just as I arrived.

The DIC's Bold Air Rights Plan

The railroad that intersects downtown High Point was once the city's lifeblood. By the early 2000s, its below grade (i.e., depressed below street level), trash-littered tracks had become difficult to maintain. City leaders had long discussed these blocks at the center of the downtown. In fact, city leaders pitched a plan very similar to the DIC's ambitious idea in 1965 during the urban renewal era. In 2002, the city's Amtrak depot was undergoing a painstaking, nearly seven-million-dollar renovation.

Meanwhile, DIC chair Clinard had concluded that the ballooning furniture showroom footprint, by then the size of four Empire State Buildings in area, was completely off-limits to residents in the minds of both showroom owners and the new Market Authority. Residents generally considered themselves "materially and symbolically" excluded from this "landscape of power."[56] It would take a major stimulus to care about the downtown again. It was a seemingly intractable dilemma: a formidable yet ambiguous foe and few allies to fight it. In late 2002, a DIC member asked Clinard, "How do you convince high-end retailers to come to High Point unless there is a market [lowercase *m*] here already?"

"I guess you convince them that 'if you build it, they will come,'" Clinard responded. He believed that this would require "new real estate that might be considered off-limits to furniture showrooms."[57] Unlike Mendenhall, Clinard did not intend to confront existing showroom development but, remarkably, to craft a work-around solution: to "*create* developable land" for resident-centered purposes.[58] This off-limits real estate would allow other uses to develop—uses that, as he would say, "just couldn't afford the dirt" of showroom speculation. The property

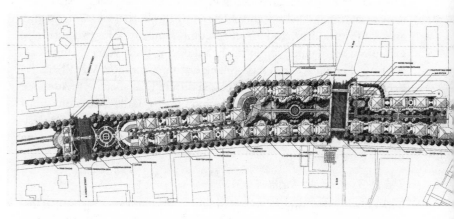

Rendering of the plan to "cover the tracks" for six blocks in downtown High Point in order to provide spaces dedicated to residents. Courtesy of landscape architect Perry Howard of North Carolina A&T University, with students Orient Au'Vang, Carrie Burkert-Kelly, Walter Royster, and Patricia Scudiere.

would be explicitly set aside for "purposes other than furniture related, such as retail, restaurants, entertainment, housing, and public space."[59] To attract shoppers, the new real estate would need enough resident-centered space to make it an instantly appealing destination.

This new real estate would come from the air rights of the city's depressed and exposed railroad tracks. Inspired by Chicago's Millennium Park, which was under construction at the time, Clinard imagined a pedestrian plaza that bisected Main Street, flanked on either side by retail establishments. Determined to establish his vision as plausible, Clinard led several contingents of city leaders, including Mayor Arnold Koonce, to visit the air rights projects of other cities and held promising exploratory meetings with the Georgia Southern and North Carolina railroads. Early on, the mayor, city manager, historic preservation chair, the newspaper, and Judy Mendenhall (just starting as the first president of the new public–private High Point Market Authority) all backed the proposal to cover the tracks.[60]

The city and the North Carolina Railroad split the cost of an extensive feasibility study to examine issues of overhead clearance, vibration, ventilation, and the possibility of a high-speed rail system.[61] It estimated the price to create buildable land in the railroad air rights at sixty-nine million to one hundred million dollars.[62] Absent a huge philanthropic gift, this would be a money-losing, government-funded, public–private

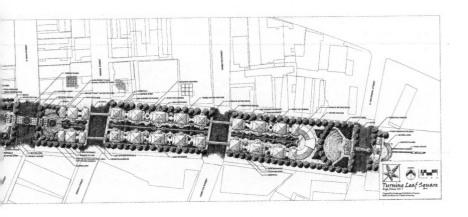

Turning Leaf Square
High Point, NC

partnership for the "public good" of a resident-centered downtown. The economic payoffs—if they ever came—would be long down the line. Lacking political and social will to see the Market-centered downtown as a problem in need of intervention, the proposal failed. High Point had an attractive, clean, fully leased downtown. The idea of pinning well over one hundred million dollars on the hope of attracting visitors that most showroom owners wanted to keep out seemed quixotic.

The DIC's Aesthetic Campaigns

As we walked past the messy downtown windows in 2010, community college business professor and resident Waymon Martin wondered aloud if "the city could *demand* in a nice way" that exhibitors leave the showrooms tidy. They had, I responded. After suffering the defeat of the functional railroad air rights project, the DIC led a series of initiatives to improve the aesthetics of the downtown for both marketgoers and residents. Not surprisingly, initial interest in these innocuous campaigns was strong. Who would resist "beautification"? To the degree that growth leaders can focus on symbolic issues, they are able to deflect public scrutiny from the major (usually boring) decisions that truly affect growth.[63]

"When you go down Main Street, you see closed-up and vacant buildings except during Market, and then it looks great," said entrepreneur Coy Willard at a DIC meeting in early 2003, sounding nearly identical to Mayor Mendenhall in 1986. Willard had a much more conservative goal, however. He wondered whether exhibitors, when departing their space for the six-month inter-Market period, "could be encouraged to leave it set up." For decades, said marketing professional Sarah Simpkins, leaders have been "trying to get across to all of these private land owners: 'you may not live here, but please make your space always reputable.'"

For the 2004 Spring Market, the DIC sent beautification campaign letters to the merchandising administration of firms with downtown showrooms politely reasoning that a well-kept storefront during inter-Market periods "leaves our city looking like the Furniture Capital of the World" and serves as an "opportunity to market your company while you are away." The committee asked firms to consider leaving a "prominent display," of their product line in their storefront, possibly lit up. "Our goal is to make it look like someone's home," a DIC member said at one meeting.

At another meeting in 2004, Shankle reported on the subcommittee's follow-up visits to the individual showrooms during the Market. "It was an interesting experience," she told the group as Clinard showed Mayor Smothers the initial letter. To a room full of knowing laughter, Shankle deadpanned what the follow-up visits revealed: "Whoever had made the commitment failed to follow through with the last person who was going to be there," she said. Showroom staff had no incentive to invest effort in following through—neither carrot nor stick.

Smothers, then serving her second stint as mayor, suggested taking photographs of messy windows and including the photographs with a note. She dryly offered some possible passive-aggressive text: "This is yours. We are so sorry that your product is not being displayed in a way that is complimentary to your line."

What did display matter, though, when "no one" was seeing it? Furniture firms seemed to understand the interests of High Point residents during the "days that do not matter" in the same way that a developer bent on gentrification sees the interests of residents in a pre-gentrification neighborhood. That is, with nothing currently of value on the table but the developer's plans, everyone should be grateful for the development these plans bring—regardless of the ramifications.

A second aesthetic campaign focused on plaques and statues to insert residents' place within the city's sought-after identity as a global downtown. Clinard would repeatedly emphasize that the DIC's campaign was to reestablish the "substance" of High Pointers. Reestablishing cultural markers documents "we are here" to visitors; they state that "before you come and after you are gone, this is our space too."[64] One could argue, then, that this campaign sought to slow the "momentum towards the total disempowerment" of residents—and their originality or vernacular—through the "reconstruction of place-based meaning."[65]

This interpretation may overstate the resistance represented within the plaques and statues. Part of the goal was also to establish the city's significance by employing the most "worthy" of local vernacular to the eyes that matter.[66] This process of making local vernacular digestible is often understood in the present context through the lens of gentrification and cultural displacement (e.g., the marketing of Black neighborhoods to white gentrifiers).[67] Landscapes intended for outsiders can "pose significant problems for people's identity, which has historically been founded on place."[68] Here, the audience was not new middle-class residents but middle- and upper-middle-class marketgoers. "To have sculpture changes the face of how a community looks," said Easter, Showplace's chief and chair of the statuary subcommittee. "It is a more enlightened look," she added.

Although Clinard was happy to settle for plaques and statues for the moment, his real interest was trained on something more functional. The DIC had observed a design trend favoring dense, pedestrian-friendly, diverse, mixed-use neighborhoods. Andrés Duany's idea of new urbanism and Richard Florida's creative class notion were finding their way to North Carolina's city leaders. Florida had just held a high-profile series of meetings in Greensboro, where plans were unfolding for a large-scale, new urbanist project in its Southside neighborhood.

In a DIC meeting in 2004, then, Clinard wanted to clarify that a vibrant downtown required more than statues and plaques. "Mayor Smothers, I will tell you this," he began. "This committee has voted to recommend to council to strongly pursue the idea of the downtown development zone." He said this had been his goal "early on, since we organized this committee." Qualifying the "development" in development zone with a tentative laugh, he clarified his announcement to Smothers: "not *showrooms,* but *other* types of development." This downtown development zone would involve instituting an incentive program encouraging social benefits, a departure from the narrowly defined addition of manufacturing jobs that had historically been the city's main priority.

The Party on the Plank Era (2000s and 2010s)

"I think that each new generation is going to see blind spots about the generation before," observed Rev. Lovejoy, thinking about the perception that the downtown excludes most residents. "And they're gonna kind of rebel against those blind spots," he concluded. One of the well-intended cultural undercurrents driving gentrification is a response to the twentieth century's dismantling of communities and its accompanying fixation on exchange value. In the dense urban neighborhoods celebrated by Jane Jacobs, some thinkers saw hope for a "subjectively effective present" that privileged the use values of a community.[69] One way to challenge the dysfunctional obsession with exchange value in a place, Lovejoy reasoned, was to have residents *experience* its use value. He believed that changing the city's dynamics of power entailed first removing the psychic walls that High Pointers had erected.

Lovejoy Takes on Community Disenfranchisement

When I happened upon a Magic Block party under the Mendenhall Transportation Terminal in 2010, I had not yet met Lovejoy. It was one of the most surreal experiences of my time in High Point, perhaps second only to my first Market opening. I was so giddy at the sight of the unexpected activity in the downtown—it seemed like a mirage—that I actually considered moving back to High Point. The idea was rash, but it shows how deeply what I was seeing affected me.

Reflective and deliberate, the soft-spoken Lovejoy explained that as an "observer of people, places, and culture," he set out to systematically research the "soul of the city." He dubbed this informal research "pneumagraphics" and felt it uncovered a recurring lament: a "desire for life" in the city's downtown. His very intentional campaign to immerse himself in all things High Point began when he arrived in 2007. He joined the Chamber of Commerce and completed its leadership institute, he registered for the Rotary Club, and he started working at the YMCA. "I've always had a fascination with places, the ethos of a place, the personality of a place, the soul of the place," he told me shortly after we met in 2010. And High Point, he concluded, was a place in need of a party. "The time that there *is* a big party in downtown High Point is during Furniture Market," he explained. "All the stops are pulled out."

Recalling my own time as a young single person new to High Point, this sentiment hit home. It stung to watch a dead city—a downtown I perceived as my home, where I lived, worked, and often wandered—come to life strictly for the benefit of outsiders. I observed revelry, I heard music, I watched people of various ethnicities from all over the world, dressed to the nines, rushing to their next destinations. Before I had a pass giving me permission to stay, I used to get asked to leave these hot spots. Later, I was serving as the front desk clerk at Showplace during Market when a resident wandered in and said, "I have always loved this building; I just want to see what it looks like from the inside." That responsibility of dealing with the "intruder" was mine. "When intruders enter" the frontstage, as Erving Goffman explains the performance of everyday life, they can sometimes be "quite unceremoniously asked to stay out."[70] (I allowed him to gape for a moment, but, conforming to my perceived role, not to enter.)

Sally Bringier, a Market leader with local roots, talked about her desire to host parties for residents during the exposition. "We've been trying to do a community day of the Market. Like letting people into the showrooms and seeing what we really, really do," she said, describing her idea for a Market tour and "hot dog roast." "But I will *tell* you, we get pushback from the buildings—*big* time," she added. Resident showroom tours had been attempted before; in the late 1970s, for instance, they were made available by raffle.[71]

Lovejoy's therapy for High Pointers did not include the oft-heard suggestion to open Market showrooms to residents. His effort was called Party on the Plank. The name drew on High Point's history as the "highest point" on the geological survey of what was then believed to be the longest plank road in existence. He conceived of this temporary "town square" as a "cultural convergence," bringing together art, food, retail, and music into one place, along with what he called a "Vision Center," which would solicit community input on key issues. Just as the Market created a temporary visitor-centered city, Lovejoy sought to engender a temporary resident-centered city through what some call *tactical urbanism,* a strategy that employs inexpensive grassroots projects intended to make a place more livable for residents and, in so doing, to promote more lasting change.

Lovejoy Takes on the Tidal Wave

"Why did you choose downtown, the middle of the Market district, for Party on the Plank?" I asked Lovejoy.

"I think for people—in my mind—downtown is psychologically hostile territory," he explained. Lovejoy intended the party to help residents overcome the "psychological barrier" that made them perceive the downtown "as the area that they are not allowed to go into," the area where "there's nothing for them." He believed that mindset not only breeds apathy in residents but also reinforces an "almost toxic business environment." In his opinion, "Business follows people and people follow . . . a sense of life, a sense of vitality." High Point, he said, lacked all the above.

"When [residents] try to start a business in that area," he declared, "you're asking [a consumer] to come to a place where their overall perception is 'that's not for me, it's for this $1.2 billion interest.'" Lovejoy raised the example of a coffee shop owner who invests $40,000 and then hopes residents will visit. Continued Lovejoy, "Forty thousand dollars versus $1.2 billion . . . I mean, come on. You're fighting a tidal wave to try to get people to come down there."

Lovejoy saw a rational descent into apathy, as he called it. "I don't like being rejected, I am tired of resenting," he reasoned, "so that is what leads to apathy." But what are High Pointers apathetic toward? "Anything happening in downtown High Point," he answered. This reflex of apathy is self-preserving, said Lovejoy and others, stemming from decades of experience. In civic affairs, explained politician Bernita Sims, residents stopped believing that "*whatever* it is you're doing, it's for me.'"

The place where Lovejoy set his sights on creating a center of life and vitality was the Magic Block, which he noted was "*designed* to be . . . a town square," albeit for the Market. Using the adjacent Mendenhall Market Terminal as a temporary band shell delivered a symbolically forceful statement reasserting local vernacular into High Point's glossy global landscape. He augmented such symbolic statements with a more explicit philosophy that he articulated through a periodic guest column in the *Enterprise*.

With billions of dollars in play and only three to four months of truly "non-Market" times each year, the space for critical reflection is minimal. This is what Lovejoy was working to inject. "There's a lot of pride that we have the Market, that it brings a lot of business to town, that we are the world market, [that] it's an international furniture market," community college administrator Janette McNeill said. "The other side is that Market hurts us," she continued. "Everybody knows that it's not good for the overall health of the city." Nothing rallies family loyalty, however, like a common goal and a common opponent; High Point has had decades of both. "The moment Market's here, we've got to clean up, we've got to spruce it up, we put out the welcome mat, we get the buttons that we can wear and there's a lot of civic pride in our Market," McNeill added.

"Here's a guy who . . . didn't have any power," said resident and retired furniture industry professional David Williams of Lovejoy. "And he was able to paint a picture that brought people together. Now, why was he able to do it and other people didn't do it or couldn't do it?" Williams wondered. To me, the answer was simple: the more I lived in High Point, the more normalized its arrangement became to me. Lovejoy, however, remained committed from the outset to calling out what he understood as abnormal. "The only thing I fear is that Elijah will get smart one of these days and leave," Williams worried.

The Party on the Plank attracted twenty-six sponsors that included local radio stations, Krispy Kreme Doughnuts, and Budweiser and featured local food favorites such as Brewster's Real Ice Cream. The Vision Center table at the event provided a place for residents to discuss the future of High Point. Clinard and Wendy Fuscoe staffed one Vision Center table, where they solicited residents to answer the question: "What is the first thing we should do to create a place in town for pedestrian friendly shopping, dining, and living—a place that is urban in style and inviting for people?"

Sentiment versus Capital

"They want a downtown, like, like when? Tell me. Was it when you were a little child? You want a downtown like that?" Smothers asked. "The thing that is a concern—I guess for any public official who has been in office for a period of time and seen their community grow so—is the challenge of trying to get a cohesive dream and not one that just seems to be for my backyard," she added. In her view, such a "cohesive dream" was apparently untenable, leading me to ask her, "If a downtown is a social heart of a place, what is High Point's downtown?" Replied Smothers: "I don't think we have a central place. But to me, that's not a disgrace. And I'm not trying to put a spin on it. Because I think we've got lots of High Point heart," she continued, shifting the meaning of "heart" from geography to sentiment. "It's just in different places."

Like the proponents of a resident-centered downtown, she listed the various sections of High Point whose disaggregation in her estimation constituted an asset rather than a liability. "In this era of people who move around and don't have those deep southern roots anymore, I'm not sure that the mythical heart that everybody is looking for isn't just in their imagination," she concluded.

Smothers's critique included a class-based perspective as well: that not all social life, after all, involves "seeing and being seen" in the restaurants and public spaces envisioned by leaders looking for a "living room." "It's kind of where you want to spend your life," she said. "Do you want to spend it at a street festival? Or would you rather have a neighborhood party? I don't know. Whatever trips your trigger."

I asked Wagner about Mayor Smothers's suggestion that High Point did not need a center, that a polynucleated city without a "mythical" living room was just fine. "You see, you asking me this question says a lot," Wagner answered. "Because the reason we are talking about and planning all of these different areas is because the elephant in the room is *downtown*." Wagner's use of the word *planning* is worth noting. What some would call "natural" was to Wagner also planning, merely with different priorities. "All of these things we're talking about *ought* to be downtown," he said. "But they're not. So we're forced to decide, where do we put an arts center? If we're going to build a new police department, where is it going to be? If we're going to have a park, where's the park going to be?

"That's not to say that you can't have neighborhood business centers that essentially serve those neighborhoods," Wagner continued. "But as far as a place where everyone is going to feel comfortable coming? I don't think we have that unless we do something about our downtown. I think we're going to continue to further divide ourselves into groups: by income or by race or by ethnicity.

"The thing about a downtown is that it's your city's front porch. Everyone in the city feels an ownership to their downtown . . . It belongs to everybody. It *should* belong to everybody." Wagner was speaking about a downtown's unique potential to unite what had become, at best, a very weak version of a polynucleated city. Architect Peter Freeman agreed. "The real important aspect of what can happen in downtown is to create connectivity from the other sections of the city," he said.

When I showed a photograph from Lovejoy's Party on the Plank to residents, it was always jarring to them, whether they were familiar with his event or not. "They got Market going on!" said Trish Perkins with feigned excitement, before I told her that this was actually a Lovejoy party for residents. "Really?" she replied. "That's where our hope lies," said resident and shuttle driver John Butt, discussing the downtown event. "They're making memories."

"Now *that's* what I like to see," agreed Glenn Chavis. "To me that's like New Orleans, that's like Charleston, South Carolina, like Savannah, Georgia. Places I enjoy going to. Asheville's gotten into it big time. As long as it's diverse in terms of variety."

At Party on the Plank, local vendors and residents take over the Mendenhall Transportation Terminal.

Given High Point's distinct history—really, the distinct history of the South—"the move to create a core city population and nurture place identity . . . may indeed provide a welcome antidote to the sprawling, deracinated character of regional urbanization in the past half century."[72] Of course, this was not yet a common sentiment. Once while I was interviewing residents in City Hall, I noticed a city official glancing at me. He asked me to come and speak with him, so I poked my head into his office.

"It ain't happening," he said, dismissing those who envisioned a resident-centered downtown as "dreamers." Explained the official: "This is the goose that is laying the golden eggs." His sentiment echoed the long-standing attitude that nobody would be so foolhardy as to upset the goose dispensing the good fortune. "High Point's good," the official repeatedly assured me, suggesting that it didn't need my meddling.

In the end, as we can see clearly in the charrette and the Downtown Improvement Committee, residents' power has been "essentially consultative" and devalued within battles that "frequently pit capital against sentiment."[73] The mechanisms established to "mollify urban residents' desire for community control" have been either too weak to take on the dominant development strategy or are "subverted at higher levels of decision."

Sentiment versus *capital* captures the framing of the lopsided mobilizations for a resident-centered downtown we saw in this chapter, efforts that employed activism, municipal power, civic engagement, and grassroots intervention in the built environment. In the next chapter, I examine a public–private partnership whose efforts were founded on urban planning, but the response of growth leaders will be similar.

Despite their very different orientations, all of these resident-centered efforts would ultimately be portrayed by their adversaries as naive sentimentality promoted by a small number of dreamers meddling in business and governmental affairs beyond their grasp. Community college business professor Martin saw something different. "Some younger people are going to start running for city council," he predicted, "so you can't be one-dimensional."

9

The City Project and the Pursuit of a Living Room

A Stack of Plans

Rosa Mae's Cafe on Main Street was surrounded by showrooms. It was time for the restaurant to succumb, owner Jim Davis decided. "If you're gonna have a retail district, you need to have a *retail district*," he said sitting in his new Rosa Mae's location in Thomasville, ten miles away from his original spot in downtown High Point. "You need to stick to it . . . You know the Belk building? It turned into a showroom. The Wright building? Showroom."

As I walked past the shuttered storefronts of Rosa Mae's and Perkinson's Jewelers with twenty-something resident Nic Ruden, he voiced one version of the High Point common sense interpretation of Market regulation. "You can't . . . force [businesses] to do things that they shouldn't be forced to do," Ruden said, "but I think there's certain things that you need to have as part of a viable approach." Looking at the recently vacated Rosa Mae's, he unwittingly repeated Mayor Judy Mendenhall's argument from 1986: "Small things like this should switch over to other uses than showrooms."

By the 2000s, High Point was confronting the paradox of deregulation whereby "it failed once it succeeded, becoming the problem where once it was the solution."[1] *Is it incumbent on government to fix the problems that past deregulation had created?* Celebrity urbanist Andrés Duany seemed to think this a reasonable expectation. "Because government policy has played a major role in getting us to where we are today," Duany argues in his 2000 book, "it can also help us to recover."[2] He added, "The promotion of community may seem to be an obvious role for the public sector, especially at the local level; some would suggest that it is the public sector's primary responsibility."[3]

The Downtown Improvement Committee "worked hard for several years to pursue improvements to the downtown"; this was the assessment of the Walker Collaborative, a Nashville firm led by planner Philip Walker that drafted the city's 2007 master plan. However, concluded Walker, the DIC's efforts couldn't work because "it has never had the authority or resources—financial or human—to implement its ideas. Consequently, this committee should be transformed into a stronger entity."[4]

This charge provided the impetus for what ultimately became the City Project, a public–private partnership created by the city to carry out the master plan of the Walker Collaborative (hereafter referred to as the Walker Plan), which called for strict regulation of the Market. The first and most important task for this new organization, headed by engineer, humanitarian, and nonprofit leader Wendy Fuscoe, was to pass what came to be known as the "Market Overlay District." The Overlay Plan, the first campaign that is followed in this chapter, was an attempt by civic leaders to harness the "wild animal let out of the barn," as observers described it. Their goal was straightforward: separate the internationalized sector of furniture real estate from the local sector of resident-centered real estate in order to resurrect local usage.

The second campaign outlined in this chapter emanated from the Walker Plan, which is not to say the plan endorsed it. The Walker Plan had noted "a 'de facto' downtown had evolved along North Main Street."[5] It advocated for the development of this northern "uptown corridor," as the plan called it, to "provide the community with an alternative to" and even blend with the central business district one mile south once the CBD began to "function . . . with retail, restaurants, services, offices, housing, and institutional uses."[6] The City Project led this effort as well, hoping that this neighborhood might become a substitute, rather than a complementary, downtown.

A plan by Duany, invited to High Point by the City Project, is the third campaign taken up in this chapter. Although divided about the development of Uptowne, High Pointers' growing sense that they needed a "living room" was powerful enough for the City Project to raise the $410,000 necessary to bring Duany and his Miami architecture and planning firm Duany-Plater-Zyberk (DPZ) to town in 2012. High Point

University, the city, and the local realtors association contributed half the fee, with business leaders and individuals providing the other half.[7]

"I see a stack of revitalization plans that have never been enacted," Jay Wagner said at the time, trying to remain optimistic about yet another new plan. "My fear," Wagner continued, "is that he will come and we will spend money, and he will tell us something that we don't want to hear, and nothing will happen."

Caging the Goose with the Overlay District

The Walker Plan stated that an approach as drastic as Aaron Clinard's plan to cover the tracks would be "a more critical project" if it "was High Point's only option for achieving a bonafide downtown in light of the furniture showrooms' domination."[8] Rather than create new land, the Walker Plan recommended putting the power of government behind a zoning effort to take back the downtown.

Each time I ran into Clinard, ever the stalwart advocate, he wanted to schedule a realtor to show me a unit in one of the upscale residential loft renovations primarily used for Market rentals. The problem remained, however, as politician Bernita Sims noted, "you can't expect people to live downtown and not put [in] the things that allow them to live downtown." While some "pioneers" move into environments with low amenities, downtown High Point lacked the other factors that usually attract such a group—namely, a low price. I felt invested enough in the cause of a resident-centered downtown that I would have considered supporting High Point by purchasing a unit. However, the real estate prices were not low enough to account for the downtown's inconveniences or dearth of public and private amenities; they revealed only the area's centrality and value to the furniture world. Unless I rented out the unit to marketgoers, owning it would be like throwing money away.

The Internationalized Rent and Local Rent

The Walker Plan pinpointed two of the same blocks as Mendenhall had in 1986: those on both sides of Main Street immediately north of the railroad tracks. It proposed to create a boundary beyond which "new showrooms would be prohibited in the future . . . to avoid this area becoming a single-use area that lacks around-the-clock vitality."[9] Walker foresaw the boundary as the engine for the development of a local real estate market within downtown's global real estate market, one that would be "accessible to restaurants and shops" for residents.[10] Clinard called these two markets, for residents and for the furniture industry, the "real" and the "false" markets, respectively.

The "internationalized sector" is a local economic sector of intense interest to buyers and sellers around the world and thus disconnected from other, more localized sectors within the same city.[11] The resulting price inflation is seemingly unfounded or "false." Explained by the Walker Plan, the "inflated real estate prices driven by . . . [showroom] real estate speculation . . . unnecessarily discourages beneficial land uses."[12]

"Landlords would rather have it sit empty than lease it for a cheaper rate," *Enterprise* editor Tom Blount noted. This speculation resulted in the "warehousing" or "mothballing" of properties, creating what Lee Burnette, the city's planning director, called "an edge of uncertainty" where landowners indefinitely postponed making any improvements while they waited for the showroom footprint to expand. Some buildings caught in this limbo of uncertainty had great potential for resident-centered usage. "An analysis of land rents . . . showed that clearly people were holding out for the potential of a Market showroom," Burnette confirmed.

Market speculation was going "outward rather than upward," he said, devouring the area. It made sense to "force it to go a little more upward" to leave some of the downtown area for High Pointers. But "force" meant regulation and proactive planning, and these were fighting words.

An anti-regulation argument common in debates over neighborhood development emerged in High Point. It goes like this: if all these vocal people really cared enough about the community, then they should "put their money where their mouth is" and privilege a restaurant over a showroom. People only say such things, Blount snickered, when dreaming up uses for somebody else's money. Yes, he believed High Pointers could ultimately support resident-centered businesses in the downtown, and, yes, he recognized that these businesses would be more beneficial to High Point in the mid- and long-term. But that did not mean it would *ever* be in anyone's self-interest to start a resident-centered business in isolation. For an individual to walk into what Elijah Lovejoy called a "tidal wave" without a large, coordinated, trustworthy plan would be foolish.

Gabriele Natale showed a sincere desire to open his renovated portion of the old Adams-Millis plant to the community, as seen in chapter 4.

Although his isolated efforts were doomed to fail, what if the third place this cosmopolitan High Pointer desired for the community had been launched in coordination with other synergistic efforts or incentivized in some other way? Over the years, several developers would eye the Adams-Millis plant. Fuscoe discussed her experience with one developer. "He was interested in turning them into lofts—loft apartments with retail at the bottom," she recalled. "We took him around and he's like 'what else you got down here?'" The answer was clear: nothing. And, as Duany concludes, "No one activity can flourish in the absence of any other since they are all mutually reinforcing."[13]

The allure of the city's greenfield corridor for business, residential, and office development also had to be considered, now with two additional decades of infrastructure since it was identified as a "warring force" in the Smothers charrette in 1994. "Why would a [resident-centered] developer buy land when they could go out [to North High Point] for a third or a fourth of the price?" asked realtor Ed Price. "And they don't have to tear down a whole building. And they don't have to worry about contamination," he added.

Fuscoe also shared the story of a potential year-round retail tenant who tried to lease a property in the showroom district, but was turned down because the owner—someone who favored a resident-centered downtown in theory—decided to wait instead for the low wear-and-tear Market tenants. "And she's a High Pointer born and bred," Fuscoe added. Similarly, Audie Cashion was frustrated by the year-round, resident-centered uses that often got "squashed" during the time when he was a realtor. I asked Cashion if he had used his role to promote the resident-centered, market-centered balance he supported. "Um, my *heart* is that," he told me, then added, "Really, my fiduciary responsibility as a real estate broker is to work for the highest and best price for my client."

The Walker Plan centered on a sustained, systemic questioning of exchange values' "domination" so that hopes of pro-resident uses were not left up to the good-heartedness—charity, really—of individual agents like the property owner, the landlord, the realtor, or the condo buyer. Most small economic players do not have the financial flexibility to readily sacrifice short-term revenue for their business or compromise their household budget in the name of unspecified, long-term community well-being.

The Rise and Fall of Walker's Overlay District

When the City Project moved forward with the Walker Plan, the *Enterprise* published four editorials in firm support. In this battle over the future development of the Market area, Blount took on the role of mediator or diplomat. No longer simply a mouthpiece for the growth machine, the paper endorsed the tack John Logan and Harvey Molotch called "restraining the short-term profiteers in the interest of more stable, long-term, and properly planned growth."[14]

The Walker team approached Market regulation cautiously. As Burnette explained, they knew that Market would be tough "to tackle, and wrestle, and hold on to, and control." The Walker Plan proposed a mixed-use district made up of space for showrooms, residential, office, and retail (perhaps on the ground floor of showrooms). The Walker Plan recognized that any proposal proclaiming "no showrooms past this point" would face a huge backlash. However, the committee overseeing the overlay proposal nevertheless wanted to boldly establish its commitment to a firm boundary that would prohibit showrooms. "That was a mistake," Wagner said in hindsight.

In September 2009, the city council approved boundaries for the overlay district, much to the chagrin of attending property owners with buildings outside the district. Mayor Smothers would not sign off on the plan. The city council clarified that concessions would be made for showrooms in the "edge of uncertainty." Those currently in showroom use would have the right to expand, and, also, a strong grandfather clause allowed them to cease use for two years before losing their property to resident-centered use. The two-year-use window reflected "concern because of the recession" at that time, said Burnette.

The concessions were not enough to appease opponents. "The perception was from the beginning that we're building a fence around the showrooms and anyone that's outside of that is screwed," observed Wagner. "In a perfect world for a planner, you take a magic marker and say 'inside this line is showroom, outside is retail,'" explained Price from the realtor's perspective. But "that doesn't mean that private enterprise is going to follow and build boutiques and restaurants and bars outside that red line," he added.

Meanwhile, Wagner, Clinard, and Fuscoe continued to shepherd their idea through the process, attending planning and zoning as well as city council meetings. During that time, said Wagner, "the opposition [was] probably five to ten property owners and tenants who were in the fringe areas." Some of these were mothballing property owners who "anticipated someday *that* being their 401(k): that they would cash out, go and retire, and sell their property for a showroom," Burnette said. Showroom was the "only viable option they saw," he said, and they needed to fight. Market showroom realtor and strategist Ivan Garry agreed. "I had some people that had property listed and the only real chance that they could ever sell that property would be for a showroom," he said. "And if you say that *no showroom* could be built there?!" He let his question answer itself.

Wagner anticipated negotiations with such stakeholders. "Not *one* of them ever said 'we don't want the Market overlay district,'" he recalled. They did not care about the resident-centered boundary as long as they were in the showroom area. "I said this in all of the different venues that we had—that's *fine* with us. We don't mind if you bring in [an excluded] property, that's fine. Just expand the boundary line," he continued. "But what we want," Wagner said with emphasis, "is that *boundary line* so that from henceforth we can say to [potential] retailers 'look, there are not going to be any more furniture Market showrooms here.'" As the back-and-forth dragged into December, the *Enterprise* warned the council to stop "machinating" and "get on with . . . approving creation of the overlay district."[15]

Recollections of the January 2010 vote provoked still-raw emotions from those involved. "So, we did not even go to the last city council meeting when the decision was gonna be made because we had been told that Lee Burnette's office had been instructed to expand the boundary lines," Wagner explained. "Every other vote all the way through the plan had been unanimous in supporting everything the plan had asked for."

No one fully grasped how the efforts of a local interior decorator with a strong allegiance to the Market—and to the free market—would influence the process. The decorator had contacted furniture showroom owners who lived outside High Point to rally resistance to the project. "The people who were able to mobilize effectively, the people who filled the room, were furniture showroom owners, furniture showroom representatives, furniture showroom lawyers," explained Lovejoy. "The room was basically filled with some local downtown property owners, but [also] a lot of out-of-town interests," he continued. "At one point during the debate, John Faircloth . . . asked the question: 'is there anybody in the room, in City Hall Chambers, anybody here who is present to speak in favor of the Market overlay district?' And there was dead silence in the room. And that was the moment that the debate turned. He turned to somebody and said 'if there's nobody here to support it, I'm not even sure why we're doing it,'" Lovejoy recounted.

Wagner regretted not attending the meeting. "Had we been there, we would've asked them just to table it for a while, study a little more, and come back with something better rather than voting the whole thing down," he said.

Instead, Michael Pugh, a member of the city council, told those in attendance: "As far as I'm concerned, abolish the whole overlay and let the market [lowercase *m*] dictate where showrooms are."[16]

"I agree with Mr. Pugh," Mayor Smothers declared. "I think the market will decide where the Market needs to be."[17] Applause filled the room.

"The Market overlay debate was a glimpse into . . . the battle of the reversing of the tidal wave" of downtown development, noted Lovejoy. Disagreeing with its own unscientific poll of its readership, the *Enterprise* published a scathing editorial after the defeat. "City council just didn't have the stomach for pushing something like that through," Blount told me. "And now the property is just too expensive for anybody to do something with, so it's just going to sit."

Long the champion of growth, the *Enterprise* failed to rally a community that was unmotivated to fight. "The groundwork wasn't laid for them to care," said Lovejoy. "In reality, they've already moved on. They've already gone to the Palladium, they've already gone to Greensboro, they've already gone on to Winston-Salem, so what we're talking about is reversing twenty-five years of tide flowing away. It's hard to turn back twenty-five years of the tide of being evacuated."

Growth machine theory anticipates that for "local individuals and groups with only weak resources," the weight of *past* decisions and "the routines they imply" establishes "the terms for adjustments that must be made—however unhealthy, inegalitarian, or otherwise troubling these adjustments are."[18] As we have seen here, they "are further ratified through the assumption that others will presume and act" in step with these unhealthy adjustments to injustice in the *present*.[19] Social structure affects *future* actions and perceptions because out of these adjustments come places, rules, norms, and so forth that "impose upon us ways of thinking and doing which reinforce existing patterns of social life."[20]

The Free Market Philosophy of Unfettered Control

One New York City stakeholder made an argument against the overlay that particularly struck Lovejoy. "'If you pass this plan, High Point is going to lose its reputation and advantage for being a business-friendly place. The one advantage you have is that people don't have to worry about all of the baggage and restrictions when they come to High Point,'" Lovejoy recounted.

It was remarkable to me to hear this; it was exactly how I had first learned of High Point ten years earlier. At that time, Manhattan showroom owners saw in High Point a government that would privilege the protection of prime space and the principle of "highest and best use" more than New York City. "It's the rare moment that you get to have an outside perspective on your own city, your own culture," said Lovejoy. "It's sad, because it's a nice way of saying 'we want to do whatever we want, to take advantage of whatever we want to take advantage of, without your interference.' And it just means there's nobody strong enough to resist that," he added.

When prime land becomes subject to regulation, we can expect stakeholders to argue that the resulting context will not be malleable enough to do business.[21] Within High Point, this argument for maintaining malleability has had three components. First, the current arrangement of malleability is *natural*. Second, this arrangement is in a *state of equilibrium*. Third, agents who unwisely compromise this equilibrium are High Point's main threat. That is, if growth leaders can successfully *fight interference*, the downtown will function properly.

As I discussed the overlay proceedings with County Commissioner Bruce Davis over a cup of coffee, I realized that I had wrongly assumed he had been in favor of the overlay's regulation. The Democrat's words echoed that narrative. "A building sitting there that's paying premium tax and rent that no one is using? That's probably not a bad thing," he told me. "My objection was—and I made it known to the city council—that with the natural growth of the Market, that's *natural*," Davis explained. "Then you're trying to do something that's unnatural, trying to put something *else* in there. You could throw off the entire balance of what really should be a blessing. If it's got that much of an economic impact, why fool with it? Leave it alone and count it as a blessing."

The sentiment underlying Mayor Mendenhall's unsuccessful 1986 effort was that fiddling with showroom development was unwise during a time of economic growth because "anything that hurts the exhibitors hurts High Point."[22] The sentiment in 2010, a time of national economic decline, was that regulating in an era of contraction was more reckless still. "They felt it wasn't the right time to do it because the economy was so bad," Wagner said. "But my feeling was 'when is the right time to do it?' Do you do it when the economy is booming and they're building new showrooms and you try to hold them down?" It was the *regulation dilemma* again. But if the city buckled just because the public–private partnership it chartered to limit Market growth faced a group that "brought pitchforks and banged pots," as he put it, then how could regulation *ever* work? "To me, that's a complete lack of political courage and leadership," Wagner added. "There's the natural tendency to not want to tell people what they can do with their property—and I understand that," he continued. "You've got to have people who are going to do what's right for the city and believe in what they're doing and believe in their vision and understand that what they're doing is bigger than their politics."

Lovejoy noted that the local owners at the hearing came to speak against the overlay. "So it wasn't 'locals versus big city.' It was pretty much everybody against the idea. And even the people who *were* arguing for revitalization downtown? They weren't arguing in favor of the Market overlay district." To my great surprise, many of the observers who staunchly opposed the showrooms' domination of the downtown were also against the overlay.

"You can't let these showrooms go here and here and here and here and then say 'Y'all can't be here anymore. You have to come back *here* now.' How dumb is *that?* . . . If they wanted it to be encapsulated, they should have done that in the beginning," said one longtime critic of the city government's passivity in regard to showrooms.

And Rosa Mae's owner Jim Davis had the same attitude: "You've already let it happen. It's too late. You can't turn it back."

"I think it would have been pretty devastating to the Market. It's kind of a wild animal that you can't really enclose," agreed Sarah Simpkins, a resident-centered advocate and former showroom leader. "The cow is already out of the barn," echoed Cashion.

"I don't say I would necessarily agree that the Market should take over the whole town—build Chinese buildings everywhere, you know?" explained Trish Perkins. "But if it's growing and thriving, there's no way it's going to work. The forces of capitalism are too powerful to make the Market shrink when it isn't already shrinking."

Fleeing the Goose with the Uptowne Plan

When leaders of a political fight face sustained resistance, it implies a particular set of calculations they must make. These calculations relate to the amount of time they have invested, the success they perceive to be possible, and the costs they have incurred. The costs can be quite personal: the loss of time for other pursuits, the effects on physical and mental health, the lack of attention to family responsibilities, the loss of income or savings, and so on. *Do I have the power to succeed? Should I use my agency to fight a different battle? Will my stubborn resistance pay off?*

After the overlay campaign died, Clinard said that it was like he was "beating [his] head against a wall," both on the Downtown Improvement Committee and with its successor the City Project. With the defeat of the Market overlay district, City Project director Fuscoe and chair Clinard developed a twist on the Walker Plan's advocacy for "uptown."

The Uptowne Plan Becomes "Plan A"

"We did all we can do with plaques and statues," Clinard remarked wryly of his work with the DIC. "One of the reasons that I am still involved in this," he said in his office after the overlay defeat, "is because I think we now have the plan to be able to create—for lack of a better term—a substitute downtown. I don't think we are ever going to be able to reclaim what we call the traditional downtown."

"Wow!" I said, shocked by his about-face. "When did you come to *that* conclusion?"

"I think that it is so far gone with furniture Market, I think that what we need to do is concentrate on the border areas so that we create that same downtown environment, but just on the fringes of the core downtown," Clinard said. The City Project was now focusing on the development of the substitute downtown they called Uptowne (now a proper noun with an "e"), the area where the 1933 Art Deco–style apartment building that I lived in during my years in High Point was located.

While Uptowne had long *looked* like a gentrifying neighborhood, it hardly was. Uptowne's location, once prime space central to the downtown, had become more peripheral, marginal land, not particularly close to either employment or amenities. One key reason that space gentrifies is its revalued centrality. But High Point's prosperous downtown, as we know, held little centrality to residents' life spaces. The twenty-two-unit property where I lived had a tax value of only about six hundred thousand dollars at the time, the total for all twenty-two units. I rented the same apartment various times during the first decade of the millennium and paid just under three hundred dollars a month each time.

"Uptowne, that ten-block area, has 170 businesses, it's got three churches, the Furniture Library, the J. H. Adams Inn, it's got three 1930s apartment buildings, it's got Krispy Kreme, it has a satellite post office, it has thirty-two restaurants from barbeque to bouillabaisse. It really has the potential—really our only potential now—to create, in some cases restore, a vital shopping, retail, family-friendly, and pedestrian-family district," Paul Siceloff explained.

In my conversation with Fuscoe and Clinard, I got into a side conversation with the latter about the potential of this substitute downtown and how it might eventually benefit the Market with amenities as it "creeps toward the traditional downtown" one mile south.

"*This* area is what we are focused on being the downtown area. We are not thinking about *that* ever being the downtown," Fuscoe excitedly broke in. "So all these efforts to streetscape are to make it pedestrian-friendly, walkable, urban, and the Market is secondary to that. This effort is for the one hundred thousand people who live in High Point," she declared. "We're happy to have the Market, but this effort is not so that the Market people have a place to walk to. It's so that the one hundred thousand people in High Point have a place to go to," she made clear.

"Wow," I replied again. "Do you feel comfortable saying that on the city payroll?"

"I do, because I think that is what it's about. So many times it's 'Market, Market, Market, Market,'" she added firmly. "It's not that I . . . don't support the Market, but not everything the city's going to do has to be with an eye to pleasing visitors who come to the city two weeks out of the year."

Clinard and Fuscoe then began an enthusiastic account of Uptowne's recent Beach Music Blast Festival, beach music being the style of music popularized by bands like the Beach Boys. The final concert drew more than 2,500 people.

"'Finally there's something for *us*,'" Fuscoe recalled people saying. "It was so amazing to hear almost everyone say 'We finally have got something that we can go to, and enjoy, and be with one another,'" added Clinard. He saw the festival concerts as marking a "transition from 'it can never happen in High Point' to now an expectation that 'it can happen and it *will* happen.'"

It was hard to push the resident-centered ball uphill, as Fuscoe and Clinard put it, but they seemed to be approaching the crest. Like Love-joy, they felt residents needed to regain a sensitivity to use value, local vernacular, and meaningful life space. "They have to demand it," Clin-ard continued. "Because when they demand it, the city council has to respond." Otherwise, he believed the council would stay "married to their theory of [resident-centered] economic development being out there in North High Point" (northeast of Uptowne), since "that's where they see the quickest return on money."

But could Uptowne ever be the city's shared living room? "It's really a question of can they coordinate, can they collaborate, and can they be team players?" said Lovejoy. Glenn Chavis could envision himself spend-ing leisure time in Uptowne if its implementation was inclusionary in its programming, food, and other amenities. "That's something *you* enjoy. You think *other* people enjoy it. That's what I think is going on down there. You're seeing avocado salad with shrimp . . . and I'm seeing a chili dog and a Budweiser," he explained.

"It doesn't sound like you want *me*. You're doing things that please *you*," he continued. "Now, I am not going to go down there and dance to bluegrass music. Forrrrrrrr*get* it. *Hee-haw?* When I hear hee-haw, I'm gone," he laughed.

When I cited Clinard's and Fuscoe's excitement about the success of Beach Music Blast to Mayor Smothers, she commented: "Black people don't generally listen to beach music." To her, Uptowne could only ever be one social gathering place among many. Neither it nor any other place was destined to be the shared "mythical" heart, living room, cen-tral gathering place, or substitute downtown some leaders dreamed of.

Still Searching for a Living Room

"You're talking about new infrastructure, you're talking about new prop-erty purchase, you're talking about new buildings, new facilities," Lovejoy said of Uptowne. "I mean, basically you're talking about transplanting your heart from scratch to a whole new location. But that's how far the debate has gone, psychologically, and that's how little is left, civically, downtown."

Despite his reservations about Uptowne, Lovejoy felt that he needed to adapt to some things in order to change others. "Just because something has been our downtown historically, does it have to keep being our downtown?" he asked, apparently also feeling like he was butting his head against a wall. Like Clinard, Lovejoy was compromising with the structure of downtown constraints in the best way he knew how.

"Are the people supposed to serve a structure or are the structures supposed to serve the people?" Lovejoy asked, outlining an elegant sociological argument. "I don't think you can force people into structures," he continued. Structures are "made up" or "structured" by the individual decisions of residents or, as Lovejoy said, "formed by people in a contemporary context." He felt that the structure constraining residents' decisions was harmful, but that didn't change the fact that more people preferred Uptowne to downtown. "People like *people*," as Fuscoe shrugged.

Lovejoy eventually took Party on the Plank to Uptowne, where he sensed structural momentum and a critical mass of activity. Although this shift may appear as vacillation, such seeming contradictions characterize the actions of all ground-level actors as they grapple with myriad factors on multiple scales. This is why it is hard to pin down the ideologies of urban leaders. They rarely have the luxury of an allegiance to abstraction that a national leader might. We could say the same of Republican Jay Wagner's seemingly anticonservative call for regulation of the Market. The pragmatism demanded of local leaders can make charges of hypocrisy based on their seemingly contradictory actions seem naive—even sophomoric. The job requires flexibility and a broad range of tools.

As Lovejoy was attempting to sustain his one-person, event consulting firm formed around his Party on the Plank events, he sought projects in Greensboro. The fourth annual run of his ten-week Greensboro skating installation called "Winterfest" attracted an estimated fifteen thousand skaters and twenty-three thousand spectators. The local news declared it a community "mecca."[23] "In some ways I kinda feel like I got spoiled," said Lovejoy, recalling his Greensboro experiences, "because I saw what could happen when businesses, and nonprofits, and organizations, and foundations, and the public really got behind something. I saw how it could take off. I saw how it could create a sense of community."

Lovejoy had invested considerable time and money into Party on the Plank and he knew that a High Point skating rink would be a much larger effort. "It was really a gut check for me. Is High Point ready to support an event of this magnitude? And, if not, who is going to be left holding the bag?" In free market High Point, that question was rhetorical: *Lovejoy*, of course, would be the one to pay the resulting debts.

Lovejoy had given his best efforts to High Point, including an unsuccessful bid for city council in 2012. Eventually, he and his family decided to leave the area. Yet Lovejoy's cultural approach—social interventions supplemented by public dialogue, including a periodic column in the *Enterprise*—made a lasting impact. Whether people agreed with his ideas or saw him as a dreamy outsider, Lovejoy had planted his message into the public dialogue: the city lacked a "living room," it needed a place to "gather," and it had "sold its heart."

Meanwhile, Wagner was also regrouping. "Do I think Uptowne means that we've taken our ball and gone home?" asked Wagner as we sat in his Uptowne law firm, the same firm as Clinard's. "No. *I hope not.* And I hope that people who don't have any desire to see things change downtown won't use it as that. This area has the ability to be a very nice niche neighborhood, mom-and-pop sort of business district. It can be high-end. It can be where your nicest restaurants are, where you have fancy boutiques, where you have great little places to go shopping, sip coffee, push baby in a stroller—it can be *aaallll* that," he said.

"But if we're going to have the things that Greensboro has, and Winston has, and Greenville, South Carolina has, it *ain't* gonna happen here," Wagner continued. "You've already got the building stock downtown. You've got old buildings there that are just *waiting* to not be showrooms, to be something different."

Tiptoeing around the Goose via the DPZ Plan

The City Project hoped that Duany could lead High Point into that something different. After spending several days with High Pointers in May 2013, he offered his sizable High Point audience some tough love in his introductory lecture at HPU's Hayworth Auditorium. For anyone who had read Duany's writings, the writing was on the wall. High Point's development had proceeded in direct opposition to his new urbanist planning principles. Take the greenfield development of North High Point, for instance. It violated a tenet Duany cherished from designer Norman Bel Geddes that city development not be allowed to sprawl around highways. High Point also ignored a related tenet that highways that flow into the city "must take on the low-speed geometries of avenues and boulevards."[24] In direct opposition to this, High Point's Main Street was a wide road that encouraged higher speeds.

To Duany, High Point posed even more foundational challenges. His new urbanism design movement envisions a diversity of residents comingling in a dense, walkable, inclusive, mixed-use, vibrant common space. "The same sidewalks, the same parks, and the same corner store serve everyone from the C.E.O. to the local librarian," he wrote. "Sharing the same public realm, these people have the opportunity to interact, and thus come to realize that they have little reason to fear each other."[25]

Duany was especially mindful of the mistakes represented in the single-use, pedestrian-isolating downtowns of the 1970s and 1980s and the sprawled dormitory suburbs surrounding them.[26] Jacobsian champions of community-focused city planning like Duany linked design to active sidewalks, successful commerce, and robust community life. They viewed this type of development as a win for both social productivity and economic vitality, a combination that yields a synergy between exchange value and use value.

Developments of the second half of the twentieth century—such as the construction of downtown convention centers that ate up huge amounts of real estate in inorganic, pedestrian-repelling superblocks—frustrated Jane Jacobs. Downtown High Point offered the opposite: an exhibition space that husbanded the existing building stock.[27] This unorthodox example of urbanism-done-well while becoming wholly exclusionary presented Duany with a confounding dilemma. He had never seen an influx of profit-seeking investment create such an organic, human-scale, walkable design that explicitly excluded residents.

Downtown High Point's highest and best use was to keep the "immaculate" downtown in "hibernation." As Duany told his High Point audience, when most people hear "empty downtown," they imagine "the pictures of Detroit," not an immaculate landscape such as High Point. "They don't really die," he mused of High Point's buildings. No Detroit-esque ruin porn tarnished the pictures of downtown High Point because there was no economic death, yet socially and culturally it was just as lifeless.

One of Duany's solutions was to recommend that High Point adopt an interim building code he called the Pink Code, a name suggesting the lightening of "red tape."[28] Much of what Duany would propose for High Point—"the only feasible type" of development for the city, he said—could not be implemented without gutting city building codes. This philosophy was not new to Duany.

Six years earlier, Duany had famously declared that "New Orleans is not among the most haphazard, poorest, or misgoverned American cities, but rather the most organized, wealthiest, cleanest, and [most] competently governed of the Caribbean cities."[29] In this philosophy, Duany advocated celebrating and emulating what he saw as productive deregulation in places like New Orleans and Detroit. The haphazard clash between centrality and marginality that Duany ascribes to the developing world—here the Caribbean—is something High Pointers have long identified within their city's landscape. He suggested that High Point exploit, not eliminate, such traces of the global South's informality.

Duany argued that informal development would enable the United States to compete with countries like China, Malaysia, Mexico, and Brazil, but warned that it would entail the adoption of some practices deemed illegitimate under traditional city building codes. The growth machine approach anticipates demands for deregulation that wield globalism "as an ideological prop for the ever-widening 'race to the bottom': If we don't lower our standard first, somebody will beat us and they will get us," as Molotch describes.[30]

Duany felt that High Point was positioned to launch a campaign of intentional deregulation. Duany said that a state like North Carolina was "just waiting for this to happen . . . in fact, I think that the *nation* is waiting. . . . By the way, the Chinese are not waiting, okay? They're not waiting. Nobody's waiting. Only the Americans are stuck in their own bureaucracy. And we cannot compete worldwide when you can't get anything done efficiently. We cannot compete in this world."

Perfect profit maximization requires, among other things, a frictionless, footloose economic maneuverability that urban space cannot fulfill because its built environment can never change "as fast as the pace of economic development demands."[31] Nevertheless, Duany wanted cities to approximate this maneuverability, which he likened to "the agile deal flow of the Internet."[32] Coincidentally, I began using this same internet analogy to describe High Point when I first examined the city. Just like web developers reshape or reorganize a site on the internet simply by wiping out and replacing the HTML, downtown High Point minimized bureaucracy and democracy to accommodate the efficiencies of highest and best use.

Duany pointed out a similar agility in Detroit. There, innovators enjoyed wide latitude in setting their own rules because the city was desperate for investment and held little leverage to influence the rules of the development game. "Detroit can no longer supervise crime, let alone gainful economic activity," he quipped, and city inspectors show up merely to tell entrepreneurs, "'Go ahead, just don't hurt yourselves.'"[33] Its emerging coolness was a fortuitous, "unintended consequence of its impoverishment."[34] He admonished High Point to learn from Detroit, a place that—beyond its "archipelago of vitality and potential"—was a "pornography of ruins."[35] For High Point, Duany recommended an agenda of proactive deregulation spearheaded by local government and institutions rather than, as he saw in Detroit, an involuntary one born out of desperation.

Duany proposed projects for four separate geographic areas or nodes of the city. Like Mayor Smothers's polynucleated status quo, each of Duany's four nodes served a distinct population. The first plan focused on Uptowne, which he described as serving "the older folk, who also need their restaurants, their walkability." Duany's highest priority went to narrowing or "dieting" Main Street through the heart of Uptowne to bring it more in line with Bel Geddes's thinking. This had also been a core component of the Walker Plan. The three remaining nodes were unique to the plan pitched by DPZ, hereafter the Duany Plan. They addressed the center city (Downtown), the High Point University area (College Town), and the dead Oak Hollow Mall (Shantytown).

Duany's Downtown Plans

Although furniture industry interests, predominantly IMC, owned most of the downtown, Duany felt that it needed "cool" and "fun" places during backstage months for residents and visitors. But how? Duany's first strategy was to rework two existing spaces owned by IMC to simultaneously serve both residents and marketgoers. One project was straightforward: build an outdoor amphitheater in front of the white office building. The other involved Showplace's parking lot on the Magic Block, where Duany would restrict parking to the perimeter of the lot and open up the middle. Here he envisioned a site suitable for a farmers market where vendors could back up their trucks to their displays. The Duany Plan called this a "multipurpose public green," but there would be nothing public about the site. Duany seemed to use "public green" as a design term for a public green *look* connoting warm meanings.[36]

Interestingly, although pre-Bain Showplace had hardly been a resident-centered space, Duany said his team detected nostalgia for the exhibition hall. I term this tension a *nostalgia gap*. For example, while I was researching in High Point from 2002 to 2005, residents could hardly identify any community assets downtown; to them, the proverbial nail was already in the coffin and the goal was luring potential assets. Yet when he arrived in 2007 Elijah Lovejoy sensed a nostalgia among residents for the businesses that had departed the downtown in the previous few years. Similarly, during my interviews of residents before the IMC/Bain purchase in 2011, residents did not exactly praise Showplace's resident-centered capabilities. Yet the visitor Duany sensed a nostalgia for Showplace when he came in 2013. "We miss our ability to meet," residents told him. "We could have the fly fish conventions, the kids could have their senior proms, like you could actually do things downtown." He added that "Bain Capital has a different business model," one that "locks it up." There are two commonalities in these anecdotes: first, the query came from an outsider, and second, it was the absence of an asset that prompted appreciation for its value. A third more general lesson was that things can always get worse.

In contrast with his more traditional approach to the amphitheater and public green, Duany's second strategy was to develop downtown gathering spaces by leasing downtown land in the Market's backstage months. This land would be used for *guerrilla* or *tactical urbanism,* generally meaning temporary, cheap, small, illegitimate, or barely legitimate grassroots projects intended to make a place livable and prompt more enduring change. Guerrilla urbanists, for example, might occupy a metered parking spot on the street and set up chairs for a book club meeting. Like the book club on the street, Duany's suggested interventions would be strictly temporary and the space would eventually have to be returned to its owner.[37]

"We can *build* nothing," Duany reiterated. His challenge was to make downtown High Point "sufficiently cool" without the benefit of traditional construction. "We literally have nothing to work with except parking lots," he reasoned. His answer? Bolt shipping containers onto the parking lots and sublease them using creative lease structures coordinated by the city. In this section, I outline four downtown shipping container projects: retail shops, an outdoor space, a children's play area, and an arena.

The Duany Plan, just as the Walker Plan, considered the storefront architecture on MLK Drive—the "Main Street, USA" stretch residents gushed over in chapter 5—best suited for resident use. With most of these shops already committed to furniture use, Duany's plan would "liberate" them for conventional retail use.[38] "Facing these pretty nice storefronts on [MLK Drive] is open parking lots," Duany continued. "You can't have a 'Main Street' that's not two-sided." With the existing internationalized real estate sector occupying the south side of the street and parking lots on the north side, what solution might exist?

Local leaders had concentrated on the south side of the street and had sought incentives to bring down the price of the storefronts to attract retailers. They figured that if that worked, developers might start building new resident-centered uses on the parking lot sites on the north side. Duany opposed the idea that High Point's government should "subsidize everybody to do everything."[39]

His plan focused on the north side of the street instead. A hip section of shipping containers on that side of the street would attract retail uses profitable enough to rival Market uses and increase the rent that retailers would be willing to pay for the storefronts across the street, he reasoned. Retailers would end up renting the "Main Street" south side for resident-centered purposes. "It's a beautiful sight, totally cool in its layout," he exclaimed, pointing to the renderings.

There remained the generations-old problem of attracting a critical mass of activity. The people shown in Duany's renderings would not come to a few shops simply because they existed. To Duany, the area also needed an edgy, gritty space, not as "an end in itself but a means of positioning downtown High Point in the minds of the young," an anchor to lure a first wave of young, gentrifying, creative residents.[40]

Duany's answer was called "the Pit." This unused space in the center of the downtown's 100 south block where Main Street and the railroad intersect was envisioned as the site for outdoor entertainment integral to his plan to revive "the cultural reputation of a dead area."[41] I understood

Duany's shipping container shops intended for the parking lots on the north side of Dr. M. L. King, Jr. Drive. Courtesy of DPZ CoDESIGN.

why Duany was drawn to this block. I had heard residents daydream about the interesting courtyard bounded by the back of the Center Theatre on one side and the back of Natuzzi and a city parking garage on the other. It was a meld of global and local, and to Duany it showed "every indication of being a superb location" to resurrect a "derelict" area.[42]

The Pit site should be reworked a bit, but not enough to lose those attributes that lent it its grit, Duany warned. Those in the "first wave" are always the "risk oblivious," Duany advised, marshalling examples of the pioneers of New York's SoHo in the 1970s and "on the Left Bank of Paris in the 1870s."[43] The pioneer's "taste for roughness cannot be overestimated," he writes, adding that if "the walls of the elevator are covered with Formica paneling, better to rip it off and just leave the glue."[44] For the Pit, the Duany Plan recommended a few shipping containers as well as "fencing, lighting, speakers, movable furniture (such as cleaned up old tractor tires, pickle buckets, and spools), first-rate wall art, food trucks, and clever programming."[45]

Besides shipping containers on MLK Drive and development of the Pit, Duany also designed a shipping container play space called Playtown in the center of downtown. He intended this space to be "the heart of the family activity node," which would support cafés and other downtown businesses.[46] In lieu of a children's museum, an idea that residents had submitted during the DPZ charrette, Playtown would provide kids with "slightly dangerous things to do" while adults are "drinking coffee and having beer and having a chat."[47]

The final shipping container project for the downtown differed from the other three. In those, the shipping containers served as entire structures (such as the retail spaces). In Duany's plans for a basketball arena and civic space, however, shipping containers would serve as massive bricks with windows built between them. These windows would be very deep, given the width of a shipping container. "What you have is a really big building with an eight-foot thick wall, you know, just like the French cathedrals," he said. "It's beautiful, casting shadows everywhere."

The land on which Duany proposed to construct the arena was owned by IMC. Despite the arena's size, the city would be "leasing rather than owning the land," just as with the other projects, and must provide ample reassurances to IMC that it would pull out if IMC asked. Although obviously much more substantial than the other shipping container projects, the arena would also be merely resting on and affixed to the ground: "just a slab and you put bolts in it." Once complete, the outside would be covered in the dryvit. "This isn't—you know—Rome, okay?" Duany said, tempering expectations. "You know, so it's not the most solid thing in the world . . . But again, it's a temporary building."

Duany argued that the arena, like the other shipping container projects, would rebrand High Point. "High Point is cool, because High Point is moving, you know, fast and inexpensively and quickly and it's 'the talk of the town,'" he said. As for IMC, "What is it to them?" Duany asked. "They don't have a better idea what to do with the parking lot. Why not [have IMC] make a little, you know, a fee off it?"

Duany's College Town Plan

Before Nido Qubein became president of High Point University, it was commonly held that the city was leaking its local wealth, that the elite would bequeath their money to their kids who would promptly leave town with it. President Qubein's success at raising funds for the university showed that previous fundraisers either had not solicited the right people or had not proposed the right ideas. As a distinctly local booster, he has combined his personal wealth, the university's funds, and his personal network of contacts to sponsor risky projects that—at least at first—few outsiders would consider supporting financially.

Duany thought the Qubeinized campus was "surreal." He wasn't alone. Andrew Kelly of the American Enterprise Institute said that "both the left and right should be angry" about its "ridiculous array of amenities that would make the manager at a Four Seasons blush." *Business Week* labeled the campus "Bubble U."[48] Early in his first visit to High Point, Duany thought that perhaps the students were "so comfortable here within their campus that they never come downtown."

Over time, he changed his mind. "The problem is that there's nothing to *do* downtown," Duany concluded. As a result, HPU had to "internalize an unusual number of its activities that normally would occur in a college town because there isn't a college town," he realized. This resonated with High Point thinkers of various ideological backgrounds. HPU's ostentatious "extraordinary" branding aside, much of Qubein's contributions addressed a lack of community that everybody knew had hurt the university's prospective enrollments and student satisfaction for decades.

Duany wanted to see a "proper college town" for HPU, developed from the College Village strip mall adjacent to the campus. The core of this new college node would be constructed in the parking lot of the L-shaped mall that, like many such malls, was fronted by nothing but a sea of parking spaces. Duany's plan exploited the mall's location at an intersection. Four separate square blocks of buildings would fill College Village's former parking lot, forming two new intersecting streets. The two largest of the new blocks would be partly lined with apartments stylized in new urbanist fashion to echo the French Quarter in New Orleans. The word *lined* is important: the apartment edifices would be only one housing unit deep, thus allowing plenty of room for parking in the center, behind these "liner buildings." The remodeled L-shaped strip mall would hug the four new residential blocks.

This was a creative transformation of a strip mall into a potentially lively street grid. Duany is indisputably adept at creating the indicators of meaningful places (e.g., pedestrian activity) from nonplaces; he is skilled at transforming marginal space into prime space. In encouraging HPU to take the lead, Duany cited the role of private universities in developing vibrant places. He noted that Palo Alto, California, was built for and by Stanford University and Princeton University built Princeton, New Jersey.

"Of course it'll grow," Duany added, "and so what we'll have is the— kind of—village growing to college town." The plan included aspirations for the adjacent area, a low-income but stable neighborhood that was majority renter-occupied, where homes sold for under seventy-five thousand dollars and poverty rates were around 30 percent.[49] There had long been a chorus of voices urging the university to buy up area housing and sell it to professors. This resonated with Duany's hope for the emergence of a proper college town, but potentially conflicted with his priority, noted thirteen years earlier, to preserve quality affordable housing where it exists.[50] The last plan I discuss centered on affordable housing intended for one group in particular: new college graduates.

Duany's Shantytown Plan

Recurring parallels between High Point and cities in the developing world surface in the plans discussed thus far. Duany's shipping container spaces recall the semi-legitimate structures constructed on the margins of prime areas in developing world cities where vendors informally sell their goods. Their hold on their location is tenuous: they are subject to removal at the whim of real estate developers or city inspectors.

Duany's plan discussed in this section bears similarities to the informal settlements or semi-formal encampments of developing world cities. Duany's shantytown, however, would be a maker village for college graduates with the catchy name of Inc. Pad, a live/work craft and artisanal center for the pool of 330,000 college students located within a seventy-five-minute drive, as identified by the Duany plan. It would be sited at Oak Hollow, High Point's dead regional shopping mall owned by HPU.

This was not to be a typical repurposing of a traditional shopping mall into a new generation mall-cum-downtown "town center" with retail, hotel, residential, and office uses. No, Duany envisioned the dead mall resurrected as a place of deregulated residential and commercial development for college graduates with "lots of skills and nothing to do, who can't find a job. And when they find a job, they're detailing stair rails." Inc. Pad would cater to digital natives who embrace minimal living and getting their hands dirty. "Rather than facing a stretch of under-employment" as they cover the cost of a traditional postcollege apartment, these recent graduates would enjoy more financial freedom within "a self-perpetuating youth culture that allows them to stay in High Point, and provides a seed for revitalization."[51]

Duany's Inc. Pad plan to provide affordable shipping container housing and business incubation for recent college graduates at the mostly closed Oak Hollow Mall owned by High Point University. Courtesy of DPZ CoDESIGN.

The mall buildings, the core of the new Inc. Pad, would become a marketplace for the makers' goods. "There's a junkyard from which the metal guys can actually make things," he said. This would be no generic maker village, but one that would utilize the expertise of furniture cluster craftspeople who are "eager to transfer their skills to the next generation," Duany noted. "And then there's of course a place where they can actually grow food . . . and the food you can actually cook in a legal kitchen because there's the food court."

The parking lot would become the residential area. In this trailer park with a twist, young people could build "really incredibly cool little" shipping container houses. "Once the commerce is successful inside the mall, they can actually come out and build a proper street with two-story buildings," Duany predicted. Units on these legitimate streets, to be built later where the shantytown residences first stood, would "actually [have] mortgages," while "the other stuff doesn't."

I have never shown Duany's plans to a class of twenty-something college students without eliciting an enthusiastic "I would *soooo* live there" response, even from students critical of Duany's philosophy. They valued the plan's economical incubation of a craft economy and a community that could grow with makers' rising household incomes.

"Young people deserve a context where initiative is possible at, say, the level of 1904, when High Point began its rise to become the furniture capital," he said. "It is astounding to understand what an individual could achieve then and how very little they can achieve today, principally because of the regulatory burden."[52] High Point, like the rest of the United States, had lost "the slack that once allowed revitalization to evolve organically" because it was "exterminated" by a "rising tide of regulation," he argued.[53] The answer? Young people needed a "free zone" where "the initiative of youth can be in play."[54] This was a targeted laissez-faire informality for a specific young and educated population that Duany felt needed a stable place to nurture and develop their talents.

"Really, tactical urbanism is how most cities are built, especially in developing nations," says one new urbanist proponent.[55] In such contexts, some plots are bulldozed when their previously marginal land gains value and is redeveloped as prime. Other plots may rise in value in their current form and even gentrify, also becoming formal, municipally legitimated spaces. The Inc. Pad incorporates this sense of evolving places minus the initial phase where poor households occupy the marginal land. Just as the public green Duany planned for the downtown was not really public, this was not really an informal encampment. It would be owned and managed by High Point University, which Duany claimed was uniquely suited to pull off such a plan. "It's not exactly a democracy, you probably know," he said to knowing laughter from the audience hearing him pitch his plan in the HPU auditorium.

Ready for Revolt

I had been extremely optimistic when, in December 2012, Democrat Bernita Sims took the oath of office and became High Point's first Black mayor. I was also excited that Republican Jay Wagner was sworn in as a new city council member. All my conversations with Sims and Wagner led me to expect the start of a historic era favorable to resident-centered development. My optimism was short-lived. Less than a year later, Sims pleaded guilty to writing a worthless check to her sister, a charge that marred her administration and led her to resign under pressure in September 2014.[56]

A month after the guilty plea, High Point Partners, a longtime alliance of local business leaders, urged the community to support Duany's plans and not "let the momentum and the energy die down."[57] Indeed, after Duany left, each of his highest-priority projects endured sustained criticism. One member of the city council, Britt Moore, jibed that Duany's plan was "using the empty containers" that imported furniture to the United States, only to fill them with "retail stores that sell imported products."

The City Project leased a renovated shipping container and displayed it in the Mendenhall Terminal during the High Point Cycling Classic to stimulate public interest. The annual event used High Point's smooth, empty, well-maintained downtown streets as the setting for a major road race and the terminal as the grandstand. Residents visiting the Classic were impressed with the dwelling, until they discovered that the chic shipping container's cost was greater than many of the homes surrounding downtown.[58] Duany's Pink Code acknowledged that shipping containers "cannot meet conventional codes, except by becoming so expensive that they approach conventional construction."[59]

After going unused for more than a year, the property intended for the Pit outdoor entertainment area saw some life when a midtwenties Greensboro social entrepreneur and podcaster held a summer event there called "Dinner with a Side of Culture" without city permission.[60] Citing liability issues, the city council suspended use of the space shortly afterward. Not only could injury occur on the city land, they argued, but the private property surrounding it could face damage.

When estimates to complete the Pit project came in, Mayor Jim Davis, who finished out the remaining four months of Sims's term in 2014, "was kind of shocked."[61] Davis (not the same Davis who owned Rosa Mae's) had thought the whole point was to spend "relatively little money, and then it bloomed up to one million dollars."[62] The cheap version of Duany's informality was simply not legal. Duany did not pitch small-scale interventions to a clandestine band of guerrilla millennials, as proponents of tactical urbanism might expect. Instead, he promoted wholesale institutional change to the city's code enforcers. "You have to be legally sure-footed," said Planning Director Lee Burnette, caught between Duany's laissez-faire dreams and the actual laws that proscribed his agency.[63]

"You just have to allow it to happen," Duany wrote in a 2014 *Enterprise* op-ed, where he made his case for narrowing the road and upgrading the streetscape in Uptowne.[64] Meanwhile, the city's transportation director, Mark McDonald, expressed misgivings about that stretch in Uptowne, noting that current traffic conditions were already "pushing the capacity of the road" even before any narrowing of it.[65] In May 2014, the City Project used monies left over after paying Duany's fee to bring in Asheville-based consultant Joseph Minicozzi and his firm Urban3 to make an economic case for the viability of the road diet. After his presentation to the city council, Minicozzi left City Hall accompanied by City Project director Fuscoe.

Later that day, the two appeared at the High Point Theatre, where Minicozzi made his presentation to the public. That's when he saw someone hurry into the auditorium. It was council member Wagner, who had come to break the news that the council had just voted to dissolve the City Project. In the decision, the city retained Fuscoe as an employee. The vote followed a meeting of the council's finance committee held in a conference room with no reporters present.[66]

"What I'm telling you is if you want to see this happen," Wagner told the forty or so people assembled, "you need a new Council because the folks who are there are not going to make this happen. They're not interested in this. They think that we can do Band-Aid approaches, that we don't need to do anything transformational."[67] Indeed, after the decision, council member Smothers reiterated her decades-old theme: when Uptowne was ready to develop, the market [lowercase *m*] would take care of it.

"It's time for a revolt," Clinard entreated the audience. "I don't like using that word, but right now our City Council is dysfunctional."[68]

During its regular Monday evening meeting in October 2014, the city council voted to suspend its rules in order to "hold the meeting open" and add the Uptowne road proposal to a special meeting later that week.[69] There, the council voted to kill the road diet, with Wagner the sole dissenter. Wagner accused the council of systematically dismantling the progress made by the City Project outside the public eye.[70] "This is nothing but a straight-up abuse of power," Wagner told the group. "What else do you all want to take the wrecking ball to before [council member Smothers's] term is up?"[71] What Wagner had feared before the Duany visit had transpired: High Point had another glossy plan on the City Hall shelf and nothing to show for it.

"It needs political will and leadership," said furniture blogger Ivan Cutler, looking back at the City Project's failure to facilitate change. This chapter examined those failures, from the inaugural effort of the overlay district to its final defeat in the road diet. "Wendy Fuscoe can't do it on her own. And Aaron [Clinard] is beating his head against a wall. Unless this Wagner guy runs for mayor and he drives it through," Cutler added provocatively.

10

High Pointers Plan a Downtown for Themselves

Everybody is doing the same darn thing . . . I don't know what that answer is going to be. But I do absolutely in the core of my being believe that there is a unique solution for High Point.

—City Project head Wendy Fuscoe, on copying other successful cities

When enough people run into enough brick walls, something happens.

—Rev. Elijah Lovejoy, after the first Party on the Plank

How do we bring these two worlds together? It's like they're always clashing.

—Local historian Glenn Chavis, on marketgoers and residents

The Rise of Both/And

"I don't want to sound like I am downing the Market because the Market is good," city leader Angela McGill assured me. "But the Market has dominated—family life, small business prosperity—it's dominated everything." McGill was articulating a fundamental question often unspoken. *What are the economic, social, political, and cultural opportunity costs of a city's growth strategy?* "Does the furniture Market bring in enough revenue to compensate for all of the other losses?" she asked.

Development is not a bad thing, of course. Communities must distinguish between positive change and regressive change. Local growth initiatives need to prove that they make sense for local economic, social, political, and cultural health "as well as in more macro or cosmopolitan terms."[1]

Prominent leaders in High Point had long scoffed at this line of reasoning. Although High Pointers critical of the Market-centered downtown were quick to point out that they were not against the Market, real estate interests historically had little patience for such nuance. Why pose the distant promise of a more lucrative hypothetical when a lucrative Golden Goose seemed a virtual certainty? As County Commissioner Bruce Davis warned overlay advocates, "Why fool with it? Leave it alone and count it as a blessing."

Yet the case for a different downtown development strategy was becoming about more than sentiment. The assessed tax value of the core area surrounding the downtown had been deteriorating by dozens of millions of dollars each year since 2008—long enough, by 2013, to qualify as a trend.[2] Some leaders and consultants argued that the Market might not only fail to benefit surrounding neighborhoods: it could be strangling them.

Charles "Seemore" Simmons, one of High Point's most enduring civic voices, has long supported dual Market and resident use of the downtown. He shared some strong opinions one day very early in Wendy Fuscoe's tenure at the City Project. "She almost gets mad because Market takes over everything," he told me. But he wondered whether Fuscoe had the disposition to find the way toward a "win–win" for both interests, Market and residents, if that path arose.

"That's what it is," the then octogenarian said emphatically at the strip mall Starbucks a mile from downtown where we talked. "Try to figure out how to laminate to it and synergize with it and graft a new body to it like a stock car racer does," he declared in poetic cadence. Here was yet another metaphor for the Market, a fitting one for this NASCAR region. Market is a stock car, perhaps a factory-made family sedan, that racing engineers have to somehow deal with—take "what it is"—and turn into something that suits their new purposes through "laminating, synergizing, and grafting."

"I can get my back up quickly about some of these things, because I hear so many people talk about an *either/or*," said Market official Sally Bringier, another mixed-use (Market/resident) advocate with High Point roots. Like Simmons, she interpreted the shrug of "oh well, what can we do?"—common from both pro-Market and pro-resident interests—as rooted in complacency. "We either have the Market *or* we have a downtown. That's what we hear. That's the negativeness we get toward Market from people who say 'but I want a *downtown*.'

"You can *have* a downtown," she added. "But you've already *got* a Market. And your Market can help your downtown. Now, we have to be careful about how we *do* this, but there has to be a way to do it and it's not an either/or." She, Simmons, politician Jay Wagner, and Planning Director Lee Burnette all believed that there must be a narrow, unconventional way forward that could accommodate both elements.

"Do you know how many phone calls we get in this office from the average Joe Blow business owner in this community . . . that has these words: 'how do I *access* Market?'" another Market leader asked me. Given the Market's history of exclusion and the downtown's dearth of entrepreneurs, this question is nearly impossible to answer unless coming from a caterer, food truck operator, florist, real estate agent, musician, shoe shiner, or someone else with a specific Market role. It is difficult for any organization outside the Market's production process to position itself for the Market. A common longing heard in High Point begins with "We have all of these people here from more than 110 nations and . . ." All lament the tantalizing opportunities for retailing, fundraising, design school recruiting, art exhibiting, and so forth lost to them for want of a way in.

Wagner agreed that High Pointers should have access to the Market-dominated downtown, but he also wanted marketgoers to see more "High Point" in the downtown. "It's an opportunity for us to show who we are to the whole world twice a year," he said, contemplating downtown's potential to meld the local and the global. "And, in that sense, every Market that we have, every Market that occurs, there is just, in my opinion, a huge missed opportunity for us."

Added Wagner: "In the past, I've had people tell me that folks downtown who own the showroom buildings don't want anything downtown because they don't want people leaving the buildings during Market, which I think is incredibly shortsighted and borderline stupid." Market stakeholders have used this argument both to dismiss the idea of a resident-centered downtown and to disparage the presumed advantages of High Point's larger rivals. The argument goes all the way back to the Market's defeat of Chicago in the early 1960s: "furniture men" did not want or need the distractions of amenities and nightlife. "It's why they come here: to do *business*. Just because they sit in a restaurant and have dinner doesn't mean they're not going to do business," Wagner retorted.

Resident-centered stakeholders sometimes return to a generations-old policy idea for balancing Market showrooms and resident-centered uses: establish a mandate requiring all showroom buildings to reserve the first floor for year-round uses. Barring such a requirement, every square foot of potential retail space is in competition with showroom space. In practice, a downtown landlord may actually feel the need to demand *more* money from a restaurant or retail store than from a showroom due to the increased wear and tear that year-round use would presumably bring and the oversight it would require from the owner. This, despite the fact that a restaurant or retail store owner may actually need *lower* rent than they would pay for spaces elsewhere in the city because of the downtown's current lack of year-round consumer traffic. The resulting discrepancy is substantial: even high retail rent is still less than showroom rent.

This seemingly intractable dilemma is why pro-Market politicians have viewed such zoning as ridiculous. "We're going to go in and say to someone, 'You have to keep this open six days a week until 2 a.m. in the morning'? Okaaay!" Becky Smothers said after the overlay battle. "That would go over real well."[3] This is a framing of capital versus sentiment, realists versus dreamers. It is easy to forget that the Walker Plan argued that a synergy between Market and residents in the downtown held promise not only for residents but also for the Market. "Real estate speculation at the fringes of the Showroom District precludes the future development from supporting districts that could serve as amenities for the High Point Market, such as an entertainment district, a shopping district or a residential district," it stated.[4]

The Rise of Buzz and Friction

Amid the tumultuous overlay battle of 2010, I asked Market Authority president Brian Casey what the downtown and the High Point Market would ideally look like in 2025. I was very surprised by his response. "Ideally?" began Casey. "You know, ideally, it would be even more concentrated than it is, with outside showrooms consolidated more in the downtown area. There would be more bars and restaurants open in the area so that it would have a natural flow for entertainment," he continued. "Probably more urban dwellers, so that you had people actually living in and around the area. Because you find that that's what supports those types of activities." Perplexed by his unique response, I was about to ask *what about Market?* when he answered first.

"But most important, while Market is going on, you've got that hustle and bustle on top of it. . . . If you have it 365 days a year and then you have the Market on *top* of it, then you have some denseness and that's what people—it becomes a pain in the butt—but it's what they like because it creates buzz," Casey concluded. Residents and merchants as *important?* This was new to hear coming from a Market leader, but it made sense, to an extent, considering that the bulk of Casey's experience had been in large city conventions.

What Mayor Smothers called war and tension, Market leader Casey labeled buzz—a buzz that would benefit the Market enough to justify what he understood as the accompanying "pain in the butt." The benefits worked both ways. With plans like Uptowne, noted Bringier, the High Point native and Market official, "you lose the benefit of Market being here." In contrast, she pointed to the "Main Street, USA" stretch of MLK Drive storefronts identified by Andrés Duany and others where she thought resident-centered uses would "have a huge bonus from having it so close to Market."

Of course, just because they were citing these synergies did not signal that Market leaders would be leading any resident-focused revolutions. Given the choice between a vibrant downtown and the current situation, some leaders might choose "buzz." However, the Market Authority felt little urgency to promote this vision of the ideal environment. We know from chapter 6 how an elaborate mini-Manhattan fix made the current "next six days that matter" arrangement work.

"Right now," said Wagner, "[downtown's] almost like Disney World during Market. And I, for one, refuse to give up on having something downtown for those folks to do when they are here so that when they walk out of those buildings they have a place to go to eat, they have a place to go to socialize. They have a place to go in their down time to enjoy themselves. And do it in a way that it can exist between Markets for people who live here."

I had never heard the two camps—resident-centered and Market leaders—speaking such similar language. Whereas people like J. J. Cox argued in the 1970s that Market-centered uses downtown benefited the residents of High Point, I was increasingly hearing the argument that a downtown with resident-centered uses benefited the stakeholders of Market. Of course, resident-centered uses would also bolster the elusive "Plan B" for an alternative downtown economy. "If you are making the statement that the furniture Market is the engine, then by all means, highest and best use is showroom," said architect Peter Freeman, arguing that others engines were needed. "I think furniture Market is the Golden Goose, but it is only a platform to create the next chapter of the city," he added.

Reclaiming a Portion for Ourselves

"If we're willing to take the steps necessary to reinvent that area for ourselves and reclaim a portion of that for ourselves . . ." Wagner began sharing with me shortly after my conversation with Casey. He stopped and started to laugh, perhaps in response to the skeptical look on my face. "Just a *portion* of it, not the whole thing," he continued with a chuckle.

"If we are willing to reclaim a portion of that for ourselves, it would help build a sense of community in our city that just doesn't exist right now," he finished. He had personal experience of that community not only from the downtown retail his relatives once owned but also through its residues in the businesses surrounding his law office (located in the white building until the late 2000s). "You've got to have this mixture of what you'd normally have in a downtown. It's got to develop a life of its own. And *then* you're going to have that friction," Wagner continued, referring to the same messy bustle of activity that Casey envisioned. "You're going to have that creativity that can flow. Bouncing ideas off other people," Wagner explained.

There's not enough critical mass," reflected Audie Cashion, drawing on his experience with both furniture expositions and real estate as we discussed a resident-centered downtown. "You've got to have all three legs of the table," he said, meaning residential, retail, and office uses. "If one landlord or, you know, showroom owner decides they want to do it, they're going to get destroyed," echoed millennial-aged furniture executive Jason Phillips. "But if everyone does—which, how do you get *that* to happen?—it could succeed."

Planner Burnette understood such conundrums. "We will revisit this Market [overlay] district at some point in time," he predicted. And while it might be "five or ten years" away, he was certain that High Point would come to realize that a resident-centered gathering place was necessary, was best located downtown, and that government involvement, whatever form that took, was the only way to foster it.

"Sooner or later, it takes on a life of its own, and it grows organically on its own," agreed Wagner as he envisioned this intervention. But Wagner knew that only in hindsight could the growth he admired in places like Greenville be considered "organic" and "market-driven." "What you *don't* see so much is behind the scenes: what the city has done in key properties in key places to help to create the stage where that growth and that organic city life can occur," he added of the South Carolina city.

"I think that's where we are: How do we set the stage for that to happen? Because it doesn't just happen. You look at any great city of any size, they're planned," Wagner continued. He firmly felt that the city's initial decision not to zone the downtown for resident-centered uses had structured the community's passivity. That structure largely ensured that the passive stance, to do nothing, produced active wins for the most powerful voices. After all, the growth machine manufactures outcomes. The resulting sociopolitical environment treated any alternative as a threat, with little room for debating the merit of both/and plans. "For too long we've sat back and just let things happen," Wagner concluded.

The notion of long-standing structures leading to unfair outcomes was foreign to many Guilford County Republicans, as local conservative bloggers actively attested. However, Wagner understood that the peculiarities of facts on the ground called for a hodgepodge of different policy approaches from across the political continuum. When navigating urban development in a global context, no tidy continuum exists. There are countless examples of urban leaders using the specific cards dealt them in unique ways that belied their politics. "I mean, they may take a hit for it, but they've got to be willing to do what's right for the city in the long term," Wagner said.

He and I had often remarked on how many designers of national stature lived in the High Point area and how many more regularly visited. If a reclaimed downtown were to serve High Point's resident design community, furniture business visitors, marketgoers, and residents at large, it would have to reckon with both local vernacular and the cluster's design aesthetic. Wagner believed this could happen organically— the new downtown business owners would realize, as he said, "'I've got to find someone with design ability.'" If they didn't, the city might need to appoint "a designated person . . . dedicated to downtown" who becomes a liaison for local "designers who are willing to lend their expertise."

A place drawing resident traffic, Market traffic, the design community, and multiple types of investors and users seemed like an exciting mix— it always had. This would be no disingenuous illusion of a "creative," "international" city, but a visible reflection of High Point's actual fabric. Was this time any different? To architect Freeman, it was. It seemed the moment for "an in-the-trench, last-ditch effort from a group of people that really want to see something happen." Still, it seemed impossible in High Point.

Risk-Taking Elite

"Greensboro didn't *go* by the money," resident Larry Diggs explained from a bench in the Mendenhall Terminal. In his opinion, Greensboro's civil leaders weren't scared off by a pricey project with resident-centered goals. "They got a lot of successful people over there: investors who are willing to take a risk," seconded civic leader Richard Wood in another conversation, as he contemplated Greensboro's civic environment. Indeed, development in southeastern cities such as Greensboro, Winston-Salem, Greenville, Asheville, and Charleston was more orchestrated than in High Point, with local boosters and government leaders making coordinated, strategic bets on their city. "We don't have much of that here," Wood lamented.

High Point may have lacked the sophistication of Greensboro's and Greenville's philanthropy, but it did not lack access to networks of wealth. For proponents of a resident-centered downtown, it stung that Nido Qubein's fundraising for the university laid this bare. Diggs challenged High Point's civic leaders: "They *know* the people—I mean, all these people that are making these donations to High Point University. Many of them have money that they would put up if they would see that the city was sincere and really reached out."

"Nobody has painted a picture [of the downtown] like Nido was able to paint at the university with what it *could* look like," Fuscoe observed. Instead, High Point leaders to date had been content to serve as cogs in the Market machine. They had rarely presented their own vision— merely the maintenance of order and a very limited definition of a good business climate. The official who dismissed all the dreamy "living room" talk at the end of chapter 8 by telling me "High Point's good" also asserted that High Point residents judge the local government's performance not by its downtown gatherings but by whether water comes out of their faucets, their trash is picked up, and High Point keeps the Market. To some residents, however, HPU was a stinging reminder that innovative development, beyond the mere maintenance of order and stability, was possible.

The Hair-N-Stuff District

I was never surprised to hear residents' assumption that IMC had little interest in resident-centered downtown projects. Why would they? "They're not going to do it. 'Cause it's strictly a business decision," said realtor Ed Price. "When it was local families, it was a little bit different." Although it makes logical sense that local people would care more about local life spaces, growth machine theory eschews such optimism. More important, High Point history had clearly shown that local ownership opposed resident-centered downtown development.

Some furniture industry thinkers wondered whether IMC might shake things up in a good way—or perhaps even harbor business motivations for caring about the future of High Point's urban core. "I think that is something that is already on their radar," Jason Phillips said, as he contemplated resident-centered uses one year after IMC's big purchase. After all, private equity had sunk half a billion dollars into High Point's downtown.

"It is frustrating to me that there is a ring of 'urban blight' around the . . . Market district," explained IMC CEO Bob Maricich. Like the New York showroom owners who had challenged Mayor Rudy Giuliani, IMC as a stakeholder questioned High Point's resolve to maintain the Market district as "prime" space and a cohesive landscape of experience. The free hand of the (lowercase) market had allowed what residents have called "pimples" and "lost teeth" to remain. The downtown landscape seemed to Maricich, a conservative like Wagner, to demand intervention.

"You know, it's a nice area, a nice stretch," resident Nic Ruden had said during our downtown walk as he surveyed Elm Street's Market Square, Commerce and Design, and Natuzzi buildings—a stretch he called Universal Studios. Then he turned north. "But when you look down there, you start getting into bad zone," he said. We were facing Hair-N-Stuff, discussed in chapter 5. "I mean, it's just . . ." he started. "I think it's moving people in around downtown that's going to change this, in a way," Ruden added as he reconsidered his suggestion that somebody should put a showroom on the unappealing-looking property. Residents like Ruden were embarrassed and even angered by the sight of prime Market spaces alongside marginal spaces like Hair-N-Stuff.

Maricich, however, had an even deeper concern than Ruden or the Manhattan showroom operators. This "only in High Point" twist envisioned that buyers traversing an IMC building might not only be seeing an abandoned gas station during Market but actually conducting business in it. The ring of marginal space around the Market allows "for every vacant building to be a 'showroom' on the cheap," Maricich said. He thought that the unregulated Market cried out for some controls to reassure its major investors. Here was IMC, a firm funded by global private equity, taking the role of a "glocalised place entrepreneur" using the traditional community-level channels identified by growth machine theory.[5]

And so the story returned to what I might as well call "The Hair-N-Stuff District" (given how many times residents commented on it). The rent gap here—the difference between current worth "as is" and what it could be worth redeveloped—along with its centrality to major buildings like the Natuzzi headquarters and Market Square offered the potential of local redevelopment. This northwest quadrant of the downtown still had important potential assets. The "Main Street"-looking block of MLK was only half a mile away and the white office building was not far, either. The Adams-Millis hosiery mill renovated by Gabriele Natale, which had interested condominium developers, was located there. So was a regional telecommunications firm's headquarters, which had remained downtown. Outside the area's northern tip was High Point Medical Center, with its eye-catching postmodern design of curvy silver glass, and the surrounding medical district. The area also included North Elm, discussed in chapter 6, where edgy Market exhibitors who identified as "the makers" were renovating real estate.

Certainly, Maricich was singing a different song from the penny-pinching, locally rooted growth machine players of the past. Did it matter? *Was the takeover of High Point by faceless private equity presenting new opportunities, new cards for perceptive city leaders to play? Could High*

Point exploit IMC's purchase for the advantage of the public good? Could the city both diversify the downtown and retain Market? With so many interests to navigate, the situation seemed to call for a specific brand of leadership: community-minded and seasoned with local experience.

People for the Job

"They need a strong leader that is autonomous," said furniture blogger Ivan Cutler, meaning independent from the Market, "with the political force of the city and the state." Cutler wanted a leader who would not view government as an arm of the Market that merely did its bidding. Could the new ownership arrangement, using the words of urbanists H. V. Savitch and Paul Kantor, "embolden local officials to impose new demands" strengthened by the confidence that High Point's niche is "difficult to duplicate"?[6]

"You want to belong to this?" Cutler continued, explaining his version of this emboldened orientation. "If you have a showroom in High Point, you're in the industry and you participate in the Market—guess what? You're under our control," he said. Cutler felt that previous local leaders allied with the Market had helped stymie the rise of politicians with a long-term vision and the mettle to execute it. They had surrendered, rather than asserted, control.

"What do you think allowed Greenville to go from vision to action in a way that High Point hasn't—with these visions [by outside consultants] stacking up?" I asked Wagner. "Leadership. Plain and simple. They have had leadership that had enough courage to reinvent themselves," Wagner replied.

Resonating with what Savitch and Kantor call the falsehood that "cities cannot choose," Wagner was suggesting that Greenville leaders dispelled the myth that because business is mobile and cities are stationary, cities are constrained from making meaningful choices.[7] To the contrary, the urbanists observe, "experience teaches cities to sense their vulnerabilities" as well as utilize their assets.[8] City leaders with vision can draw on this specific, local wisdom to reassess, take stock, and innovate.

Leaders in Greenville "were willing to pay a political price to get things done," Wagner explained. "They started early, they had a clear vision, they knew what they were shooting for, they had buy-in from the business community, and someone to lead them. . . . They had a guy like Max

Heller," Wagner said. Heller, Greenville's mayor from 1971 to 1979, came to the city in 1938 after fleeing the Nazi invasion of his native Austria.

The dynamic Heller was a favorite of the DIC and City Project crowd. However, when other High Pointers thought of leadership, the person often brought to mind was Qubein, a "compact, white-haired 63-year-old who favors dark suits and vividly colored silk ties" and "moves with a dancer's grace," as *Business Week* described. The magazine called him "captivating."[9] High Pointers "are blinded by Neon Nido," said Cutler. Another Greensboro journalist gushed (and I must agree), he "seems to relish every millisecond of his work."[10]

Qubein's term *extraordinary* was not only HPU's catchword but captured the attitude toward daily life he promoted. One resident described an HPU employee appreciation event at Showplace. "Nido spread out rugs for every faculty member and staff member in High Point University. And then, with this very elaborate system based on how long you've been there, what your seniority was, you could go in and pick [one] out," she recalled. "And when he came in [to the presidency], he presented everyone on the staff and faculty with fifteen pounds of Ghirardelli chocolate. It's crazy. It's Nido: master of the grand gesture."

Until he assumed his post at High Point University, some residents had questioned whether his leadership style and positive thinking amounted to "smoke and mirrors." However, his one-billion-dollar overhaul of High Point University—for better or for worse—had concretized his philosophy into buildings, roads, sidewalks, events, employment, and, very slowly, curriculum. It was not difficult to imagine how Qubein's connections to Market leaders, government leaders, and High Point's old furniture and textile money that served him so well at the university could benefit the community beyond his school's black wrought iron gates.

"I've always believed that you've got to create something that's fantastically wonderful to have people want to be a part of it—first—not at the end, but first," said Raymond Waites. "Make High Point an artistic center," Waites continued. "Let's declare that. You have to *declare* something before you can make it happen." His emphatic "de-*clay*-uh" fully exposed the Alabama roots that preceded his ascent as a designer in Manhattan. "Qubein declared in his mind, if nobody else's mind, what he was going to do and he stayed focused," added Waites. "Now, you've got the city of High Point that's fragmented—good stuff, ugly stuff—and nothing hinging it together. Nothing," he said.

Turning to HPU's master-planned campus, Waites noted, "I'm telling you . . . every New Yorker that I bring down there, they are amazed that this is in *High Point*. It changes your perception of High Point. It's so outrageously luscious, with all those fountains, all those neoclassic buildings. They're all built in a certain way: water, pavilions everywhere. You go 'wow, I'd like to be a part of this.' Take that philosophy and bring it *downtown*," he said.

While some residents wondered where the next wave of resident-centered momentum could come from, leaders at City Hall were brainstorming as well. In a 2014 City Hall email exchange uncovered by journalist Jordan Green, council member Jason Ewing told colleagues one of his primary concerns was "containing the beast" of the Market.[11] He longed for "an area that investors, developers, and business owners can have comfort in knowing that adjacent space will not be turned into a Market showroom." This sounded very familiar. "I'm in," said his fellow conservative Wagner. "But let's do it right this time," he added.

In the mayoral election held after Bernita Sims's resignation (and Jim Davis's four months as interim mayor), the city swore in Republican Bill Bencini in December 2014. Bencini was a furniture industry executive who had not been exceedingly vocal about downtown issues as a council member, but nonetheless served as a resident-centered ally for many years. He won with a decisive 54 percent of the vote, well ahead of State Representative Marcus Brandon, a Democrat who got 36 percent of the vote in the three-candidate race. The size of Brandon's healthy share of the vote was significant for resident-centered proponents too, as he had taken an even bolder stance than Bencini on restricting downtown showrooms.

In the same election, the two candidates for city council advocating for downtown reform won even more decisively. Republican Alyce Hill, who got involved in High Point politics during the excitement of the Duany visit, had more than double the votes of her main opponent, political veteran Judy Mendenhall, and Wagner nearly tripled the count of his primary rival. It was no surprise when Bencini appointed Wagner to chair the comprehensive planning committee. When Bencini developed the seating assignments for the dais, he placed himself between

Wagner and Hill. It was an exceedingly young council, with no member having served more than two years, although one member had done a previous stint. Significantly, both Mendenhall and Smothers retired at that point. "We know a lot of the folks who won ran on the revitalization issue," Aaron Clinard said at the swearing-in ceremony of the new council.[12] "I hope that's going to go a long way towards this Council making some good decisions," he added.

New Blood

While major fluctuations were occurring in High Point's downtown plans between 2012 and 2014, German-born woodworker Miro Buzov quietly opened a creperie on the oft-discussed "Main Street USA" stretch of MLK Drive. The showroom real estate market had been struggling since the Great Recession and the idealist Buzov bought into the ideas of resident-centered thinkers. He established his Penny Path Cafe and Creperie as the sole resident-centered business on that promising stretch of hibernating MLK storefronts. His gamble paid off. Buzov's six-hundred-square-foot restaurant overcame the challenges of its isolated downtown location and his loyal supporters throughout the Triad region (and among marketgoers) would later allow him to open two additional eateries. His success in a location and a business climate previously considered impenetrable offered hope for proponents of a resident-centered downtown. "Have you been to Penny Path?" became the new question the downtown dreamers would ask me.

The new city council voices supporting a resident-centered downtown immediately began nudging and prodding the newly emerging downtown alliances. In 2015, the city restructured the City Project into a new public–private partnership called Forward High Point Inc. Later that year, High Point's private economic development alliance, High Point Partners, merged with the Chamber of Commerce to create Business High Point–Chamber of Commerce, which would become, in their words, "the united voice of the private sector." Significantly, IMC's executive vice president served on this new board. Business High Point president Patrick Chapin, the city manager, and a BB&T Bank vice president were on the boards of both the new Forward High Point and the new Business High Point. With the former High Point Partners, the former Chamber of Commerce, the new Forward High Point, and the city leadership now all interlocked, High Point had a tight, both/and-minded, resident/Market-centered coalition that could bargain with a unified voice.[13]

In March 2016, by a unanimous 7–0 vote, the city council announced a strategic goal to produce 15–20 new restaurants and shops, 250 housing units, and a central gathering space downtown.[14] Forward High Point hired Ray Gibbs, the former president of Downtown Greensboro Inc., as the first executive director. Gibbs wasted no time in bringing elements of the Greensboro model to High Point. He understood what several eras of leaders before him had understood: downtown rents would continue to prohibit small businesses.

"We can live together [with the Market], but we need street-level activity along Main Street," Gibbs said. "It would be nice if we could convince some of the showroom owners that if they opened up the first floor of their buildings to retail or restaurants, it would be in everyone's best interest," he added.[15] The idea was not new, but both the position and the person articulating it was. Gibbs was a veteran of downtown development success with government backing and a sense of what "convince" might mean. He was reintroducing an idea that then mayor Smothers had heartily mocked just three years earlier.

In 2016, Buzov was looking for a larger downtown location for his two-year-old creperie and believed that he had found the ideal spot. However, he ran up against a decades-old problem: his desired location had been redeveloped as a furniture showroom. Buzov was not able to compete amid a new wave of building investment that had set in over the intervening two years, and he remained where he was. "I love High Point," he said in 2017. "I can't leave the city. I think there's absolutely an opportunity here."[16]

The properties that were available on MLK's "Main Street" section when the downtown was still in a recessional malaise had slowly fallen back into Market hands after the overlay defeat. From 2016 to 2018, about five hundred thousand square feet of new showrooms were constructed. "In my opinion, the city missed an opportunity," said Buzov after he lost his relocation effort. "Most of that land has been bought up by showrooms."[17] While the situation was similar—a local business hemmed in by showroom investment—the changing political environment in High Point promised a different end for Penny Path than what Rosa Mae's, Nobles, and others had faced.

A Downtown for Baseball?

At the urging of Gibbs, in April 2017 the High Point City Council approved fifteen million dollars to purchase land downtown for the construction of a small baseball stadium half a mile from the MLK storefronts where Buzov's creperie stood. The hope, it seemed at the time, was that a baseball team and stadium would attract resident-centered retail, restaurants, and residences. In typical High Point fashion, and ignoring years of intervening research, this bet sounded twenty years out of date.

In May, at the annual meeting of the High Point Convention and Visitors Bureau, Forward High Point announced that HPU president Qubein, who was also on the board of Business High Point, would lead the stadium project and its related endeavors. Qubein pledged to raise thirty-eight million dollars for the downtown plan, which he said would also include amenities such as an events center, a children's museum, an urban park and playground, and an educational cinema.[18] "I am happy here [at HPU], and I love my city," he told an audience at the country club. "I have no financial interest or stake in this development project in any way," clarified Qubein. "My sole interest is helping High Point thrive."[19] Although it seems quite likely that he would personally benefit at some point if the downtown overhaul succeeded, it appeared that Qubein was indeed acting as a local booster: an entrepreneur and university president employing his money, power, and reputation in the name of his city and his local legacy.

Four months later, in September, Qubein assembled a crowd at High Point University's Hayworth Auditorium to update them on his fundraising progress. Projected on a screen behind him was a huge image of the pledge he had made months earlier: "$38,000,000 By SEPTEMBER 15." Pausing dramatically, Qubein announced: "We raised $50 million." At that moment, another giant projection changed to "$50,000,000" to gasps and applause from the audience of nine hundred people.

Qubein declared that the project would be considerably larger in scope than just a baseball arena—with apartments, a hotel, and other year-round amenities in line with city council goals. Maryland-based Tim Elliott would be the master planner. "Raising the $50 million was not that difficult, really," Qubein commented after making formal remarks. "What was more important was to state with clarity why we needed those funds," he added, as if directly challenging High Point's history of visionless, growth-chasing leadership that Diggs, Fuscoe, and others had outlined.[20] The fifty million dollars came from eleven contributors, including Qubein and High Point University. Single-minded players such as Gibbs and Qubein—linking expertise with access to networks of philanthropists—were uncovering previously hidden synergies.

The city paid sixteen million dollars to assemble plots of the under-valued land in the downtown's northwest quadrant. The state approved the city's request to issue up to thirty-five million dollars in limited obligation bonds to build the stadium.[21] The City of High Point asked Guilford County to allocate future tax revenue generated from the 649-acre economic development area into bond repayments, but in September 2017, the Guilford County commissioners would not even second the request for a vote.

A Downtown for Residents

After the disappointment at the county commissioners meeting, High Point leaders vowed to go at it alone if they must, and a new political action committee, the High Point Political Alliance (HPPA) led by a local attorney who was the Business High Point chair-elect, pledged to forge ahead. HPPA's stated mission was "advocating pro-business and pro-growth positions," which was not particularly surprising. Its objectives spanned seven broad issue areas: downtown, the university, the Market, transportation, taxes, education, and the attributes of a great city.[22] Besides fighting for a strong resident-centered downtown, HPPA articulated a Market-centered objective to pass "beneficial tax and zoning laws that enhance the Furniture Market's national and global competitiveness."[23] The both/and message was clear: the city was doubling-down on resident-centered uses, but it would continue to privilege the Market.

Most interesting were HPPA's social goals. Among what it called its "ten elements of a great city," one notable aim was to develop "places and events where the community can meet." Even more surprising was a goal that the "entire community become more civically active and informed regarding the affairs of government."[24] The statement of these goals codified the shift that had occurred over the past decade and asserted HPPA's implicit recognition of the city's poor civic climate. Did this represent a nod to "a capacity for informed citizenship," a shift away from leaders who quietly enjoyed the agility that disenfranchisement afforded decision-makers?[25]

There were additional shifts occurring in High Point's political life. Mayor Bencini declared that he would not seek another term. In the November 2017 mayoral election, HPPA-endorsed Jay Wagner narrowly beat County Commissioner and Democrat Bruce Davis. This was Davis's first campaign for High Point mayor, and while his platform espoused downtown plans, his previous position—recall "leave [Market] alone and count it as a blessing"—left the resident-centered downtown crowd skeptical. Even so, the fact that Davis now endorsed downtown renewal was evidence of the changing political climate.

Around this same time, the city council approved a plan developed by Burnette and his planning team for a 131-acre area of the downtown that included the fourteen acres of the stadium project area. This northwest downtown quadrant constituted a new mixed-use zoning district that excluded new Market showrooms but grandfathered in nearly thirty existing showrooms. The city, Forward High Point, and High Point University would be sharing investment and development responsibilities in what would become a two-hundred-million-dollar project. It appeared that the "Nido aesthetic" might escape the campus walls after all.

The local Samet Corporation built the stadium where the new High Point Rockers of the Atlantic League threw their first pitch in May 2019. The developing stadium district was named The Outfields. The first building to open, in late 2021, was 275 North Elm Street, which mimics the brick, steel, and glass of the nearby factory lofts. The building includes the Stock + Grain Assembly food hall, developed and managed by a Baltimore-based firm, as well as thirty-six-thousand square feet of office space overlooking the stadium. The planned development also includes a plaza, a 120-room hotel with a restaurant, a 200-unit apartment building, and mixed-use space.

High Point's artists and designers were also staking a claim to the city's West End neighborhood one and a half miles from downtown where John Muldoon was assembling a coalition to renovate the city's former Melrose Hosiery Mill. In Muldoon's vision, the mill and the remnants of the small merchant district that had surrounded it would combine into a project called Cohab.Space. "We're trying to bring in other artists, other community venues for people such as restaurants, such as other living spaces, and office spaces for designers and architects . . . to help develop the community," said JK Gallery owner Jim Koch, who had been on the block for three decades.[26] Muldoon, the owner of Clubcu, which produced handmade reclaimed furniture, had relocated from a space in the North Elm District. Part furniture showroom, part maker space, part garden, and part third place, Muldoon's concept of the "co-working and co-living" innovation community was still evolving.

In early 2019, Qubein announced that the Factory, the Quebecois-owned loft showroom building constructed in 1910 and the oldest building in the Adams-Millis hosiery complex, would be the linchpin for another major project. Supported by a gift from local trucking executive David Congdon, then chair of Business High Point, it would be combined with a second Adams-Millis building (discussed in the next section) to create a two-hundred-thousand-square-foot complex called Congdon Yards. A newly formed High Point Chamber of Commerce Foundation would operate the events center, across the street from Hair-N-Stuff, whose own site interestingly was denoted as "residential" on Elliott's conceptual plan.

At the same time, just east of downtown, plans were underway for the fifty-thousand-square-foot Nido & Mariana Qubein Children's Museum. Designed in the High Point University aesthetic and supported by a gift from the university president, it was to be located on the outskirts of

John Muldoon's plan for Cohab.Space, a co-working and co-living artist and creative space west of the Market district in a former hosiery mill complex. Courtesy of John Muldoon.

downtown on the still-public section of Montlieu Avenue (the street HPU had acquired). The museum had the potential to provide a transition between the HPU area and the new Outfields district. Quebin's plan gains added significance when contrasted with Duany's response to residents' desire for a children's museum: a play space constructed from shipping containers.

The various building projects in progress all had a goal of injecting street life into the downtown. Elliott was a seasoned architect and designer who specialized in creating "Main Streets" out of marginal land, exactly what Forward High Point wanted for "The Hair-N-Stuff District." He described himself as "a bonafide and admitted 'Disneyholic'" who visits the Orlando theme park three or four times a year to study the details of its design.[27] For some urbanists, Elliott's allegiance would raise reasonable concerns that the new district will be Disneyfied, marked by generic structures with a veneer of ersatz vernacular.

A Disneyfied district does not seem like a place that furniture aesthetes would embrace, especially when the downtown already had an authentic (though Market-centered) "Main Street" storefront district on MLK Drive. The question remained open. In the meantime, a formulaic intervention to generate street life might not be a bad first step toward the more "organic" iteration expected to follow later, as Wagner had argued. After all, this was no infill project but the creation of a destination district where none had existed—in a city that had not had one for a half century.

The reasonable skepticism that a lone small baseball stadium would be able to turn the tide of downtown use was, in the end, irrelevant. It was just one piece within a larger puzzle, Gibbs later clarified. Elijah Lovejoy's idea in chapter 8 to generate a mobile town center via his Party on the Plank had, in just seven years, evolved into the will for a permanent town center. As the previous chapters should heartily attest, this was no small feat. The civic energies invested in the overlay plan, the Uptowne plan, and the Duany plan had cultivated both an awareness of what was possible and a sense of efficacy among a broader group residents.

After years of talking about it, the time seemed right to Charles Simmons—whose half century of civic brainstorming earned him the nickname "mayor of Main Street"—to align his assets with his aspirations for the downtown. Simmons's brick and marble building, built by his grandfather in 1912, was across from the white building. In late 2019,

Simmons offered the use of his building rent-free to a group of artists ranging in age from the midtwenties to early thirties, some of whom were also involved in Washington Street's Gallery 512 project. One early contributor to the Gallery on Main, a newcomer to the city, quickly discovered for himself what Lovejoy had dubbed the High Point riddle. "That is why this town is dominated by showrooms," he explained. "[Building owners] don't have to deal with any renters or businesses coming in or anyone else except these entities that have these large amounts of cash." Without interventions like Simmons's, he said, this capital "drowns out any kind of local community organization" from getting a foothold.[28] Just before the Covid-19 pandemic, Sabrina Tillman McGowens and Sheena Dawkins took over Gallery on Main to establish an inclusive, creative, downtown hub for Black creatives like themselves. "I keep saying that music, art, design, fashion, and spoken word—they all go hand in hand. It's all creative," McGowens said.[29] "One of the things that I wanted to do is have a place for African-American artists and artists of color to feel at home, and at the same time, making sure that we keep everything open for everyone."[30]

Meanwhile, on the political front, High Point reelected Wagner mayor and voted to seat four Black men on the city council, all Democrats. The election of Tyrone Johnson, Michael Holmes, Cyril Jefferson, and Chris Williams represented the first time the council had four Black members. Each was sympathetic to downtown redevelopment to varying degrees. With two of the new council members also having furniture ties, Holmes at Ikea and Williams at IMC, a broad coalition of support for the both/and approach seemed possible. At-large council member Johnson, a pastor, had won a citywide contest. "When we have a healthy downtown that is vibrant and alive, then we can have a healthy neighborhood," he said.[31]

A Downtown for the Cluster

The new resident-centered efforts beginning to unfold in the late 2010s did not outpace the furniture-related innovations. Business High Point launched HP365, an initiative to develop an industry incubator to cultivate the remains of High Point's furniture economy into the "Silicon Valley of Furnishings."[32] Tim Branscome, a former executive with Oaktree Capital Management and IMC, was the CEO and developer of the project. He partnered with Chapin, of Business High Point, to form the nonprofit HP365.

"People tend to think the furniture industry went off to Asia, but if you think of the ecosystem around the industry—marketing, design, production, logistics, IT—there's an enormous infrastructure here that is alive and well, it's just not branded and it doesn't raise its flag during Market," Branscome said, echoing our exploration of High Point's cluster in chapter 7.[33] HP365 was established with funding from a $1.5 million grant from the North Carolina Department of Commerce and $1.5 million from private donors, including International Market Centers, High Point University, and Bill Millis (of the original hosiery family that operated the plant). The initiative sought to help the cluster's "suppliers, entrepreneurs, and small businesses" as they "strive to redefine themselves and adapt to an ever-changing marketplace."[34]

In June 2018, seven months before his announcement of what would become the larger Congdon Yards project, David Congdon announced he would lease the rear building of the old Adams-Millis plant—the section that Gabriele Natale and designer Sid Lenger had considered renovating for residents in 2000—for one dollar annually to Business High Point. It would house Plant 7, a globally minded furniture industry incubator and platform. Together, Plant 7 and the Factory would make up Congdon Yards. Branscome noted that the project's "scale could not be pulled off in any city other than the furnishings capital of the world." There, "product designers and engineers, craftsmen, finishers, photographers, logistics companies, professional services, and others" would engage in the "'cross-pollination' of ideas and techniques."[35]

"The real beauty is this: this project is global in scope and it perfectly serves as a platform for new start-ups, while also supporting the large number of active designers, producers and service companies already located in the High Point region," Branscome said.[36] Plant 7 is important to the cluster as a physical symbol of High Point's year-round furniture presence. It sends an unprecedented message to furniture creatives that High Point sees their needs and their potential. "This particular community was fragmented," Branscome added, a profound understatement.

"Just like you have craft beer, you have craft furniture," Mayor Wagner remarked at an early event.[37] *This Is Not a Chair,* an art furniture exhibit displayed at Plant 7 before the Fall 2018 Market, featured celebrated Brooklyn designers such as Asa Pingree and Chen Chen & Kai Williams.

Plant 7 furniture art and design, entrepreneurship, and innovation center, within the Congdon Yards complex. Photograph by Louis Cherry.

"Am I wrong to think that we might be at the beginning of a . . . new appreciation for limited quantity, for passion-inspired furniture?" asked one Plant 7 exhibitor.[38]

Branscome left Plant 7 in 2019 and the facility underwent a major renovation. It includes not only coworking space and a café, but also two million dollars of pay-per-use industrial-grade woodworking machinery for prototyping and small-batch production (through a partnership with Italian firm SCM) and a furniture materials library called Material ConneXion. There is no doubt that Plant 7 is positioned to make an impact, although the facility's specific role as an "incubator" remains undefined. In late 2021, the global fabric firm Culp, Inc. leased the entire top floor for its innovation and design roles—giving "innovation" a decidedly corporate connotation.

Meanwhile, Arkansas-based Riverside Furniture planned and completed an overhaul of the city's seventy-thousand-square-foot YMCA building that included both year-round offices and a "Collab Lab." In this innovation center, product developers and merchandisers would collaborate on Riverside's latest projects.[39] As with Culp, the firm followed common practice in locating only the most innovation-sensitive jobs—rather than its whole headquarters—within an industry cluster.

Just before the Covid-19 pandemic, a group of furniture industry professionals began to develop their own vision for High Point as a year-round design hub. What emerged was HPxD, an association of about fifty showrooms, some open to the trade only and others open to the public. With the tagline "Design Never Goes Dark," the new group understood their campaign as well-timed for "design in the time of Covid," when there was an industry-wide affirmation that "nothing replaces a showroom visit for an unfiltered brand experience" along with an understanding that the pandemic made broader access to showrooms a necessity.[40]

The inertia around year-round use enveloped the city's longtime institutions as well. The Home Furnishings Hall of Fame announced plans to build a 23,500-square-foot glass, steel, and concrete center with a clerestory roof one block from the Big Building. Designed by High Point architect Peter Freeman, it is intended not only to be an homage to furniture but also to serve as a dedicated, year-round gathering space for the industry and larger public. The center, due to open in 2023, is slated to include space for exhibits and a theater as well as an archive and research area housing furniture history artifacts. Another major furniture industry resource, the Bernice Bienenstock Furniture Library, established an ongoing venue to highlight the city's design functions when it held its first Designers Summit in fall 2021, bringing thirty college students to the city for a three-day conference.

Good for High Point Is Good for Market

"This building actually tells a really long story about the history of this industry." Furniture journalist Francine Liddelle was talking about downtown High Point's vacant white office building on South Main Street, a structure Duany celebrated in 2013 as "one of the greatest loft buildings in the world." With its subsequent handover to IMC, Duany expressed regret that now it was likely to be demolished for costly code violations. To Duany, the enemy was regulation. "Why have we tortured this building?" he asked.

This lament of the white office building's demise turned out to be premature. In October 2018, International Market Centers revealed the magnitude of the city's seismic shift when it donated the building to Forward High Point, considering it in their best interest. IMC's chief strategy officer expressed that the white building "will be a valuable addition to both the community and to High Point Market upon redevelopment," and added, "What's good for the city is good for the Market."[41]

This was a jarring inversion of High Point's half-century-old adage, "what's good for Market is good for High Point." Like other transformations then under way in the city, it represented the dismantling of High Point's unswerving dedication to immediate-term exchange value for a slightly longer-term view. "A thriving downtown creates a more inviting and accommodating destination for the tens of thousands of visitors that come to Market twice a year, so IMC is very supportive of the downtown revitalization efforts," IMC's chief strategy officer continued.[42] In the past, the largest downtown showroom landowners were never "very supportive" of any resident-centered downtown plan—and this was the largest showroom landowner ever.

CEO Maricich had stated early on that his firm would benefit from the downtown as "a place of vitality and energy."[43] In donating it to the city, IMC did not merely delete a line from its spreadsheet to let the white building become a hulking ruin. It instead sought to reintegrate the showroom space with community uses while it continued to invest in its anchor showroom buildings. In relation to the latter, IMC even had a plan, delayed by the Covid-19 pandemic, that would strip off the corrugated brown aluminum cladding of the Big Building and rework both its exterior and interior. "We are moving away from the 80s," joked IMC's executive vice president, confirming that the building had been frozen in time during the cash cow era.

Meanwhile, Forward High Point invited site proposals for the white building from mixed-use developers. The Request for Proposals outlined several unprecedented deed restrictions, most notably a prohibition banning use as a "showroom for the display and wholesale sale of furniture, home décor and related accessories."[44] It was the ultimate evidence of a sea change. For generations, individual small showroom owners had sought to shield their cash cows from both wear and tear and liability by excluding community uses from the downtown. Over time, it became clear that some of these local real estate beneficiaries were essentially furniture slumlords, wringing as much revenue as they could from their investment while investing minimally in upkeep.

After several potential deals fell through, in 2021 a New York–based development firm acquired the white building for a project it dubbed the Hive, projected to include restaurants, office, retail, residential units, and e-sports gaming. In the past, there was no government or civic will to corral the growth machine's drive for highest and best use because their ranks had swallowed both the government and the civic. Even showroom owners like Pasquale Natale and others who showed some concern for the community fabric saw the embers of their resident-centered dreams suffocated by civic leaders with little interest in fanning them. Instead, the political culture at the time encouraged citizens to withdraw and then celebrated them for it, as if passivity indicated civic pride and a respect for leadership.

"If we don't confront the question of what we have already lost, how we lost it, and what alternative forms of ownership might keep them in place, we risk destroying the authentic urban places that remain," sociologist Sharon Zukin stated, warning us to not be stubborn and narrow-minded in our solutions to contemporary problems of community spaces.[45] One lesson the High Point story illustrates is that even when it seemed the downtown could not get more dead, the loss of breakfasts at Rosa Mae's, proms at Showplace, and dinners at Nobles showed that it could. This was the *nostalgia gap*: residents were looking back to "time A" with nostalgia for a downtown that they, in "time A," had considered emptied and hopeless. This variation on the old truism "you never know what you've got 'til it's gone" reinforces the asset-based community development tenet that even amid the bleakest situations, assets remain—to be inventoried and cultivated by an engaged community.

By discouraging engaged citizenship, High Point's leadership sacrificed the benefits to be derived from local wisdom and know-how.[46] In contrast to High Point's exclusive governance, an *inclusive* local government is one in which "citizens and their values can play a critical role in stewarding a place and its economy to serve long-term goals with broad benefits."[47] Multiple Black High Pointers aged fifty and over commented to me over the years about the far-reaching control of officials they sensed within the constrictive mill town patriarchy.

"What has happened in the past, and I know it to be true, is they've always had someone to infiltrate it, get in the middle of it, act like they're a part of the thing," noted resident Larry Diggs. We were talking about past committees ostensibly created to solicit citizen participation in community visioning. "But they're [actually] there to get information to take it back to the city so they can get a jump on what's going on," he concluded. Fears of such reconnaissance and leaders' desire to corral public engagement are understandable and legitimate given the city's historic fixation on order and its heritage of mill town patriarchy. This was hardly an environment to invite creative problem solving.

"That's almost like going to counseling to talk about your parents and having your parents sitting there in your face," said Angela McGill. Although younger than Diggs, she expressed the identical distrust. "What are you really going to say?" she laughed. "You're not going to say anything that you're going to have to deal with later." Glenn Chavis, a retired pharmaceutical salesperson, felt keenly aware of a cost in voicing the wrong opinion. But as the outspoken Chavis liked to point out to local officials, his livelihood (now in retirement) came from distant Chicago and did not depend on their networks of power.

The legacy bred by such a political culture is rational disenfranchisement. Recall how Sims characterized the atmosphere in High Point: "Whatever it is you're doing, it's not for me." High Point's leadership has exploited this disenfranchisement for so long that even good-intentioned and inquisitive politicians have had difficulty overcoming it. Most officials have simply enjoyed its conveniences.

Ironically, at the moment, the "impulsive roamings" of global investors were fostering local decisions to reembed and reintegrate resident-centered and community-integrated uses into High Point.[48] While the entrance of private equity can be characterized as a "capital-led colonialization of urban space" headed by powerful "financial, corporate, and state interests" that were displacing a rich, authentic local life, it is also important to recognize the state of the community that global capital entered.[49] It is safe to say that for some the main concern in High Point is not colonization by outside elites (such as Vornado, Bain, or Blackstone) but the local brand of domination.[50] From this perspective, although external investment in High Point brings great disadvantages, the addition of outside eyes focused on the city's goings-on could potentially include new benefits.

As Duany enjoyed craft beer and brick-oven pizza at the Factory in 2013, the Bermex furniture executives who operated it shared with him their "dream to be open to the public all year round" just like Pasquale Natale had dreamed before them.[51] Duany encouraged the Quebec firm to "bypass government" in pursuing this goal.[52] In the end, after multiple free market efforts by furniture interests to offer resident-centered space in those old Millis loft buildings, it was ultimately civic philanthropy and government-endorsed public–private initiatives that assigned the old mill to a new, valuable hybrid function. Jane Jacobs did not believe in using government intervention to, as Zukin states, "break the great power of those who own, and those who can zone, the land."[53] This hyperlocal organic approach is why some of Jacobs's followers today can overlook preservation of the *social* environment in their privileging of the *built* environment, celebrating buildings and sidewalks while, due to more structural factors, the way of life that animated them disintegrates.

Duany has written that local "common sense" activism, like that displayed in Part III by the proponents of a resident-centered downtown, is "a necessary foil against the technical expertise of specialists."[54] While Duany deferred to the downtown's tidal wave of real estate investment with a plan to bolt residents' life spaces—arenas, stores, playgrounds—to private parking lots, Wagner was affirming High Pointers' right to claim spaces that nurture community life even in the midst of High Point's prime Market real estate. He believed residents had a right to expect a mutual respect between the internationalized sector of the downtown's Market real estate and its more localized functions.

Conclusion

Integrating Frontstage and Backstage

The ironic thing is that [the showroom strategy] was foresight, it was progressive, it was cutting edge. It was preparation for future generations to have a little something to do, business-wise. But now it's like that foresight has hit a dead end. Who's doing the foresight now?

—Rev. Elijah Lovejoy

Comparing the Downtown Mobilizations

Elton Cox's nonviolent direct actions in the 1960s, including his "ace in the hole," the threat to have one thousand Black men lie on the street during Market, were the first mobilizations over downtown use. They awakened an apathetic public through orchestrated direct actions that threatened the image High Point leaders were working to portray. We have not seen a similar pressure exerted since. None of the mobilizations described in Part III employed the tools of protest, and rarely did they publicly identify and focus on an adversary. Like Rev. Cox's protest, Elijah Lovejoy's tactics targeted social and cultural domains. The Downtown Improvement Committee's plaques and statues campaign also focused on cultural ends. The remaining seven campaigns were similar in that they involved specific plans regarding land use policy. I have diagrammed these approaches in this figure and briefly review each one.

The *targeted takings* diagram shows how in the 1980s Mayor Judy Mendenhall targeted key downtown properties for resident-only uses before showrooms dominated the center city. The approach would graft little "solution strands" into the community fabric before the mounting issue—showroom speculation—became overwhelming. Rather than managing growth through zoning or planning a large, high-impact, "big

307

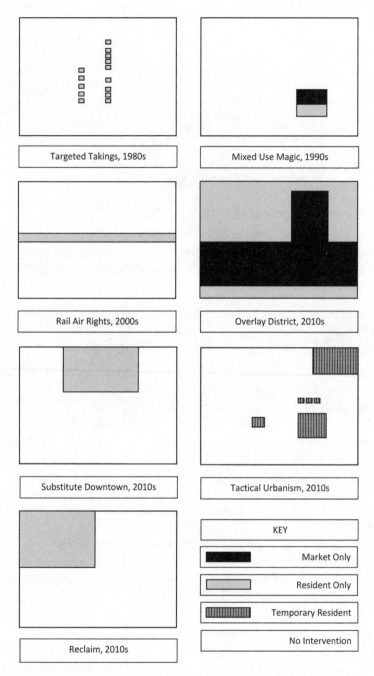

Diagram representations of the seven land use plans discussed in Part III, with Market only, resident only, and temporary resident only spaces denoted.

bang" project, it invoked the use of eminent domain on particular buildings in order to scatter resident-centered uses throughout a concentrated area.

Mayor Becky Smothers's Magic Block charrette, in *mixed-use magic,* adhered to a big bang approach with discussion of a mixed-use (resident and Market) development that focused on an entire central block. However, that project also was aborted by the city's failure "to seize some control" by rezoning the land, as land use attorney Tom Terrell explained. It illustrated local government's refusal to serve as a "connective tissue between idea and action" to balance resident and Market uses. If such balance was meant to be, said the underlying logic, the free market would respond, bringing use value and exchange value into alignment. Such approaches are politically palatable partly because they are politically impotent: charrette as charade.

Represented by *rail air rights,* Aaron Clinard's campaign to regain resident-centered use sought to create real estate by utilizing the air rights above the downtown railroad tracks for building. Such an orientation entails the insertion of major government or philanthropic projects to produce a quick transformation of the urban fabric—another big bang plan. New York City's Hudson Yards, Chicago's Millennium Park, and the Sacramento Railyards are the result of similar schemes.

The *overlay district* plan proposed an area of Market-only and resident-only zones. Even the overlay plan's proponents admit they were not savvy in this battle. "I'm not telling you the city did not go out and try to talk to these people, but I don't think [it] talked to them in the way they expected to be contacted," one Market leader reflected. High Point's collective leadership just didn't get it. "They're from all over the world," she said, referring to showroom stakeholders. "You can't have a public hearing at the High Point City Hall and sit down and put your hands"—she raised her hands in the air and shrugged in resignation—"and say 'Oh! No one came.' No one came because if you live in New York, you probably didn't know." When the "New Yorkers" did hear, they were understandably up in arms, she added. "Times like that, I think the city forgets to act like an international center," another leader observed. Yet it ultimately was not the style of the overlay's approach that provoked resistance, but the plan's substance. Local leaders, developers, and voters believed that supporting the plan would stunt investment or, worse, cause it to depart for another setting with less government interference.

The overlay was a type of "hotspot" strategy, sometimes applied in antigentrification efforts to prevent displacement, which offers special protection to a stipulated amount of less profitable uses (often affordable housing) within a highly profitable fabric. If implemented in a nurturing rather than an exploitative way, the community fabric potentially triumphs.[1] However, for profit-minded investors who already owned downtown High Point property, the seeming unfairness that one property is banned from showroom use while the one across the street is not was a predictable point of resistance.

As a response to the overlay defeat, the Uptowne effort, represented in *substitute downtown,* focused on ceding the entire capital-inundated downtown to Market and encouraging resident-centered uses elsewhere using policy tools such as a road diet and grants for facade improvements. Like the failed overlay effort, this plan assigned a place for the internationalized sector of real estate to prevent it from pricing out local real estate players. However, while the overlay plan confronted the internationalized sector, the Uptowne effort exited the confrontation to embrace a neighborhood that had two benefits: it already had resident-centered uses and did not interest showroom investors. Whereas the overlay approach explicitly encouraged the mixture of very different uses, the Uptowne approach privileged highest and best use: showrooms *belonged* in downtown and boutiques *belonged* in Uptowne. The latter made potential synergies between resident-centered uses and showrooms functionally impossible.

Andrés Duany's *tactical urbanism* approach inserted temporary resident uses into prime properties, adapting shipping containers as temporary quarters for novel resident-centered uses. The free market orientation Duany advocated for High Point required agile government, small business, and resident actors willing to stay out of the way of big capital. This approach granted resident-centered uses a status downtown, albeit a quasi-legitimate, temporary one. Rather than challenging the showrooms' domination of downtown, it encouraged precarious interventions.

Although it shares the overarching orientation of other mobilizations discussed in Part III—the reprivileging of resident-centered uses—Forward High Point's plan to "reclaim" reflects the lessons and battle scars of previous planning efforts. *Reclaim* shows a region of the downtown that is restricted to residents only.

The approach echoes Mendenhall's 1980s plan in its acquisition and sale of land to specific developers for resident-centered uses. That makes it quite unlike Smothers's approach in the 1990s: it has no illusions that a critical mass of resident-centered uses can be profitable enough to displace showroom uses without government intervention into real estate markets. It also bears similarities to Clinard's railroad air rights plan from the early 2000s. Instead of using regulation alone to support resident-centered uses, both plans called for new construction dedicated to resident-centered uses within a multiblock area of underutilized real estate adjacent to prime land. Embellishing Clinard's hope: "If you build enough of it all at once, they will come." Both endeavors, a decade apart, shared the belief that their resident-centered spaces would both benefit the Market and benefit from the Market.

The Forward High Point plan was quite different from that of the overlay. While the overlay would have created a protected area where resident-centered uses could emerge, it did not actually designate resident-centered projects. As realty owner Ed Price noted of that effort, just because the city draws a line "doesn't mean that private enterprise is going to follow." In the Forward High Point plan, the driving force is not maximum profit but a socially minded public–private partnership committed to assembling a curated mix of sufficiently profitable resident-centered uses.

One lesson derived from the many debacles of the urban renewal era in the United States was that local governments used federal funds to condemn, acquire, and clear land only to discover that developers did not wish to "follow," as Price put it. The Magic Block's early history bears out the difficulty that city leaders face in finding a mutually beneficial balance of community and developer input. Not soliciting developer input can lead to sites of deteriorating buildings or razed rubble sitting for years due to lack of interest.[2] Yet overprivileging developer input can lead to the ceding of control to advantaged developers as "experts," giving them the latitude to bend the rules toward their own personal gain. Despite these difficulties, in High Point's case it would be hard to imagine any resolution of the downtown riddle without a willingness on the part of elected officials to collaborate carefully with property developers on resident-centered plans. To dismiss High Point leaders who collaborate on resident-centered uses as the mere pawns of business interests is to ignore a century of context.

The Forward High Point plan was completely unlike the two efforts that directly preceded it: the Duany and Uptowne plans. Duany paid obeisance to the "Golden Goose" by proposing temporary construction in the shadow of the Market. The Uptowne plan deferred to the goose by exiting its habitat altogether. Forward High Point's emphasis on "reclaiming," fully relegitimating and reprioritizing resident-centered uses, was unprecedented. But the plan's philosophical underpinnings were far from revolutionary.

As Duany writes, "To the degree that government policies influence the market, this influence must consciously support community, not inadvertently destroy it."[3] He could be describing High Point, especially with his assertion that the act of intervening in the (lowercase *m*) market—including with incentives such as free leases and land—should not be framed as socialism but as "the city operating competitively within the reality of a cutthroat marketplace."[4] Despite this wise and prescient admonition years before his visit, Duany did not lend his pedestal to amplify the High Point voices who articulated these very arguments.

Although this new rendition of the card game has only begun to unfold, the Forward High Point plan marked a profound shift in the dynamics of local politics. The City of High Point was using the power of government and public–private partnerships to limit showroom development rather than to clear a path for it as it had done in the past. Economic, social, political, and cultural shifts had coalesced into an expanding movement that empowered city leaders to steer rather than trail development. For decades, High Point officials had pitted the certainty of capital against the folly of sentiment. Now, the prospect of pairing the two no longer induced scorn and ridicule.[5]

The Common Threads and the Right to the City

The right to the city is inherently "a collective rather than an individual right."[6] Ultimately, it is power that a democratic collective must exercise "over the processes of urbanization."[7] It is the reassertion of human worth in calculations of economic value. We have seen the agitation of alienated actors such as Elijah Lovejoy who understood these processes "as preventing adequate satisfaction of their human needs," in the words of planning scholar Peter Marcuse.[8] Over the past two decades, I observed High Point as a community beginning to grasp that—despite differences within that community—they were being pitted against a structure that ill-served the majority.

What is their common enemy? Marcuse would call it a "one dimensionality [that] eats away at their humanity."[9] Ten years ago, resident Waymon Martin had used the same phrase to describe a new generation of High Point leaders on the horizon that would not stand for "one dimensional" growth. The one dimensionality that Lovejoy also discerned and fought was the "huge fixation with business and money" that formed contemporary downtown High Point. Some it affected more in the wallet, others more in the heart, but their discontent was trained on a common adversary.[10] High Pointers of different persuasions and from different perspectives articulated a desire for both a robust public realm and an inclusive economy; the showroom-dominated downtown was a touchpoint that allowed them to identify some of their shared grievances. A new generation of High Point leaders played with some new cards, but they were also playing with a renewed dynamism.

The High Point story echoes the experiences of other places across the world where citizens are resisting decades of privileging highest and best use with calls to "reclaim," the word used by both Clinard and Jay Wagner. The threads constituting the fabric of this story represent defining urban issues of our era. These four common issues, woven throughout the narrative of this book, relate to exchange value, exclusion, globalizations, and users. As I overview key lessons from the book, I attempt to artificially disentangle these four threads, which are intricately interrelated in practice.

Thread of Exchange Value:
The Unavoidable Costs of Ridiculing Use Value

In a run for mayor in 2014, Democratic state legislator Marcus Brandon called High Point a "good-old boy network that has really isolated downtown for themselves."[11] Both candidates in this election criticized the extreme degree to which the Market extracted local exchange values without contributing to community life. It seemed clear that the loss in property values in the neighborhoods surrounding the downtown was at least partly the result of a downtown offering no local centrality and anchoring no local use value. For local interests, being proximate to the downtown brought zero benefit. It explained why I could continue to enjoy my inexpensive 1930s apartment in Uptowne without the cost pressures of gentrification.

Very early on in my research, residents would tell me the growth of the High Point Market was not about the well-being of the furniture industry at all. They said it was strictly a matter of real estate development. Furniture-centered growth would have actually looked much different; it would have been more oriented to use value. Sociologist Lorenzo Vicario observed the same thing in Bilbao. "It's not culture-led redevelopment," he said paradoxically of the boom that surrounded the culture-anchored Guggenheim. "It's property-led redevelopment."[12]

In a similar way, it has become apparent just how little downtown High Point offers the furniture world. How many potential employees of various levels of skill and income could High Point have developed for local firms if city leaders had cultivated the extant furniture cluster rather than allow it merely to persist as a residue of the city's craft past amid low regulation? Recall the idea that architecture scholar David Crane raised during the Smothers charrette in 1996 to house a school for the industrial arts on the Magic Block. What effect would such intentional cross-fertilization have had over the past twenty-five years?

It is always a straw man argument to portray a battle of economic growth versus no economic growth, capital versus sentiment; such arguments rarely capture messy realities. The details make all the difference. *What time horizon is a community using? What type of growth is it pursuing—one aimed at producing fulfilling jobs that offer the dignity of a local livelihood? Specific to High Point, how do various types of potential employment complement the components of its fragile furniture cluster or, as locals say, its furniture DNA?*

We can only loosely approximate the mid- and long-term economic costs of the city's "any Market growth is good growth" orientation. One measure of the cost is in lost property value beyond the downtown. It is also in the lost potential of the myriad jobs that a year-round furniture innovation center could have fostered and in the value that high schools, two-year colleges, and four-year colleges might have contributed by offering courses to prepare students for these jobs. We can find it, too, in the robust cultures of innovation that companies would have developed in such collaborations. Also, consider the more far-reaching effects. Any calculation of costs must include all the funding High Point will now invest in the core city's vacant homes, impoverished households, workforce retraining, and policing. How many of this small city's nearly seventy homicides from 2018 to 2021 could have been prevented by more inclusive growth and community wealth?

High Point presents an enduring lesson: complete disregard of use value now will lower exchange value later. Balance undoubtedly has a place; this is hardly a case of "do-gooder" social-centered sentiment versus "realistic" revenue-centered capital. If governments merely privilege isolated short-term fiscal injections, then they should expect little in the way of sustainable economies and communities. If this is the goal, to adjust Mayor Roy Culler's retort in 1988, I wonder why we even have governance.[13]

For many decades, the city's civic leadership brought a parade of experts and consultants to town in hopes of sparking an idea for a both/and downtown that would not interfere with the profit machinations of the real estate market. It was Duany with his shipping container interventions who actually delivered such a plan. Yet, when the Miami-based designer suggested things like the city turning its dead mall's parking lot over to new college graduates and filling its downtown with shipping containers, it felt to some like Duany was using the town as a canvas for his own abstract daydreams. As one resident acerbically commented on the latter: would the downtown now be filled with port-a-potties to service the temporary retail?[14] "We see them as some kind of carpet-baggers or boondoggle-sellers," said conservative Jim Davis, echoing his constituents' apparent view of Duany and his ilk.[15]

To be sure, Duany's plans were an affront to some in this city of craft and construction. Duany proposed a temporary arena for HPU basketball made of stacked shipping containers bolted to the ground. Later, Nido Qubein would go on to break ground for a $130 million Qubein Arena where basketball legend Tubby Smith came to coach. Duany said High Point did not have the critical mass to sustain a children's museum and suggested a playground of sand and shipping containers. A few years later, the city greenlighted Qubein's plans for a brick-and-mortar version.

The failure of city leaders to leverage their competitive advantage by championing a unique High Point vision has long annoyed Glenn Chavis. "We think, 'oh no, we're going to upset 'em too much,'" Chavis complained. "This is *your* business. You know more about it than any-one in the *freaking* world." Duany has espoused this bold view, writing, "Civic leaders must develop a physical vision for their city which they commit to and then actively promote. Rather than being victimized by the self-interest of the private sector, they must determine the type, scale, and quality of new growth and then act as the lead booster for that growth."[16]

A new coalition anchored by Forward High Point and Business High Point has built a homegrown downtown community development apparatus. With a city council amenable to a resident-centered downtown, local community development experts on the payroll, a stronger coalition of the High Point business community, and full investment from Nido Qubein and anchor institution High Point University, sufficient momentum had formed to develop a community vision for downtown High Point that did not rely on the advice of outside experts or investors. The agile elite championing this plan, although it was still the product of a local growth machine, clearly had tempered short-term exchange value calculations with a concern for the community fabric—or at least a concern for more sustainable, longer-term exchange value calculations.

The changing narrative of downtown High Point and its Market point the way forward to a more careful and inclusive brand of community development that values "the human experience of growth and not just seeing it as a set of abstract economic metrics."[17] In communities from conservative Salt Lake City to progressive Barcelona, citizen mobilizations have emerged to proclaim that "how we grow matters."[18] Enlisting active resident participation in that growth can occur only through a "democratic stewardship" of it.[19] In High Point, philanthropists and public–private partnerships were working to establish local use values by offering one-dollar leases for small business and artists. Space for local use values could also be taken up more directly by government via a type of inclusionary zoning in which mom-and-pop business are protected amid what Lovejoy called "tidal waves" of investment.[20]

After years of promoting market-centered plans that assumed a side effect of community benefit rather than stewarding plans centered on community benefit, a new generation of High Point leaders learned by repeatedly banging their head against a collective wall that—without strong action—their downtown economy would consistently encourage the extraction of a community's wealth for the benefit of a select few.[21]

With a new set of leaders taking the initiative to understand the issues and longtime voices continuing the fight, it appeared that the High Point community was willing to be intentional about setting the stage for a more inclusive growth.

Thread of Exclusion: The Frontstage, the Backstage, and the Absorption Continuum

Nearly two decades of discussions with Market leaders make me appreciate Michael Moore's caustic comment about the 1980s tourism campaigns of his hometown, Flint, Michigan, that people do not want to see "human tragedy while on vacation."[22] Or on a business trip for that matter. In the current climate of event planning, most organizers—even for a convening of lefty urbanists who study these matters—will mindfully or unconsciously labor to insulate their guests from experiences that might undermine the event's intended messaging. Although the motive is understandable, leaving it unchecked empowers event planners and local tourism and convention leaders to hold an entire community hostage for the sake of a curated visitors' gaze.

Expanding on the lack of a metaphorical living room lamented by High Point's resident-centered advocates, you could say downtown High Point has had plenty of formal *sitting rooms*—most prominently the shiny frontstage exposition spaces. They are formal because nobody enters these spaces without preparation and rehearsal. High Point as a community also has had *bedrooms*. Unlike the sitting room, in the bedroom vernacular flourishes and only intimates can enter. The boundary between sitting room and bedroom is stark and strictly enforced, separating the glossy performance of landscape from the locally particular comforts and complexities of vernacular.

A *living room* dwells somewhere in the messy in-between—a place where the intersection of frontstage and backstage is not a "breach." It is a place that a geographically, ethno-racially, and class-diverse array of residents intuitively consider the most "central gathering place" in the city, the public realm that hosts a community's intersections.

The brilliance of the growth machine strategy is that its underlying logic is invisible and not made available for discussion, making responses to the most pressing questions seem commonsensical (i.e., "there is no alternative") and hardly requiring discussion. One major Market-related issue undiscussed is to what degree the community should tolerate the

separation between the frontstage it presents to the world and the backstage places it hides. In 1967, when Rev. Cox threatened to bring the dirty
laundry of High Point's white racism to the frontstage of the Market
through a community-rooted effort that would pierce the glossy sheen
of Market, the compromise ultimately reached followed precedent: city
leaders prevailed and the traces of resident life were vanquished from
the Market area during the "days that matter."

Shielding visitors from the community by confining them to a sanitized tourist experience is not optimal.[23] Ideally, visitors would be incorporated as "a permanent, even mundane feature of everyday life" and
simply blend into streets that "absorb tourists seamlessly."[24] In practice,
the "bubble" versus "blending" comparison exists on what we can call an
absorption continuum. Not every city can be Paris—much less a small
city. But High Point is obviously on the wrong end of the continuum
that ranges from zero osmosis between community and visitor on one
end to unhindered osmosis on the other.

An engaged citizenry must have a venue to challenge the calculations undergirding the backstaging and frontstaging of particular places,
people, and times. The alternative is to permit the implicit agreements
enforcing such segregation to become accepted practice and unques-
tioned common sense. If an issue—such as a neighborhood's deterioration—is legitimately disconcerting enough to steer visitors away from
it, it should be serious enough to warrant some kind of action when
visitors are *not* present. Energy invested in averting users' gaze away from
an issue rather than addressing it head-on will eventually diminish the
well-being of the community at large in the name of short-term convention and visitor revenue.

As historian Glenn Chavis well knew, the rerouting of state and federal roads around Black neighborhoods, essentially *delinking* them from
the cognitive maps of people who had no reason to go there and *containing* those who lived there, helped foster their deterioration across
the United States.[25] Today, that deterioration—not the racial history of
Washington Street or its current racial composition—is offered as the
reason to isolate this backstage from the frontstage. The tendency for
decisions like these to become about abstractions such as the "not so
great" impressions of deterioration rather than the explicit racist decisions that created the issue highlights what sociologist Mary Pattillo
calls "the genius of systemic racism." As "past racism has so distorted

the functioning of institutions and markets," an overtly racist motive "is no longer even necessary" to maintain an unjust status quo, she argues.[26]

Once leaders pronounce a particular place—here Washington Street—unfit for the visitor's mise-en-scène, two poles define the possible responses: remake or remove. First, they can try to *remake* it, perhaps into a diluted, themed version of its former self with Coltrane-themed clubs and museums, to make it legible, comfortable, and consumable for marketgoers and prime real estate for exhibitors. Citing Washington, D.C., as an example, Chavis described this approach as "sanitizing neighborhoods" so that "we [Black residents] can't live in 'em." He sensed that this was the preferred plan for Washington Street. "Go over to the development office and tell them to show you the first poster that came out regarding Washington Street depicting how it was going to look. Guess what? The figures are on the street, strolling up and down the street? They're all white. *White,*" Chavis repeated. "I went before the city council and I said: 'That's what you *want.*'" On the other end of the continuum, leaders may attempt to further *remove* what they deem unsightly from the marketgoer's map—the predominant approach in High Point. In deciding which places will be the illuminated frontstage and which will be the contained backstage, High Point officials make decisions that distribute not only resources but also dignity.[27]

To this *remake/remove* discussion, I would also recall Jane Jacobs's lesson on the inevitability of interaction between neighborhoods—and more broadly, destinies. No "artificial haven," no maintaining of "turf," can be created to successfully wall off and contain one particular population from another.[28] Issues troubling the areas beyond protected citadels will eventually require reckoning. And when they do, the situation will be worse and more complex than what prompted the original separation.

High Point's current contradiction between the continuously renovated, exclusively used, and excessively controlled downtown and its ever-deteriorating surroundings—regularly compared to a campy scene out of science fiction—would be better confined to fiction. Yet this contrast afflicts cities from Detroit to Lagos to Bilbao. "Many people see [it] from the outside; only a few experience it from the inside," Vicario observed about the disparity between visitor areas and resident areas in Bilbao. "What kind of regeneration is this?" he asks.[29]

This does not argue that High Point's securing and maintaining the Market—or Bilbao's developing the Guggenheim—were poor decisions.

Ultimately, they may well be net positives considering what might have transpired otherwise. "The city becomes a place you choose to stay in, as opposed to being the place you want to escape," said urbanist Beatriz Garcia in reference to the sociocultural effects of Bilbao's regeneration campaign. "It's an act of storytelling."[30] We cannot overlook these "soft" benefits to all residents. Smaller towns that have lost an identity altogether and developed sagging branding campaigns (e.g., Flint's attempt at an indoor automotive theme park called Autoworld) would trade places with High Point or Bilbao in a New York minute. However, "success" is always rife with "question marks," as Garcia noted of Bilbao, and more than twenty years after the museum opened, the community legacy of Bilbao's campaign remains "a work in progress."[31]

Strategies like those deployed in Bilbao continue to inspire other cities. In 2018 Dundee, Scotland, opened an offshoot of London's Victoria and Albert Museum whose boat-shaped edifice designed by Kengo Kuma would look at home docked alongside High Point's Natuzzi ship, by Mario Bellini. "'If you build it, they will come,'" the local *Courier and Advisor* newspaper advised Dundee in 2012 when the project was under consideration. Invoking the success of Australia's iconic Sydney Opera House, the newspaper encouraged local government to "build it," warning leaders that "the converse [of that axiom] is also true."[32] The culture strategy articulated by the newspaper draws on two strains of classic growth machine rhetoric: "We must do it now or another city will beat us to it" and "this will make us world class."[33] Clinard used the "if you build it, they will come" idiom in chapter 9, but he was speaking of the residents of High Point and the region, highlighting just how unique High Point's situation is. This is very different from Bilbao and Dundee, which were courting an international population of city users. High Point had plenty of those.

Thread of Globalizations: The Need for Small City Expertise in Forging a Glocal

When they formulated their plan, Bilbao's visionaries did not know what was in store. "Back then, we didn't really understand what we were talking about," recalled Guggenheim Museum Bilbao director Juan Ignacio Vidarte. "What was happening was that the world was becoming global."[34] Likewise, even when the Kennedy family's MMPI outbid High Point local Ivan Garry for his National Furniture Mart, the industry's turbulent period ahead was not fully apparent. The High Point leaders of that era, caught up in their growth strategy, could not have imagined the doubling of the Market's floor area or the specter of Bain and Blackstone acquiring the controlling interest in their downtown. They were riding the exchange value wave as hard as they could in case that wave subsided. That wave carried them into the thick of uncharted waters in the global economy.

Global waters are tumultuous. With one private equity firm controlling most of the downtown, the area will remain to some degree subject to the formulations and whims of financial formulas. Global financial capitalists have representatives seated in the local small city conference room.[35] *How will the city maneuver within this relationship? Will the city subject investment to the levers of democracy and mediate it with inclusive planning?* Without community oversight, Forward High Point's "success" in increasing the value of the core city could have drastic effects. For instance, it could incentivize the bundling and purchasing of properties, many of which are currently valued in the tens of thousands of dollars. The more than 1,400 vacant acres surrounding the downtown are worth only around one hundred million dollars altogether.

Unsurprisingly, High Point has not developed the network of activists, organizations, and other voices of reflection that its complex intersection of rural-style poverty and global-city-style real estate investment requires. Without such watchdogs, there's "no political price for caving" to development interests.[36] Localized interests in globally central, small U.S. cities—be they corporate headquarters such as Bentonville, Arkansas, or less conventional variations such as High Point—do not have the same structural capacity as their larger peers to make demands of the powerful global interests that may increasingly choose to locate in them. Nor do they enjoy the support of state, provincial, or national governments that small cities in other nations receive to help them mediate the resulting complexities and pressures.

In most small U.S. cities, the people leading the charge for the right to the city are volunteers with very different day jobs. In fact, even many full-time, development-related professionals lack expertise in real estate, community development, or the workings of big finance. They often largely rely on either the benevolence of business or the synergies existing between the community's interests and those of profit-seeking enterprises to broker resident-centered benefits. With those enterprises increasingly internationalized and disembodied, such benevolence and synergies will likely emerge not automatically but as the result of debate and negotiation. Locals must request, demand, or require them. Local universities—if they are able to act as a liaison rather than a growth booster—can be a good incubator for these asset-based strategies particularly suited to the small-city context.

As small cities become more deeply embedded in global circuits of commerce and investment, they will increasingly need to employ tools such as the ones that larger cities wield—zoning, deed restrictions, and community benefits agreements, among others—to capture benefits from local development. Until higher levels of government also privilege the local community fabric, however, small city leaders take on extra risk with such an approach. An emphasis on interests tied to use value jeopardizes two key advantages that small cities like High Point have historically offered global capital: malleability and low costs. Recall Lovejoy's read on the New York landowner who resisted the overlay plan in chapter 9: "We want to do whatever we want, to take advantage of whatever we want to take advantage of, without your interference."

High Point's new glocal nexus is demanding both preparation and shrewdness from High Point's current leaders. For the first time in generations, the global economy has evidently dealt High Point leaders new cards to play. Where the loose furniture coalition that previously dominated the Market Authority had agreed on little but showroom growth, IMC has presented local authorities with a more complex constellation of interests that includes the social vitality of the downtown.

IMC's investment in downtown High Point is wed to a sense of place, giving IMC reason to be an active player in manipulating the local context of its assets.[37] High Point's success rests on its branding as a creative design, merchandising, and fashion center as never before. If downtown High Point as a brand begins to lose value, IMC's asset values and revenues are put at risk. What would it mean to IMC for marketgoers to see downtown High Point as an opulent citadel amid a struggling ghetto? Or what would it mean if marketgoers interpreted the downtown as the center of a backwater, patriarchal, parochial mill town? In either case, one could imagine IMC having to confront major barriers. Recall the "dirty little secret" that a city council member shared with me in chapter 4: "People don't come because High Point has the Market. High Point has the Market because people come."

The possibility always exists that city users will not use or will condition their use with demands for change. The threat of "users not using" emerged in 2016 when the North Carolina General Assembly passed HB2, a state bill requiring people to use the public bathroom corresponding to the gender listed on their birth certificate. Revealingly, a disproportionate amount of the conversation surrounding the statewide impact of HB2 centered on the High Point Market. National, state, and local journalists quoted Market leaders among the interests that distanced themselves from North Carolina's state legislature and the bill. "How embarrassing for us that people don't want to come to our state," said Mitchell Gold, the gay co-owner of the nationally known, North Carolina–based manufacturer Mitchell Gold + Bob Williams. "It's such a dark blemish on our state and our people,"[38] agreed IMC CEO Bob Maricich. "We as an industry have always been supportive of gays and lesbians and view our diversity as a strength. By the way, I'm a conservative Republican," he noted. "I haven't had one outreach from a buyer or a tenant who said, 'I'm glad they did that. Good for them.'"[39]

Thread of Users: The Imperative of Both/And

Consultants proffering advice on the creative industries would be astounded to hear how few benefits High Point has reaped from its designer-laden region. In finally recognizing this strength, High Point is not merely manipulating its industrial past into a gritty backdrop, chasing the latest trends in "maker culture" or "craft." Its assets predate this mania. Design, merchandising, small-batch manufacturing, product development, marketing—these are all specializations that local leaders have allowed to scramble for survival for decades. Nobody seized the threads that could weave these extant fibers into a coherent, sustainable fabric that integrated High Point's locally rooted expertise with its functions that draw users from elsewhere. Plant 7 is one thread: a strategic, long-term investment in High Point's unique global niche and its most aggressive effort toward staking a claim as the world's furniture innovation center.

Plant 7 is not isolated in a new furniture complex for visiting users, however, but is next door to the city's new baseball stadium. With tickets to a baseball game going for the price of a movie ticket, independent league baseball is about as "local" an artifact of Americana as a small city can have. The priorities of the new Congdon Events Center next to the stadium will be the opposite of Showplace's: *allowing* Market-related events, but *designed* for the community. Blocks away is the white office building, controlled in succession by three private equity companies, now with a restrictive deed for resident-centered uses.

In a comment echoing those raised by High Point's resident-centered proponents, the former curator of Scotland's Dundee Contemporary Arts noted that while that institution aspired to drawing an international audience, the museum must also serve as "a new living room for the city."[40] The breadth and depth of residents' participation in efforts such as these will depend largely on day-to-day decisions made by city leaders including who gets to create, sit at, and lead the decision-making table, what uses the projects privilege, and which local and supralocal organizations are invited to run programming within these living room spaces. An inclusive space holds the potential to become a central nexus for both residents and its temporary users from around the world.

While it is hard to imagine the furniture world giving up its global meetings, the Covid-19 pandemic and the specter of future pandemics have certainly increased the possibility of High Point's visitor traffic evolving from two huge seasonal spikes of pedestrian activity to something more spread out. This would further the goal of making the downtown a more active, year-round community. If the city center transforms into a place that functions year-round, visits by workers in creative occupations from design cities such as Milan, New York, or Antwerp will likely increase, and some of these workers will decide to live in High Point. Even a small uptick in such migration or the length and frequency of visits by outsiders will have a significant impact. Out of this transforming sociopolitical environment, new types of decisions will emerge. Newcomers—both individuals and firms—will decide to what degree they will engage in difficult "big picture" discussions. The alternative, evident in previous eras, is to allow growth leaders to insulate them from these discussions as it privileges their interests.

To what degree will local culture encourage, evoke, or demand dialogue about the effects of development? For instance, developers have begun pitching new downtown residences for locals, but others have made such promises in the past. Will High Point leaders step in if furniture companies lease apartments en masse or if downtown condominiums amount to little more than lucrative Airbnb properties?

What if city users are not even present? As furniture expositions evolve, the term *city users* could take on a twenty-first-century twist, as physical spaces are represented in online showrooms, complete with virtual reality headset capability. This is an emerging niche in High Point and, with the January 2020 launch of IMC's Digital Innovation division, one can only imagine the potential. The ability for marketgoers to visit showrooms virtually presents a potential for a frictionless melding of physical and virtual spaces. This was quite valuable for those not able to come to the Market during the pandemic. In normal times, however, a buyer might make in-person visits to one Market to touch, feel, and see the furniture and supplement them with virtual visits later. If this hybrid practice becomes standard, downtown High Point's twelve million square feet may eventually exist as both an online and physical space for the same users.

As always, new success brings new issues. New users with higher education and income introduce the potential for an entirely different variety of polarization, especially evident in cities with increasing amenity-centered investment in their city centers. Examples include not only Greenville, South Carolina, the object of Clinard and Wagner's affection, but also more globally connected small cities like Bilbao and its protégés like Dundee. Activists in each of these places regard them as dual cities, with regions of isolated joblessness and poverty hidden from the gaze of the gentrifier and the tourist.[41]

This does not have to be. Just as with encouraging strategic investment, attracting new educated residents need not be a bitter pill with inextricable, violent side effects. A community does not have to accept injustice as the inevitable partner of success. It can choose to do this, but can also mitigate or fight possible polarization between longtime and newer residents—just as it can carefully navigate the tensions in exchange and use value, frontstage and backstage spaces, and global and local considerations. A democratic collective has the option to carefully navigate a path of both/and.

TATA for Now

The lesson to be derived from this book is certainly not that "High Points" as a type will or should emerge all over the world, although I do believe that smaller global *niche cities* will continue to rise to prominence.[42] I see a much simpler foundational lesson. If High Point could become a world leader in furniture exposition—competing against Chicago, Dallas, Las Vegas, and other much larger cities—to create "the last bastion of free market capitalism" and then later develop the political will to aggressively limit the free market development it enticed, urban agendas *must* be more malleable than we sometimes recognize. The High Point growth machine argued forcefully that "there is no alternative" (TINA) to privileging their brand of Market growth. However, as many thinkers have noted, "there are thousands of alternatives" (TATA).

Understanding these alternatives requires an immersion in the local circumstances, history, and players. Immersion offers a set of tools of a breadth and depth that a consultant's toolkit—with its particular orientation, biases, and agenda—often cannot match. The tool of ethnography afforded me these tools, and with them I was able to discern the threads that precipitated each of the mobilizations of the past dozen years. That is not to say that I successfully predicted what has occurred in High Point.

In fact, I initially was ready to write the book about how the Las Vegas market eviscerated downtown High Point. When the Market overlay district failed, I prepared to write the tragic account about how the High Point community finally identified its fatal flaw but failed to respond. Then, I was set to write the story about how, in the Uptowne plan, High Pointers left downtown High Point to give the Golden Goose free range. When Bain Capital funds suddenly absorbed the majority of the downtown in the IMC transaction, I assumed I would illuminate how High Point ceased governing altogether and willingly faded into the Greensboro hinterland in exchange for a stable stream of tax revenue. After the baseball stadium was proposed, I was going to chronicle how High Point leaders thought they could seize on a generic, off-the-shelf medication to reverse the effects of the city's rare disease.

All the while, the pieces were being laid for what Clinard apprehensively called "a revolt"—although he would be the first to admit he does not fit the part of the typical activist. Of all the High Pointers I identify as mobilization leaders, only Rev. Cox fit my own preconceptions of an activist. Throughout this research, colleagues would ask me "who are the activists leading the fight against the colonization of downtown High Point?" This simple question belies how long it actually took me to identify how the characters this book presents constituted the players in a coherent movement.

These leaders shared a desire for their community to value itself beyond the metrics of highest and best use. All were willing to incur personal costs as they rallied less committed people in pursuit of their goals.[43] They did not lead marches, plan direct actions, or passionately confront opponents. They wore no T-shirts stamped with messages of the movement. If there were any such trappings of "activism," my task would have been much easier.

Neither were there tidy categories to mark the boundaries of this battle. Republican Mayor Mendenhall argued that government intervention was precisely what downtown High Point required during the conservative Reagan–Thatcher era. I witnessed the stubborn pragmatism of Wagner, to the dismay of local conservative bloggers, making the same argument long before he won an elected office. I saw that fight in Bernita Sims—a Democrat who worked in the home furnishings industry—before her election as mayor. Such leaders expressed a willingness to use what they considered the necessary tools, regardless of their affiliations with conservatism, progressivism, or any other orientation.

Urban politics is inherently nonpartisan. Theory and abstractions are important when examining macro-level solutions, but may lose some significance when dealing with urban governance. A point of governance occurs somewhere between national heads of state and the neighborhood council member where facts on the ground become more important than allegiance to philosophies and theories. This brand of governance often entails using a both/and toolkit. While outsiders tend to frame important events (a factory leaving, an organic grocery store coming) as good or bad, it is local leaders who are most equipped at pivotal moments to address the nuanced question: "What is the alternative" (WITA)?

One interesting facet of this case is that the very people we might label as part of the growth machine, to use Logan and Molotch's formulation, are those who have questioned the effects of unregulated urbanization. There is Tom Blount, now editor emeritus of the *High Point Enterprise*, who all but explicitly over the past dozen years has been asking the paper's readers to think beyond exchange value. Growth machine theory allows for such agency, but characterizes it as a narrow path to navigate. We can consider Phil Phillips—a furniture businessperson, showroom property developer, and former U.S. ambassador—in a similar light.

Although it is now almost forgotten, when Phillips heard about the Bain transaction in 2011, he pressed residents to "borrow a chapter out of the Green Bay [Packers] playbook" and consider a "public owner-ship" of High Point showrooms in order to block the purchase.[44] "Let's not capitulate to this takeover attempt," he warned. Instead, Phillips called on residents to "purchase and . . . manage the market" and thereby "control [their] future."[45] Globalization brought this certified Republican to the point of riffing on the idea of municipal socialism. In this moment of economic destabilization, Phillips sought to take the delocalized mach-inations of private equity financialization and reground them in the local. It would have been a monumental event—a publicly owned downtown championed by a Reaganite and Bush appointee. Perhaps this portends what could occur when IMC bows out of High Point.

Just as "many Southern conservatives jettison their faith in free-market globalization" the moment it starts hurting their business interests, civic and government leaders need to demonstrate similar flexibility when the free market is creating dysfunctional dynamics in communities as it did in High Point.[46] Like furniture manufacturer John D. Bassett III, who sought to ward off Chinese furniture makers using tariffs two decades before the more recent tariff war, Phillips was attempting to soften the impact that the vagaries of the global economy posed to his business and town. In both cases, their regulatory reflexes ran afoul of their con-servative economic philosophies. Just as with several of the land use plans discussed to start the chapter, such strategizing illustrates how levees of regulation (e.g., for small business, for affordable housing, for local ownership) can be espoused even by a leadership that generally favors the unfettered "tidal waves" of the free market.

Although the tumult of the global processes of urbanization is well established, "what is not a given is the local interpretation of this real-ity."[47] Ample room remains for locally rooted contingencies, dialogue, and decision-making. Without allowing this room, it is easy to assume that local places are "responding to a global imperative," a view that sim-ply "imputes too much rationality to the world."[48] Local agency endures even amid the apparent dominance of macro-level forces. Places diverge from each other and even from their own enduring trajectories, as this story shows.

All of this ideological messiness, less surprising at the level of local politics, points a promising way forward for a more inclusive form of urban governance. Capital can take the form of thousands of variations toward a place, and, correspondingly, there are thousands of variations in a place's potential approach toward capital. This is not to exalt the virtues of a middle ground between laissez-faire and government intervention but to promote an end to thinking in terms of this continuum. Urban agendas—certainly, small-city urban agendas—are more open and malleable than urbanists often allow.

While not all local agents will have the foresight to perceive the best way to situate their city within this array of possible futures, those who do are extremely likely to be locally seasoned and rooted. Those who own the problem own the solution. Social analysts, policy wonks, and consultants can play a vital role in strategizing, but without immersion in ground-level intricacies and local wisdom, they cannot be expected to adequately assess a place. For their part, local urban leaders must consider all the tools available to them, leverage all the local wisdom at their disposal, and develop home-rooted policies that, although they may be applauded from afar, are truly too local to travel.

Acknowledgments

My study of High Point began in my graduate courses at New York University with Harvey Molotch and Neil Brenner, two supportive mentors who each have their own distinctive strengths. Harvey has invested his time to provide feedback on this project for two decades. His charming wit enabled me to laugh through any challenge: I have never asked Harvey for feedback without receiving notes in return that were all at once critical, caustically dry, encouraging, and hysterical. He has always been willing to read my arguments at their earliest stages, held together by duct tape and bubble gum. Jason Patch, a student of the same two urbanists, has been my research partner and friend. His insights can be found on each page of this book—there would be no chapter 5 without him. Over the past two decades, these three scholars have never tired of talking about this project, or perhaps they just didn't let on.

My DePaul colleagues Larry Bennett and Black Hawk Hancock have been gracious in giving their time to various iterations of this manuscript, Larry in the early days and Black Hawk more recently. Peter Marcuse was good enough to critique early drafts of this book and is responsible for broadening my definition of gentrification (although many tried before him) in a way that illuminated the High Point case. Richard Lloyd has been effusive in his advice and coaching since he first became aware of this project in 2014. He read early versions and invited additional requests for feedback. Christopher Andrews was a Houston-based urban planner I became familiar with on social media when I learned that he was relocating to the city of High Point for work. An urbanist new to High Point, his willingness to share his perspective on the draft manuscript was precious. Jeff Muckensturm, a member of the Next City family that I joined as a Vanguard fellow in 2016, offered invaluable feedback. Jodie Draut read a near final version, while Gerald Beecham and Francesco Tassi help me wordsmith areas related to their expertise.

Pieter Martin of the University of Minnesota Press and Globalization and Community series editor Susan E. Clarke valued my treatment of High Point as an in-depth case study very early on. They, along with my (once) blind reviewer Leonard Nevarez, were patient, supportive, and properly critical as I developed the manuscript. Linda Levendusky's expert editing eyes arrived on this project at just the right moment. Once she recognized that I invited her harshest critiques, she probed ever deeper into excavating the book's compositional weaknesses. Paula Dragosh was extremely flexible in providing the final edits. I am grateful for the strong support of my community at DePaul University, which furnished Linda's expertise through the Faculty Scholarship Collaborative, several grants from both the University Research Council and the College of Liberal Arts and Social Sciences, and the expertise of my undergraduate readers Quinn, Deyana, Marina, Ryan, and Franco through the Writing Center. I must also note the great encouragement and support that a National Science Foundation grant lent to my early work (Award #0327474).

I am deeply indebted to the people of High Point, especially those who make up this book's cast of characters. They opened every aspect of their lives to me and helped make High Point one of a handful of places my heart calls home. I'll never forget how the late councilman Aaron Lightner took me to City Hall the moment I finished unloading my U-Haul from Brooklyn—I didn't even get a chance to shower! Martin Sinozich gave me a job at his gym with two four-hour shifts, 6–10 a.m. and 6–10 p.m., so that I had the core of my day for research. There are so many whose help and perspective benefited my research, but I must single out Aaron Clinard simply for the way he welcomed me as a young ethnographer and, with complete humility, sought only to grant me access. He believed that the good in the High Point he loved would ultimately show in whatever story I told; I believe it did. Glenn Chavis was always a caring but critical voice of the High Point I was uncovering. Without the work of both him and Phyllis Bridges relating to High Point's Black history, this would be a different book.

My gratitude to the people who became my High Point family, especially Ron, Rashad, Melvin, Tripper, Donna, Larry, Treaver, Mike, and

Akin. I am thankful, also, for my church and choir families in High Point, New York, and Chicago (and especially to John Swain Jr.), who lent listening ears and offered encouragement in my research while I worked to walk as a Christian, pursue justice, and be an academic. I am grateful for the support of my mother, Mary, and late father, Bill, whose love for architectural engineering (learned on the job as a young man in New York and Chicago) seeped into me through countless "war stories." When my father arrived for a visit to downtown High Point, he said the juxtaposition of buildings looked like a hurricane had ripped through the pages of architecture coffee table books. And as I look at this project that has spanned so much of my life, I thank God, the keeper of mind, body, and spirit; I must agree with Solomon that "excessive devotion to books is wearying to the body!"

My interest in High Point evolved with my interest in a firecracker from Brooklyn named Monique Bobb. On one visit to High Point, she casually pointed out that the JH Adams Inn would be a great place for our wedding—ours happened there in 2006 with a reception following at J. Basul Nobles. High Point has always been a topic of discussion for us (guess who always brought it up!), and I could not have completed this book without her patience (a hint), conversations, inspiration, and support.

Appendix

The People in Showroom City

Name	Role (Organization)
Abernathy, Ralph	civil rights activist (Southern Christian Leadership Conference)
Allen, Heidi (pseudonym)	temporary Market worker
Bellini, Mario	architect and designer
Bellizaire, Arianne	interior designer
Bencini, Bill	politician (city council, mayor)
Blount, Tom	newspaper editor
Branscome, Tim	furniture industry veteran
Bringier, Sally (pseudonym)	Market leader
Brown, Joe	newspaper editor
Burnette, G. Lee	urban planner (City of High Point Planning Director)
Butts, Beka	illustrator
Buzov, Miro	restaurant owner, woodworker (Penny Path)
Campbell, Al	politician (city council)
Casey, Brian	Market leader (Market Authority president and CEO)
Cashion, Audie	consultant, real estate agent
Chapin, Patrick	business leader (Business High Point president and CEO)
Chavis, Glenn	local amateur historian
Clapp, Paul	politician (city council, mayor)

Clinard, Aaron	civic leader, attorney
Cox, B. Elton	civil rights activist, Freedom Rider
Cox, J. J.	multi-tenant Market showroom executive (National Furniture Mart)
Crane, David	architect, academic
Cutler, Ivan	furniture industry veteran, blogger
Davis, Bruce	politician (county commissioner)
Davis, Jim	restaurant owner (Rosa Mae's)
Davis, Jim	city council, interim mayor
Dickins, Geraldine (pseudonym)	advertising professional
Diggs, Larry	civically engaged resident, political candidate
Duany, Andrés	architect, urban planner (New Urbanism movement)
Easter, Joanna	multi-tenant Market showroom executive (Showplace)
Elliott, Tim	community designer (Elliott Sidewalk Communities)
Everitt, Callie (pseudonym)	showroom designer
Freeman, Peter	architect
Froehlich, Jake	furniture sector leader, showroom developer
Fuscoe, Wendy	public–private partnership leader (The City Project)
Garry, Ivan	furniture showroom realty strategist
Gibbs, Ray	public–private partnership leader (Forward High Point)
Gruenberg, Bob	multi-tenant Market showroom executive (Big Building)
Heer, Leo J.	multi-tenant Market showroom executive (Big Building)
Hood, Phil	furniture product developer, executive
Hsieh, William	furniture executive (Lifestyle Enterprises)
Johns, Trina (pseudonym)	engaged High Point resident
Johnson, Kevin	economic development professional (HP Economic Development Corporation)

Kennedy, Chris	multi-tenant Market showroom executive (Merchandise Mart Properties)
Khoury, Emil	showroom operator
Lambeth, Candy	multi-tenant Market showroom executive (Radio Building)
Lambeth, William	furniture product developer, executive
Lenger, Sid	furniture designer
Liddelle, Francine (pseudonym)	furniture industry journalist
Lovejoy, Elijah	pastor, political candidate, and activist (Party on the Plank)
Maricich, Bob	multi-tenant Market showroom executive (International Market Centers)
Martin, Waymon	community college professor
McGill, Angela	real estate and development leader (Housing Authority)
McNeill, Janette	community college professor
McPherson, Holt	newspaper editor
Mendenhall, Judy	politician (mayor, city council); public–private partnership (Market Authority)
Millis, Jim	hosiery industry executive and philanthropist (Adams-Millis)
Muldoon, John	furniture industry executive (COHAB.SPACE)
Natale, Gabriele	furniture industry executive (Natale Furniture, Manwah USA)
Natuzzi, Pasquale	furniture industry executive (Natuzzi Group)
Nixon, Jason	designer and furniture executive (Madcap Cottage)
Perkins, Trish	consultant and civically engaged resident
Phillips Jr., Earl ("Phil")	furniture finance executive
Phillips, Jason	furniture industry executive (Phillips Collection)

Phillips, S. David ("Dave")	furniture finance executive, showroom developer (Market Square)
Price, Ed	realty and development
Qubein, Nido	motivational speaker, business and education executive (High Point University)
Reed, Ray	furniture analyst, journalist
Ruden, Nic	civically engaged resident
Shuford, Harley F. ("Buck")	furniture industry executive (Century Furniture)
Siceloff, Paul	nonprofit, civic leader
Simmons, Charles	showroom operator, civic leader (Gallery on Main)
Simpkins, Sarah (pseudonym)	furniture industry executive (Big Building)
Sims, Bernita	politician (city council, mayor)
Smothers, Becky	politician (city council, mayor)
Stout, Carson	politician (city council, mayor)
Tallon, Matthew (pseudonym)	real estate and showroom developer
Terrell, Tom	attorney, civic leader
Tillman, Otis	physician, civic leader
Wagner, Jay	politician (city council, mayor)
Waites, Raymond	furniture designer
Walker, Philip	urban planner (Walker Collaborative)
Willliams, David	furniture industry veteran and documentary filmmaker
Williams, Tom (pseudonym)	pastor and civic leader
Wood, Richard	floor covering industry veteran, civic leader (The City Project)

Notes

Introduction

1. Debra Phillips, "Twenty Best Cities for Small Business," *Entrepreneur Magazine*, October 1997, https://www.entrepreneur.com/article/22732.

2. Donald McNeill, "The Bilbao Effect," in *The Global Architect: Firms, Fame, and Urban Form* (New York: Routledge, 2009), 162–76.

3. Elaine Markoutsas, "Raymond Waites Translates Personal Style into American Style," *Chicago Tribune*, March 24, 1985, https://www.chicagotribune.com/news/ct-xpm-1985-03-24-8501160692-story.html.

4. The Market was quarterly (January, April, July, October) from the 1950s until 1982. Although High Pointers and people in the furniture industry often use *Market* as a lowercase proper noun, for clarity I capitalize it when used as a proper noun even when the original source did not and dispense with brackets for readability, despite convention. Nor do I capitalize the commonly used term *marketgoer*, which is used as a simple noun.

5. Sharon Zukin, *The Cultures of Cities* (Cambridge, Mass.: Blackwell, 1995), 9.

6. Andrés Duany, "Closing Presentation: Ignite High Point," High Point University, 2013.

7. Andrés Duany, "Opening Presentation: Ignite High Point," High Point University, 2013.

8. Duany, "Opening Presentation."

9. Fredric Jameson, *Postmodernism, or, the Cultural Logic of Late Capitalism* (Durham, N.C.: Duke University Press, 1991); Saskia Sassen, *Cities in a World Economy*, 5th ed. (Thousand Oaks, Calif.: SAGE / Pine Forge, 2019), 89.

10. Robert Marks, "City Challenged as Market Center," *High Point Enterprise*, October 26, 1967.

11. Richard Lloyd, "Urbanization and the Southern United States," *Annual Review of Sociology* 38, no. 1 (2012): 484.

12. Lloyd, "Urbanization and the Southern United States," 491.

13. Enterprise Staff, "Bond Said Vital to City's Growth," *High Point Enterprise,* April 21, 1964.

14. Gay Carter, "Asian Survey Market for Export Possibilities," *High Point Enterprise,* October 24, 1978.

15. Jerry Epperson, "Viewpoint," *Furniture Supplier Spotlight,* Spring 2003.

16. Beth Macy, *Factory Man: How One Furniture Maker Battled Offshoring, Stayed Local—and Helped Save an American Town* (New York: Back Bay Books, 2015), 163.

17. David Held and Anthony G. McGrew, *The Global Transformations Reader: An Introduction to the Globalization Debate* (Malden, Mass.: Polity, 2000); Coltrane Jazz Fest, "Festival History," http://www.coltranejazzfest.com/about-us/history/.

18. Barry Bluestone and Bennett Harrison, *The Deindustrialization of America: Plant Closings, Community Abandonment, and the Dismantling of Basic Industries* (New York: Basic Books, 1982), 17–18.

19. Bluestone and Harrison, *Deindustrialization of America.*

20. Bluestone and Harrison, *Deindustrialization of America.*

21. Bluestone and Harrison, *Deindustrialization of America,* 12.

22. Duany, "Opening Presentation."

23. Joseph Alois Schumpeter, *Capitalism, Socialism, and Democracy* (New York: Harper, 1942).

24. Bonnie Nichols, *Valuing the Art of Industrial Design: A Profile of the Sector and Its Importance to Manufacturing, Technology, and Innovation,* Research Report No. 56 (Washington, D.C.: National Endowment of the Arts, 2013), https://www.arts.gov/sites/default/files/Valuing-Industrial-Design.pdf; Richard L. Florida, *The Rise of the Creative Class* (New York: Basic Books, 2002); Michael E. Porter, "Clusters and the New Economics of Competition," *Harvard Business Review,* November–December 1998.

25. Allen Scott and Michael Storper, "Regions, Globalization, Development," *Regional Studies* 37, nos. 6–7 (2003); Porter, "Clusters and the New Economics of Competition"; Gilles Duranton and Diego Puga, "Micro-Foundations of Urban Agglomeration Economies," in *Handbook of Regional and Urban Economics,* edited by J. V. Henderson and J. F. Thisse (Amsterdam: Elsevier, 2004), 2063–117.

26. Saskia Sassen, *Expulsions: Brutality and Complexity in the Global Economy* (Cambridge, Mass.: Belknap Press of Harvard University Press, 2014), 2.

27. Jamie Peck and Nikolas Theodore, *Fast Policy: Experimental Statecraft at the Thresholds of Neoliberalism* (Minneapolis: University of Minnesota Press, 2015); Malcolm Tait and Ole B. Jensen, "Travelling Ideas, Power and Place: The

Cases of Urban Villages and Business Improvement Districts," *International Planning Studies* 12, no. 2 (2007).

28. H. Molotch, W. Freudenburg, and K. E. Paulsen, "History Repeats Itself, but How? City Character, Urban Tradition, and the Accomplishment of Place," *American Sociological Review* 65, no. 6 (2000): 793.

29. H. V. Savitch and Paul Kantor, *Cities in the International Marketplace: The Political Economy of Urban Development in North America and Western Europe* (Princeton, N.J.: Princeton University Press, 2002), 171.

30. Savitch and Kantor, *Cities in the International Marketplace,* 43.

31. Savitch and Kantor, *Cities in the International Marketplace,* 45.

32. Savitch and Kantor, *Cities in the International Marketplace,* 270.

33. Paul L. Knox, "Globalization and Urban Economic Change," *Annals of the American Academy of Political and Social Science* 551, no. 2 (1997): 21.

34. Quotations from these interviews are not footnoted. See Douglas Harper, "An Argument for Visual Sociology," in *Image-Based Research: A Sourcebook for Qualitative Researchers* (London: Falmer, 1998), 24–41; Margarethe Kusenbach, "Street Phenomenology: The Go-Along as Ethnographic Research Tool," *Ethnography* 4, no. 3 (2003); Kevin Lynch, *The Image of the City* (Cambridge, Mass.: MIT Press, 1960); P. J. Bettis, "Urban Students, Liminality, and the Postindustrial Context," *Sociology of Education* 69, no. 2 (1996).

35. R. L. Polk & Co., *High Point, North Carolina City Directory* (Livonia, Mich.: Polk, 1963); R. L. Polk & Co., *High Point, North Carolina City Directory* (Livonia, Mich.: Polk, 1983); R. L. Polk & Co., *High Point, North Carolina City Directory* (Livonia, Mich.: Polk, 2003).

36. Harvey Molotch, "Growth Machine Links: Up, Down, Across," in *The Urban Growth Machine: Critical Perspectives Two Decades Later,* ed. Andrew E. G. Jonas, David Wilson, and Association of American Geographers Meeting (Albany: State University of New York Press, 1999), xiii, 312, 248.

37. Loretta Lees, Hyun Bang Shin, and Ernesto López-Morales, *Planetary Gentrification* (Cambridge: Polity, 2016), 223.

38. Molotch, "Growth Machine Links," 248.

1. The Common Threads in High Point's Uncommon Fabric

1. John R. Logan and Harvey Luskin Molotch, *Urban Fortunes: The Political Economy of Place* (Berkeley: University of California Press, 1987), 292.

2. Molotch, "Growth Machine Links," 249.

3. Logan and Molotch, *Urban Fortunes,* 292.

4. Molotch, "Growth Machine Links," 248.

5. Eric Clark, "The Order and Simplicity of Gentrification: A Political Challenge," in *Gentrification in a Global Context: The New Urban Colonialism,*

edited by Rowland Atkinson and Gary Bridge (London: Routledge, 2005), 256–64.

6. Then called the International Home Furnishings Market Authority. I use the most recent name throughout the book.

7. Molotch, "Growth Machine Links," 251.

8. Appraisal Institute, *The Dictionary of Real Estate Appraisal,* 5th ed. (Chicago: Appraisal Institute, 2010).

9. John Friedmann, "Life Space and Economic Space: Contradictions in Regional Development," in *Life Space and Economic Space: Essays in Third World Planning* (New Brunswick, N.J.: Transaction Publishers, 1988), xi, 322.

10. Charlie Lehman, "Boiler Room Bar Declared Unsafe," *High Point Enterprise,* October 24, 1984.

11. Edward W. Soja, *Thirdspace: Journeys to Los Angeles and Other Real-and-Imagined Places* (Cambridge, Mass.: Blackwell, 1996).

12. David Harvey, *The Urban Experience* (Oxford: Blackwell, 1989), 43.

13. Ada Louise Huxtable, "The Problems of Zoning," *New York Times,* July 30, 1980.

14. Friedmann, *Life Space and Economic Space.*

15. Friedmann, *Life Space and Economic Space.*

16. Mike Robertson, "Market Rules City's Downtown," *High Point Enterprise,* October 10, 2000.

17. John Urry, *Consuming Places* (London: Routledge, 1995), 179.

18. E. P. Thompson, *The Making of the English Working Class* (New York: Pantheon Books, 1964); Tamara K. Hareven and Randolph Langenbach, *Amoskeag: Life and Work in an American Factory-City* (New York: Pantheon Books, 1978).

19. Eviatar Zerubavel, *Hidden Rhythms: Schedules and Calendars in Social Life* (Chicago: University of Chicago Press, 1981), 14.

20. Eviatar Zerubavel, *The Seven Day Circle: The History and Meaning of the Week* (New York: Collier Macmillan, 1985), 91, 17, 99.

21. Callie Everitt is a pseudonym.

22. John Friedmann and Goetz Wolff, "World City Formation: An Agenda for Research and Action," *International Journal of Urban and Regional Research* 6, no. 3 (1982): 325.

23. Teresa Pires do Rio Caldeira, *City of Walls: Crime, Segregation, and Citizenship in Sao Paulo* (Berkeley: University of California Press, 2001).

24. David A. Snow and Leon Anderson, *Down on Their Luck: A Study of Homeless Street People* (Berkeley: University of California Press, 1993), 103.

25. Andrés Duany, "The Pink Zone: Why Detroit Is the New Brooklyn," *Fortune,* January 30, 2014, http://fortune.com/2014/01/30/the-pink-zone-why-detroit-is-the-new-brooklyn/.

26. Stephen J. Sills, "Market Segmentation and Targeted Revitalization: High Point Core City," Center for Housing and Community Studies: University of North Carolina at Greensboro, 2016.

27. Sills, "Market Segmentation and Targeted Revitalization."

28. Sassen, Cities in a World Economy.

29. Manuel Castells, ed., The Rise of the Network Society (Cambridge, Mass.: Blackwell, 1996), 412.

30. David Bell and Mark Jayne, "Conceptualizing Small Cities," in Small Cities: Urban Experience beyond the Metropolis, edited by David Bell and Mark Jayne (London: Routledge, 2006).

31. Bell and Jayne, "Conceptualizing Small Cities."

32. Bell and Jayne, "Conceptualizing Small Cities."

33. Bell and Jayne, "Conceptualizing Small Cities"; John Joe Schlichtman, "The Niche City Idea: How a Declining Manufacuring Center Exploited the Opportunities of Globalization," International Journal of Urban and Regional Research 33, no. 1 (2009): 105–25.

34. Donald Lyons and Scott Salmon, "World Cities, Multinational Corporations, and Urban Hierarchy: The Case of the United States," in World Cities in a World-System, edited by Paul L. Knox and Peter J. Taylor (Cambridge: Cambridge University Press, 1995), xi, 335, 9.

35. Schlichtman, "Niche City Idea."

36. Richard L. Florida, The New Urban Crisis: How Our Cities Are Increasing Inequality, Deepening Segregation, and Failing the Middle Class—and What We Can Do About It (New York: Basic Books, 2017); Knox, "Globalization and Urban Economic Change," 23.

37. Neil Brenner and Roger Keil, "Introduction to Part Five," in The Global Cities Reader, edited by Neil Brenner and Roger Keil (London: Blackwell, 2000), 217; Peter Marcuse and Ronald van Kempen, Globalizing Cities: A New Spatial Order? (Oxford: Blackwell, 2000), 263.

38. Castells, Rise of the Network Society, 442.

39. Guido Martinotti, "Four Populations: Human Settlements and Social Morphology in Contemporary Metropolis," European Review 4, no. 1 (1996): 1–21.

40. Saskia Sassen, "On Concentration and Centrality in the Small City," in World Cities in a World-System, edited by Paul L. Knox and Peter J. Taylor (Cambridge: Cambridge University Press, 1995), 71.

41. Sassen, "On Concentration and Centrality."

42. Sassen, Cities in a World Economy, 119.

43. Saskia Sassen, "Locating Cities on Global Circuits," Environment and Urbanization 14, no. 1 (2002): 92.

44. Castells, Rise of the Network Society, 443.

45. Andy Merrifield, "The Entrepreneur's New Clothes," *Geografiska Annaler: Series B, Human Geography* 96, no. 4 (2014): 4.

46. Allen J. Scott, "City-Regions Reconsidered," *Environment and Planning A: Economy and Space* 51, no. 3 (2019): 554–80.

47. M. B. Aalbers, "Financialization," in *The International Encyclopedia of Geography: People, the Earth, Environment, and Technology*, edited by D. Richardson, N. Castree, M. F. Goodchild, A. L. Kobayashi, and R. Marston (Oxford: Wiley, 2019), 1–12.

48. Saskia Sassen, "Who Owns Our Cities—and Why This Urban Takeover Should Concern Us All," *Guardian*, Friday, May 11 2015, https://www.the guardian.com/cities/2015/nov/24/who-owns-our-cities-and-why-this-urban -takeover-should-concern-us-all.

49. Sassen, "Who Owns Our Cities."

50. Sassen, "Who Owns Our Cities."

51. Sharon Zukin, *Landscapes of Power: From Detroit to Disney World* (Berkeley: University of California Press, 1991), 139.

52. Zukin, *Landscapes of Power.*

53. Harvey Molotch, "L.A. as a Design Product: How Art Works in a Regional Economy," in *The City: Los Angeles and Urban Theory at the End of the Twentieth Century*, edited by Allen John Scott and Edward W. Soja (Berkeley: University of California Press, 1996), 225–75.

54. Molotch, "L.A. as a Design Product."

55. Molotch, "L.A. as a Design Product."

56. Molotch, "L.A. as a Design Product."

57. Molotch, "L.A. as a Design Product."

58. Martinotti, "Four Populations."

59. Martinotti, "Four Populations," 8.

60. Leslie Sklair, "The Transnational Capitalist Class and Contemporary Architecture in Globalizing Cities," *International Journal of Urban and Regional Research* 29, no. 3 (2005): 485.

61. Martinotti, "Four Populations," 7.

62. Clark, "Order and Simplicity of Gentrification."

63. Manuel Aalbers, *Subprime Cities: The Political Economy of Mortgage Markets* (Malden, Mass.: Wiley-Blackwell, 2012), 257.

64. Clark, "Order and Simplicity of Gentrification."

65. I am indebted to Peter Marcuse for insights about gentrification in this paragraph and the next. John Joe Schlichtman, Jason Patch, and Marc Lamont Hill, *Gentrifier* (Toronto: University of Toronto Press, 2017).

66. Peter Marcuse, "A Note from Peter Marcuse," *City: Analysis of Urban Trends, Culture, Theory, Policy, Action* 14, nos. 1–2 (2010): 193.

67. Marcuse, "Note from Peter Marcuse."

68. David Harvey, *A Brief History of Neoliberalism* (Oxford: Oxford University Press, 2005), 1–2.

69. Marcuse, "Note from Peter Marcuse," 190.

70. Marcuse, "Note from Peter Marcuse," 195, 90.

71. John Rawls, *A Theory of Justice* (Cambridge, Mass.: Belknap Press of Harvard University Press, 1971), 458, 63.

72. Molotch, "Growth Machine Links," 258.

73. Wendell Berry, *The Unsettling of America: Culture and Agriculture* (San Francisco: Sierra Club Books, 1977), 7–8.

74. Berry, *Unsettling of America.*

75. Savitch and Kantor, *Cities in the International Marketplace,* 23.

76. Savitch and Kantor, *Cities in the International Marketplace.*

77. Savitch and Kantor, *Cities in the International Marketplace.*

78. Berry, *Unsettling of America,* 7.

79. Snow and Anderson, *Down on Their Luck,* 103.

80. Zukin, *Landscapes of Power,* 199.

81. Mark Davidson and Loretta Lees, "New-Build Gentrification: Its Histories, Trajectories, and Critical Geographies," *Population, Space, and Place* 16, no. 5 (2010): 403.

2. Hollowing Out

1. U.S. Bureau of the Census, "Summary Statistics for Greensboro—Winston-Salem—High Point, Nc Msa 1997 Naics Basis," in *Economic Census,* 1997.

2. R. L. Polk & Co., *High Point, North Carolina City Directory* (Livonia, Mich.: Polk, 1963); R. L. Polk & Co., *High Point, North Carolina City Directory* (Livonia, Mich.: Polk, 1983); R. L. Polk & Co., *High Point, North Carolina City Directory* (Livonia, Mich.: Polk, 2003).

3. Ray Oldenburg, *The Great Good Place: Cafés, Coffee Shops, Bookstores, Bars, Hair Salons, and Other Hangouts at the Heart of a Community* (New York: Marlowe, 1999).

4. John Joe Schlichtman and Jason Patch, "Contextualizing Impressions of Neighborhood Change: Linking Business Directories to Ethnography," *City and Community* 7, no. 3 (2008): 193.

5. Forrest Cates, "Blight in Law Building Block Now Estimated at 68 Percent," *High Point Enterprise,* October 23, 1967.

6. Adelaide Wendler, "Urban Renewal Discussed," *High Point Enterprise,* April 16, 1964.

7. Jane Jacobs, *The Death and Life of Great American Cities* (New York: Random House, 1961).

8. Dow Shepperd, "Court Considers Urban Renewal Effort Here," *High Point Enterprise,* April 29, 1964, https://www.newspapers.com/clip/35796844/the_high_point_enterprise/.

9. John Nagy, "Magic Block Awaits Plans for Its Future," *Greensboro News and Record,* July 20, 1993, https://www.greensboro.com/magic-block-awaits-plans-for-its-future/article_528fb668-1d0e-57ed-8033-944e67d78c8e.html; Tim Webb, "The Magic Block: College's Investment Materializing in Sears," *Hi-Po,* September 30, 1966, https://archive.org/stream/Hi-Po_1966_V_40_Issue_1-27/Hi-Po_1966_V_40_Issue_1-27_djvu.txt.

10. Nagy, "Magic Block Awaits Plans for Its Future"; Robert Marks, "Buildings Slated for Demolition," *High Point Enterprise,* October 21, 1964.

11. Forrest Cates, "No Relief in Sight for Slum Area Here," *High Point Enterprise,* October 30, 1967.

12. Aldon D. Morris, *The Origins of the Civil Rights Movement: Black Communities Organizing for Change* (New York: Free Press, 1984).

13. Ta-Nehisi Coates, "The Case for Reparations," *Atlantic,* June 2014, https://www.theatlantic.com/magazine/archive/2014/06/the-case-for-reparations/361631/.

14. Heather Fearnbach, "National Register of Historic Places Registration Form: Washington Street Historic District," edited by Department of Cultural Resources: Office of Archives and History, 2010, https://www.highpointnc.gov/DocumentCenter/View/13477/Washington-St-NR-Nomination-Report.

15. John Lowe, "Radisson Will Give Downtown Boost, Merchants Say," *High Point Enterprise,* September 5, 1982.

16. Richard Rothstein, *The Color of Law: A Forgotten History of How Our Government Segregated America* (New York: Liveright, a division of W. W. Norton, 2017).

17. Ray Hubbard, "School Segregation Plan Still Not Found," *High Point Enterprise,* October 24, 1969.

18. Sharon Zukin, *Loft Living: Culture and Capital in Urban Change* (Baltimore: Johns Hopkins University Press, 1982), 171.

19. Arthur J. Vidich and Joseph Bensman, *Small Town in Mass Society: Class, Power, and Religion in a Rural Community* (Garden City, NY: Doubleday, 1960), 217, as quoted in Logan and Molotch, *Urban Fortunes,* 64; Harold D. Lasswell, *Politics: Who Gets What, When, How* (New York: Whittlesey House McGraw-Hill, 1936).

20. Logan and Molotch, *Urban Fortunes,* 292.

21. Forrest Cates, "Plans for New Showroom," *High Point Enterprise,* October 16, 1978.

22. Jeff Johnson, "Merchants Rap Downtown Construction," *High Point Enterprise,* October 17, 1978.

23. Johnson, "Merchants Rap Downtown Construction."

24. Johnson, "Merchants Rap Downtown Construction."

25. Molotch, "Growth Machine Links," 261.

26. Reggie Greenwood, "A History of Economic Development Efforts in High Point during the 1970s," City of High Point, 1980.

27. Joe Brown, "Focus on Downtown," *High Point Enterprise*, October 10, 1983.

28. John Lowe, "Businesses Told to Move: Furniture Complex Rumored," *High Point Enterprise*, October 16, 1985.

29. Andrés Duany, Elizabeth Plater-Zyberk, and Jeff Speck, *Suburban Nation: The Rise of Sprawl and the Decline of the American Dream* (New York: North Point, 2000), 87.

30. Pete Austin, "Mayor Proposes Pause on Corridor Growth," *High Point Enterprise*, October 28, 1988.

31. Austin, "Mayor Proposes Pause on Corridor Growth."

32. Duany, Plater-Zyberk, and Speck, *Suburban Nation*, 19.

33. Duany, Plater-Zyberk, and Speck, *Suburban Nation*, 224.

34. Andy Matthews, "Developers Target Eastchester," *High Point Enterprise*, October 21, 1993.

35. Matthews, "Developers Target Eastchester."

36. Paul Dillon, "Sprucing Up Downtown: Group Studies Area's Aesthetic Appeal," *High Point Enterprise*, October 24, 1993.

37. Thomas Russell, "New Restaurant Fills Space Left by Chick-Fil-A," *High Point Enterprise*, October 11, 1985.

38. Edward W. Soja, "Inside Exopolis: Scenes from Orange County," in *Variations on a Theme Park: The New American City and the End of Public Space*, edited by Michael Sorkin (New York: Hill and Wang, 1992), 94–122.

39. Andrea Monroe, "Scenes from a Mall: City's Focal Point," *Greensboro News and Record*, July 8, 1995, https://www.greensboro.com/scenes-from-a-mall-city-s-focal-point-when-a/article_5d840bd0-8936-5228-a635-727e156 18340.html.

40. Natasha Geiling, "The Death and Rebirth of the American Mall," *Smithsonian Magazine*, November 25, 2014, https://www.smithsonianmag.com/arts-culture/death-and-rebirth-american-mall-180953444/.

41. Marie Byerly, "Letter: City Gives Developers a Free Hand," *High Point Enterprise*, October 30, 1997.

42. Duany, Plater-Zyberk, and Speck, *Suburban Nation*, 145.

43. Don Kirkman, "Triad Gets Approval to Expand Foreign Trade Zone," *Triad Business Journal*, July 2, 2007, https://www.bizjournals.com/triad/stories/2007/07/02/daily12.html.

44. Matt Harrington, "Developer Plans More Retail, Office for N. High Point," *Triad Business Journal,* September 4, 2006, https://www.bizjournals.com/triad/stories/2006/09/04/story2.html.

45. Apartment List, "Palladium Park," https://www.apartmentlist.com/nc/high-point/palladium-park.

46. Duany, Plater-Zyberk, and Speck, *Suburban Nation,* 101.

47. Harrington, "Developer Plans More Retail, Office for N. High Point."

48. Duany, Plater-Zyberk, and Speck, *Suburban Nation,* 25.

49. Bernard J. Frieden and Lynne B. Sagalyn, *Downtown, Inc.: How America Rebuilds Cities* (Cambridge, Mass.: MIT Press, 1989), 51.]

50. Jordan Green, "Becky Smothers Looks Back at Three Decades of Public Service," *Triad City Beat,* December 14, 2014, https://triad-city-beat.com/becky-smothers-looks-back-at-three-decades-of-public-service/; Charlie Lehman, "Does High Point Have a Class in the Middle?" *High Point Enterprise,* October 9, 1983.

51. Green, "Becky Smothers Looks Back at Three Decades of Public Service"; Lehman, "Does High Point Have a Class in the Middle?"

52. Green, "Becky Smothers Looks Back at Three Decades of Public Service."

53. Jill Rosen, "High Point Ponders LADD Loss," *Greensboro News and Record,* January 23, 1997, https://www.greensboro.com/high-point-ponders-ladd-loss/article_b6ac2ecf-cofc-51ae-8b63-423bba3e8ffd.html.

54. Lloyd, "Urbanization and the Southern United States," 494.

55. Lloyd, "Urbanization and the Southern United States."

56. Monroe, "Scenes from a Mall."

57. News and Record Copy Desk, "Greensboro Timeline," http://nrcopydesk.wikifoundry.com/page/Greensboro+timeline.

58. Donald Patterson, "Crane in the Skyline Signals Downtown's Regaining Its Health," *Greensboro News and Record,* October 23, 2003, https://www.skyscrapercity.com/showthread.php?t=403737.

59. Deanna Thompson, "Bryan Foundation Helps City Help Itself," *Triad Business Journal,* December 28, 1998, http://www.bizjournals.com/triad/stories/1998/12/28/focus2.html?page=all.

60. Lloyd, "Urbanization and the Southern United States," 494.

61. Florida, *Rise of the Creative Class,* 68.

62. Heidi Allen is a pseudonym.

63. Richard Craver, "HPU President Says Trust the Process with BB&T-Suntrust Merger," *Winston-Salem Journal* February 16, 2019, https://www.journalnow.com/business/hpu-president-says-trust-the-process-with-bb-t-suntrust/article_8912cfcc-dc3a-56cc-bd75-75c5d8d98f81.html.

64. Office of the President, "Marching Onwards with Faithful Courage," High Point University, news release, 2018, http://www.highpoint.edu/president/marching-onwards-with-faithful-courage/.

65. Peter Marcuse, "Gentrification, Abandonment, and Displacement: Connections, Causes, and Policy Responses in New York City," *Journal of Urban and Contemporary Law* 28 (1985): 195–239.

66. Carol Matlack, "Bubble U: High Point University What Happens When You Run a College Like a Growth Business?" *Bloomberg*, April 19, 2012, https://www.bloomberg.com/news/articles/2012-04-19/bubble-u-dot-high-point-university; Andrew Kelly, "A College Both Left and Right Should Be Angry About," *AE Ideas*, May 14, 2012, https://www.aei.org/education/higher-education/a-college-both-left-and-right-should-be-angry-about/.

67. Sally Bringier is a pseudonym.

68. Duany, Plater-Zyberk, and Speck, *Suburban Nation*, 12.

3. The Golden Goose

1. Molotch, "Growth Machine Links," 258.

2. Molotch, "Growth Machine Links."

3. Marks, "City Challenged as Market Center."

4. Logan and Molotch, *Urban Fortunes*, 71. Gene Burd, "The Selling of the Sunbelt: Civic Boosterism in the Media," in *The Rise of the Sunbelt Cities*, edited by David C. Perry and Alfred J. Watkins (Beverly Hills, CA: Sage, 1977), 129, as quoted in Logan and Molotch, *Urban Fortunes*.

5. Burd, "Selling of the Sunbelt," as quoted in Logan and Molotch, *Urban Fortunes*.

6. Mark Boyle, "Growth Machines and Propaganda Projects: A Review of Readings of the Role of Civic Boosterism in the Politics of Local Economic Development," in *The Urban Growth Machine: Critical Perspectives Two Decades Later*, edited by Andrew E. G. Jonas, David Wilson, and Association of American Geographers Meeting (Albany: State University of New York Press, 1999), xiii, 312, 61.

7. Holt McPherson, "Furniture Market Worth Holding Onto," *High Point Enterprise*, October 23, 1973.

8. Southern Furniture Exposition Building, "Smile and Say 'Hi,'" *High Point Enterprise*, October 19, 1973.

9. Joe Brown, "The Benefits of Warm Welcome," *High Point Enterprise*, October 19, 1973.

10. Brown, "Benefits of Warm Welcome."

11. Ray Reed, "Rambling with Ray," *Home Furnishings Daily*, October 18, 1963.

12. Reed, "Rambling with Ray."

13. Leo Heer, "World Perspective of Furniture Shows Here," *High Point Enterprise*, April 19, 1964.

14. Heer, "World Perspective of Furniture Shows Here."

15. Holt McPherson, "Good Afternoon," *High Point Enterprise,* April 3, 1964.

16. Holt McPherson, "Good Morning," *High Point Enterprise,* October 17, 1965.

17. McPherson, "Good Morning"; Bell and Jayne, "Conceptualizing Small Cities," 1.

18. McPherson, "Good Morning."

19. Reed, "Rambling with Ray."

20. Holt McPherson, "Furniture Achieves Its Style Ambition in South," *High Point Enterprise,* October 20, 1963.

21. Reed, "Rambling with Ray."

22. Jim Hawkins, "Growth of High Point Cited at Dedication of New Mart," *High Point Enterprise,* October 24, 1964.

23. Faye Marks, "Joyce Typifies Market Spirit," *High Point Enterprise,* October 27, 1967.

24. Jim Hawkins, "New Exhibition Building Ready for Fall Market," *High Point Enterprise,* October 18, 1964.

25. Robert Marks, "Size of Market Worrying Manufacturers," *High Point Enterprise,* October 20, 1967.

26. Joe Brown, "Whose Market Is This?," *High Point Enterprise,* October 23, 1975.

27. Robert Marks, "New Culture Center Long in Making," *High Point Enterprise,* October 5, 1972.

28. Robert Marks, "Theater Opening Begins 'New Era,'" *High Point Enterprise,* October 6, 1975.

29. Jim Hawkins, "Furniture Row Goes North," *High Point Enterprise,* October 20, 1972.

30. Hawkins, "Furniture Row Goes North."

31. Bob Jessop, Jamie Peck, and Adam Tickell, "Retooling the Machine: Economic Crisis, State Restructuring, and Urban Politics," in *The Urban Growth Machine: Critical Perspectives Two Decades Later,* edited by Andrew E. G. Jonas, David Wilson, and Association of American Geographers Meeting (Albany: State University of New York Press, 1999), xiii, 312; Molotch, "Growth Machine Links," 250–51.

32. Molotch, "Growth Machine Links," 251.

33. Boyle, "Growth Machines and Propaganda Projects," 58.

34. Geraldine Dickins is a pseudonym.

35. Michael McGuire et al., "Building Development Capacity in Nonmetropolitan Communities," *Public Administration Review* 54, no. 5 (1994): 426–33; Gary P. Green et al., "Local Self-Development Strategies: National Survey

Results," *Journal of the Community Development Society* 21, no. 2 (1990): 55–73; Andrew Smith, *Events and Urban Regeneration: The Strategic Use of Events to Revitalise Cities* (London: Routledge, 2012).

36. Dennis R. Judd, "Constructing the Tourist Bubble," in *The Tourist City,* edited by Dennis R. Judd and Susan S. Fainstein (New Haven: Yale University Press, 1999), 340; John Hannigan, *Fantasy City: Pleasure and Profit in the Postmodern Metropolis* (London: Routledge, 1998).

37. David Harvey, *The Urbanization of Capital: Studies in the History and Theory of Capitalist Urbanization* (Baltimore, Md.: Johns Hopkins University Press, 1985), 21.

38. Holt McPherson, "City's Need: Attraction for Year Round," *High Point Enterprise,* October 23, 1976.

39. McPherson, "City's Need."

40. Zukin, *Loft Living,* 78.

41. The Design Tourist, *High Point Market Part 1,* vol. 1, November 21, 2013.

42. Anh-Minh Le, "Henry Adams: Brains behind Design Center," *San Francisco Chronicle,* July 5, 2013, https://www.sfgate.com/homeandgarden/article/Henry-Adams-brains-behind-Design-Center-4649188.php.

43. Charlie Lehman, "Consumers Told to Object to Restrictions on Imports," *High Point Enterprise,* October 20, 1983.

44. Lehman, "Consumers Told to Object to Restrictions on Imports."

45. Zukin, *Loft Living,* 127.

46. Cinde Stephens, "Furniture Analysts Continue to Eye Import Problem," *High Point Enterprise,* October 19, 1986.

47. Zukin, *Loft Living,* 15.

48. Adelaide Wendler, "New Kind of Showroom Ready for Viewing at Market," *High Point Enterprise,* October 13, 1978.

49. Zukin, *Loft Living,* 67–68.

50. Sharon Zukin, *Naked City: The Death and Life of Authentic Urban Places* (New York: Oxford University Press, 2010), 14.

51. Zukin, *Loft Living,* 72.

52. Zukin, *Loft Living,* 62.

53. Zukin, *Loft Living,* 2.

54. Charlie Lehman, "Survey: Manufacturers Glad They Moved," *High Point Enterprise,* October 22, 1984.

55. Francine Liddelle is a pseudonym.

56. Christopher Breward and David Gilbert, *Fashion's World Cities* (Oxford: Berg, 2006).

57. Zukin, *Loft Living,* 188.

58. Zukin, *Loft Living,* 151.

59. Wes Cashwell, "No Skywalk Access Perplexes Exhibitors," *High Point Enterprise,* October 22, 1987.

60. Tom Inman, "Market Square Tower to Satisfy Triple Need," *High Point Enterprise,* October 19, 1989.

61. S. Davis (Dave) Phillips, interview by Joseph Mosnier, January 27, 1999, Interview I-0084 (#4007) Wilson Library, University of North Carolina at Chapel Hill.

62. Wes Cashwell, "Huge New Showrooms Will Enhance Market," *High Point Enterprise,* October 14, 1987.

63. Quoted in Cashwell, "Huge New Showrooms Will Enhance Market."

64. Quoted in Tom Inman, "IHFC Plans Expansion of Showroom Complex," *High Point Enterprise,* October 18, 1989.

65. Inman, "IHFC Plans Expansion of Showroom Complex."

66. Matthew Tallon is a pseudonym.

67. Sarah Simpkins is a pseudonym.

68. Joe Brown, "Welcome to the Market," *High Point Enterprise,* October 17, 1985.

69. Bobbi Martin, "Bobbi Martin," *High Point Enterprise,* 1988.

70. K. R. Cox and A. Mair, "Locality and Community in the Politics of Local Economic-Development," *Annals of the Association of American Geographers* 78, no. 2 (1988): 319.

71. Cox and Mair, "Locality and Community in the Politics of Local Economic-Development."

72. Boyle, "Growth Machines and Propaganda Projects," 32.

73. Martha Clontz, "Market's Impact Hard to Measure," *High Point Enterprise,* October 20, 1977.

74. Richard E. Foglesong, *Married to the Mouse: Walt Disney World and Orlando* (New Haven: Yale University Press, 2001), 191.

4. The Cruise Ship and the Forbidden City

1. Tom Blount, "In Plain Talk, Market Matters," *High Point Enterprise,* October 17, 1993.

2. Blount, "In Plain Talk, Market Matters."

3. Tom Blount, "Hospitality," *High Point Enterprise,* October 17, 1994.

4. Josephine Goodson, "High Point Rolls Out the Red Carpet for Market," *High Point Enterprise,* October 27, 1998.

5. Goodson, "High Point Rolls Out the Red Carpet for Market."

6. Nick Maheras, "Candidates for at Large Seats Split on Oak Hollow Mall Issue," *High Point Enterprise,* October 1, 1989; Election Coverage, "Judy Mendenhall," *Yes! Weekly,* August 21, 2012, https://yesweekly.com/judy-menden hall-a18629/.

7. Tommye Morrison, "Exhibitors Open in Old Theater," *High Point Enterprise,* October 18, 1991.

8. Andy Merrifield, "The Urban Question under Planetary Urbanization," *International Journal of Urban and Regional Research* 37, no. 3 (2013).

9. Molotch, "Growth Machine Links," 254.

10. Held and McGrew, *Global Transformations Reader;* Coltrane Jazz Fest, "Festival History."

11. Zukin, *Landscapes of Power,* 5.

12. PRN News Wire, "Vornado-Realty Trust to Acquire Merchandise Mart and Other Properties from the Kennedy Family," 1997; Maura Webber Sadovi, "A Chicago Exit Strategy?," *Wall Street Journal,* July 31, 2012, https://wsj.com/articles/SB10000872396390444130304577559731999895366.

13. PRN News Wire, "Vornado-Realty Trust to Acquire Merchandise Mart"; Sadovi, "Chicago Exit Strategy?"

14. Justin Catanoso, "New Kid May Challenge IHFC Dominance," *Triad Business Journal,* January 4, 1999, https://www.bizjournals.com/triad/stories/1999/01/04/tidbits.html?page=all.

15. Ada Louise Huxtable, *The Unreal America: Architecture and Illusion* (New York: New Press, 1997), 26.

16. Zukin, *Landscapes of Power,* 45.

17. Paul L. Knox, *Cities and Design* (Abingdon, UK: Routledge, 2011), 183–84.

18. Andrew Dickson, "Is the Bilbao Effect on Urban Renewal All It's Cracked Up to Be?" *Financial Review,* December 21, 2017, https://www.afr.com/world/europe/is-the-bilbao-effect-on-urban-renewal-all-its-cracked-up-to-be-2017 1211-h02fru.

19. Jeff Holeman, "Magic Block Finds Buyer," *High Point Enterprise,* October 4, 1996.

20. Chris Gels, "Could It Be Magic? Area's Development Might Boost Downtown," *High Point Enterprise,* July 24, 1994.

21. Jeff Holeman, "Magic Block Finds Buyer," *High Point Enterprise,* October 4, 1996.

22. Holeman, "Magic Block Finds Buyer."

23. Benjamin Briggs to Preservation Greensboro, 2007, https://preservationgreensboro.org/2007-the-year-g/.

24. Eric Whittington, "Showrooms Continue to Flourish," *High Point Enterprise,* January 13, 1998.

25. Richard Craver, "Natale Showrooms Show Their Readiness for Furniture Market," *High Point Enterprise,* October 17, 2000.

26. Beth Macy, *Factory Man: How One Furniture Maker Battled Offshoring, Stayed Local—and Helped Save an American Town* (New York: Little, Brown, 2015), 222–23.

27. HFN, "Museum/Showroom Underscores China's Presence in High Point," *Home Furnishings Weekly,* April 12, 2004.

28. Zukin, *Naked City,* 232.

29. Boyles, "Growth Machines and Propaganda Projects," 66.

30. Richard Craver, "Buyers Suggest Market Improvements," *High Point Enterprise,* October 24, 2000.

31. Lloyd, "Urbanization and the Southern United States," 492; Neil Brenner and Nik Theodore, "Cities and the Geographies of 'Actually Existing Neoliberalism,'" *Antipode* 34, no. 3 (2002); Harvey, *Brief History of Neoliberalism.*

32. Harvey, *Urban Experience,* 240.

33. Editorial Staff, "High Point Established New Market Authority Corporation," *Triad Business Journal,* February 2, 2001, https://www.bizjournals.com/triad/stories/2001/01/29/daily13.html.

34. Richard Craver, "Opinions Differ on Authority Role," *High Point Enterprise,* October 21, 2001.

35. Richard Craver, "Market Pricing Gets Focus: Many Urge Moderation," *High Point Enterprise,* October 17, 2000.

36. Craver, "Opinions Differ on Authority Role."

37. Craver, "Opinions Differ on Authority Role."

38. Logan and Molotch, *Urban Fortunes,* 64–65.

39. Richard Craver, "Vegas Crew Eyes Share of Market," *High Point Enterprise,* October 3, 2000.

40. World Market Center, "World Market Center Media Kit," October 1, 2008.

41. World Market Center, "World Market Center Media Kit."

42. Morris Newman, "Developers in Las Vegas Put Money on Furniture," *New York Times,* February 23, 2005.

43. Newman, "Developers in Las Vegas Put Money on Furniture."

44. Ivan Saul Cutler to InsideFurniture, July 28, 2005.

45. Sassen, *Cities in a World Economy,* 106.

46. Valerie Miller, "High Point Far from Throwing in Towel," *Business Press,* February 13, 2006.

47. Zukin, *Naked City,* 222.

48. Herbert Muschamp, "Remodeling New York for the Bourgeosie," *New York Times,* September 24, 1995; Zukin, *Loft Living,* 190.

49. David Grazian, *Blue Chicago: The Search for Authenticity in Urban Blues Clubs* (Chicago: University of Chicago Press, 2003); Richard Lloyd, "Neo-Bohemia: Art and Neighborhood Redevelopment in Chicago," *Journal of Urban Affairs* 24, no. 5 (2002); Gina M. Pérez, *The Near Northwest Side Story: Migration, Displacement, and Puerto Rican Families* (Berkeley: University of California Press, 2004).

50. Jacobs, *Death and Life of Great American Cities.*

51. M. Buraydi, "Introduction: Downtowns and Small City Development," in *Downtowns: Revitalizing the Centers of Small Urban Communities,* edited by M. Burayudi (New York: Garland, 2001); T. Paradis, "The Political Economy of Theme Development in Small Urban Places: The Case of Roswell, New Mexico," *Tourism Geographies* 4 (2002); Kent A. Robertson, "Can Small-City Downtowns Remain Viable?" *Journal of the American Planning Association* 65, no. 3 (1999).

52. John Urry, *The Tourist Gaze: Leisure and Travel in Contemporary Societies* (London: Sage, 1990).

53. Walter Benjamin and J. A. Underwood, *The Work of Art in the Age of Mechanical Reproduction* (London: Penguin Books, 2008).

54. Dillon, "Sprucing Up Downtown."

55. Larry Thomas, "Update: High Point's Showplace Could Be in Receivership for Years," *Furniture Today,* August 26, 2009.

56. Georg Simmel, "The Metropolis and Mental Life," in *On Individuality and Social Forms: Selected Writings* (Chicago: University of Chicago Press, 1971), lxv, 395, 12.

57. Sadovi, "Chicago Exit Strategy?"

58. Phil Phillips, "Public Ownership—It's Time for High Point Area Citizens to Take Charge of Market," *High Point Enterprise,* February 20, 2012, https://www.furnituretoday.com/business-news/high-point-should-take-page-from-green-bays-playbook/.

59. IMC, "Launch of International Market Centers Creates Premier B-to-B Platform for the Home Furnishings and Gift Industries," news release, May 3, 2012, https://prnewswire.com/news-releases/launch-of-international-market-centers-creates-premier-b-to-b-platform-for-the-home-furnishings-and-gift-industries-121155344.html.

60. IMC, "Launch of International Market Centers Creates Premier B-to-B Platform for the Home Furnishings and Gift Industries."

61. IMC, "Launch of International Market Centers Creates Premier B-to-B Platform for the Home Furnishings and Gift Industries."

62. Quoted in Matt Evans, "High Point Ponders Impact of Showroom Sales," *Triad Business Journal,* March 11, 2011, https://www.bizjournals.com/triad/print-edition/2011/03/11/high-point-ponders-impact-of-showroom.html?page=all.

63. Jordan Green, "Who Owns Downtown High Point?" *Triad City Beat,* July 9, 2014, https://triad-city-beat.com/who-owns-downtown-high-point/.

64. Atif Shafique et al., "Inclusive Growth in Action: Snapshots of a New Economy," in *Inclusive Growth Commission* (London: Royal Society for the Encouragement of Arts, Manufactures and Commerce, 2019), 46.

65. Berry, *Unsettling of America,* 7–8.

66. Elvin Wyly et al., "Cartographies of Race and Class: Mapping the Class-Monopoly Rents of American Subprime Mortgage Capital," *International Journal of Urban and Regional Research* 33 (2009): 338.

67. Wyly et al., "Cartographies of Race and Class."

68. Green, "Who Owns Downtown High Point?"

5. Hibernation

1. Douglas Harper, "An Argument for Visual Sociology," in *Image-Based Research: A Sourcebook for Qualitative Researchers* (London: Falmer, 1998), 24–41; Margarethe Kusenbach, "Street Phenomenology: The Go-Along as Ethnographic Research Tool," *Ethnography* 4, no. 3 (2003).

2. Molotch, Freudenburg, and Paulsen, "History Repeats Itself, but How?" 257. See Kevin Lynch, *The Image of the City* (Cambridge, Mass.: MIT Press, 1960); P. J. Bettis, "Urban Students, Liminality, and the Postindustrial Context," *Sociology of Education* 69, no. 2 (1996).

3. Schlichtman and Patch, "Contextualizing Impressions of Neighborhood Change."

4. Schlichtman and Patch, "Contextualizing Impressions of Neighborhood Change."

5. D. W. Meinig, "The Beholding Eye: Ten Versions of the Same Scene," in *The Interpretation of Ordinary Landscapes,* edited by D. W. Meinig and John Brinckerhoff Jackson (New York: Oxford University Press, 1979), 6.

6. Erving Goffman, *The Presentation of Self in Everyday Life* (Woodstock, N.Y.: Overlook, 1973), 22.

7. Sklair, "Transnational Capitalist Class and Contemporary Architecture in Globalizing Cities," 28.

8. Urry, *Consuming Places,* 179.

9. Urry, *Consuming Places,* 179.

10. Huxtable, *Unreal America,* 98.

11. Castells, *Rise of the Network Society,* 412.

12. Castells, *Rise of the Network Society,* 418.

13. Jura Koncius, "Furniture High Points from High Point," *Tampa Bay Times,* October 9, 2005.

14. Tom Williams is a pseudonym.

15. Molotch, Freudenburg, and Paulsen, "History Repeats Itself, but How?" 793.

16. Castells, *Rise of the Network Society.*

17. Lynch, *Image of the City,* 4.

18. Castells, *Rise of the Network Society,* 418.

19. Sharon Zukin, "The City as a Landscape of Power: London and New York as Global Financial Capitals," in *Global Finance and Urban Living,* edited by Leslie Budd and Sam Whimster (New York: Routledge, 1992), 195–223.

20. Huxtable, *Unreal America,* 98.

21. Huxtable, *Unreal America,* 27.

22. Susan Sontag, "Notes on 'Camp,'" *Partisan Review* (1964); Robert Venturi, Denise Scott Brown, and Steven Izenour, *Learning from Las Vegas: The Forgotten Symbolism of Architectural Form* (Cambridge, Mass.: MIT Press, 1977).

23. Huxtable, *Unreal America,* 121.

24. Huxtable, *Unreal America,* 26; Michel de Certeau, *The Practice of Everyday Life* (Berkeley: University of California Press, 1988).

25. Boyle, "Growth Machines and Propaganda Projects," 32.

26. Huxtable, *Unreal America,* 97.

27. Sklair, "Transnational Capitalist Class and Contemporary Architecture in Globalizing Cities," 27.

28. Huxtable, *Unreal America,* 25.

29. Boyles, "Growth Machines and Propaganda Projects," 67.

30. Trina Johns is a pseudonym.

31. Richard Craver, "Showplace Makes Market Debut: Opening Energizes Town," *High Point Enterprise,* October 20, 2000.

32. Michelle Boyer, "Cities for Sale: Merchandising History at South Street Seaport," in *Variations on a Theme Park: The New American City and the End of Public Space,* edited by Michael Sorkin (New York: Hill and Wang, 1992), xv, 252, 188.

33. Zukin, *Naked City,* 17.

34. Andrew Ross, *No Respect: Intellectuals and Popular Culture* (New York: Routledge, 1989), 153.

35. Sontag, "Notes on 'Camp'"; see also Venturi, Scott Brown, and Izenour, *Learning from Las Vegas.*

36. Sontag, "Notes on 'Camp'"; see also Venturi, Scott Brown, and Izenour, *Learning from Las Vegas.*

37. Walter Benjamin, *One-Way Street, and Other Writings* (London: NLB, 1979).

38. Molotch, "Growth Machine Links"; Stephen L. Elkin, *City and Regime in the American Republic* (Chicago: University of Chicago Press, 1980), 95; J. Dewey, *The Public and Its Problems* (Athens, Ohio: Swallow Press, 1991); C. E. Lindblom, *The Intelligence of Democracy. Decision Making through Mutual Adjustment* (New York: Collier-Macmillan, 1965).

39. Molotch, "Growth Machine Links"; Elkin, *City and Regime in the American Republic,* 95; Dewey, *Public and Its Problems;* Lindblom, *Intelligence of Democracy.*

40. Molotch, "Growth Machine Links"; Elkin, *City and Regime in the American Republic,* 95; Dewey, *Public and Its Problems*; Lindblom, *Intelligence of Democracy.*

6. Choreographing Mini-Manhattan

1. Jura Koncius, "Name-Dropping Our Way through High Point," *Washington Post,* October 27, 2005.

2. Arianne Bellizaire to Inspired to Style, October 28, 2014, http://www.inspiredtostyle.com/high-point-market-fall-2014-recap/.

3. High Point Market Authority, "Places to Go: IHFC," https://www.highpointmarket.org/news-and-videos/places-to-go/ihfc.

4. The Design Tourist, *High Point Market Part 1,* video, Design Network, October 16, 2013.

5. Editor at Large, *The Designers' Guide to High Point Market: High Point Market Spring 2015,* https://editoratlarge-production.s3.amazonaws.com/class_images%2F134%2Fimages%2Foriginal%2FHigh%20Point%20Market%20Guide%20Spring%202015.pdf.

6. Terri Tysinger, "Market Parade: Colorful Event Entertains Local Folks," *High Point Enterprise,* October 28, 2000.

7. Goffman, *Presentation of Self in Everyday Life,* 72.

8. Andrew Matthews, "Market's Scope Inspires Awe," *High Point Enterprise,* October 10, 1993.

9. Cinde Stephens, "Jury Still out on Success on Market," *High Point Enterprise,* October 22, 1986.

10. Bryan Haislip, "High Point Is Fashion Center," *High Point Enterprise,* October 23, 1970, 5; Adelaide Wendler, "Decorators Setting the Stage for a Big Production," *High Point Enterprise,* October 15, 1972.

11. Goffman, *Presentation of Self in Everyday Life,* 124.

12. Goffman, *Presentation of Self in Everyday Life,* 22.

13. Carol Wilson, "Dallas—High Point Competitors or Complementary Market Hosts?," *High Point Enterprise,* October 22, 1978.

14. Guido Martinotti, "The New Social Morphology of Cities," in *UNESCO/MOST* (Vienna: United Nations Educational, Scientific and Cultural Organization, 1994).

15. Goffman, *Presentation of Self in Everyday Life,* 19.

16. Harvey, *Urban Experience.*

17. Donald Taylor Jr., "Big Events Like Furniture Market Often a Magnet for Sex Trafficking," Duke Social Science Research Institute, October 14, 2015.

18. Charlie Lehman, "Market Plays Those Homecoming Blues," *High Point Enterprise,* October 23, 1984.

19. Editor at Large, *Designers' Guide to High Point Market.*

20. Goffman, *Presentation of Self in Everyday Life,* 33.

21. Carole Nicksin, "A Man of Many Phases: After Thirty Years of Home Furnishings and Design, Raymond Waites Is Still a Work in Progress," *HFN,* December 13, 2003, https://www.thefreelibrary.com/A+MAN+OF+MANY+ PHASES%3B+AFTER+30+YEARS+IN+HOME+FURNISHINGS+DESIGN %2C . . .-a0111400240.

22. Vicki Bridgers, "Marketfest Put on Hold for October," *High Point Enterprise,* October 16, 1986.

23. Lukas Brun and T. William Lester, "The Economic Impact of High Point Market," Center on Globalization, Governance, and Competitiveness, Duke Social Science Research Institute, 2013.

24. Editor at Large, *Designers' Guide to High Point Market.*

25. Editor at Large, *Designers' Guide to High Point Market.*

26. Editor at Large, *Designers' Guide to High Point Market.*

27. Jim Hawkins, "Demand Grows for Housing at Fall Furniture Mart," *High Point Enterprise,* October 21, 1964.

28. Holt McPherson, "Good Morning," *High Point Enterprise,* October 23, 1969.

29. Charlie Lehman, "City Ready for Influx of Buyers," *High Point Enterprise,* October 13, 1982.

30. Don Wrenn, "Rooms Being Sought for Market Visitors," *High Point Enterprise,* October 20, 1971.

31. Holt McPherson, "Good Morning," *High Point Enterprise,* October 23, 1969.

32. Thomas Russell, "Home Rental Tax Plan Draws City Opposition," *High Point Enterprise,* October 3, 1995; Nick Maheras, "Helms Helps Erase Market Rent Tax Bid," October 20, 1995; Eric Whittington, "Rental Tax Remains Issue in Congress," *High Point Enterprise,* October 16, 1997.

33. Jane Renalter, "Hospitality International-Style: Motel Guests Represent Eight Countries," *High Point Enterprise,* October 26, 1988.

34. Sontag, "Notes on 'Camp'"; Venturi, Scott Brown, and Izenour, *Learning from Las Vegas.*

35. Bob Burchette, "Bob Market Renters Now 'Like Cousins,'" *Greensboro News and Record,* April 8, 2005, https://www.greensboro.com/news/market -renters-now-like-cousins/article_0ba6173a-a691-53c2-8c85-befc7e18a895 .html.

36. Burchette, "Bob Market Renters Now 'Like Cousins.'"

37. David Wachsmuth and Alexander Weisler, "Airbnb and the Rent Gap: Gentrification through the Sharing Economy," *Environment and Planning A: Economy Space* 50, no. 6 (2018).

38. Jim Hawkins, "Car 'Attendance' Might Be Record," *High Point Enterprise*, October 26, 1966.

39. Forrest Cates, "Lack of Parking Threatens City's Core," October 14, 1966.

40. Joe Brown, "Great Parking Snafu," *High Point Enterprise*, October 28, 1966.

41. Keith Pugh, "Give Me Shelter: The Story of Mendenhall Station," in *NCSITE Annual Meeting* (2007).

42. Richard Craver, "New Authority Confronts Uncertain Market," *High Point Enterprise*, October 7, 2001.

43. Pugh, "Give Me Shelter."

44. Newman, "Developers in Las Vegas Put Money on Furniture."

45. Brun and Lester, "Economic Impact of High Point Market," 14.

46. Goffman, *Presentation of Self in Everyday Life*, 22.

47. Goffman, *Presentation of Self in Everyday Life*, 32.

48. Richard Craver, "Opening Day? Officially, Market Begins on Thursday," *High Point Enterprise*, October 10, 1999.

49. Editorial Staff, "Maricich Calls High Point Premarket 'Stupid and Destructive,'" *Furniture Today*, March 26, 2014, https://www.furnituretoday.com/business-news/maricich-calls-high-point-premarket-stupid-and-destructive/.

50. Carl Wilson, "Premarket Event Sets Tone for High Point's Big Furniture Market in October," *Greensboro News and Record*, September 15, 2020, https://greensboro.com/news/local/watch-now-premarket-event-sets-tone-for-high-points-big-furniture-market-in-october/article_138772fc-f45b-11ea-922f-f7b383057b76.html.

51. Wilson, "Premarket Event Sets Tone for High Point's Big Furniture Market in October."

52. HPEDC, *Annual Report*, High Point Economic Development Corporation, 2018.

53. Sontag, "Notes on 'Camp.'"

54. Sontag, "Notes on 'Camp.'"

55. Sontag, "Notes on 'Camp.'"

56. Sontag, "Notes on 'Camp.'"

57. United States Securities and Exchange Commission, "International Market Centers, Inc.," in *Registration Statement for Registration under the Securities Act of 1933 of Securities of Certain Real Estate Companies*, 2014.

58. Jordan Green, "Smaller Furniture Companies Stake Identity in Ned District," *Triad City Beat*, October 20, 2015, https://triad-city-beat.com/smaller-furniture-companies-stake-identity-in-ned-district/.

59. Green, "Smaller Furniture Companies Stake Identity in Ned District."

60. Lloyd, "Neo-Bohemia: Art and Neighborhood Redevelopment in Chicago."

61. Green, "Smaller Furniture Companies Stake Identity in Ned District."
62. Zukin, *Loft Living,* 28.
63. Brun and Lester, "Economic Impact of High Point Market," 14.
64. Jeff Johnson, "In Focus: Studio Industry Rooted in Furniture," *High Point Enterprise,* October 22, 1978.
65. Kreber, "Services," accessed December 18, 2015, https://www.kreber.com/services.
66. Lees, Shin, and López-Morales, *Planetary Gentrification,* 64.
67. Goffman, *Presentation of Self in Everyday Life,* 18.
68. Zukin, *Loft Living,* 190.
69. Burning Man, "The Event," accessed January 10, 2020, https://burningman.org/event.
70. Goffman, *Presentation of Self in Everyday Life,* 22.
71. Sontag, "Notes on 'Camp'"; Venturi, Scott Brown, and Izenour, *Learning from Las Vegas.*
72. Goffman, *Presentation of Self in Everyday Life,* 14.
73. Reed, "Rambling with Ray."

7. The Fragmented Year-Round Design Cluster

1. Kaitlin Petersen, "Is High Point the New Brooklyn?" *Business of Home,* March 29, 2018, https://businessofhome.com/boh/article/is-high-point-the-new-brooklyn.
2. Nichols, "Valuing the Art of Industrial Design."
3. Duranton and Puga, "Micro-Foundations of Urban Agglomeration Economies," 4; Scott and Storper, "Regions, Globalization, Development."
4. Molotch, Freudenburg, and Paulsen, "History Repeats Itself, but How?" 794.
5. Michael J. Piore and Charles F. Sabel, *The Second Industrial Divide: Possibilities for Prosperity* (New York: Basic Books, 1984), 17.
6. Macy, *Factory Man,* 128.
7. Ruth Simon, "The U.S. Furniture Industry Is Back—but There Aren't Enough Workers," *Wall Street Journal,* December 5, 2019.
8. Deloitte and the Manufacturing Institute, "Deloitte Skills Gap and Future of Work in Manufacturing Study," 2018; Katherine S. Newman and Hella Winston, *Reskilling America: Learning to Labor in the Twenty-First Century* (New York: Metropolitan Books, Henry Holt, 2016).
9. Simon, "U.S. Furniture Industry Is Back."
10. GTCC, "Guilford Technical Community College Launches Furniture Sewing Class," news release, August 14, 2017, https://www.gtcc.edu/about/news-and-events/2017/05/guilford-technical-community-college-launches-furniture-sewing-class.php.

11. Andy Pratt, "New Media, the New Economy and New Spaces," *Geoforum* 31 (2000); David C. Harvey, Harriet Hawkins, and Nicola J. Thomas, "Thinking Creative Clusters beyond the City: People, Places and Networks," *Geoforum* 43, no. 3 (2012).

12. Eileen Finan, "Painted Ladies," *Chicago Tribune,* June 10, 1999, https://www.chicagotribune.com/news/ct-xpm-1999-06-10-9906120002-story.html.

13. Pat Kimbrough, "Duany Ignite Plan Being Brought Down to Mediocrity," *High Point Enterprise,* May 6, 2014.

14. Cindy Hodnett, "Pandora's Manor Adds Panache to Downtown High Point," *Furniture Today,* March 27, 2017, https://www.furnituretoday.com/business-news/pandoras-manor-adds-panache-downtown-high-point-2/.

15. Duany, "Pink Zone."

16. Petersen, "Is High Point the New Brooklyn?"

17. Jill Ann Harrison, "Rust Belt Boomerang: The Pull of Place in Moving Back to a Legacy City," *City and Community* 16, no. 3 (2017).

18. Alex Marshall, "The Human Casualties of 'Winner-Take-All Urbanism': Are We Doing Enough for the People Left Behind in Cities?" *Governing,* June 2017, https://www.governing.com/columns/transportation-and-infrastructure/gov-winner-take-all-urbanism-cities.html.

19. Sills, "Market Segmentation and Targeted Revitalization," 149.

20. Lloyd, "Urbanization and the Southern United States," 78.

21. Zukin, *Naked City,* 99; emphasis mine.

22. Susan Ladd, "Renewal Key to Southwest High Point Vision," *Greensboro News & Record,* November 6, 2012, https://www.greensboro.com/news/renewal-key-to-southwest-high-point-vision/article_37845941-6e2f-51ba-ba6f-fd4466c5fcdo.html.

23. Cinde Ingram, "West End Holds Hidden Artistic Gem," *High Point Enterprise,* July 31, 2020, https://hpenews.com/news/10206/west-end-holds-hidden-artistic-gem/.

24. Derek S. Hyra, *Race, Class, and Politics in the Cappuccino City* (Chicago: University of Chicago Press, 2017).

25. Eric Ginsburg, "Arts Collective Flourishes in Salvaged Space," *Triad City Beat,* August 13, 2014, https://triad-city-beat.com/arts-collective-flourishes-in-salvaged-space/.

26. Michael Storper, *Keys to the City: How Economics, Institutions, Social Interactions, and Politics Shape Development* (Princeton, N.J.: Princeton University Press, 2013).

27. Florida, *Rise of the Creative Class.*

28. Zukin, *Naked City,* 237.

29. Zukin, *Naked City,* 245.

30. Paul Johnson, "Furniture Job Erosion Shows No Sign of Waning in North Carolina," *High Point Enterprise,* August 23, 2004.

31. Lloyd, "Urbanization and the Southern United States," 493.

32. Lloyd, "Urbanization and the Southern United States," 493.

33. Marcus Doel and Phil Hubbard, "Taking World Cities Literally: Marketing the City in a Global Space of Flows," *City: Analysis of Urban Trends, Culture, Theory, Policy, Action* 6, no. 3 (2002): 365.

8. Poking the Golden Goose

1. Larry Isaac, "Movement of Movements: Culture Moves in the Long Civil Rights Struggle," *Social Forces* 87, no. 1 (2008): 33–63; Lloyd, "Urbanization and the Southern United States," 489.

2. Phyllis Bridges, dir., *March on an All-American City* (Yalik's Modern Art, 2017).

3. Bridges, *March on an All-American City.*

4. Bridges, *March on an All-American City.*

5. Bridges, *March on an All-American City.*

6. Bridges, *March on an All-American City*; Kerry Robinson, "High Point Students Protest for Theater Integration, 1960–1964," Global Nonviolent Action Database, 2014, https://nvdatabase.swarthmore.edu/content/high-point-stu dents-protest-theater-integration-1960-1964; Frank Warren, "Negroes Ask Injunction against Theater," *High Point Enterprise,* June 19, 1963.

7. Frank Warren, "Demonstrators Go on Trial; Stout Speaks," *High Point Enterprise,* April 22, 1963.

8. Editorial Staff, "Tear Gas at High Point," *Iola Register,* September 12, 1963.

9. Bridges, *March on an All-American City.*

10. Bridges, *March on an All-American City.*

11. Bridges, *March on an All-American City.*

12. Bridges, *March on an All-American City.*

13. Bridges, *March on an All-American City*; Editorial Staff, "Tear Gas at High Point."

14. Bridges, *March on an All-American City.*

15. Glenn Chavis, "'Colored Mill' Gave Blacks Opportunity," *Greensboro News and Record,* January 23, 2004, https://www.greensboro.com/news/col ored-mill-gave-blacks-opportunity/article_132c78c3-b0ff-5d3e-8004-b6be 6f0bff3d.html.

16. Bridges, *March on an All-American City.*

17. Bridges, *March on an All-American City.*

18. Bridges, *March on an All-American City.*

19. Associated Press, "Unrest Grips All-America City," *Bridgeport Post,* September 10, 1963.

20. Lloyd, "Urbanization and the Southern United States," 490.

21. Holt McPherson, "High Point's Uneasy Truce," *High Point Enterprise,* September 14, 1963.

22. Holt McPherson, "Good Morning," *High Point Enterprise,* April 24, 1966.

23. Robert Marks, "New Human Relations Group Selection Set," *High Point Enterprise,* September 16, 1963.

24. Clarence N. Stone, *Regime Politics: Governing Atlanta, 1946–1988* (Lawrence: University Press of Kansas, 1989); Davison M. Douglas, "The Rhetoric of Moderation: Desegregating the South during the Decade after 'Brown,'" *Northwestern University Law Review* 89, no. 1 (1994): 92–139; Gavin Wright, *Old South, New South: Revolutions in the Southern Economy since the Civil War* (Baton Rouge: Louisiana State University Press, 1996); John Dittmer, "'Too Busy to Hate': Race, Class, and Politics in Twentieth-Century Atlanta," *Georgia Historical Quarterly* 81, no. 1 (1997): 103–17; Jason Sokol, *There Goes My Everything: White Southerners in the Age of Civil Rights, 1945–1975* (New York: Alfred A. Knopf, 2006).

25. Bridges, *March on an All-American City.*

26. Bridges, *March on an All-American City*; Forrest Cates, "Council Handed Negroes Threat to Demonstrate," *High Point Enterprise,* April 21, 1966; McPherson, "Good Morning."

27. Bridges, *March on an All-American City.*

28. Joe Brown, "Threats of Protest Marches Voiced," *High Point Enterprise,* May 16, 1966; Bridges, *March on an All-American City.*

29. Holt McPherson, "Blessings on Market's Unsung Heroines," *High Point Enterprise,* October 24, 1974; Robert Marks, "Mr. Furniture Buyer," *High Point Enterprise,* October 25, 1964; Lolita Hilton, "Women's Zest Sparks Urban Improvement," *High Point Enterprise,* October 2, 1969; Heidi Coryell, "Panelists Tour Role of Women," *High Point Enterprise,* October 17, 1999.

30. Thomas J. Sugrue, *The Origins of the Urban Crisis: Race and Inequality in Postwar Detroit* (Princeton, N.J.: Princeton University Press, 1996).

31. Robert Marks, "In Racial Chaos: Waynick Guides City through Critical Time," *High Point Enterprise,* June 16, 1963.

32. Mike Robertson, "Market Rules City's Downtown," *High Point Enterprise,* October 10, 2000.

33. Zukin, *Loft Living,* 175.

34. Logan and Molotch, *Urban Fortunes,* 320.

35. Eric Reis, "Battle Lines Drawn in Dispute over Downtown Plans," *High Point Enterprise,* October 26, 1986; Joe Brown, "Creative Solutions" *High Point Enterprise,* October 2, 1985.

36. Reis, "Battle Lines Drawn."

37. Reis, "Battle Lines Drawn."

38. Reis, "Battle Lines Drawn."

39. Reis, "Battle Lines Drawn"; Eric Reis, "Move for Downtown Redevelopment Encouraged," *High Point Enterprise,* October 2, 1986.

40. Reis, "Battle Lines Drawn."

41. Reis, "Battle Lines Drawn."

42. R. D. McKenzie, "The Neighborhood: A Study of Local Life in the City of Columbus, Ohio. I," *American Journal of Sociology* 27, no. 2 (1921): 362.

43. See Karl Marx and Martin Nicolaus, *Grundrisse: Foundations of the Critique of Political Economy (Rough Draft)* (London: Penguin Classics, 1993), 224–25.

44. Reis, "Battle Lines Drawn."

45. Chris Gels, "Could It Be Magic? Area's Development Might Boost Downtown," *High Point Enterprise,* July 24, 1994.

46. Gels, "Could It Be Magic?"

47. Harvey, *Urban Experience,* 240.

48. Tom Blount, "Designing Men Map Battle Plan," *High Point Enterprise,* August 28, 1994.

49. Blount, "Designing Men Map Battle Plan."

50. Blount, "Designing Men Map Battle Plan."

51. Gels, "Could It Be Magic?"

52. Gels, "Could It Be Magic?"

53. Paul Dillon, "Sprucing Up Downtown: Group Studies Area's Aesthetic Appeal," *High Point Enterprise,* October 24, 1993.

54. Dillon, "Sprucing Up Downtown."

55. Tom Blount, "Change: Downtown Improvement Groups Seeks Public's Help," *High Point Enterprise,* October 8, 2000.

56. Zukin, "City as a Landscape of Power."

57. Walker Collaborative, "High Point Core City Plan," 2007, 33.

58. Walker Collaborative, "High Point Core City Plan"; emphasis mine.

59. Walker Collaborative, "High Point Core City Plan."

60. Tom Blount, "City Sees a Bold Plan for Downtown Revival," *High Point Enterprise,* July 1, 2002.

61. Amanda Young, "City Awaits Railroad Track Study," *High Point Enterprise,* August 13, 2003.

62. Walker Collaborative, "High Point Core City Plan," 33.

63. Logan and Molotch, *Urban Fortunes,* 64; Peter Bachrach and Morton S. Baratz, "Two Faces of Power," *American Political Science Review* 56, no. 4 (1962): 947–52; Maxwell E. McCombs and Donald L. Shaw, "The Agenda-Setting Function of Mass Media," *Public Opinion Quarterly* 36, no. 2 (1972): 176–87.

64. Schlichtman, "Niche City Idea," 113.

65. Jerome Krase, *Seeing Cities Change: Local Culture and Class* (Farnham, UK: Ashgate, 2011), 21; Zukin, "City as a Landscape of Power," 139.

66. Boyle, "Growth Machines and Propaganda Projects," 32.

67. Hyra, *Race, Class, and Politics in the Cappuccino City*; Brandi Thompson Summers, *Black in Place: The Spatial Aesthetics of Race in a Post-Chocolate City* (Chapel Hill: University of North Carolina Press, 2019).

68. Urry, *Consuming Places*, 21.

69. Jon Caulfield, "'Gentrification' and Desire," *Canadian Review of Sociology / Revue canadienne de sociologie* 26, no. 4 (1989): 139.

70. Goffman, *Presentation of Self in Everyday Life*, 140.

71. Jim Hawkins, "Furniture Market Showrooms to Be Open for Public Tours," *High Point Enterprise*, October 5, 1977.

72. Lloyd, "Urbanization and the Southern United States," 494.

73. Zukin, *Loft Living*, 186.

9. The City Project and the Pursuit of a Living Room

1. Foglesong, *Married to the Mouse*, 112.

2. Duany, Plater-Zyberk, and Speck, *Suburban Nation*, 218.

3. Duany, Plater-Zyberk, and Speck, *Suburban Nation*, 218.

4. Walker, "High Point Core City Plan," 158.

5. Walker, "High Point Core City Plan," 158.

6. Walker, "High Point Core City Plan," 158.

7. Fox 8 Digital Desk, "City Project Board Adopts Resolution in Support of Ignite High Point Master Plan," *Fox 8 News*, December 9, 2013, https://myfox8.com/news/city-project-board-adopts-resolution-in-support-of-ignite-high-point-master-plan/.

8. Walker, "High Point Core City Plan," 158.

9. Walker, "High Point Core City Plan," 4.

10. Walker, "High Point Core City Plan," 4.

11. Sassen, *Cities in a World Economy*, 119.

12. Walker, "High Point Core City Plan," 4.

13. Duany, Plater-Zyberk, and Speck, *Suburban Nation*, 156.

14. Logan and Molotch, *Urban Fortunes*, 71.

15. Editorial Staff, "It's Time for Overlay District Action," *High Point Enterprise*, December 17, 2009.

16. Pat Kimbrough, "Council Scraps Market Plan," *High Point Enterprise*, January 5, 2010.

17. Kimbrough, "Council Scraps Market Plan."

18. Molotch, Freudenburg, and Paulsen, "History Repeats Itself, but How?" 817.

19. Molotch, Freudenburg, and Paulsen, "History Repeats Itself, but How?" 817.

20. Harvey, *Urban Experience,* 250.

21. Molotch, "Growth Machine Links," 251.

22. Reis, "Battle Lines Drawn."

23. Taft Wireback, "Downtown Ice Skating Stays on Feet: The Portable Rink and New Ice Coaster Are on Track to Attract Fifteen Thousand Customers This Season," *Greensboro News and Record,* January 5, 2014, https://www.greensboro.com/downtown-ice-skating-stays-on-feet/article_40ad0a11-18c7-5ccc-8f17-7edc568f7682.html?mode=jqm.

24. Duany, Plater-Zyberk, and Speck, *Suburban Nation,* 87.

25. Duany, Plater-Zyberk, and Speck, *Suburban Nation,* 87.

26. Frieden and Sagalyn, *Downtown, Inc.,* 58.

27. Roberta Brandes Gratz, *The Living City: How America's Cities Are Being Revitalized by Thinking Small in a Big Way* (New York: John Wiley & Sons, 1995).

28. Freeman Kennett and Duany-Plater-Zyberk, *The Master Plan: Ignite High Point,* 2013, 140.

29. Andrés Duany, "New Orleans: The Wealthiest City of the Caribbean," *Bloomberg,* February 26, 2007.

30. Molotch, "Growth Machine Links," 259; Jeremy Brecher and Tim Costello, *Global Village or Global Pillage: Economic Reconstruction from the Bottom Up* (Boston: South End, 1994).

31. Lees, Shin, and López-Morales, *Planetary Gentrification,* 58.

32. Duany, "Pink Zone."

33. Duany, "Pink Zone."

34. Duany, "Pink Zone."

35. Duany, "Pink Zone."

36. Boyer, "*Cities for Sale,*" 188.

37. Kennett and Duany-Plater-Zyberk, "Master Plan," 71.

38. Duany, "Opening Presentation."

39. Duany, "Closing Presentation."

40. Kennett and Duany-Plater-Zyberk, "Master Plan," 71.

41. Kennett and Duany-Plater-Zyberk, "Master Plan," 71.

42. Kennett and Duany-Plater-Zyberk, "Master Plan," 71.

43. Kennett and Duany-Plater-Zyberk, "Master Plan," 71.

44. Duany, Plater-Zyberk, and Speck, *Suburban Nation,* 171.

45. Kennett and Duany-Plater-Zyberk, "Master Plan," 71.

46. Kennett and Duany-Plater-Zyberk, "Master Plan," 11.

47. Kennett and Duany-Plater-Zyberk, "Master Plan," 34.

48. Matlack, "Bubble U"; Kelly, "College Both Left and Right Should Be Angry About."

49. Sills, "Market Segmentation and Targeted Revitalization," 132–35.

50. Duany, Plater-Zyberk, and Speck, *Suburban Nation,* 43–55.

51. Kennett and Duany-Plater-Zyberk, "Master Plan," 87.

52. Duany, "Closing Presentation"; Kennett and Duany-Plater-Zyberk, "Master Plan," 87.

53. Duany, "Pink Zone."

54. Duany, "Closing Presentation"; Kennett and Duany-Plater-Zyberk, "Master Plan," 87.

55. Nate Berg, "The Official Guide to Tactical Urbanism," Bloomberg City-Lab, March 2, 2012, http://www.bloomberg.com/news/articles/2012-03-02/the-official-guide-to-tactical-urbanism.

56. This is a perplexing series of events for me. There are almost certainly dynamics of racial identity and bias at play here, as there is in all U.S. politics. I have worked to understand the events of 2013 and 2014 better, especially concerning what injustices had transpired in this scandal, but it seems to me all sides have decided to move on. For me, Sims remains a vital part of the High Point story.

57. Jordan Green, "Revitalization Proponents Plan to Ask City of High Point for $700,000 for the Pit," *Yes! Weekly,* October 30, 2013, http://yesweeklyblog.blogspot.com/2013/10/revitalization-proponents-plan-to-ask.html.

58. Chanel Davis, "Sea Can Opens for Its First Preview," *High Point Enterprise,* July 25, 2013.

59. Duany-Plater-Zyberk, *The Pink Code: Interim Code,* 2014.

60. Tom Blount, "Our View: Showing Us How It Starts," *High Point Enterprise,* July 2014, http://www.hpe.com/opinion/x143262745/Our-View-Showing-us-how-it-starts; Jordan Green, "Library Plan Ousts Markets and Other Public Gatherings," *Triad City Beat,* July 23, 2014, https://triad-city-beat.com/library-plans-ousts-markets-and-other-public-gatherings/.

61. Pat Kimbrough, "Pit Cost Estimate One Million," *High Point Enterprise,* November 17, 2014, http://www.hpe.com/news/x2082482258/Pit-cost-estimate-1-million.

62. Kimbrough, "Pit Cost Estimate One Million."

63. Sam A. Hieb, "The Future of High Point: Shipping Containers? Planning Star Duany Offers a Dramatic Remake of Downtown," *Carolina Journal,* January 23, 2014, https://www.carolinajournal.com/news-article/the-future-of-high-point-shipping-containers/.

64. Andrés Duany, "In Support of the Road Diet," *High Point Enterprise,* March 16, 2014.

65. Editorial Staff, "Will Main Street Get Skinny?" *High Point Enterprise,* January 2.

66. Jordan Green, "City Project Leaders Try to Figure Out Initiative's Future," *Triad City Beat,* May 28, 2014, http://triad-city-beat.com/city-project-leaders-try-to-figure-out-initiatives-future/.

67. Jordan Green, "Stung by Firing, Some High Pointers Want a New City Council," *Triad City Beat,* May 19, 2014, https://triad-city-beat.com/stung-by-firing-some-high-point-citizens-want-a-new-city-council/.

68. Green, "Stung by Firing."

69. Jordan Green, "Road Dieting Vote Blindsides Dissenting High Point Councilman," *Triad City Beat,* October 28, 2014, https://triad-city-beat.com/road-dieting-vote-blindsides-dissenting-high-point-councilman/.

70. Pat Kimbrough, "Council Rejects Road Diet Proposal," *High Point Enterprise,* October 24, 2014, https://www.wxii12.com/article/high-point-city-council-rejects-road-diet-on-main-street/2057039.

71. Kimbrough, "Council Rejects Road Diet Proposal."

10. High Pointers Plan a Downtown for Themselves

1. Molotch, "Growth Machine Links," 263.

2. HPEDC, *Annual Report.*

3. Green, "Who Owns Downtown High Point?"

4. Walker Collaborative, "High Point Core City Plan," 158.

5. Stephanie Farmer and Chris D. Poulos, "The Financialising Local Growth Machine in Chicago," *Urban Studies* 56, no. 7 (2019): 1404–25.

6. Savitch and Kantor, *Cities in the International Marketplace,* 35–36.

7. Savitch and Kantor, *Cities in the International Marketplace,* 36.

8. Savitch and Kantor, *Cities in the International Marketplace,* 36.

9. Matlack, "Bubble U."

10. Allen Johnson, "What Happens When Nido Qubein Leaves HPU?" *Greensboro News and Record,* September 12, 2017, https://www.greensboro.com/blogs/thinking_out_loud/what-happens-when-nido-qubein-leaves-hpu/article_1d4b391c-0f0f-5f2b-8f2f-a0e663923c39.html.

11. Green, "Who Owns Downtown High Point?"

12. Jordan Green, "Goodbye Becky Smothers and Judy Mendenhall, Hello Bill Bencini," *Triad City Beat,* December 10, 2014.

13. Editorial Staff, "Triad Business Journal," *Two Major Triad Business Groups to Merge,* July 7, 2015, https://www.bizjournals.com/triad/blog/morning-edition/2015/07/two-major-triad-business-groups-to-merge.html.

14. City of High Point, "City Council Minutes," High Point City Council, High Point, N.C., 2016.

15. John Brasier, "Is Downtown High Point Ready to Play Ball?," *Triad Business Journal,* March 24, 2017, https://www.bizjournals.com/triad/news/2017/03/24/is-downtown-high-point-ready-to-play-ball.html.

16. Brasier, "Is Downtown High Point Ready to Play Ball?"

17. Brasier, "Is Downtown High Point Ready to Play Ball?"

18. Thomas Russell, "HPU President Nido Qubein to Raise Funds for Downtown Baseball Stadium," *Furniture Today,* May 17, 2017, https://www .furnituretoday.com/business-news/hpu-president-nido-qubein-raise-funds -downtown-baseball-stadium/.

19. Russell, "HPU President Nido Qubein to Raise Funds for Downtown Baseball Stadium."

20. Nana-Séntuo Bonsu, "Downtown High Point Update with Dr. Qubein," WXLV News, 2018.

21. Dan Way, "High Point Getting Closer to Bringing Taxpayer-Funded Stadium Home," *Carolina Journal,* December 8, 2017, https://www.carolina journal.com/news-article/high-point-getting-closer-to-bringing-taxpayer -funded-stadium-home/.

22. HPPA, "Prosperity for All: 2017 Platform," High Point Political Alliance, 2017.

23. HPPA, "Prosperity for All."

24. HPPA, "Prosperity for All."

25. Molotch, "Growth Machine Links," 58.

26. COHAB Space, "Cohab: Live-Work-Thrive," 2019.

27. Carley Milligan, "In the C-Suite: Why Developer Timothy Elliott Looks to Disney for Planning Inspiration," *Baltimore Business Journal,* September 18, 2018, https://www-bizjournals-com.cdn.ampproject.org/c/s/www.bizjournals .com/baltimore/news/2018/09/17/in-the-c-suite-why-developer-timothy-elliott -looks.amp.html.

28. Katie Murawski, "The Millennials behind High Point's Renaissance," *Yes! Weekly,* December 4, 2019, https://yesweekly.com/the-millennials-behind-high -points-renaissance/#comments.

29. Chanel Davis, "Art and Artists Go Main, Bring Traffic Back to Downtown," *Yes! Weekly,* July 28, 2021, https:// www.yesweekly.com/news/art-and -artists-go-main-bring-traffic-back-to-downtown/article_1a2d4198-efb1-11eb -a0fd-2fa8d1316caa.html.

30. "Making Art Happen in High Point, *High Point Discovered,* June 22, 2021, https://highpointdiscovered.org/magazine/making-art-happen-in-high -point/.

31. Jordan Greene, "Candidates for At-Large High Point City Council Seats Vie for Votes," *Triad City Beat,* August 14, 2019, https://triad-city-beat.com/ high-point-city-council/.

32. Business High Point, "HP365," Business High Point—Chamber of Commerce, https://www.bhpchamber.org/entrepreneurship.

33. Hadley Keller, "Plant Seven, a New Creative Space, Aims to Bring Small-Batch Design to High Point," *Architectural Digest,* October 5, 2018, https://

www.architecturaldigest.com/story/plant-seven-creative-space-high-point-small
-batch-design?verso=true.

34. Business High Point, "HP365."

35. Business High Point, "HP365."

36. Pat Kimbrough, "'Global in Scope': Entrepreneurship Hub Launches Downtown," *High Point Enterprise,* June 12, 2018.

37. Scott Yost, "Plant Seven Brings New Energy to Furniture Business," *Rhino Times,* December 26, 2018, http://www.rhinotimes.com/news/plant -seven-brings-new-energy-to-furniture-business/.

38. Sayaka Matsuoka, "Old World Craftsmanship Revitalized at High Point's Design Space," *Triad City Beat,* March 28, 2019, https://triad-city-beat.com/ old-world-craftsmanship-revitalized-at-high-points-design-space/.

39. Nic Ledoux, "Riverside Furniture to Restore Historic 1925 YMCA in High Point Market Downtown District," *Furniture World,* October 18, 2019.

40. "About Us," HPXD, https://hpxd.org/about-us/.

41. IMC, "International Market Centers Announces Donation of Downtown Property to Forward High Point," news release, October 3, 2018, https:// www.imcenters.com/news-and-media/international-market-centers-announces -donation-of-downtown-property-to-forward-high-point/.

42. IMC, "International Market Centers Announces Donation of Downtown Property to Forward High Point."

43. Pat Kimbrough, "Maricich Weighs In on Market," *High Point Enterprise,* October 20, 2014, http://www.hpe.com/news/x1154811507/Maricich -weighs-in-on-market.

44. Forward High Point, "The Showplace West Building: Request for Proposals," 2019, 8.

45. Zukin, *Naked City,* 27.

46. For a multi-faceted account of repeatedly ignored local wisdom, see Mary E. Pattillo, *Black on the Block: The Politics of Race and Class in the City* (Chicago: University of Chicago Press, 2007).

47. Shafique et al., "Inclusive Growth in Action," 58.

48. Clark, "Order and Simplicity of Gentrification," 266.

49. Merrifield, "Urban Question under Planetary Urbanization."

50. There is a parallel here to exploited groups seeing some benefits in outside imperialism as in Gail Omvedt, *Dalits and the Democratic Revolution: Dr Ambedkar and the Dalit Movement in Colonial India* (New Delhi: Sage India, 1994).

51. Doug Clark, "Outsiders Show High Point Some Fun," *Greensboro News and Record,* April 22, 2013, https://www.greensboro.com/opinion/outsiders-show -high-point-some-fun/article_ee720d9a-380d-58f4-ad46-a239b8412d97.html.

52. Clark, "Outsiders Show High Point Some Fun."

53. Zukin, *Naked City,* 244.

54. Duany, Plater-Zyberk, and Speck, *Suburban Nation,* 241.

Conclusion

1. Berry, *Unsettling of America.*
2. Frieden and Sagalyn, *Downtown, Inc.,* 43.
3. Duany, Plater-Zyberk, and Speck, *Suburban Nation,* 237.
4. Duany, Plater-Zyberk, and Speck, *Suburban Nation,* 166.
5. Zukin, *Loft Living,* 186.
6. Harvey, *Brief History of Neoliberalism,* 1–2.
7. Harvey, *Brief History of Neoliberalism.*
8. Marcuse, "Note from Peter Marcuse," 190.
9. Marcuse, "Note from Peter Marcuse," 195, 90.
10. Marcuse, "Note from Peter Marcuse," 191.
11. Jordan Green, "High Point Journal: Two Pro-Revitalization Candidates Offer Clashing Visions," *Triad City Beat,* October 15, 2014, http://triad-city -beat.com/high-point-journal-two-pro-revitalization-candidates-offer-clashing -visions/.
12. Dickson, "Is the Bilbao Effect on Urban Renewal All It's Cracked Up to Be?"
13. Austin, "Mayor Proposes Pause on Corridor Growth."
14. Bill Harris, "Your View: Container Complexes Won't Help Downtown," *High Point Enterprise,* May 30, 2013.
15. Jordan Green, "High Point Journal: Council Members Explore New Revitalization Ideas," *Triad City Beat,* June 11, 2014, https://triad-city-beat .com/high-point-journal-council-members-explore-new-revitalization-ideas/.
16. Duany, Plater-Zyberk, and Speck, *Suburban Nation,* 174.
17. Shafique et al., "Inclusive Growth in Action," 58, 70.
18. Shafique et al., "Inclusive Growth in Action."
19. Shafique et al., "Inclusive Growth in Action," 58.
20. Zukin, *Naked City,* 245.
21. CLES, "Community Wealth Building through Anchor Institutions," Centre for Local Economic Strategies, 2017; Shafique et al., "Inclusive Growth in Action," 52.
22. Michael Moore, dir., *Roger & Me* (Burbank: Warner Home Video, 1990).
23. Susan S. Fainstein and David Gladstone Fainstein, "Evaluating Urban Tourism," in *The Tourist City,* edited by Dennis R. Judd and Susan S. Fainstein (New Haven, Conn.: Yale University Press, 1999), 340, 36–37.
24. Fainstein and Fainstein, "Evaluating Urban Tourism," 37.
25. Schlichtman, Patch, and Hill, *Gentrifier,* 106.
26. Pattillo, *Black on the Block,* 182.
27. Molotch, "Growth Machine Links," 257.
28. Jacobs, *Death and Life of Great American Cities,* 49.

29. Dickson, "Is the Bilbao Effect on Urban Renewal All It's Cracked Up to Be?"

30. Dickson, "Is the Bilbao Effect on Urban Renewal All It's Cracked Up to Be?"

31. Dickson, "Is the Bilbao Effect on Urban Renewal All It's Cracked Up to Be?"

32. Jim Crumley, "If You Build It, They Will Come," *Courier and Advisor,* December 18, 2012, https://www.pressreader.com/uk/the-courier-advertiser -perth-and-perthshire-edition/20121218/282059094321580.

33. Molotch, "Growth Machine Links," 259; Brecher and Costello, *Global Village or Global Pillage.*

34. Dickson, "Is the Bilbao Effect on Urban Renewal All It's Cracked Up to Be?"

35. Farmer and Poulos, "Financialising Local Growth Machine in Chicago," 5–6.

36. Foglesong, *Married to the Mouse,* 161.

37. Farmer and Poulos, "Financialising Local Growth Machine in Chicago," 5–6.

38. Jordan Green, "Opposition to HB2 Puts a 'Dent' in Furniture Market Attendance," *Triad City Beat,* April 20, 2016, https://triad-city-beat.com/oppo sition-to-hb2-puts-a-dent-in-furniture-market-attendance/.

39. Doug Clark, "No More 'Fuel on the Fire' from Cautious High Point Market," *Greensboro News and Record,* April 1, 2016.

40. Feargus O'Sullivan, "Scotland Tries for the Bilbao Effect at the New V&A Dundee," *CityLab,* September 25, 2018, https://www.citylab.com/design/ 2018/09/scotland-tries-bilbao-effect-new-va-dundee/571000/.

41. Cindy Landrum, "Greenville's Corporate Leaders Urged to Face the Growing Problem of 'Two Greenvilles,'" *Greenville Journal,* August 31, 2017, https://greenvillejournal.com/2017/08/31/greenvilles-corporate-leaders-urged -face-growing-problem-two-greenvilles/; O'Sullivan, "Scotland Tries for the Bilbao Effect."

42. Schlichtman, "Niche City Idea."

43. Pamela E. Oliver and Gerald Marwell, "Mobilizing Technologies for Collective Action," in *Frontiers in Social Movement Theory,* edited by Aldon D. Morris and Carol McClurg Mueller (New Haven, Conn.: Yale University Press, 1992), xii, 382.

44. Phillips, "Public Ownership."

45. Phillips, "Public Ownership."

46. Lloyd, "Urbanization and the Southern United States," 14.

47. Molotch, "Growth Machine Links," 259.

48. Molotch, "Growth Machine Links."

Index

Page numbers in italics represent photos/maps/illustrations.

(*continued from page ii*)

JOHN JOE SCHLICHTMAN is associate professor of urban sociology at DePaul University and coauthor of *Gentrifier*.

HARVEY MOLOTCH is emeritus professor of social and cultural analysis and sociology at New York University.